COURT PATRONAGE
AND CORRUPTION IN
EARLY STUART ENGLAND

COURT PATRONAGE
AND CORRUPTION IN
EARLY STUART ENGLAND

Linda Levy Peck

London

First published in 1990 by the Academic Division of Unwin Hyman Ltd.

First published in paperback in 1993
by Routledge
11 New Fetter Lane, London EC4P 4EE

Simultaneously published in the USA and Canada
by Routledge
29 West 35th Street, New York, NY 10001

Printed in Great Britain by
Redwood Books, Trowbridge, Wiltshire

British Library Cataloguing in Publication Data
Peck, Linda Levy
    Court patronage and corruption in early Stuart England.
    1. Great Britain. Government. Patronage. History
    I. Title
354.420009

Library of Congress Cataloging in Publication Data
Peck, Linda Levy.
    Court patronage and corruption in early Stuart England / Linda
Levy Peck.
        p.   cm.
    Originally published: Boston: Unwin Hyman, 1990.
    Includes bibliographical references and index.
    1. Great Britain-Politics and government-1603-1649.   2. Great
Britain-Court and courtiers-History-17th century.   3. Patronage,
Political-Great Britain-History-17th century. 4. Political
corruption-Great Britain-History-17th century.   5. England-
Social conditions-17th century.   I. Title.
DA390.P43   1993
306.2'0941'09032-dc20
                                                        92-46114

ISBN 0-415-09368-6

To my mother
Arlene Levy Sitomer

Contents

Preface

The completion of a project, like the ending of the old year and the beginning of the new, is a moment for reflection. When it comes time to acknowledge one's scholarly debts, how much one owes to others becomes apparent.

This book would not have been possible without the National Endowment for the Humanities, which provided fellowship support both to me and to the research libraries at which I worked, for which I am deeply grateful. I am grateful too to the British Academy and the American Council of Learned Societies for grants for this project. The Henry E. Huntington Library provided fellowship support to use its extensive manuscript collections for which I wish to express my great appreciation to Robert Middlekauff, Martin Ridge and Mary Robertson. A fellowship from the Folger Shakespeare Library in 1988/9 enabled me to complete this book for which I wish to thank Werner Gundersheimer, Barbara Mowat and Lena Orlin. Purdue University generously allowed me to work at these research libraries and I am grateful to John Contreni, David Caputo and Varro Tyler for their support.

I learned so much by participating in the Folger Center for the History of British Political Thought, from teaching a research seminar on early seventeenth century political thought and from organizing a conference on "The Mental World of the Jacobean Court." I am deeply grateful to J. G. A. Pocock, Lois Schwoerer, Gordon Schochet and Lena Orlin for the opportunity to take part. If this book sounds as much like *Politics, Language and Time* as *The Structure of Politics on the Eve of the Accession of George III*, that may be the reason.

Both the Huntington and the Folger provided good fellowship: I especially enjoyed the Folger fellowship class of 1988/9, A. R. Braunmuller, Gail Paster and Michael Neill, who will find traces of our conversations in these pages. I am very grateful to Barbara Donagan, Mark Edwards, Elizabeth Read Foster, Caroline Hibbard, Derek Hirst, Wilfred Prest and Barbara Taft for reading the individual chapters and providing helpful comments. Deepak Lal kindly allowed me to try out some of my ideas on corruption and the economy before a World Bank audience.

Very special thanks go to A. R. Braunmuller, Stanley Engerman and John Guy who read most or all of the complete manuscript and provided extensive comments. Most of all I wish to thank John Morrill for his close and very helpful reading of the text. Even if we disagree on some of the answers I hope I have addressed his penetrating questions.

As he celebrates his eightieth birthday, I wish to acknowledge a special debt to Jack Hexter for his continuing gift of inspiration. Finally to dear friends and family who must have wondered how I had wandered so deeply into the thickets of patronage and corruption, my thanks for their support and loving kindness.

I should like to express my great thanks to the librarians and staff of the manuscript room and the North Library of the British Library, the Public Record Office, the Bodleian Library, and Duke Humfrey's Library, Oxford, the Cambridge University Library, the Library of Congress, the National Maritime Museum, the National Register of Archives. In particular I want to thank the Master and Fellows, Magdalene College, Cambridge for permission to use the Pepys manuscripts and Richard Luckett, the Pepys Librarian, and Mrs. A. Fitz-Simons and Mrs. E.M. Colemans who were so helpful to me while I worked there. I have used the resources of the Yale Parliamentary Diaries Center on many occasions for which I thank Maija Jansson and William Bidwell.

I am grateful to Sir William Gordon Cumming for permission to cite family papers at the National Museum of Scotland. *The Journal of British Studies* has allowed me to draw upon my article "For a King not to be bountiful were a fault: Perspectives on Court Patronage in Early Stuart England," vol. 25 (1986), pp. 31–61. Dr. Helen Braham, curator of the Rubens collection at the Courtauld Gallery, was kind enough to show me Rubens' *modello* of Royal Bounty overcoming Avarice which serves as this volume's cover.

How can one adequately express one's thanks? Seneca suggested that such debts cannot be repaid but they remain, living, in the memory of the recipient. I, of course, am responsible for the errors that inevitably linger in the book.

West Lafayette, Indiana
January 1990

*COURT PATRONAGE
AND CORRUPTION IN
EARLY STUART ENGLAND*

Introduction

The fountain of favor

John Webster began his Jacobean tragedy *The Dutchesse of Malfy* with a striking image of good and bad government:

> . . . a Princes Court
> Is like a common Fountaine, whence should flowe
> Pure silver-droppes ingeneral. But if't chance
> Some curs'd example poyson't neere the head,
> "Death and diseases through the whole land spread.
> And what is't makes this blessed government,
> But a most provident Councell, who dare freely
> Informe him, the corruption of the times?
> Though some o th'Court hold it presumption
> To instruct Princes what they ought to doe,
> It is a noble duety to informe them
> What they ought to fore-see . . .[1]

The magnificent fountains of Renaissance and seventeenth-century Europe symbolized the contemporary vision and rhetoric about royal patronage.[2] The metaphor of the fountain was used repeatedly in the Elizabethan and early Stuart period to describe the monarchy, especially the king's favor, to his subjects. Bountiful, free-flowing, continuous, the king granted favor to his subjects. Monarchy was a never-ending source of reward, the earthly embodiment of God, who was the original spring or wellhead, the fountain of life and justice. At the same time there was, in practice, a second aspect of a fountain: recirculation. On the one hand the fountain was continuous, visibly moving in one direction; on the other, it was based on the principle of the water returning to its source. When the king rewarded his subjects and servants, they returned loyalty and service in their turn to the king.

1

Contemporaries invoked the same metaphor to describe political corruption. The pollution of fountains, the muddying of the streams of royal patronage, "signified the corruption of the times." The minister John Stoughton preached: "The ancients were wont to place the Statues of their Kings by Fountaines, intimating they were the Fountaines of good or ill in the common-wealth, as indeed they are."[3] Corruption, identified by Webster in *The Dutchesse of Malfy* with corporeal images of death and disease, posed a significant and perennial threat to royal government and its support by both servants and people.

This book analyzes the language, context, configuration and consequences of royal patronage and corruption in early Stuart England. It examines the changing characteristics of bounty, those "pure silver-droppes" of which Webster spoke, and the structure of patron–client relationships. It also looks at contemporary norms of bureaucratic behavior and the intermingling of public and private interest, market and government in the early seventeenth century. Was early Stuart government more corrupt or merely perceived to be more corrupt than its Tudor forbears? Was English government becoming unworkable or was it mismanaged by the early Stuarts? To answer such questions, this study not only considers the general problems of governance from 1550 to 1650 as early modern government expanded its scope without an adequate financial base, and the impact of economic distress and inflation from the 1590s on, but also places these questions in the larger context of the changing values and ideology of the Crown, its officeholders and the political elite.

Historians of early modern Europe have become interested in court patronage as they have analyzed the structures of informal power that created ties between centers and localities. From the fifteenth to the eighteenth century, from the work of MacFarlane to Namier, the study of relationships between patrons and clients has been at the forefront of modern historiography. In French history the work of Roland Mousnier and his students has helped to delineate the relationships between courts and political elites, between kings and estates. In English history, the work of Sir John Neale, Wallace MacCaffrey and Sir Geoffrey Elton has shaped current thinking on the court, patronage and place. Most recently, revisionist historians, such as Conrad Russell and Kevin Sharpe, by questioning what they perceive to be Whiggish analyses of the English Civil War, have given renewed emphasis to relations of patrons and clients in Tudor and Stuart politics, shifting the focus from constitutional issues to political clientage.[4]

There are many books that can and should be written about patronage, that ubiquitous relationship that permeated early modern political, social, economic and artistic life. This book does not attempt exhaustively to map personal relationships in early seventeenth-century England but to place patronage in the context of contemporary politics and ideology. That personal and private relationships dominated contemporary politics suggests that emphasis on the emergence of the bureaucratic state in sixteenth-century England needs to be broadened. At the same time, by placing patronage in the context of wider social, intellectual and administrative developments, the book questions the sometimes simplified picture of political manipulation characteristic of recent writings on early Stuart history. But this study aims not to challenge proponents of the Tudor revolution in government or revisionism but to incorporate their insights in order to understand how the political system actually worked and how contemporaries interpreted it.

Patronage structured early modern society. At once symbiotic and symbolic, these private, dependent, deferential alliances were designed to bring reward to the client and continuing proof of power and standing to the patron. The establishment of patron–client relationships came about in many different ways: through appeal to mutual friends, to kinship ties, and to neighborhood bonds. Often, important courtiers and officials served as brokers to carry out patronage transactions. The language of patronage, situated in a theory of mutual, indeed, social benefits, and the practice of gift-giving, strongly marked political and social behavior.

Elements of patron–client relationships had existed in earlier times in the ties which bound the king to his magnates and these magnates to their feudal retainers. Beginning with the reign of Richard II in the fourteenth century and continuing under the Tudors, English kings moved systematically to build their own affinities in the counties, naming leading country gentlemen to honorific court offices that required only occasional attendance. Their purpose was to create local connections to rival and supplant affinities loyal to powerful noblemen.[5] The naming of important local gentlemen to honorific court office continued. At the beginning of James's reign a group of twelve knights, leaders in their counties, were appointed to Queen Anne's Council, but not put in commission.[6]

But in the sixteenth century the centralization of power in the hands of the monarch and the expansion of that power to regulate social and economic behavior, the break with Rome, the growth in numbers of the landed elite, and changing patterns of commerce significantly altered the contours and dimensions of patronage. Royal reward linked the newly powerful Tudor monarchy to the nobility and gentry in the countryside, establishing and reinforcing the informal relationships that maintained political power for both. As the numbers of justices of the peace who enforced the Privy Council's orders in their counties increased, pressure on the monarch to reward this voluntary local bureaucracy grew as well. The dissolution of the monasteries and chantries increased the amount of land and presentations to benefices in the hands of the Crown available for distribution. New economic privileges, which developed from the royal creation of monopolies and trading companies in the late sixteenth century, added further to the king's store of bounty. The exchange at the heart of patron–client relationships continued in traditional patterns too, such as the symbolic power inherent in the grant of a keepership of a royal park, the reputation and economic gain that flowed from government office, and the advantage that came from influencing the speed, conduct, or outcome of a lawsuit.[7]

Early Stuart England was governed by a personal monarchy which ruled through a patrimonial bureaucracy organized within a hierarchical society structured by patron–client relationships. Although Henry VIII had increased salaries, these had remained fixed despite inflation.[8] Its officials received fees paid by those who used their service, bounty such as annuities and pensions granted by the Crown and the informal payments above the traditional fees given or extracted by royal officials. Among the glues which bound together superior and subordinate were gifts, given in tribute to the power and authority of the superior and of the deference of the inferior. In early Stuart England there was often no great social distance between patrons, who might be nobility or gentry, and their clients who were other nobility and gentry as well as merchants. The great man might control access to favor but those who sought such access were, in the main, other members of the political elite.

The opening of King James's reign, in 1603, after forty-five years of the venerated but parsimonious Elizabeth, altered the dispensation of court patronage. While the Scottish king dramatically increased royal bounty, he brought with him a cluster of foreign followers who laid claim to some of that bounty for themselves and took up positions as brokers on behalf of clamoring suitors. Increasingly in the seventeenth century, the Crown's problems of allocation were solved by marketing favor and monopolizing patronage. The government's lack of funds from its own income and from parliamentary subsidies forced it to maximize its income and to cannibalize its patronage and bounty in the form of sale of honors, titles, licenses and offices. Such sales were a self-conscious effort to allocate resources through legal payments to the benefit of the Crown rather than through bribes to agents. Moreover, the monopoly of patronage exerted by the Duke of Buckingham, royal favorite to King James and King Charles, represented another solution to the problem of allocation. Although cutting back competing demands was more comfortable for the king, a single patron led to self-aggrandizement and disaffection among other patrons and unsuccessful clients. After the death of Buckingham, the trend toward monopoly of influence continued with the replacement of many patentees with a few in the 1630s.

At the heart, then, of the intertwined problems of patronage and corruption were issues of access and allocation, of office and gift. Contemporary complaint literature and later historians have labelled the Jacobean court corrupt.[9] For the analyst, the definition and issue of corruption is, however, a knotty one. Similar practices are tolerated to a different degree by divergent groups and the significance of such acts varies in different times and places. Reluctant to accept the word of contemporary complaint, Joel Hurstfield and Gerald Aylmer sought to analyze the structural causes and the incidence of corrupt practices in early modern English administration. Hurstfield argued that historians erred in applying modern bureaucratic norms to early modern administration. Aylmer in his magisterial works, *The King's Servants* and *The State's Servants*, showed that despite structural similarities, there were differences in the extent of administrative venality between the Caroline and the Commonwealth and Protectorate periods.[10]

Yet most historians' attitudes toward corruption have tended either to be moralistic, thereby placing themselves in the position of condemning behavior without concern for context, or dismissive, arguing that the charge of corruption was simply the tool of "outs" versus "ins." Unable to accept the testimony of complaint literature about venality that stretches from the Middle Ages to the present, unwilling to apply modern conceptions of corruption to early modern government, most historians have dealt with the issue by avoiding it. While recent works on the early Stuart court have deepened our understanding of its policies and processes, their focus on court faction as the major explanation of contemporary discord within the political elite has downplayed corruption as an issue central both to contemporary political ideology and to contemporary perceptions of Stuart government in England and Europe.

This book argues that corrupt practices, while characteristic of early modern administration, became a matter of increasing concern in the early seventeenth century. The extent and scale of corruption appears to have increased especially from the 1590s. The Crown mounted increasing numbers of prosecutions of under-officers, parliament revived the procedure of impeachment to remove royal officials from office and passed new statutes on bribery and sale of office. As a result, the boundaries between legitimate and corrupt transactions were redrawn. The targets and timing of some of these investigations were no doubt influenced by political considerations but, as we shall see, the evidence for general and increasing concern about corruption is manifest in statute, proclamation, language and behavior.

I

Institutional and polemical attacks on corruption were not new. Bribery, in its first English usage by Chaucer, meant a thing stolen or robbed, unlike old French and medieval Latin from which the word derived, in which it meant alms or a piece of bread given to a beggar.[11] Statutes going back to the thirteenth century proscribed a variety of corrupt practices. Magna Carta prohibited the low-level extortion of purveyors. The First Statute of

Westminster of 1275, c. 26, prohibited sheriffs and other royal officers from taking reward for doing their offices beyond what the king allowed them on pain of double damages; the second Statute of Westminster of 1285, c 44, provided for the punishment of officers of the courts for taking more than their fees.[12]

The itinerant justices in Edward I's reign were ordered to inquire about a range of abuses in local administration:

> sheriffs taking gifts for consenting to the concealing of felonies committed in their bailiwicks ... of clerks and other bailiffs of sheriffs, coroners, and their clerks ... taking gifts for removing recognitors from juries and assizes ... who by the power of their office have maliciously troubled any, thereby extorting from them lands, rents, or other payments ... who have received the king's command to pay his debts, and have taken from the creditors a certain portion for paying them the remainder, and nevertheless have caused the whole to be allowed to themselves in the Exchequer or elsewhere ... who have received the king's debts ... and have not thereof acquitted the king's debtors ... who have summoned any that they should be made knights, and have received bribes from them for favour to be shown ... whether sheriffs and other bailiffs of any liberty have ... fraudulently and insufficiently executed the precepts of our lord the king for entreaty, bribe, or favour and from what time.

The articles extended to those who carried away stone, timber or other things provided for the king's works and to those "who for entreaty, reward, or favour, have consented or consulted to sell any wardship of our lord the king, or the marriages belonging to our lord the king, for less price than they ought to be sold according to their true value."[13]

The focus of most of this inquest was the legal system and feudal obligations. Members of Edward I's bench themselves were removed for venality. A century later, in the first year of his reign Henry IV made extortion by sheriffs punishable at the king's will.[14] Tudor statutes continued to address venal practices by sheriffs and their under-officers.[15] But they did not include other issues that became important in the seventeenth century such as sale of titles, conflict of interest and monopolies.

The crucial statutes on bribery and sale of office were 12 Richard II, c. 2, and 5 and 6 Edward VI, c. 16. The first, passed in 1388, provided that appointments to office should be 'of the best and most lawful men, and sufficient to their estimation and knowledge'. It specifically forbade the Chancellor, Treasurer, Keeper of the Privy Seal, Steward of the King's House, King's Chamberlain, Clerk of the Rolls and other officials from naming any officer or minister of the king 'for any gift or brocage, favour or affection'.[16]

The Edwardian statute, enacted in 1552, tried to enforce the previous statute. Its purpose was

6

for the avoydinge of corruption whiche maye hereafter happen to be in the officers and ministers in those courts, places or romes wherein there is requisite to be had the true admynistration of justice or services of truste ... and to th'intent that persons worthye and mete to be advaunced to the place where justice is to be mynistered or any service of truste executed, sholde hereafter be preferred to the same and none other.

The statute specifically applied to the buying and selling either directly or indirectly of offices or any part of them that concerned "the admynistration or execution of justice, or receipte ... of any of the king's treasure." The seller was to forfeit title and the buyer to be disabled from holding the office. The bill had three significant exceptions. Firstly, it did not extend to "any office ... whereof any person or persons ys or shalbe seised of any estate of inheritaunce". Secondly, it did not include any keepership of any park. Finally, as if in response to protests, a separate schedule provided that the statute was not in any way to extent "or be prejudiciall or hurtfull to anye of the chief justices of the king's courts ... but that they ... maye doe in everie behalfe, touchinge or concerninge any office or offices to be given or graunted by them ... as they or anye of them myght have done before the makinge of this Acte."[17] The limitations within the bill on the sale of office were extended through judicial interpretation. In Cavendish's Case (1587) the judges decided that office could be considered property and inheritance.[18] Invoking Magna Carta, they held that the Queen's creation of a new office in the court of Common Pleas disseised present officers of their freehold.[19] Their view prevailed into the nineteenth century.[20]

II

It is instructive to consider modern definitions and models of corrupt practices. J. S. Nye, who concentrates on bureaucratic roles and norms, defines corruption as "behavior which deviates from the formal duties of a public role because of private-regarding (personal, close family, private clique), pecuniary or status gains; or violates rules against the exercise of certain types of private-regarding influence."[21] Arnold Rogow and Harold Lasswell argue that an act is corrupt when it "violates responsibility toward at least one system of public or civic order and is in fact incompatible with (destructive of) any such system. A system of public or civic order exalts common interest over special interest; violations of the common interest for special advantage are corrupt."[22] In his analysis of sixteenth-century government practice, Joel Hurstfield put forward a definition similar to that of Rogow and Lasswell.[23] But do these modern definitions find a resonance in seventeenth-century English thought and practice? To find out, later chapters

7

examine the contemporary discourse of corruption in law cases, prescriptive literature and other contemporary writings.

Economists have come at the problem of corruption from a different angle, focusing not on bureaucratic norms or civic order but on the relationship of the market to administration.

> Corruption ... involves a shift from a mandatory pricing model to a free-market model. The centralized allocative mechanism which is the ideal of modern bureaucracy may break down in the face of serious disequilibrium between supply and demand. Clients may decide that it is worthwhile to risk the known sanctions and pay the higher costs in order to be assured of receiving the desired benefits. When this happens bureaucracy ceases to be patterned after the mandatory market and takes on characteristics of the free market.[24]

Bureaucracies are concerned with tasks of allocation, contracting and law enforcement. The ways in which they carry out these tasks shape incentives to corrupt practices. Rather than examining just the forms of corruption – bribery, extortion, kickbacks – this study aims to understand the conditions under which they are likely to arise. Susan Rose-Ackerman emphasizes the notion of agency in her analysis of corruption. A "superior expresses a set of preferences which specify desired outcomes" to an agent; corruption occurs, she argues, when a third person tries to influence the agent's action by "offering him a monetary payment which is not passed on to the principal."[25] Rose-Ackerman argues that such payments do not necessarily subvert the principal's objects; indeed, sometimes they may increase satisfaction with the agent, much like the foreign pensions given to James I's privy councillors. Like a tip to a waiter, a bribe to low-level employees may improve performance. In any society some of these payments will be illegal and that fact will lower the willingness to accept or offer such payments.[26]

Bureaucracies allocate resources in several different ways, including contracting and queuing. There is a difference between bribery to gain a contract and "speed money" to maintain or speed up one's place in a queue. We shall see such distinctions in parliamentary debates on corrupt practices in the judicial system in chapter 8. Thus in early Stuart England, there was a difference between bribes paid to courtiers to gain the Great Farm of the Customs and money paid to low-ranking court officials to ensure that the legal process would be carried out expeditiously.[27]

King James was plagued by hordes of place-seekers. Thomas Sackville, Lord Buckhurst and Earl of Dorset, who served as Lord Treasurer late in Elizabeth's reign and in the first years of James's, was lauded by a contemporary for recognizing this problem of allocation and, in response, creating and enforcing a single queue.

And for his dispatches and the contents he gave to suitors, he had a decorum seldom since put in practice. For he had of his attendants that took in a roll the names of all suitors with the date of their first address, and these in their order had hearing, so that a fresh man could not leap over his head that was of a more ancient edition except in the urgent affairs of the state.[28]

III

There existed then, in 1603, statutes forbidding bribery, extortion, sale of office and advancement to office by gift and favor. At the same time, sixteenth-century judicial decisions treated office as property and made contradictory findings on the taking of fees. In the case of *Dive* v. *Manningham*, decided in Common Pleas in 1551,[29] the judges had defined extortion broadly, a definition Sir Edward Coke set forth in his *Institutes*. "Extortion . . . is a great misprison by wresting, or unlawfully taking by any officer, by colour of his office, any money or valuable thing of or from any man, either that is not due, or more than is due, or before it is due." Yet Coke took note of statutory exceptions and legal decisions, such as *Sherley* v. *Packer* in 1616, that held "reasonable fees as have been allowed by the courts of justice of ancient time to inferior ministers and attendants of courts for their labor and attendance, if it be asked and taken of the subject is no extortion."[30] Because of such limitations, extortion could adopt "the visor of vertue, for expedition of justice, and the like." Coke provided an expansive definition of extortion, declaring it "any oppression . . . by color or pretence of right."[31]

In the early seventeenth century, pressure increased in parliament to enforce statutes against corrupt practices although many members of parliament expressed the contradictory views apparent in contemporary judicial decisions. Most bills introduced against the buying of offices in the middle of the sixteenth century had concerned the abuse of simony, the purchase of church office. Indeed, Chaucer had taken deadly aim at corrupt practices in the church. The outcry against corruption in the royal bureaucracy in the sixteenth and seventeenth centuries marked the sea-change from the dominance of a patrimonial church to that of a patrimonial bureaucracy. Bills against simony continued into the early Jacobean period but were overshadowed by the number of bills concerning sale of state office. In the sessions of 1621, 1625, 1626 and 1628 bills were repeatedly brought forward to make more precise the definition of bribery and prevent the buying and selling of judicial offices. Going further, contemporary sermons and political literature argued that all offices were offices of justice and that gift, favor and affection were as corrupt as bribery in gaining office."[Not] only money, gold and silver, or presents as they call them, are bribes, but the guilt of bribery may also be justly imputed, even to exorbitant affection . . . [that] sways a man . . . from the impartial execution of justice." Another preacher argued: "I am not ignorant of the distinction of Judicature, trust and pains; but are they not all offices of Justice?. . . Offices are not livings and salaries but charges and duties: not preferments for favorites but rewards of deserts."[32]

While incentives to corrupt practices existed throughout the judicial system, contemporary complaints of corruption were followed by prosecutions both by the Crown and private individuals. Complaints were lodged against local judicial officers from the jailor and county clerk all the way up to justices of the peace. In 1617 a petition from a single parish complained of fourteen acts of extortion on eleven victims involving seven bailiffs. The assize records of Somerset show complaints against bailiffs that include extortion, bribery and acts of violence.[33] Between 1615 and 1624 seventy bailiffs were subject to complaint, some of them repeatedly, at quarter sessions or in Star Chamber. Juries found a total of twenty-one indictments for extortion against twenty different bailiffs; even so, because of the inadequacy of the evidence, it is likely that even more bailiffs were presented.[34] As the Jacobean court mounted investigations into waste and fraud, it also prosecuted under officers in the legal system and local administration.

Many charges of official malfeasance were brought in Star Chamber during James's reign: of 1,816 cases 152 were brought by the Crown. Embezzlement was alleged in 122 cases, 17 of which were brought by the Attorney-General and 575 cases of extortion were presented, 57 of which were Crown cases.[35] It is difficult to sort out the relative importance of these charges which were often part of a package that included riot and violence; official malfeasance may have been cited to bring the case within the purview of Star Chamber. Nevertheless, the cases themselves provide a vivid picture of official misconduct. In one, a group of local officials in Yorkshire were accused of using the enclosure statutes to extort money from illiterate farmers. In another, an official was accused of padding his accounts for mourning shrouds with five shillings' worth of tobacco which he "drank" with a servant of the Lord President of the Marches of Wales.[36]

Yet specific policies and practices of the Jacobean court elicited attacks on court corruption even when the policies were not themselves legally corrupt. Monopolies, begun as government policy under Elizabeth to diversify the economy, were continued and expanded under James. They figured prominently in the revival of parliamentary judicature in 1621 and the impeachment of Sir Francis Bacon. The sale of titles by the Crown began with the introduction of the baronetcy in 1611 and continued with the sale of baronies beginning in 1615. The sale of peerages as well as the sale of offices were among the charges of impeachment brought against the Duke of Buckingham in 1626. Charges of corruption were now extended to activities beyond the statutory definitions to include certain kinds of gift-giving, the sale of titles, non-judicial office and monopoly.

James's innovative efforts to solve the problems of allocation through sale and monopoly caused further political problems. By creating a market for titles and offices he evoked complaints that he was selling his honor. His efforts to place allocation in the hands of one trusted official on whom he could rely, the Duke of Buckingham, engendered a monopoly of royal patronage and what were perceived to be incentives to corruption.

But if the expanding role of government in sixteenth and seventeenth-century England and its constrained finances in the early seventeenth century created incentives to corruption, the changing values and behavior of officeholders and King James's refusal in the first half of his reign to hold high-ranking officials accountable for corrupt practices created a culture of political corruption in which everything was perceived to be for sale at the English court. If, as has been argued, "the officials" net gain from accepting a bribe is the value of the bribe minus the official's expected penalty and the moral costs of engaging in an "illegal action," the net gain was high: at the Jacobean court there were meager and intermittent penalties and apparently few moral costs.[37]

The king and his subjects shared aspects of a common discourse on corruption. Yet despite the Crown's significant investigations to stem corrupt practices, even initiating prosecution of its own servants, the perception of court corruption extended beyond its practice. The language of corruption provided a powerful mode of criticism and challenge to the court and the king in a society shaped by order and consensus. Corruption became a political issue capable of helping to undermine governmental legitimacy when it became tied to other critical issues such as religion, finance and fundamental law. Understanding how and why corrupt practices worked, who they affected, and what they were construed to mean by different groups within the political elite helps to explain why corruption became a major part of political discourse in the early decades of the seventeenth century.

If patron–client relationships bound together the king and the political elite, the language of corruption became a means of disconnection. Because contemporary politics lacked satisfactory discourses of protest and opposition, the language of corruption provided an essential vocabulary with which to criticize early Stuart government. Indeed it forged a powerful ideology that endured in one form or another at least until 1820 when its language can still be found in the writings of radical pamphleteers in the Queen Caroline tracts.[38]

In conclusion, with Webster's warning ringing loud and clear, we shall seek to discover whether and with what results James I and Charles I listened to a "provident Councell" telling them of corrupt practices and how their policies hemmed in or enhanced the perception of royal corruption. In the end, the book seeks to discover why the monarchy's "pure silver-droppes . . . poyson't neere the head."

Chapter 1

The language of patronage: a discourse of connection

In the midst of the English Civil War in the 1640s, William Dobson painted portraits of royalists in Oxford. Amongst the Cavalier soldiers, he portrayed Sir Thomas Aylesbury, Master of Requests. Dressed in his official robes, Aylesbury symbolized his position by holding a petition inscribed "to the king's most excellent majesty." As a Master of Requests, he presented petitions to the king asking for redress of grievances or for personal advancement, in short, asking for royal bounty. As Dobson's portrait signifies, such petitions were not merely the seedy clamoring of early Stuart courtiers but an open and important link between the monarch and the subject, one suitable for commemoration in portraiture. The painting makes concrete, even in the midst of civil war, the king's traditional role as guarantor of justice and giver of favor. The king's promise of justice dates from early Anglo-Saxon dooms and tenth-century coronation oaths; his giving of favor was just as old, immortalized in charter. The monarch's giving of largesse had expanded with the Renaissance monarchy of the Tudors and it was embedded in the Senecan language of James I's *Trew Law of Free Monarchies*, which spoke of the mutual benefits that flowed between monarch and subject.[1]

I

In his book *On Benefits*, the Stoic philosopher Seneca had described the good society in terms of the exchange of benefits among members of the commonwealth. Senecan ideas were important to early Renaissance

12

humanists. Neo-Stoic language and thought gained further circulation with the translation of Seneca's works with commentary by Justus Lipsius in the 1570s. Thomas Lodge translated:

> Of Benefits then we are to intreat, and to set down an order and direction in this vertue, which chiefly concerneth humane societie: we are to prefixe and set down a law of living, least inconsiderate facilitie in giving, grow in favour under the colour of benignitie; least this observation, whilest it temperateth liberalitie (which must neither be defective nor superfluous) restraine the same wholly. Men are to be taught to receive with thankfulnesse, and to restore with the same correspondence, and to procure (in regard to those that oblige them with any benefit) not only to be equall with them in will, but to over-come them with greater gratuitie: because that he who is obliged to acknowledge a good turne, requiteth not the same, except his remuneration exceede the givers merit.[2]

Such benefits, given freely, in moderation, and received gratefully, circulated throughout society.

Senecan language of benefits was central to the language of patronage.[3] Thus, Sir Arthur Chichester defined a commonwealth as "nothing more than a commercement or continual suppeditation of benefits mutually received and done among men."[4] The exchange of such benefits was crystallized in contemporary practices of gift-giving. Moreover, at Renaissance courts the scale of such gifts increased dramatically.

King James VI of Scotland and I of England has long been criticized as a spendthrift, and his courtiers as sycophantic seekers of reward. While some aspects of that portrait are correctly drawn, the picture has remained unfocused because it omits the framework of contemporary beliefs and values.[5]

Virtue in the sixteenth and early seventeenth centuries included the giving of favor and reward. "For a King not to be bountiful were a fault" was a defense made by Robert Cecil, Earl of Salisbury to criticism of James I's reward and spending in Parliament in 1610. He argued that the king held the same opinion as other learned authors, "that there is no greater a slave than money and not worthy to be accounted among wise men, it being good for nothing but for use."[6] Salisbury was not inventing an apology but echoing fifteenth-century humanist theorists who, in writing advice for princes ("mirror-for-princes literature"), stressed that "among the greatest virtues of all" were liberality and magnificence. Nevertheless, this was something of a change from the Senecan view in which benefit was seen to exist within boundaries.[7] Erasmus, for instance, wrote that "kynges must so fere extende humanitee and favour towardes their subjectes, as thei maye in the meane tyme accordyingly upholde and maintein their authoritee and estate royal. For goodnesse and favour, without ende or measure shewed is many a tyme and ofte the mother of contempte."[8] Royal bounty coincided with and confirmed notions of the godlike nature of the king. In Renaissance Europe, as in archaic societies, honor and prestige were "closely bound up with expenditure."[9] Contemporaries declared "the king is free," and acting freely, the king rewarded his subjects.[10]

At the same time, contemporaries also believed that the granting of bounty was part of a reciprocal relationship between king and subject. If Seneca articulated for Renaissance society the view that society was based on the exchange of mutual benefits, James I wrote in *The Trew Law of Free Monarchies* (1598) of the reciprocal and mutual duty "betwixt a free king and his natural subjects."[11] Salisbury went on to say "that duty is best and surest tried where it is rewarded, which is the cause and makes men the willinger to do service."[12] Indeed, the king's rewarding of the political elite, especially the nobility, was essential because he thereby reinforced the reciprocal bonds established between the Crown and its most important subjects. Claude de Seyssel, the French humanist, served as master of requests to Louis XII. In *The Monarchy of France*, published in 1508, he emphasized

> that the King should sustain and cherish the estate of the nobility, (which is the first everywhere), not only by maintaining its rights and preeminences but, further, by showing all the people of the estate that he especially loves and esteems them … men of this estate should always be preferred over those of every other … providing they are equally adequate or even where there is some slight advantage on the others' side.[13]

James I accepted Seyssel's views. In the *Basilikon Doron*, written in 1597 for his son Prince Henry, James laid out the classic case for royal bounty. Like God, the king gave freely to his people, much as he ensured justice. He honored the political elite by rewarding them with position and honors at court. While warning that the nobility must be made to keep the laws, James emphasized the importance of using court patronage to bind them to the crown.

> The more frequently that your court can bee garnished with them; thinke it the more your honour; acquainting and employing them in all your greatest affaires; sen it is, they must be your armes and executors of your laws … as may make the greatest of them to thinke, that the chiefest point of their honour, standeth in striuing with the meanest of the land in humilitie towards you, and obedience to your lawes.

Like the mirror-for-princes theorists, James celebrated royal generosity: "Use trew liberalitie in rewarding the good, and bestowing frankly for your honour and weale."[14]

The liberal dispensation of royal bounty was, therefore, the Renaissance ideal espoused by monarchs and theorists alike, not merely the behavior of the Scottish king. This ideal posited the free giving of gifts and rewards because it was virtuous. Duty and deference would then follow from grateful recipients. Moreover, such an exchange reflected political reality. By dispensing royal bounty to local governors who ruled the countryside in the king's name, the Crown made court patronage an important instrument of political control. Royal favor also rewarded royal officials to provide for their work in royal administration. These functions were crucial in the absence of a paid central or local bureaucracy and a standing army. The restoration of power to the monarchy achieved by the Tudors rested in part on the systematic use of royal patronage.

Courtesy books, guides to behavior, were popular in the late sixteenth and early seventeenth centuries; in them the symbolic behavior of the courtier was packaged and sold as a commodity.[15] One popular volume was Angel Day's *The English Secretorie: or plaine and direct Method, for the enditing of all manner of Epistles or Letters*. The book went through eleven editions between 1586 and 1639 and included letters of petition and letters of commendation, described as "the most ordinary of any sorts of letters." Day included letters to and from patrons. One, from a nobleman on behalf of a client (1586 and 1592 editions) makes explicit the mutual benefits and duality of the patronage connection:

> This bearer having of long time continued in my service, and therein at al times honestly, faithfully, and carefully behaved himselfe. I have thought good hereby to recommend unto your patronage ... by reason of your office of Lord Governour of V. in her maiesties realme of Ireland, I am enformed there are many offices and places of great commodity remaining in your gift, uppon your followers to bee bestowed ... I doe most hartely pray you, that you will not onely for my sake be contented to receave him into your service, but also ... in any place of preferment about you, do him that benefite and furtherance ... Herein if my request may prevaile ... I shall finde my selfe both greatly occasioned to thanke you, and in like manner, in whatsoever you shall have meane to use me, bee most willing to requite you.

The letter's language spells out the mutual benefits, the exchange and conditional nature of patron, client and broker relationships. Despite the letter's peremptory nature, it was possible for the recipient to say no. Day followed it with three possible responses, the negative, the positive and the equivocal. Later editions, from 1599 on, omitted direct reference to patronage while retaining the letter's references to tangible resources and to reciprocal benefit.

In the 1630s, an anonymous courtesy book appeared entitled *The Mirrour of Complements*. The volume provided several letters as exemplars for offering service to the king and his courtiers including such lines as "how much my soul doth thirst to do you service." Billing itself as "a pleasant and profitable academy," it claimed to provide "the practice of the court ... where ... the words of least importance are precogitate. Make thy profit of the present and attend the future."[16]

Day's model's, at least, reflected court usage. James I wrote a letter to the King of France that sounds remarkably like Day's exemplar. In the Elizabethan period Robert Beale compiled for his own use a formulary book for the Clerk of the Council that included models under such headings as styles of the prince's letters to all kinds of noblemen and gentlemen, supplications, requests, complaints and petitions to the council, and appointments to royal service.[17] In the 1620s a secretary to the Duke of Buckingham kept a useful group of forms, several of which concerned parliamentary elections and proxies, the creation of a bishop, the grant of the keeping of royal forests and wood sales.[18]

To fully understand early Stuart court patronage, we need to go beyond models, to enter the mental and linguistic world of the participants. The linguistic origin of the words "patron" and "client" is Roman, growing out of the word for father and meaning one who stood in relation to another as a father. "Client" and "clientage" too were Roman, deriving from the verb to hear or to listen, which came to mean a plebian who was under the patronage of a patrician.[19] In medieval Latin, "patron" signified, in addition, patron saint, and lord and master. The order in which these meanings were taken over into English was not the same, however, as in Latin. Its first usage in English was religious not secular, referring to the patron of a church, in the thirteenth and fourteenth centuries, and the presentation to a benefice. In the fourteenth and fifteenth centuries, "client" was used generally to describe one under the influence of another. By the sixteenth century, it had changed significantly. It was applied to secular relationships, coming to mean aid to a client in return for certain services.[20] In the sixteenth and seventeenth centuries, there was occasionally an identification of the client with a vassal or even a slave.[21]

To build up a picture of court patronage we need to see how the patron and client constructed and construed their relationship. Charles Cornwallis was ambassador to Spain in the first decade of James I's reign. He provided official reports to Robert Cecil, Earl of Salisbury, the king's chief minister. In addition he wrote letters to his patron, Henry Howard, Earl of Northampton, the Lord Privy Seal, and to Northampton's nephew, Thomas Howard, Earl of Suffolk. In 1607, not having heard from Northampton for several months, Cornwallis wrote anxiously to inquire if he had offended him. Northampton reassured Cornwallis that only the press of council business had kept him from writing. In exaggerated rhetoric, Northampton conjured up an idealized vision of patron–client relations.

I made election of your worth so faithfully, I affected your own person so
sincerely, I drew your love out of the bunch so particularly, I recommended
you to the grace and favor of the best and highest so assuredly, I defended
your good parts against your emulators and enviers so resolutely, embraced the
profession of your vows so confidently, I undertook your cause so laboriously,
I made your interest my own so indifferently, I settled on your faith so
constantly, to change my love, my hope and trust without some such ground
as from a person of [your] worth, integrity, and wit, I cannot expect, and
therefore the condition of the contract standing still in force you need fear
no forfeitures.[22]

Although deliberately playing on the word "contract," this explicit statement
of the patron's obligations did not reflect a contract to buy and sell but a
continuing exchange of benefits. While their relationship was asymmetrical,
the patron acknowledged the standing and ability of the client. The general
exchange of personal honor, love, hope and trust surrounded a specific
exchange between court patron and client by which to gain access to royal
bounty.[23] Moreover, Northampton built a picture not only of the patron but
also of the atmosphere of the court itself. For Northampton acted not only
as Cornwallis's patron but also as a court broker. He emphasized the heated
competition for favor at court and, in referring to the more sinister side of
court life, noted that he had defended Cornwallis against his enviers and
emulators. Northampton reflected a vision of the Jacobean court as tense and
competitive. This was indeed the portrait drawn by contemporary writers,
but it also suggests the performance of a court patron trying to heighten the
effect of the work he claimed to have undertaken for the client.

What is perhaps most illuminating is that Northampton suggested almost
a religious connection between patron and client, invoking words with a
religious resonance, such as "election," "vows," and "faith." If this seems an
odd note to strike between patron and client, we need to remember that
in a divine-right monarchy in which the king himself and many other
contemporary writers employed the metaphor of God, the free dispenser
of grace, the court patron or broker might see himself as similar to the saint
who intercedes with an all-knowing God to bring salvation and favor to the
supplicant and himself. A supplicating letter to the queen drew on the same
metaphor: "suffice it these find grace not from our merit but your bounty."[24]
How many Renaissance paintings show the patron in precisely this fashion:
small, hands supplicating the saint or Madonna, whose painting he has
commissioned from his client the artist, in order to seek favor with God?

Northampton served not only as patron but also as broker between
Cornwallis and Robert Cecil, Earl of Salisbury. "You have been very much
bound in this place to my Lord of Salisbury, whose voice in his own
element having greater force than theirs that speak in a further distance
though one harmony, has not been wanting upon all occasions that might

either improve your merit or advance your reputation."[25] In reply, his client Cornwallis spoke in similarly exaggerated and affective terms. "By that perfect unity your prince shall be served, your country secured, and my poor self shadow my head under that bay tree whereunto I wish perpetual greenness and plentiful blossom."[26]

Giving up direct efforts to secure access to favor, the client rejoiced in the triumphs of his patron that promised rewards to both. Their effusive language spoke only indirectly of concrete rewards, emphasizing personal ties and service to the state. There was magnanimity on the part of the patron and deference on the side of the client.

The dialogue between Northampton and Cornwallis provides a good example of patronage as a form of general exchange. Unlike a commercial or a market transaction, patronage partakes of more than access to material resources. The purpose of such a general exchange as suggested by Marcel Mauss in *The Gift* was to establish conditions of trust, solidarity, and the obligation to uphold one's commitments; indeed, to establish and defend one's honor.[27] Moreover, gift-giving, like patronage of which it was frequently a component, was to appear to be generous and disinterested but was, in fact, performed with formal pretense and social deception. Crucial to the success of court patronage was its disguise. While contemporaries were frank with one another about their desire for court office and titles, the rhetoric between patron and client drew on another language, one which stressed the free gift of royal patronage, the magnanimity of the patron, and the dependence of the client. It was a belief shared by all members of the political elite including the king himself. By putting together general symbols of obligation and honor *along* with concrete specific exchanges, patronage acts as "a distinct mode of ... structuring ... the flow of resources, exchange and power relations and their legitimation in society."[28]

Natalie Davis has argued that gift culture existed side by side with market culture in sixteenth-century France; the same was true in sixteenth and early seventeenth-century England.[29] Gift-giving extended throughout the social structure. New Year's gifts were traditional and members of the political elite reaching up to the monarch himself kept records over several generations of those given and received.[30] It was usual for members of the political elite to present the monarch with New Year's gifts. In the 1580s the Countess of Shrewsbury wondered what to give Queen Elizabeth. Several letters to friends at court were taken up with discussion of the issue and one wrote to say that the Queen would *not* like a gift of money. After the Countess presented the Queen with a handsome gown, her court correspondent wrote that the Queen was exceedingly pleased with it.[31] In 1610 the king gave Prince Henry £1,000 and Prince Charles £200 as New Year's gifts and gave Prince Charles's household officer, Sir Robert Carey, £100 "to be paid out upon such occasions as Duke of York shall have this New Years tide to expend in gifts, rewards, etc.;" Prince Charles was 10 years old.[32]

The relationship between patron and client was marked by a gift from client to patron which, in the Tudor and early Stuart period, ranged from venison, gloves, gilt cups and clothing to art works and books. One giver presented "a New Year's remembrance of the old years favors" to a lord, likening himself to "a beggar that presents an orange stuck with cloves."[33] The fishermen of Rye requested that Sir William Twysden, who sat for the borough, accept "a poor dish of fish" in return for his care in soliciting their suit for the amendment of the harbour.[34] The Merchant Adventurers in 1623 gave New Year's gifts to the Duke of Buckingham, the Archbishop of Canterbury, the Lord Keeper, the Lord President, Secretary Calvert and Mr Comptroller, "yearly presents to such honorable personages as they have received favors from." Because they were especially indebted to the Lord Treasurer, they gave him a larger gift than before, 200 pieces of 22s in gold and a piece of plate.[35]

Increasingly, however, the market was coming to penetrate areas of governance so that the line between gifts and bribes became more difficult to draw. In a series of fiery sermons preached before Edward VI in the 1550s, Hugh Latimer had inveighed against "a briber, a gift taker, a gratifier of rich men."[36] He endorsed the English translations of the Bible by William Tyndale and Miles Coverdale saying in his sermon, "I can commend the English translation that doth interpret *munera*, bribes not gifts."[37] Lawrence Stone has argued that gift-giving reached its apogee in sixteenth-century England, that it appears with greater frequency and importance in the sixteenth-century Lisle letters than in the fifteenth-century Paston letters, the seventeenth-century Salisbury letters, or the Walpole correspondence of the eighteenth century.[38] While exchange continued it took a new form in the late sixteenth and early seventeenth centuries.

This changing understanding of gift-giving can be demonstrated at the very highest level. Sir Thomas More accepted gloves from a litigant as a New Year's gift but refused gold and, presented with a gilt cup, returned a more valuable, though less attractive one, to a suitor.[39] William, Lord Burghley, had urged the presentation of small but noticeable gifts to great men in the Elizabethan period. At the turn of the century, Penry Williams has demonstrated, Robert Cecil wrestled with the legitimacy of taking a coach and four from the Earl of Northumberland. The reasons against it were the fear that observers including the queen might connect it to his recently aiding the earl in a suit and that "gifts of value" should not pass between "those whose minds condemn all the knots that utility can fasten."[40] On the other hand, the coach and horses had arrived. Cecil kept the gift. Shortly after the accession of James I, Sir Robert Cecil wrote to the Earl of Shrewsbury that the king had chosen the earl a justice in oyer. Presumably referring to customary practice, Cecil joked that he expected a warrant dormant for a stag and a hind as bribe.[41] The

19

line between gifts and bribes was a narrow one and often in the eye of the beholder. The language of mutual benefits so prevalent in sixteenth and seventeenth-century Europe could come into contradiction in at least two ways: firstly, when it was used in relationship to the law which rhetorically at least rejected the influence both of friendship and of gift and, secondly, when the benefits exchanged were monetary, suggesting a commercial transaction, not gift-giving.

The particular problem that the Jacobean court faced was that the Crown, under the combined pressures of clamoring suitors, increased expenses and fall-off in parliamentary funding, made explicit the basis of its allocation of resources. The Jacobean court openly sold knighthoods, titles and offices. As a result, they faced the crucial problem of the political cost of the loss of the "symbolic capital" that royal bounty represented.[42]

It must be stressed that when the free gift granted by an all-powerful monarch became transformed into a contract to buy and sell, such market-place negotiations undermined the central meaning of court patronage. The use of money had become part of the patronage system before the seventeenth century, but it had served as an adjunct to the other gifts given to the patron by his clients, perhaps the most important of which were the intangible ones of deference and service.[43] In the early seventeenth century, money assumed an increasingly central role, in part as a deliberate policy of the Crown to sell titles and offices. Such sales provided funds for king and courtiers when parliament voted inadequate subsidies and when income from Crown revenues became inadequate. Moreover, payment served as a filter for the Crown faced with too many worthy suitors. But the increasing role of money as the medium of exchange from client to patron and the control of court patronage by a royal favorite affected the relationships on which the Crown depended. Northampton may have omitted any mention of money in his panegyric to Cornwallis, but he served as broker for large cash payments made by merchant clients to the king's favorite Somerset for the lucrative farm of the customs.[44]

II

Performance was as much a part of patronage as general and specific exchange. Sir John Holles's writings partake of the same language as Northampton's and Cornwallis's. He portrays the court and its patronage from the viewpoint of an inveterate office-seeker. Through his performance as favor-seeker he conjures up for us the world of the Jacobean court and its contradictions held in uneasy balance: the continuing ties between patron and client and the multiplicity of brokers; the ritual language amounting to playacting and conflicting attitudes toward the court. These contradictions were resolved by the new system brought in by the new favorite, George Villiers, the Duke of Buckingham, but not necessarily with happy results.

In 1617 Holles wrote to a friend in the country:

> I confess this age wherein we live is fruitfull of strange, and extraordinarie accidents; and as the world in the beginning was a chaos, and confusion of all things, till the laws of God, of nature, of man gave eache creature, and thing his proper separation, the one from the other, so now, through the divine providence, all things drawing to their prefixed period, by abandoning those laws, and rules which contained them within their proper orbs, and distances, return through this corruption to their first confusion; that the ould game ended the cards may be new shuffled for that which followeth.[45]

The world view adopted by both Northampton and Holles is the same, but the conclusion is different. Did court connections have the stability of contract (or, as Holles put it, "the laws of God, of nature, of man") or had they returned to their first confusion and chaos with the accession of Buckingham?

Holles came from a gentry family in Nottinghamshire and became Earl of Clare in the 1620s. Although sometimes identified as a member of the "Country" party, Holles in fact exemplifies the connection of the court and the country in the minds and actions of Stuart gentry.[46] He attacked the Scots and the Duke of Buckingham even as he tied himself to Robert Carr, the king's naturalized Scottish favorite, and bought both a barony and an earldom during the Duke's supremacy. He fought with some of his eminent local neighbors such as the Earl of Shrewsbury and sought the influence of central government ministers in local affairs. His family exhibited the division caused by the Civil War: his son Denzil Holles was the leader of the Long Parliament presbyterians from 1640 to 1646; his son-in-law Thomas Wentworth, the court critic turned government minister, became Earl of Strafford and was condemned to death by the Long Parliament.

Holles tells us how the patronage system *had* worked. In advice for his heir, in which he set forth ten precepts concerning marriage, children, hospitality and kindred, Holles included a precept copied from Lord Burghley:

> Be sure you always keep some great man to your friend but trouble him not for trifles, compliment him often, present him with many yet small gifts, and of little charge; and if you have cause to bestow any great gratuity on him, then let it be some such thing as may be daily in sight; for otherwise you shall live like a hop without a pole, live in obscurity and be made a football for every insulting companion to spurn at.[47]

Burghley's advice adopted by Holles reflects a sixteenth-century version of patronage as performance and as general exchange: the first, by urging that the patron be complimented often; the second, by recommending the giving of many small gifts or one large present to put him in mind of the client. Payment of the patron is not mentioned at all.

The sixteenth and seventeenth centuries saw many such counsels of father to son, a favorite mode of communication whether of princes or of gentlemen.[48] Holles also informally counseled his father. In 1587 Holles told his father that the latter had been omitted from the commission of the peace not because of malice (his father's conjecture) "but only for the want of any your frend, that should at that time afore the Councell have given knowledge of your sufficiency and service for that place, which my Lord Cheef Justice [Sir Edmund Anderson] ... might have done (whose commendation, or word did ratify, or disanull for that Cuntrie) if he had been half that friend to you which he had himself to yow professed."[49]

Patronage was necessary, then, even to get small favors done. But what could the client do who had no connection with the officer entitled to grant the favor? The answer was to find a court broker. In one instance, Holles wanted to do his cousin a favor that required the intervention of the Lord Chief Justice. His quandary was this: "Understanding my waters too shallow to carry a vessel of his lordship's burden as having never by familiarity or merit interested in him, I advised with myself whom I had powerful to work this favor from him." As a result he applied to Sir Francis Bacon, "presuming rather from your love, which has been faithful to me ... whence you may believe that my fortunes being better, my service may prove also of a higher quality."[50] In this case, Bacon was only one of several patrons to whom Holles applied, using the language of love as well as suggesting, perhaps, a douceur for the Attorney-General.

If Burghley put forward the ideal of a single patron, clients at the Jacobean court often applied to many patrons. Nevertheless, they used language of extreme deference as if they were beholden to just one. Indeed, that language seems to have become more exaggerated as the quest for patronage quickened from the 1590s on. Holles served in the king's privy chamber for almost nine years and then went on to serve in Prince Henry's household. This was his most important court office. While Holles often congratulated himself on achieving court office without the help of a patron other than the king and the prince, after Prince Henry's death he earnestly sought new patrons, hoping to achieve office and title. He approached many including the Earl of Somerset, Archbishop Abbot, the Earls of Suffolk and Northampton, the Duke of Buckingham, and the Duke of Lennox. To the latter he wrote, "Eight years I served his Majesty and because I depended not elsewhere, that time wasted without acknowledgement, my fellows and inferiors on every side preferred before me, some to honors, some to employments."[51] To Sir Thomas Lake he noted that change rather than diligence brought success. Although Northampton, as patron, had invoked the stability of "contract," to a client such as Holles, Jacobean court patronage was marked by great uncertainty.

It must be remembered that Holles was not only a country gentleman; the problem of political uncertainty was of particular importance to him and to his colleagues as court officeholders. In particular, English ambassadors abroad needed to know not only the details of official policy but also the names of those who were influential at court. The letters of Cornwallis, Sir Henry Wotton and Dudley Carleton are filled with discussions of patrons and brokers at the court. Indeed, as we shall see, they reveal the influence of some court brokers who have not been sufficiently noticed by historians.

Holles served as adviser to Sir John Digby, the English ambassador in Spain. When Holles informed him of Salisbury's last illness, Digby noted his own important connection to Cecil as patron and administrator: "None will participate more of the general loss than myself whom he has bound unto him by many obligations. Besides you cannot but conceive of how much advantage it is to one in my place to have the favor and love of his director."[52] After Salisbury's death, Digby needed to know to which patron, to which network, he should now turn. He thanked Holles for his advice, noting that its performance might be difficult: "Therein much art is to be used, for changes of that kind are to be made by insensible degrees."

Adopting a pose of indifference as to who received the great offices at court, Digby wrote, "I will run the same course if my best friends have the place as if my greatest enemy had it, relying upon the integrity of my own proceedings and my diligence in the King's service and not on the friendship of a kind or favorable minister;" but he gradually admitted the importance of cultivating a patron: "though I shall not omit by all fitting means to endeavor to have their good opinion, for I well know that those by whom my services must pass unto his Majesty may by the way, if they list, give them an ill taste." He ended the letter breathlessly, "I pray you by your first let me hear how all things are disposed of."[53]

The importance of court patronage to the officeholder was as clear with Digby as it was with Cornwallis, his predecessor as ambassador. But Digby put forward contradictory ideas about the importance of a court patron to the fulfillment of his official duties. Only when he fell foul of the Duke of Buckingham during the ill-fated trip by the duke and Prince Charles to Spain to woo the Infanta did Digby fully realize the crucial importance of the "friendship" of a favorable minister.[54]

In the sixteenth and seventeenth centuries the royal court was perceived both as the center of magnificence and reward and as the siren singing subjects to shipwreck. Holles shared these views. But even as he labeled the court a labyrinth, "a place of artifice," Holles longed for reappointment to the Household and to the Bedchamber of Prince Charles. "I am loath to retire to a private condition." When he was not successful, this supposed member of the "Country" party bemoaned the fact that "henceforth the useless country swallow me up; for thither for ought I know, the torrent of my fate carries me, the anchor being gone by which I held."[55]

Patronage connections spanned Privy Council and Royal Household. Appointment to the Household meant not just private service to the monarch but a role at the center of court patronage and, often, court politics. While major decisions might be taken at the Privy Council, it was necessary, as David Starkey has suggested, for major court officials to ensure personal access to the monarch.[56] Leading court patrons therefore frequently placed clients in the Bedchamber of the monarch and his family to reinforce the positions or policies those patrons had taken. For the clients this meant a key role in the distribution of royal favor.

Holles had watched jealously as Scots took important positions in the Household; like many others, Holles believed that Scots were monopolizing royal bounty.[57] This was not an issue of private concern to a few courtiers; Holles named it a public grievance in the parliamentary session of 1610 in a speech which recapitulated several themes discussed in this chapter.

> The king wants money for which supply this Parliament is called ... The court is the cause of all for by the reception of the other nation that head is too heavy for this small body of England ... The king's equal affection to us as them would help all ... but the Scottish monopolize his princely person, standing like mountains betwixt the beams of his grace and us; yet we most humbly beseech his Majesty his Bedchamber may be shared as well to those of our nation as to them, that this seven years' brand of jealousy, distrust or unworthiness, may at the last be removed from us, and that the same chamber may have the same brotherly partition which all the other inferior forms of the court, the Presence and Privy Chamber have. From this inequality proceeds a twofold unequal distribution of benefits, of favors, for not only the King's ordinary and extraordinary receipts be exhausted by them ... all favors and honors directly or indirectly pass through their hands; for not only they possess the royal presence, they be warm within, while the best of ours starve without. Hence, as from a fountain, is fed that great and daily renewing overplus of their nation, which surrounding the whole court devours that royal hospitality and trebles the ordinary expense. Many of them be worthy; I am not lean because they be fat, only I wish equality, that they should not seem to be children of the family and we the servants; which proportion, as it will breed a mutual love, so will it close up in such measure this evacuation, that the King being abundantly supplied from his own, those words of supply and support and this fearful term of grievance shall be no more remembered and we hereafter shall live most happy subjects under a far more happy sovereign.[58]

Despite his attacks on Scots, Holles, performing the role of aspiring client, wrote frequently to the Duke of Lennox and allied himself with Robert Carr, Earl of Somerset. What appears inconsistent was, in fact, common behavior for clients fishing for favor at the Jacobean court. But once bound to Somerset, Holles remained loyal to him for more than two decades after the favorite's fall. Toward Somerset Holles at first felt critical, particularly because the favorite was the "chief workman" of Household appointments. Holles felt "a stranger at Whitehall and cannot witness but by the universal effects Somerset's greatness." In 1614 he attached himself to Somerset and through his intercession kissed the king's hand. Thereafter his attachment to Somerset did not waver. In asking for Somerset's favor, Holles explicitly solicited appointment to the king's Household, "wherein I might al so serve your Lordship in more neernes."[59] Holles was sensitive to the concern of great men to have clients in the king's Household in daily contact with the monarch.

Holles greeted with disbelief the accusations of poisoning leveled against Somerset in the Overbury murder case.[60] At the execution of Richard Weston, Holles repeatedly called on the condemned man to recant his implication of the earl in the scheme. For his behavior, Holles was committed to prison. Once free he continued his close attachment to Carr throughout Buckingham's supremacy, visiting the former favorite in the Tower, sending him news of court, and even advising him on his pardon.[61] He even suggested that Somerset's loss of favor had brought about psychologically based illness. "My Lord of Somerset's sickness questionless comes from a grounded, deep discontent in regard of the hard and unworthy usage he has received for to a good mind neglect weighs more than hatred or injury, the sense whereof smothered in him now breaks forth into this dangerous expression."[62] Once scourge of the Scots, Holles now called the former Scottish favorite "the best friend that ever I had." The statement reflects not only Holles's sentiment but also his failure to gain a better friend.

The fall of Somerset and the rise of Buckingham were blows for Holles. He saw in Somerset's fate the traditional dangers of the court and dependence on court favor. Visiting Somerset in the Tower he wrote of

> such journeys beeing necessarie sumtyms for humiliation, seeing in others miseries, as in a glass, we may behould the misfortune, to which all men that live under the will of another be subject, ... this ... which modernly is termed reason of state is an arrow, which flyeth over every mans head, and no man can escape it without miraculous fortune, if he stand in the way; for sum mens ruins ar as necessarie for Princes dessignes, as other mens services.[63]

Somerset had suffered from a new spin of the wheel of fortune, a new shuffling of the deck. The emergence of Buckingham brought a new system of court favor that gave renewed emphasis to "reason of state."

After Buckingham became favorite, Holles continued to press for court office. He was unsuccessful, perhaps because of his continued allegiance to the old favorite Somerset and his crossing Buckingham when the latter wished to marry the daughter of Sir Edward Coke to his brother. Holles supported Coke's estranged wife, Lady Hatton, in her attempt to prevent the marriage and commented ribaldly on the public notice taken of this court intrigue. Everyone, he said, was interested in it, "from the King to the favoritt, and from him to the ferriman of Putney, and a woman that sells chickens who have been examined for some scandalous words of Sir John Villiers' soar legg."[64]

Although Buckingham allowed Holles to purchase two titles, he never admitted him to court office again. Holles dwelled on his own loss of his patron Somerset, using, like Raleigh, the language of love to describe his unsuccessful search for favor. "To this fortun am I born . . . still with Tantalus to gape after the flying apples, allways sowing and never reaping. But there is a time to give over, as well as to give on, and it suffyseth to have attempted, having oft ennough wooed fortun, and favour, it beeing peradventure better for my condition to have been her souldior, then her minion."[65] Somerset's prominence had been shared with other patrons; Buckingham's control of the king and the court was total, or so Holles saw it.

> we all ar reeds, we bow with every breath, not okes which withstand the most tempestous wynds; a blynd Jesuitical obedience beeing the naturall temperature of this clymate which, though peradventure worse for sum particulars, who covett to walk by the true rules of the Kings honor, and thir owne; yet muche better for the generality, whose summum bonum is an ydle quietnes, purchased, and possessed, they ar not curious by what ways.[66]

Writing at the beginning of Buckingham's dominance, Holles touches on two elements: blind loyalty and purchase, the hallmarks of the favorite's rule that were to transform the early Stuart patronage system. Against them, Holles, who had been unable to attach himself to the new favorite, raised the issue of the king's honor, traditionally at the center of patronage. This proved a theme often repeated, for Holles and many others continued to express these views not just in private letters but also in parliament in the 1620s.

If we turn from the search for favor to the exchange between patrons and clients, it is necessary to examine the symbolic meaning of the systematic introduction of money into the transaction by which the king grants favor. The exchange of money for favor from client to broker or patron does not reflect prescriptive literature or sixteenth-century practice but was characteristic of Jacobean patronage. It became systematized under the Duke of Buckingham. Holles's own attitude toward money-making was quite clear: he kept a close eye on his own estates. Advising Lord Sheffield in 1598, he wrote, "I would always buy cheap and I covet now you sell dear."[67] Yet even as he offered money in exchange for favor and advancement, unease and tension entered his offers. This is apparent in his letter to the Duke of Lennox asking him to serve as broker between himself and the king:

> By the place your Lordship has vouchsafed me in your favor, I persuade myself my good is also interested. Of other my friends I have no assurance. These latter

years have given me experience that money prevails beyond all obligations of merit or nature, so as I wonder not that great men have cause to complain of those they term their friends for leaving them when their sunshine sets: seeing they choose neither kindred nor virtue . . . but profit only, who having their turn served will repay such ladders with the like coin. I speak not this to save my own purse, but even in that I will be found as thankful.[68]

This was not an idle promise. To Robert Carr, Earl of Somerset and to the Duke of Buckingham, Holles made similar offers. "Knowing that Princes favors ar proffitable to their favorites, as well by reflection from inferiors, as by influence descending from themselves, and when those of my rank faile of this consideration, they wrong themselves; and those great persons by whom they covett to be respected before others."[69] Holles never became a client of the Duke of Buckingham but that is not to say he did not try. Patronage required the performance of role of a devoted follower and exaggerated language of alliance even if the client did not feel it. Thus to Buckingham he wrote:

I appeal to your Lordships noblenes, and justice, and fear no tutche soever in matters of honor, and friendship, and as yow fynd me so either receave me, or throw me out of your nest, with thes bastard aiglets, which dazzel at every sunshine: neither will I befrend my self with experiences past, the world [is] not ignorant at what rates I have purchased the name of a frend.[70]

Holles's repeated use of "purchase" may appear metaphorical, but it can be argued that the language that he adopted signified not only the emotions of honor and friendship but also, simultaneously, the payment for favor.

For Holles was not unwilling to admit that he had bought his titles. After embroiling himself with Sir Edward Coke in a matter in which Buckingham was also concerned, Holles wrote in indignation to the Duke of Lennox to complain of ill usage at being questioned by the Privy Council:

I have receaved the wrong to be brought upon the stage, convented as a criminell, and censured worse by the voice of the people, who ar so just to the honors of all men, espetially to thos of the rank I purchased that they hould a man condemned, if questioned, and not to be questioned for pinns, and points, and such slight ware; princes seeking the punishment of malefactors, not to discontent their loyal, honest servants.[71]

But even as he was willing to pay, Holles begrudged such payments. We might assume that this was due to a sharp eye to his cash outflow, but something much more important was involved. Even though the sale of office had taken place for decades, and the sale of titles was greeted with a large pool of applicants decked out with appropriately gentle credentials, the expansion and institution of such sales as a system brought into question the nature of bounty itself. The contradiction between royal favor and marketplace mentality was forcefully pointed up by Holles when, as a court official, he attacked the suggested marriage of Prince Henry to a daughter of the Duke of Savoy. Holles claimed that the motive was money,

> supposed the best receivable mean for the clearing the King's debts ... But why should the heir of England be sold? ... what honor, what profit, either present or future, shall redound to this kingdom thereby? In the circumference of the word profit we may include the word honor, seeing princes be of that transcendency as none but God can add diamonds to their crowns, and their profit is of a larger latitude than to be determined with a sum of money.[72]

Commercial practice increasingly shaped some patronage relationships in the early seventeenth century but it was rejected or only dimly reflected in official acts and representations.

III

The language of patronage included the vocabularies of the masque and contemporary architecture and art. Early Stuart masques celebrated the theories of divine right and the virtues of the monarchy in visual pictures accompanied by explanatory text. Stephen Orgel has argued that the masque was presented for the king himself and reflected the virtues of his rule.[73] The Banqueting Hall, the architectural masterpiece of the Jacobean era, begun in 1619, was created as the site for court masques whose language was reflected as well in Rubens's paintings for the ceiling.

Rubens was first approached about the commission perhaps as early as 1619. The panels were installed in 1635 but Per Palme has argued that Rubens began work in the 1620s.[74] Sir Roy Strong suggests that Inigo Jones, the English artist, architect, and masque maker, Surveyor of Works to both James and Charles, who designed the Banqueting House, formulated the program. In the Baroque style admired by the court of Charles I, the Banqueting Hall ceiling celebrates the monarchy of James I as a new Solomon. The ceiling begins with a view of the Union between England and Scotland under the encouraging eye of King James and reaches its climax with the apotheosis of King James, who is drawn into heaven to be reunited with the God whose representative on earth he is. In the middle is a painting, *The Benefits of the Government of James I*, which celebrates both his bringing of peace and plenty and his overcoming of war and revolt. Side panels show wise government overcoming rebellion and royal bounty overcoming avarice.[75]

Benefits, the language of James's own *Trew Law*, encompassed plenty and abundance. Roy Strong connects the virtues of the good governor that James put forward in *Basilikon Doron* with those depicted in the ceiling, especially justice, wisdom, temperance and liberality.[76] Such rule welcomed in a golden age in which "The earth unplowed shall yield her crop / Pure honey from the oak shall drop / The fountain shall run milk."[77] It is significant to keep in mind, however, that bounty did not overcome famine or want but avarice. Seneca had emphasized that "there is a great difference ... betwixt a benefit and a negotiation of bargaining."[78] Court culture, in art as in text, emphasized liberality and bounty in opposition to merchandising and greed. At the same time the language of benefits existed alongside commercial practice.

Royal patronage was embodied not only in the language of art and the language of political theory but also that of religion. Frequently these overlapped. Sir Walter Raleigh wrote to James I asking for mercy, "the more my misery is the more is your Majesty's great mercy if you please to behold it, and the less I can deserve the more liberal your Majesty's gift. God only your Majesty shall imitate herein, both in giving freely, and in giving to such a one from whom there can be no retribution."[79] Of the Duke of Buckingham, King James said that "Christ had his John and I have my George."[80] Indeed, in the 1620s, petitions to the favorite requesting his intercession with the king increasingly emphasized the patron as saint.[81] At the Caroline court the Calvinist minister, John Prideaux, delivered a court sermon entitled *A Project for Preferment* in which he celebrated Jesus Christ as the greatest Master of Requests.[82] Thus patronage was not only central to the political life of the poetical elite but to the language in which they wrote, spoke, worshipped and symbolized themselves.

Chapter 2

The structures of patronage and corruption: access and allocation

In 1611 after the death of King James's most important Scottish councillor, George Hume, Earl of Dunbar, an unnamed official drew up "A note of such grants as were made to the Lord Dunbar by the king's majesty." These included lands in Leicestershire, Norfolk, Bedfordshire, Kent, Oxfordshire, Somerset, Northumberland and Ireland; offices in the central administration and the Household such as Chancellor of the Exchequer, Keeper of the Great Wardrobe, and Keeper of the Privy Purse, and, later, Chancellor of Scotland; keeperships of sundry royal castles and manors; the title of Baron Hume of Berwick "under which that liberty is given to him to convey away by will or otherwise that honor either consanguino or cognate," and of Earl of Dunbar; and the monopolies of all monies due the king for logwood and blockwood to be brought into the realm for forty-one years and £2,000 a year granted for ten years of the impost on seacoal.[1] The reader might be forgiven for thinking that he was looking at a Norman baron of the reign of King Stephen, an "overmighty subject," or the holdings of Cardinal Wolsey before his fall. Dunbar was, instead, the loyal servant and councillor of James VI and I of England, the leader of those Jacobean Scots who came south with the new king to claim his inheritance.

I

To understand the policies and practices of James I, it is necessary to set early Stuart patronage in a larger context. Structures of political patronage were not static but changed over time. They were sensitive to the changing political and economic power of the Crown, of different elements of the political elite and of such institutions as the church and parliament. Furthermore, important as structure and policy, the personality and behavior of the individual monarch shaped contemporary patronage relationships.

In the fifteenth century, service in the private armies and large "affinities" of magnates served as the most important way of securing access to resources.[2] The Tudors brought "overmighty subjects" under their control and secularized patron–client relationships, which were no longer primarily based on military or clerical power.[3] Moreover, patronage reacted sharply to demographic and economic as well as political changes. The structures of royal patronage in the sixteenth and early seventeenth centuries were affected by population growth and significant shifts in the ownership of land.

Between 1541 and 1641 the English population grew from approximately 2,744,000 to about 5,092,000.[4] Moreover, the number of those who could consider themselves gentlemen and, thereby, members of the political elite, grew even more dramatically in the sixteenth century. This enlarged political elite owned an increasingly large share of the country's landed wealth. In the early sixteenth century, the church held perhaps 20–25 per cent and the Crown about 5 per cent of the land in England. By the late seventeenth century, because of the dissolution of the monasteries, the dissolution of the chantries and royal land sales to finance war, those holdings had dropped to between 5 and 10 per cent. Whereas middling and lesser gentry owned perhaps as much as 25 per cent of the land in the fifteenth century, their share increased to 50 per cent. As a result, in the early sixteenth century, in counties such as Suffolk, Rutland and Leicestershire, only one village in five or so had a resident gentleman; by the 1680s over two-thirds had one or more gentleman residing in the village. In Somerset, it has been suggested that the number of gentle families quadrupled between 1502 and 1623. By the middle of the seventeenth century many shires had hundreds of gentry families.[5] While many of these were parochial gentry who might not aspire seriously to court reward, the increase in the size of the bench in the late sixteenth and early seventeenth centuries provides evidence of growing numbers of gentry whose support the Crown needed and who brought pressure on court patronage relationships to gain access to local office and royal bounty.

In addition, for centuries, important merchants had had close ties to the English Crown to which they loaned money. Increasing trade in the sixteenth century made merchant connections even more important to the Crown which wished to tap the wealth of the great trading companies and the merchant community. In return, merchants and companies sought to preserve and expand their control of overseas trade and domestic monopolies. The social mobility of the sixteenth century that saw the movement of yeomen into parish gentry also saw the continuance of the longstanding ideal of well-to-do merchants buying landed estates, thereby creating greater numbers of those who could claim membership of the political elite.[6]

The clamor of growing numbers of clients was met by a significant increase in royal bounty in the sixteenth and early seventeenth century in the form of land for lease or sale, economic privileges, such as licenses and customs farms, government offices, and status symbols of little economic value but great social prestige, such as keeperships of royal parks.[7] (Even the latter afforded the tangible gift of game.) Because of the Crown's efforts to deal with economic and social problems which threatened order and stability, many new statutes were enacted controlling different aspects of the economy. These statutes became vehicles for both formal and informal agents of the state to assert power and to make money from rents. The Tudor bureaucracy expanded thereby increasing the number of offices. Under Elizabeth the extension of monopolies created new opportunities for those seeking profits. The expansion of resources and of government in the sixteenth century created new dependence on the Crown, new officeholders, and a large increase in royal bounty. Yet the dispensation of that bounty lagged behind the exponential growth in the numbers of gentry under Elizabeth.

Royal bounty increased markedly in early Stuart England, whether calculated in honors and titles conferred, in gifts given, in lands bestowed, or in offices and privileges granted. If, as we have seen, the gentry expanded sharply as part of a general rise in population in the sixteenth and early seventeenth centuries, so did the dispensation of royal liberality. There were about 600 knights at the beginning of Elizabeth's reign, a number that had fallen to 550 in the 1590s, perhaps as many as a quarter made by the Earl of Essex during his military expeditions. James I tripled the number of knights in his first year of his reign. Indeed, the king permitted the making of 432 knights in one day to mark his coronation. Thereafter the king made about 74 a year up to 1609, about 31 a year from 1610 to 1614, a number which rose to 120 a year between 1615 and 1619, and returned to 70 or so a year from 1620 to 1625.[8] Under Charles I there was a significant decline from about 45 knights a year from 1626 to 1630 down to 22 a year from 1631 to 1640. In 1641 and 1642, the king abruptly increased the grant of knighthoods to almost 100 each in 1641 and 1642. Lawrence Stone has calculated that Elizabeth created 878 knights in 44 years; the early Stuarts created 3,281, almost four times as many.

In addition to the quadrupling of knighthoods, titles of honors increased at every level. Indeed, the Crown created a new title in 1611, the baronetage, at the price of £1,095 allocated for the plantation of Ulster in Ireland. The original creations numbered just over 90. In 1618 James created baronetages of Ireland and Scotland, accounting for 44 Irish baronets and 132 Scottish baronets, the latter to support the colonization of Nova Scotia.[9] Although King James originally promised to limit the numbers of English baronets to 200, King Charles, in the first years of his reign, increased the numbers to just short of 300. From 1629 to 1640, however, he made only 2. As with knighthoods, Charles expanded the numbers of baronets in 1641 by another 128.

The numbers of peers in the sixteenth century remained steady, ranging from 50 to 60 peers. Thus, at the accession of Queen Elizabeth there were 57 peers; at her death there were only 55. In what might be called "the deflation of honors," Elizabeth strongly resisted the creation of new nobles despite the changing demography of the landed interest. In the first few years of the new reign, King James created over 20 new peers. From 1615, when baronies began to be sold, to 1628, when such sales ceased with the death of the Duke of Buckingham, the king created 45 more peers and the English peerage totalled 126, more than double its Tudor norm. Moreover, the ranks of Irish and Scottish nobility increased too. Where there had been 25 Irish peers in 1603, there were 105 by 1641, most created between 1616 and 1630.[10] Overall, royal honors poured out in cornucopian abundance beginning in 1603 and continuing up to 1628, after which there was a sharp decline until 1640 and 1641. Then, with the calling of the Short and Long Parliaments, Charles I expanded royal honors.

Service as a justice of the peace was both a burden and a sign of status eagerly sought in Tudor and early Stuart England. The numbers of local landowners appointed to the commission of the peace steadily grew from 1558 to the 1620s. Where Kent had 44 men on the commission in 1562, the county had 97 by 1608. Anthony Fletcher has argued that James I tried to improve the quality of the work of the commissions of the peace in 1616/17 by adding barristers, with the result that the numbers increased by more than 100 in that period alone. Charles I adopted a different policy toward service on the bench, one which focused on the efficiency of a smaller number of justices. Beginning in 1625, the size of the bench was reduced and those smaller numbers maintained throughout the 1630s.[11]

Patents of monopolies, the grant of certain licenses and economic privileges, increased too. The ending of the war with Spain opened up possibilities of greater international trade, recognized by the Crown when it established the Great Farm of the customs in 1604, combining most of the different customs farms that had existed under Elizabeth. The Great Farm of the Customs tended to monopolize international trade in the hands of a few London merchants who had links to high officials. Although Queen Elizabeth had withdrawn a group of monopolies in 1601 after parliamentary debate and James I announced the curtailment of the grant of monopolies by proclamation in 1603 and in 1610, these rights to introduce new modes of economic production as well as to grant licenses to carry on all manner of trade, steadily increased up to 1621. In that year parliament received large numbers of petitions against almost one hundred different projects and in 1624 passed a statute limiting monopolies.[12] The statute exempted some such as alum, restricted the right of monopoly to inventors for fourteen years, and continued the right to grant privileges to towns and corporations.[13] As a result, new monopolies continued to be granted throughout the 1630s until 1639 when, under pressure, Charles I withdrew more than thirty.[14]

At his accession, James I established three Royal Households, for himself, for Queen Anne and for their three children, instead of Elizabeth's single Household. In later years there were additional separate Households established for Prince Henry and Prince Charles. James thereby increased not only the number of Household officials but their fees. Fees and annuities dispensed from the Exchequer to pay court officials increased from £27,000 in 1603 to £63,000 in 1608. Amongst the Household charges, fees, pensions and annuities almost doubled, jumping from £27,900 7s 8³/₄d to £48,125 19s 3d.[15] By 1614 fees, annuities and pensions had grown to £104,860. After a period of retrenchment which saw the amounts decreasing or holding steady, fees and annuities mushroomed to £116,000 in 1616 and 1617. After further retrenchment for the rest of the reign and the early years of Charles I, fees increased in the 1630s reaching £102,000 in 1638.[16]

Because royal officials were concerned about the financial cost of royal patronage, their accounts provide a picture of the increase in Jacobean bounty. Two years after King James's accession, a survey of the costs of royal bounty was undertaken, describing "increased yearly charges to the Crown by augmenting of new payments and diminutions of old receipts." New payments amounted to £117,946 1s 4d, while Crown revenue had diminished by £26,449 2s 2d. Of this diminution, almost half came from Crown lands the king had given away in fee simple, totalling over £11,000.

Household expenses as a whole grew from £64,031 in 1602/3 (which included part of the last year of Elizabeth's reign) to £86,720 in the first year of James's. This ballooned in 1610 to £113,099. Much of this increase came from the increasing and virtually unregulated growth in the costs of Prince Henry's Household from £2,743 to £35,765 after his creation as Prince of Wales. Over £33,000 went to diet, wages and stable. There were 120 officers above stairs and 113 below.[17] The death of Queen Anne only saved £10,916 in annual Household expenditure. G. E. Aylmer argues that by 1626 the size and cost of the Chamber had increased disproportionately to other royal expenses.[18]

The expansion of the numbers of officers led to some confusion about who *was* a member of the king's service. Attaching oneself to the court not only promised reward but also freedom from suit and the Lord Chamberlain's papers are filled with petitions and directives about royal servants detained by local officials. In one case the Lord Chamberlain decided that the person falsely claimed to be a royal official because he "obtayned that Title by a disguized false suggestion of beeing one of the Queene of Bohemias Playres, when in truth hee is a Carpenter and never understood or practized the quality of a Stageplayer."[19]

The great expansion in royal bounty under the early Stuarts finds further confirmation in the annuities granted by the Crown. Gerald Aylmer argues that they represent an early modern version of a pension scheme. The necessary intermixing of public and private monies by government officials also meant that patronage was necessary to pay and repay their outlays of private money for public purposes.[20]

Rewards and free gifts were abundant in the early years of James's reign, beginning in 1603 at £11,741 and reaching a high point of £78,791 19s 11d in 1611. The amounts tapered off thereafter except for the first year of Charles I's reign which saw £37,267 1s 2d dispersed by the new monarch. As we shall see, however, the largesse of King James was long lived.

In a kind of snapshot of royal favor taken in 1639, the Crown was still paying £680 10s in annuities granted by Queen Elizabeth who had died in 1603. At the same time, £40,120 19s 2d in pensions granted by James I were still being paid out.[21] In 1639, Charles I was formally responsible for over £160,000 in pensions and annuities annually, nearly 25 per cent of which had been granted by his father.[22]

This increase in officers, fees, pensions and gifts was attacked in contemporary comment. Much parliamentary complaint had to do with customs, impositions, monopolies, and the king's dearth.[23] Yet if the amount of pensions and annuities swelled in response to demand from the landed gentry, why was there an outcry against these expenditures? The reasons included the swollen scale of royal bounty, the Scottish nationality of those getting royal favor, and the fact that many of the court's clients were "double dipping."

James's Bedchamber, an important part of his Household, was divided between English and Scottish courtiers. As we saw in Sir John Holles's speech to parliament in 1610, anger among English courtiers about the share of royal bounty that the Scots were supposedly enjoying spilled over into parliamentary debate. Such criticism did not prevail upon James to change the personnel of his Bedchamber. He did however monitor Queen Anne's attendants and the Household of the French princess Henrietta Maria, who married Charles I, was restructured to eliminate many of her French attendants and replace them with English courtiers.[24]

Like the Earl of Dunbar, early Stuart clients were rewarded again and again and again. The compilers of the volume of royal annuities and pensions in 1639 took special note, perhaps with reform in mind, of the many who had more than one pension. Thus Sir Robert Ayton had three pensions granted by King James for an annual total of £840; the Countess of Monmouth had three pensions from James amounting to £700; Lord George Goring received £2,260 from several pensions granted by James; and Sir Charles Howard had two grants for a total of £1,166 13s 4d a year.

The total of plural pensions was £42,262 6s 10d and the number of those with more than one pension over 90.[25] Of these, at least 48 had been granted one of their pensions by King James and they were still being paid fourteen years after his death. Of these 48 only 14 had also received a pension from King Charles. In other words, these duplicate pensions were overwhelmingly the responsibility of King James. Finally, as to scale, the largest by far of Elizabeth's pensions was for £300 and there was just one. Charles I still owed 31 large Jacobean annuities: 15 annuities of between £300 and £500, 13 between £500 and £1,000 and 3 over £1,000.[26]

By the 1630s, annuities and pensions paid by the Crown to its officeholders amounted to £131,100 and fees another £41,600.

Diet for the three Households amounted to over £80,000 a year.[27] The Crown paid its officeholders in the 1630s a total of about £350,000 out of Crown revenues of about £618,000. Moreover, Aylmer argues that fees and gratuities paid to officeholders were of the magnitude of £250,000 to £400,000 representing an indirect tax on those using government services.[28]

Of course, theoretically, one course open to James I and Charles I was a parliamentary Act of Resumption or Revocation, to reclaim these grants as Edward IV, Henry VII and Henry VIII had done. Politically, it was impossible for James to do this at his accession. Because he claimed England's throne by hereditary right, his peaceful accession might have been challenged. Thereafter the closest his ministers came to such an Act of Resumption was *The Book of Bounty* to limit future grants.[29] Charles I, who would have benefited from such an Act, was probably inhibited by his need for parliamentary support for the war effort already under way at his succession in 1625. The bureaucratic reforms of the 1630s took the place of an Act of Resumption that could not be introduced because the king did not call parliament into session. Nevertheless Charles did attempt a wide-ranging Act of Revocation in Scotland which would have affected all alienation of Crown and church land since 1540.[30] Like the imposition of the Book of Common Prayer on the recalcitrant Scots, it was unsuccessful.

II

If the numbers of favor seekers and the amount of reward swelled in sixteenth and seventeenth-century England, the keys to control of resources, political power and social status still depended on access to the royal court and to the king, the fount of favor. Such access was personal. Court patrons acted as middlemen in transactions between the king and the political elite.

Despite some increasing bureaucratization of English government, personal attendance on royal officials up to and including the king himself remained crucial to political favor. While the king promised that those who were away from court would still be thought of, out of sight all too often proved out of mind.

The pressure of private suits never abated. Thus, in the summer of 1588, as the Crown sought to marshall its forces against the Spanish Armada, Lord Hunsdon, governor of Berwick on Tweed from 1582 to 1593, wrote regretfully from the court to his deputy, Sir Henry Withrington, that he had hoped 'to have done some good' for them both but

> both her Majesty and the whole Council have been ... continually occupied to prevent the great mischief ... resolved upon by the King of Spain against her Majesty and this realm, as neither we have had any opportunity to move any suits unto her Majesty nor she any leisure to hearken unto them ... Yet nevertheless your wife doth not cease to follow your cause as she may with all diligence ... I will not fail to do my best.[31]

There were two separate problems that faced the monarch in the fruitful dispensation of royal bounty, that of cost and of allocation. The king and his ministers tried several approaches to stanching the flow of royal bounty including the fees, annuities and pensions which, as we have seen, had quadrupled by 1614. The first approach to limiting cost was to investigate and cut back expenditure in the Household, the Navy and other departments. These investigations began as early as 1605 and, as we shall see, there were intensive investigations of the Household and Navy in 1608 and 1618 and other offices from 1618 on.[32]

The second was to try to develop a policy on royal bounty, to maintain royal revenue and prevent grants harmful to the subject or to trade. In 1592, as King of Scotland, James had the Scottish Parliament enact a statute establishing procedures to insulate him from clients.[33] In 1601 Queen Elizabeth had withdrawn certain monopolies after great complaint in parliament, and in 1603 James forbade certain types of grants (with little effect).[34]

In 1608 the Privy Council led by Robert Cecil developed criteria for those grants that the king would consider giving and those that were off limits to suitors. *The Book of Bounty*, published in 1610, ruled out grants that were against the law or "are fitt to be wholey to our owne use untill our estate be repaired," including the benefits of penal laws, royal land, leases and rents, leases in reversion, pensions and freedom from customs duties. In addition, the *Book of Bounty* sought to prevent the king from giving away royal privileges which were oppressive to the subject such as fines and inquiries into defective titles. Permissible grants included offices, keeping of parks, forfeiture of lands and goods stemming from felonies, debts due to the Crown before the thirtieth year of Elizabeth and projects or new inventions, "soe they be not contrary to the lawe nor mischeevous to the state by raysing pryces of commodities at home, or hurt of trade."[35]

The king's officials considered a draconian order identified as "a French ordinance concerning petitions and suits," touching gifts and recompense to the king's subjects and servants. The order went to great lengths to prevent undue largesse to importuning suitors. Were the king to make such grants, the Secretary of State was not to expedite and the Chancellor and Keeper of the Seals not to grant them.[36] Whether or not such an order was ever promulgated, it was never put into practice.

Charles I also developed a policy on bounty. In the 1630s, he consistently replaced several clients with one of high rank and systematized procedure. Yet in 1639, under pressure he, too, like Elizabeth and James was forced to renounce grants of monopoly because

> divers grants ... have been procured from his Majesty ... upon pretences that the same would tend to the common good and profit of His Subjects, which since upon experience have been found prejudiciall ... to His people, contrary to His Majesties gratious intention in granting the same ... far from those grounds and reasons whereupon they were founded, and in their execution have been notoriously abused.[37]

Thirdly, King James and his advisers tried to put the allocation of patronage on a paying basis. All members of the political elite including the king himself believed that one of his most important roles was to grant office and honors to his subjects. To do so, the king expanded his administration and the annuities, pensions and other benefits paid to members of the political elite. When it became clear that these would not stanch the demand, the king put bounty on the market. The Crown's sale of titles, however, brought honor and market too closely together. Sales of office among officeholders were characteristic of early modern bureaucracy and regarded as legal by judicial decision. The particular problem that the Jacobean court faced was that the Crown, under the several pressures of clamoring suitors, increased expenses, and decreased parliamentary funding, made explicit the basis of its allocation of resources. As a result, they faced the political cost of the loss of the "symbolic capital" that royal bounty represented.[38]

As we have seen, gift-giving was intrinsic to the exchange of patronage. The expansion of the scale and scope of official gift-giving in the early Stuart period provides just one illustration of the increased cost of bounty that could cause confusion between gifts and bribes and led to the loss of "symbolic capital." It was usual for the King of England to present gifts to departing ambassadors of foreign nations. The Crown annually spent about £4,000 a year on such presents between 1627 and 1641.[39] Among the tasks of his Master of Ceremonies was to ensure that the Spanish and French ambassadors received gifts of the same value and that all others received presents of lesser value depending on their status. Such "gifts" had precise monetary values. The ambassador from a monarchy was to receive 2,000 ounces of silver plate worth 8 shillings an ounce amounting to £800; the ambassador from a lesser state £410; and an agent a medal and gold chain worth £210.[40] In 1638 the Agent of Savoy complained that his £210 chain was worth only £150; it was short thirteen ounces of silver plate. The ambassador from Poland complained that his gift of plate, supposed to be worth £800, was worth only £600 and that Sir Henry Mildmay, Master of the Jewel House, had then asked for a gratuity of £40.[41] Mildmay had bought his office in 1618 for £2,000 or £3,000 from the previous holder, presumably with the blessing of his friend, Buckingham,[42] and his demand for a gratuity of 5 per cent may serve as a baseline for fees and graft in the early Stuart period.

Such official gift-giving was reciprocal and indeed expanding in the late sixteenth and early seventeenth centuries. At the end of the Anglo–Spanish war in 1604 the Spanish ambassador gave presents to all the English negotiators. These gifts soon became settled pensions provided to several high ranking English officials including Robert Cecil, Earl of Salisbury, the Secretary of State and later, Lord Treasurer, of which the king approved.[43] Large gifts from foreign states were not unique in the Renaissance. What caused comment in early seventeenth-century England was their scale, scope, and timing. Robert Cecil wrote to Sir Thomas Parry, ambassador in France, that "the French Ambassador hath lately presented to the Queen, the Prince and to diverse Councilors and Ladies very fair and rich presents such (I assure you) as for so many I have not seen fairer." He enclosed the names of those that had received them. Cecil conveyed an order from the king that Parry deliver the thanks of his councillors and servants as a group and of James himself to the King of France. Cecil ended:

> And so much for ... the matter of our presents, wherein you shall understand this one particular, which you may reserve to your self, that it is here conceived that this humor of giving hath risen much from an action of the Ambassador of Spain, who in the Christmas presented some ladies about the Queen with some presents to the value of £100 a piece, and some rewards given to every officer in the king's house. A matter not usual except where Ambassadors do lie in the King's house, and are attended by his officers.[44]

The Earl of Worcester, a Jacobean privy councillor, also commented on the unusual nature of these gifts. Writing to the Earl of Shrewsbury that the French Queen had sent costly gifts to the Queen and to several of those at Court, he added that he did not know the meaning of it.[45]

This intrusion of the market into the giving of honors and the enlargement of normal gift-giving practice was extended to settled pensions paid by the Spanish and probably the French.[46] When the English ambassador in Spain learned of them in 1613 he was outraged; when it became public knowledge in 1620, one pamphleteer accused the king of being bribed against himself.[47] Yet such expansion of official gift-giving was a fact of life of seventeenth-century Europe. In the same period, Cecil ordered Parry to try to bribe French ministers, wrote to Sir Charles Cornwallis that he was thought to be bribed by the Spanish, and the English were accused of demanding payments from everyone.[48]

III

In early Stuart England, changes in patronage practices and bureaucratic structures had an important impact on the form that corrupt practices took. The clamor of demand was expressed both in queuing before one patron and, increasingly, seeking influence through many different patrons. Clients continued to use the rhetoric of dependency on a single patron but applied to many at once. The successful pressure of demand was reflected in the variety and number of courtiers who, as we shall see, signed off on grants issued by the signet office.

Access to resources at the early Stuart court was controlled by major patrons. Access to *them* was often controlled by brokers. While major patrons had their own networks of clients, they were often solicited for favor by people of whom they knew little. Thus it was important for a would-be client to obtain some sort of entree to the patron. The process of brokering went on from the lowest clerk to the highest official. When the king served as patron, his privy councillors and favorites might intercede as brokers. In other cases, the secretaries of prominent patrons might serve as brokers.[49] The system was fluid and, as we saw in the case of Sir John Holles, in the early seventeenth century clients often turned to more than one patron to secure their ends even while invoking the language appropriate to a single dependent relationship. Despite the supremacy of the patron, he was often more acted upon than acting.

The books of the signet office record the bounty dispensed by the Crown and suggest some significant aspects of early Stuart brokerage. Under the Act of 27 Henry VIII, c. 11, entitled "An Acte concernynge Clerkes of the Signet and Privie Seal," grants from the king were signified to the principal secretary or one of the clerks of the signet who prepared a warrant to the keeper of the privy seal. This was followed by a warrant under the privy seal to the keeper of the Great Seal authorizing the affixing of the Great Seal to the grant.[50] The purpose of the signet books was not only to record the names of grantees and the business of the office, but also the fees to be paid and distributed to the clerks.

The signet books show more often the output side of the patronage system: that is, those officials who "signed off" on the grant, not those who successfully gained the favor. The names most often seen are, then, those of the secretaries of state and the clerks of the signet. Masters of Requests, heads of departments or superiors frequently procured offices under them. For example, the Lord Chamberlain and Master of the Horse signified Household appointments and the Bishop of Peterborough subscribed to the presentation to a parsonage in the diocese of Lincoln for one of the king's clerics. Presenting suits and signing grants was a profitable business. Under Elizabeth, Sir John Fortescue, Chancellor of the Exchequer, profited both from "the signing of most books that past of land or any grants out of the Exchequer" and his right to move the Queen to obtain suits for important petitioners such as the Earl of Essex which netted him a park in Buckinghamshire.[51]

In the early Stuart period, the books of the signet office record the subscribers and procurers of grants. At times, these records can be an important key to understanding patronage ties and their implementation at the court because they bring us into contact with courtiers, especially those who were members of the royal Household, whose influence has not always been apparent to historians.[52] Administrators and Household officials co-operated in the dispensation of patronage. Secretary of State, Sir Edward Conway, wrote to Henry Gibb, a member of the king's Bedchamber, about a suit towards which Gibb had already expressed his "good affection." Alexander Stuart had been granted the forfeiture of the goods of the Duchess of Richmond. Some of those who had bought plate stolen from the Duchess wished to compound with Stuart for their pardon. Stuart was, therefore, a suitor to the king to pardon three people who had bought the plate. Conway asked Gibb to move the king in Stuart's suit "and, when the occasions shall present themselves wherein I may be usefull to you my readie endeavours shall give you proofe how much I am yours."[53]

Neal Cuddy has demonstrated the importance of the king's Bedchamber in politics and patronage under James I. The role of Jacobean Scots who had taken up a considerable number of the Bedchamber posts as patronage brokers finds reflection in the signet book records.[54] Thus the presentation to the parsonage of Haseley Magna, Oxford, which was in the king's gift, subscribed by the Bishop of Bristol and Thomas Lake, Secretary of State, was procured by Thomas Erskine, Viscount Fenton, one of the king's longtime Scottish followers who served as Captain of the Guard and Groom of the Stool.[55]

Jacobean Scots, who held court positions not only in the Bedchamber and the Household but also the Privy Council, included George Hume, Lord Berwick, and later, Earl of Dunbar, Keeper of the Great Wardrobe, Privy

Councillor and Lord High Treasurer of Scotland; Ludovic Stuart, Duke of Lennox, Privy Councillor, Gentleman of the Bedchamber and Lord High Steward of the Household; Edward Bruce, Lord Kinlosse, Privy Councillor and Master of the Rolls; Sir John Ramsay, Viscount Haddington, and later Earl of Holderness; Robert Carr, Viscount Rochester, and later Earl of Somerset, Gentleman of the Bedchamber and later Privy Councillor; John Murray and George Murray, Gentlemen of the Bedchamber. They, as well as other Scots, all procured grants. Thus, in October 1612, the office of the Comptroller of the great and small customs in Poole granted to Thomas Robarts was procured by John Murray, and Viscount Haddington procured a pardon for Edward Vaux.[56]

The process by which grants were procured and signified in the early Jacobean period was incoherent. Although Cuddy has argued that Sir Thomas Lake probably procured most of the grants before 1614, the process was actually in flux and the signet books graphically show how confused the process of patronage was at the beginning of James's reign. Indeed, more than fifty different people signified grants during the twenty-two years of James's reign. The early years of the reign were marked by a multiplicity of brokers and a contradictory process: on the one hand, important Household officials, especially members of the Bedchamber, secured grants and, on the other, privy councillors stopped grants once they had been obtained from the king.

In the first months of the reign, the entries do not show who subscribed or procured the grants. Thus grants subscribed by Stephen Bull and Mr Conner, whose authority apparently was questionable, were stayed. Clerks noted when they had received the order by word of mouth rather than by warrant and, occasionally, wrote that they had nothing to do with certain entries.[57] At times, grants were stayed either because they had already been made to others, or because reforming administrators such as Robert Cecil, Earl of Salisbury and Henry Howard, Earl of Northampton were trying to cut down on royal expenditure.[58]

Thus, Salisbury stopped grants such as the warrant to pay two men wages and allowances for the keeping of the king's spaniels, which had been procured by John Murray, a member of the king's Bedchamber, and wages and livery to a man who had the reversion of the position of one of his Majesty's falconers.[59] Salisbury stayed the king's free gift to William Steward of 1,000 marks out of fines inflicted in any court for notorious crimes, even though it had been commanded by the king and communicated to his Secretary of State.[60] Presumably he urged the king to leave such monies in the Exchequer. Among more than forty grants that Northampton stayed both before and after Salisbury's death were the grant in reversion of the office of keeping his Majesty's hare warren at Hampton Court, subscribed by the Earl of Nottingham in 1612, and the pension of 18d a day for Thomas Browne for his service and skill in making iron ordnance, subscribed by Lord Carew, Master of the Ordnance.[61]

Thus while statute fixed procedure, practice in the Jacobean period belied it. In the early years of the reign, notes are occasionally found saying "that nothing pass that may concern the Earl of Shrewsbury, either in Derbyshire, Yorkshire or Nottinghamshire, where his lordship is named steward, tenant or officer to his Majesty."[62] The clerks made notes of specific caveats that certain grants not be issued until certain nobles and officials were notified. Nothing was to pass concerning the East Indies "before Mr Secretary Winwood be acquainted with it;" no presentation to the Rectory of St Matthew in Friday Street, London was to pass "before Mr Barton, clerk of the prince's closet, have notice of it."[63]

In fact, most of these special notices seem to have concerned suits in which Household officials had an interest. For instance, Secretary Lake was to be made acquainted with any bill for the forfeiture of the goods and lands of William Price or pardon of his life for killing one William Estrig because the king had already promised Prices' goods to Saunder Stevefor, his Highness's servant at Theobalds. The signet clerks carefully noted the benefit of legal and recusancy fines and defaults which had already been granted to gentlemen of the privy chamber, a page of the Bedchamber, one of the king's chaplains and the king's plasterer.

After the death of Salisbury in 1612, the king did not immediately appoint a new principal secretary, using Robert Carr, Viscount Rochester, his favorite and Gentleman of his Bedchamber, as his secretary. The roles of Carr and other members of the Household in carrying out policy are reflected in the signet book between 1612 and 1614. Thus, Humphrey May, Groom of the Privy Chamber, continued to serve as the king's instrument to deal both with Irish policy and Irish patronage. May signified the king's careful instructions to the Lord Deputy of Ireland for the 1613 session of the Irish parliament while transmitting orders for lay and ecclesiastical patronage in Ireland.[64]

At the same time as the King relied more and more on his Household, the Earl of Northampton increasingly stopped grants between 1612 and 1614 as part of his efforts to control expenditure and court patronage. These ranged from a monopoly to make artificial stones resembling marble to be used for buildings and tombs; an office of filer and keeper of bills in the Court of Exchequer at Chester to Robert Strickland "granted to him by the late Prince;" a lease to Henry Sherfield and Michael Dalk "by order from diverse lords of the Privy Council;" a pardon for a robber subscribed by Mr Warburton,[65] and a pardon to Isabel Constantine of corporal punishment for her practice with others to steal away and have married the only daughter of Elizabeth de la Fountane, widow.[66]

These stays were frequently temporary and most of these grants were later passed. Northampton had stayed a grant of 1,000 marks to Rowland

White who had close connections with Robert Sidney, Viscount Lisle, once Northampton's ally as a follower of Essex but later, under James, an opponent allied with the Earl of Southampton. White received a different grant in 1614.[67] A pardon granted Sir Thomas Hervet "for any adultery, fornication or incontinency" (with exception of rapes, incests, and buggeries), signified by Sir Christopher Parkins, has a marginal note saying "stayed at the privy seal" which has been crossed out.[68] The reason for such stays of bills was to determine the authority of those who had subscribed and to provide the opportunity for another discussion with the king on the merits of the grant. In one case, Northampton stayed a grant to Sir William Woodhouse of all goods, chattels and debts forfeited to King James by attainder of John French for felony. In this case Northampton's own nephew, Thomas Howard, Earl of Suffolk, was the broker who wrote to Lake to beg him not to obtain benefit of pardon of French, the horse stealer, having obtained a grant of it long before for Sir William Woodhouse.[69] This grant was never passed. These stays of royal grants reflect concern for order and financial stability as well as for political power.

The problem of allocation of reward was solved in a new way with the rise of the Duke of Buckingham as the king's favorite. Now most patronage came through the Duke. As before, the signet books reflect patronage connections only obliquely. Members of the Bedchamber, such as Archibald Hay, Henry Gibb, and Mr Livingston, continued to procure grants, often under Buckingham's direction. The creation of Ulrick Bourke as Earl of Clanricard was procured by the Duke of Buckingham in April of 1624. The creation of Sir William Brereton, Baron Breton of Laghlyn in Ireland, was procured by Christopher Villiers, Earl of Anglesey. Warrants to pay close to £29,000 to the Treasurer of the Navy were discharged by order of Buckingham as Lord Admiral and procured by Mr Palmer of the Bedchamber.[70]

Jacobean Scots continued to be important both as middlemen in the patronage process and as receivers of royal bounty. A warrant to the Exchequer to pay Sir Patrick Murray £500 for his private service was procured by James Murray, the Earl of Annandale and Keeper of the Privy Purse. In 1624 a warrant to the Exchequer and Duchy of Lancaster gave direction for passing to James Ramsay, Earl of Holderness, £100 a year, £500 year in fee farm or any parcels of his Majesty's honors after the Prince had filled up £1,300 in rents. It was subscribed by the Attorney-General and procured "by the said Earl." *The Book of Bounty* and other such strictures were no longer read. In the same month, the king granted lands from Overton in York although he "hath received no certificate from the Lords of the Privy Council as prescribed by the indenture of annexation of lands to the Crown."[71]

Under Charles I, the administration of the signet was tightened. In the 1630s there appear to be fewer grants to individuals than under James. At the same time, the papers of Attorney-General Bankes show that the Crown was replacing a multitude of low-level grantees with a single one of high degree in various projects.[72] Most Caroline grants went through channels, prepared variously by the Attorney-General, the Lord Treasurer, and the Secretary of State, and few were stopped. Again, those who had administrative charge participated in procuring and subscribing grants: Archbishop Laud signified presentations to benefices, elections of bishops and Oxford appointments; the Lord Treasurer and Chancellor of the Exchequer presented leases of Crown lands. The Master of the Horse, the Marquis of Hamilton, and the Lord Chamberlain, dealt with appointments of his Majesty's footmen and other household posts.[73] Members of the Bedchamber continued to work with administrators to execute royal policy as well as to dispense court patronage. Thus Patrick Maule, by order of Secretary Windebank, subscribed a warrant to pay George Vaughn, a merchant, £500 a year "to be employed for his Majesty's secret service and to advance unto him £500 every year before hand."[74] Letters to the Lord Deputy of Ireland were subscribed and procured by Sir Harry Holcroft. Although he pleaded ignorance of Irish affairs, Holcroft advised others on how to obtain grants from the crown.[75] Christopher Villiers, Earl of Anglesey, advised by Holcroft, mounted a campaign to obtain for a relative the wardship of her children.[76] Mr Livingston of the Bedchamber procured a warrant for Adam Crosley, one of the king's footmen, to recover an Elizabethan debt.[77] James Maxwell, Groom of the Bedchamber and gentleman usher of the parliament chamber, Patrick Maule, Groom of the Bedchamber, George Kirke, Groom of the Bedchamber and Gentleman of the Robes, all procured grants during Charles's reign.[78]

The Jacobean Scots did not fare as well under Charles I. While William Murray remained a presence in the royal Bedchamber, John Murray, Earl of Annandale, and under James, Keeper of the Privy Purse and in charge of the king's stamp, appealed to Secretary Conway to move the king that his pension might be paid. Money was not his sole object. He was concerned "that the world may not notice that he is neglected and forgotten."[79]

As before, many Caroline grants were made to royal household servants. A pension of £450 a year was granted to Mrs Cecily Crofts, maid of honor to the Queen Henrietta Maria, subscribed by the Attorney-General upon signification of the king's pleasure by the Lord Treasurer, procured by a member of the king's Bedchamber.[80] A pension of £1,200 a year out of the farm of gold and silver thread was settled by the king on the Countess of Roxborough and her assignees for thirty-one years from 1636 in lieu of £5,750 arrearage of the pension granted her by King James. This large grant was subscribed by the Attorney-General, upon signification of his Majesty's pleasure by Mr Secretary Windebank and procured by Mr Maxwell of the Bedchamber.[81]

Perhaps because bureaucratic routine was more carefully worked out and adhered to under Charles I, there appear to be fewer stays of grants. Those that were halted ignored bureaucratic guidelines. Thus a grant to Colonel

Scott of the office of borough-master in Winkeworth, Derby, with profits for fifty years and a rent of 26s 8d signified to be the king's pleasure by the Chancellor of the Duchy, subscribed by the clerk of the Duchy, and procured by the colonel himself, was stayed.[82] So, too, was the presentation of Henry Salmon, BD, to the rectory of Paul's Purie in Northamptonshire, void by simony and, therefore, in the king's gift, although ordered by Sir Sidney Montagu and procured by Mr Secretary Coke.[83] Others stopped included another presentation to a rectory that, like Salmon's, was not subscribed by Laud, a grant to the soapmakers, and a gunner's room. In addition, the office of Clerk of Court of Wards, in reversion after Richard Chamberlain, Hugh Audley and James Maxwell, subscribed by the Attorney-General and procured by the Duke of Lennox, was stayed.[84]

By 1636 the signet was less occupied with royal bounty and grants to Household servants. It was increasingly concerned with commissions for forest laws, for execution of laws against unlawful importing of wood, and with offenders against the statute of 31 Elizabeth, c. 7, touching cottages erected within any honors, manors, boroughs, towns, forests, parks, chases, hundreds.[85] If the Jacobean Scots and royal favorites had influenced the granting of favor earlier, by the 1630s the hallmarks of "Thorough" (the reform of administration and increased fiscal extraction through the enforcement of royal rights) was shaping not only royal policy but the structure of royal patronage.

Chapter 3

Court patronage networks

On April 24, 1623, Lucy Harrington, Countess of Bedford, wrote to Sir Dudley Carleton, the English Ambassador to the Low Countries, that she had transmitted his letters to the Duke of Lennox, the king's longtime Scottish friend and member of the Privy Chamber, and the Earl of Pembroke, the Lord Chamberlain, who was with the countess when Carleton's despatches arrived. She then turned to the burning question of the moment: who would receive the provostship of Eton, a position which Carleton very much coveted.

> Since Mr Thomas Murray's death nobody believes Sir William Becher shall enjoy the fruits of his hope of Eton; for which though there are too many worthier pretenders, yet by our skillfulest courtiers, it is supposeth Freeman that is one of the Masters of Requests, and an ally of my Lord Admiral's, [George Villiers, Duke of Buckingham] is like to carry it, claiming a former promise of his. I dare neither advise you to persist nor desist ... as I can make no judgment of any thing, all wonted grounds failing and I assure your Lordship even those that are nearer the well head, know not with what bucket to draw for themselves, or their friends.[1]

Court brokers and patrons, "even those near the well head," wondered how to tap the fountain of favor for themselves and their clients. With this pungent phrase the countess captured the fluidity and fragility of court patronage connections even at the time of dominance of the great Stuart favorite, the Duke of Buckingham. Furthermore, her letter suggests several important themes that this chapter will take up: first, the character of patrons, favorites and factions; second, the search by the client for a patron; third, the mobilization of patron–client relationships in the quest for a single post, and finally, the usually veiled role of women as patrons, clients and

47

brokers who wove a web of political connections across the Privy Council and royal Households. The Countess of Bedford's letter demonstrates that the early Stuart court was structured by male–female patronage networks within which male favorites and women brokers played important roles.

I
Patrons and favorites

Renaissance patrons sought to extend their political power in time and space. They created networks of followers to enforce their will and harnessed literature and art to document and testify to their greatness. Controlling access to resources of all sorts, patrons received in exchange from their clients signification and reinforcement of power and prestige. Clients presented gifts that testified to the court patron's honor and superiority; observers marked his or her standing in direct proportion to the numbers of his or her dependents; the patron celebrated self and family, in art, literature and politics. Theophilus Field, a minister who wished to be transferred to another diocese, wrote to the Duke of Buckingham: "I desire it . . . be it Eli or Bathe and Wells; and I will spend the remainder of my days in writing an history of your good deeds to me and others."[2] As our earlier examination of the language of favor showed, patron and client made a compact of mutual benefits.

In early Stuart England, patrons ranged from the king, his Privy Council and nobility to central and local officials, while clients included individuals, towns and corporations. The distance in status between patron and client, often both members of the political elite, was frequently exaggerated by rhetorical geesture. Much court life and political energy was taken up with reading the signs of court favor and the dissemination of court news throughout the country.[3] Patronage networks spanned court, household and council, and center and locality. Two significant additions in early seventeenth-century patronage networks were the wildcards of the Scots as brokers and the increasing importance of royal favorites.

Private networks linking lord, vassals and followers had long existed in England. These connections, originally based on military relationships, expanded in the high Middle Ages into affinities, broad-based groupings resting on geographical and family connections by which a leading lord provided favor to his military and civilian followers in return for their loyalty.[4] Such networks in the sixteenth century changed with the emergence of the Crown as the central source of reward and Renaissance notions of the patron.

The transformation of magnate politics into court-centred patronage finds an exemplar in Henry Percy, ninth Earl of Northumberland. Scion of the

Percys whose control of the northern borders with Scotland had marked their influence in English politics, Northumberland was also the owner of Sion House, described as "a heap of benefits" given to the Earl.[5] After the Queen's death Northumberland attended a meeting of Elizabethan privy councillors accompanied by a large retinue. He questioned the authority of the councillors and pressed the role of the nobility in announcing the new monarch. Immediately after the king's accession, others thought Northumberland an important court patron and solicited his aid. When Northumberland heard that the king was to appoint a commission for the examination and granting of suits, he wrote Cecil that he would feel it a disgrace were he not one of the commissioners.[6] Northumberland's pretensions to military and civil power died, however, with his imprisonment by the king after the Gunpowder Plot in which a close relation, Thomas Percy, was a conspirator. Northumberland had corresponded with James VI of Scotland while Queen Elizabeth was still alive, telling him that Elizabethan peers were discontented "that ofices of trust are not laid in there handes to manage as thay were wont; that her maiestie is percimoniws and sloe to reliefe there wants." James responded to such complaints with liberality, but his own writings reflect a wariness toward a powerful nobility independent of the Crown.[7]

In contrast to magnates like the Percys, the power of favorites was based on the personal affection of the monarch. Favorites had existed in Europe and in England throughout the Middle Ages and the sixteenth century. Contemporaries viewed their emergence as part of the cycle of court life. A reflection of personal monarchy, the rapidity of their rise and fall was a symptom of the changing affections and unpredictable behavior of the monarch.[8] Edward II had Piers Gaveston, Elizabeth had Leicester and Essex. Bacon wrote "it is no new thing for Kings and Princes to have their privadoes, their favorites, their friends."[9] While favorites were frequently criticized, they played an important role in the early modern court in two ways: they became the focus of petitions for favor thereby insulating the monarch from incessant demands, and they substituted for a nobility whose institutional power made it a greater threat to the monarch than the favorite who was his "creature." These functions were understood by contemporaries. James, it was said, "strengthened himself ever with some favorite, whom he might better trust than many of the nobility tainted with this desire of oligarchy."[10]

Queen Anne perceptively described the position of favorite to Archbishop Abbot, her ally in her project to supplant Robert Carr, Earl of Somerset, one of James's most influential favorites, with George Villiers. She pointed out that "the King will teach him to despise and hardly entreat us all, that he may seem to be beholden to none but himself."[11] Sir John Holles did not believe that Villiers would be able to replace Somerset and his father-in-law Thomas Howard, Earl of Suffolk, both great officeholders; as Holles put it, to "raze a Chamberlain and a Treasurer (both rooted by long service and many offices of great latitude in our state) out of the book of life, and turn the stream down another channel." But James raised Villiers far above all others, saying to the Privy Council "he loved the Earl of Buckingham more than any other man, and more than all those who were here present."[12]

Although a member of the Privy Council, Buckingham did not attend often, waiting more frequently on the king himself. James's use of Buckingham as chief broker of royal patronage was calculated to insulate himself and he noted Buckingham's "continued attendance upon my service, your daily employments in the same, and the incessant swarm of suitors importunately hanging upon you without discretion or distinction of times."[13] Roger Lockyer argues that James used Buckingham as a filter for the many demands made by suitors and officeholders upon him.[14]

Sir Francis Bacon, who served as an adviser to Villiers at the beginning of his ascendancy, described with considerable acuity the position of favorite, its privileges and pitfalls in language that evoked simultaneously sex, sale and theology. Buckingham had become James's favorite through God and "the King's favor (purchased by your noble parts, promising as much as can be expected from a gentlemen)."[15] The favorite served as a mediator between subjects and king, a theological vision of brokerage implied by the contemporary advice to William Trumbull to direct himself to the "right saint."[16] "The whole Kingdom hath cast their eye upon you as the new rising Star, and no man thinks his business can prosper at Court unless he hath you for his good Angel or at least that you be not a *Malus Genius* against him."

Such a saint could also serve as a sacrifical lamb. The king was above the people's censures but his courtiers were not. Bacon advised Buckingham that "you may be offered as a sacrifice to appease the multitude."[17] (While Bacon correctly understood this to be a traditional fate of a favorite, Charles I did not.) The favorite held a position of great trust as the king's sentinel, to provide him with intelligence and to speak for those who did not have access to the king.

According to Bacon the principal functions of the favorite were to give good service to the king and good dispatch to suitors. Bacon laid down a series of very specific rules for Buckingham on how to organize the granting of petitions and the dispensing of royal bounty, even instructing him on how to underline the petitions. These rules reflected the usage of the Privy Council under Robert Cecil in the first decade of James's reign. Firstly, important suits were to be put in writing and a day appointed for their answer, noted by Villiers' secretary, thereby relieving the favorite of the suitor until then. Secondly, Bacon urged Buckingham to set aside an hour or two a day to sort the petitions into categories, of religion, law, matters of state, diplomacy, war, foreign plantations and colonies, trade and the court, "which will be easily done if your Secretary draw lines under the matter." Instead of relying on himself or one or two private friends, two or three copies should be sent to several trustworthy men in appropriate professions. Another hour or two a week devoted to perusing the petitions and opinions of the referees and "within a short time you shall be able to judge of the fidelities of those you trust and return answers to petitions of all natures as an oracle."[18] Bacon pointed out that "next to the granting of the request, a reasonable and a fair denial is most acceptable."

Such an organized system to consider petitions had been in effect under Salisbury who had established a council subcommittee to survey suits and referred petitions to experts and learned counsel.[19] In the early Jacobean period this inner group included Cecil himself, Northampton, Worcester, and Suffolk. After Cecil's death Robert Carr functioned as the king's secretary when the king refused to appoint a new Secretary of State and continued the practice of referring petitions to other privy councillors.[20]

On each of the eight categories, Bacon had specific advice to proffer. He strongly urged Buckingham to avoid suits on religious doctrine, referring these to eminent divines. No doubt Buckingham's mother's catholicism made the issue particularly dangerous. Were any question raised about "the doctrine of the Church of England expressed in the thirty-nine articles, give not the least ear to the movers thereof. That is so soundly and so orthodoxally settled as cannot be questioned without extreme danger to the honour and stability of our Religion." Regulation of those who disagreed, whether papists, anabaptists or sectaries should be left to Parliament.

In appointments to court office, Bacon urged Buckingham to rely on merit, to choose learned lawyers and able privy councillors. "Although to some persons of great birth, the place of princes' councilors may be bestowed as an honour unto them, yet generally the motive should be the parts of the man and not his person." Diplomatic missions were best handled by men of honor and eminence as was the practice under Elizabeth; because they undertook the mission "as a work of favor," were "willing to undertake it at an easy rate the expense of the Crown (which hath not often been so of later times)."[21] Bacon's allusion was probably to the expensive embassies undertaken by James Carlisle, Lord Hay, the extravagant Master of the Wardrobe.[22]

While Bacon could prescribe procedures for dealing with policy and petitions, he admitted "for the affairs of Court, you are much better able to instruct yourself than any man else can ... In the disposing of the offices and affairs of Court, the King hath a latitude for his affection, which in matters touching the public he must deny to himself: Here he is more properly *Paterfamilias*, in the other *Pater Patriae*."[23]

While the position of favorite was a personal one, Buckingham managed the unusual feat of inheriting a new king. Sir Henry Wotton observed "he had now gotten (as it were) two lives in his own fortune and greatness; whereas otherwise the state of a favourite is at the best but a tenant-at-will and rarely transmitted."[24] His career belied the meteoric rise and fall which usually described the parabola of a favorite. With the Thirty Years War, the Duke moved beyond the position of favorite, and now bestrode both patronage and policy. In 1624 as James I fell terminally ill and Prince Charles moved to take power, one observer described Buckingham: "if you saw the fashion of his treating of suitors (whereof he is as full as ever), and with what elevation he comports himself with the greatest that have to do with him, you would say he hath gained *le hault bout* and that he knows himself fixed past jeopardy of relapsing."[25]

Bacon's bureaucratic approach to patronage was belied by the favorite's practice. In a break with contemporary mores, Buckingham insisted that those to whom he gave favor recognize him as their singular patron as a means to procure financial gain and, even more, to ensure dependence. The favorite's control of access to the king exalted the position of patron to saint. Indeed, Catholic language of intercession became common in addresses to Buckingham.[26] After Lord Keeper Williams lost favor in 1625 he asked to be revived naming himself the Duke's "creature." "I was never hitherto brought into the praesence of a Kinge by any Saint beside your selfe; turne me not over (most noble Lord) to offer my prayers at newe aulters."[27] When Sir Humphrey May petitioned both Pembroke and Buckingham, Buckingham saw this not as the Jacobean norm but as double dealing.[28] When Bacon got caught up in the imbroglio over the Coke–Villiers marriage negotiations, even he had to apologize to the favorite whom he had tutored. Buckingham replied graciously "I do freely confess that your offer of submission ... battered ... the unkindness that I had conceived in my heart for your behavior towards me in my absence."[29] Sir Henry Yelverton, who wished to become Attorney-General, found that he too needed to voice complete dependence on Buckingham. The favorite declared that he would not have opposed him had Yelverton sought access through him first. Because he did not, Yelverton caused people to think Buckingham's favor was waning "and he not thought to be of that power he had been."[30]

Such concern proved unnecessary. As we shall see, Buckingham controlled court patronage even while in Spain with Prince Charles in 1623. Buckingham's power never waned. And it is not too strong to say that King James *begged* Lord Treasurer Cranfield to find money for the Duke in 1621.

Milorde, Shame stayed me from refreshing youre memorie concerning Bukkinghame's busienesse upon Sunday last, having so ofte and earnestlie delt with you in it before, but now upon the occasion of his wyfe's going to London, his mother putte him in mynde of preparing things for her lying in quhiche I chawncing to overheare, I askid earnestlie and conjured him to tell me the trewth of his estait, for ye knowe how loathe he is to doe it and alas I finde he muste paye twentie thowsande powndis for his lande at Burghlie and these provisions for her lying in and meubling are lyke to cost tenne thowsand besydes three thowsande for his newe house and all this he must borrowe ... doe quikkelie thairfore quhat ye are to doe for him and remember that a thing done in tyme is twice done, comforte me with some present goode news in this point for till then I proteste I can have no ioye in the going well of my owin busienesse.[31]

Writing in his own hand, the king's plea demonstrates the dominance of the favorite over the monarch's affections.

II
Faction

In recent years, court faction has come to dominate analysis of early Stuart political history.[32] As part of a new emphasis on personal relationships in politics, faction has come to seem the most important, indeed the only, major shaper of events. In a series of articles in *History Today* a group of revisionist historians analyzed the political meanings of the term and drew attention to an important aspect of national politics before the age of party, the informal power of the court faction.

Factions, portrayed perjoratively by classical political theorists, Roman historians such as Tacitus, and contemporary European observers, were networks of patrons and clients who, at the least, were viewed by others as connecting and co-ordinating their political behavior. The faction might be animated not only by mutual self-interest but by similar views on foreign policy and religion. In that case they would use their power to press a specific political agenda and define themselves in opposition to other groupings at court. Charles I maintained "the ill of aristocracy is faction and division, just as its good ... is the conjunction of counsel in the ablest persons of state for the public benefit."[33] Sir Thomas Parry, English Ambassador to France, described divisions between French and Scots guards within the French king's household at odds over their places. Such differences might be expected but factions were a sign of political discontent. "Soyssons is now farther out then before ... And thus factions heere begyn to spring and wil grow dangerouse if the king in his regal prudence prevent not in tyme."[34] Simon Adams has pointed out that faction was a term of derogation and was never used by the group to describe themselves.[35]

How important, how fixed were factions? Early Stuart historians have traditionally described the court as divided into factions grouped around

Robert Cecil, Earl of Salisbury, Secretary of State and later Lord Treasurer; around the Howards or "Spanish" faction consisting of Henry Howard, Lord Privy Seal, Thomas Howard, Lord Chamberlain and their allies such as the Earl of Worcester and Lord Knollys and, after 1611, Robert Carr, Earl of Somerset, the royal favorite; the French faction led by the Duke of Lennox, other Jacobean Scots and the Earl of Carlisle, and an explicitly anti-Spanish faction which included the Archbishop of Canterbury, George Abbot, and Queen Anne, the Earl of Pembroke, Lord Chancellor Ellesmere and Sir Ralph Winwood, Secretary of State.[36]

Such firm boundaries between groups and such close linkages to foreign policy do not, however, reflect the ambiguities and shifting sands of court politics. Foreign powers sought to influence domestic politics through English factions. Yet a word of caution is necessary. Although there were supporters of Spain at the early Stuart court, the Spanish faction tends to melt away when analyzed.[37] Much of our knowledge of factional politics comes from the evidence of diplomatic correspondence in which foreign policy matters, of course, dominated. Gondomar, the Spanish Ambassador, felt that the only member of the "Spanish" faction devoted to Spanish interests was Henry Howard, Earl of Northampton; all his other "confidants" were in it for the money.[38] Most of the leading Jacobean courtiers took gifts and pensions from the Spanish, the French and the Dutch, often from more than one at the same time.

The fluidity and fragility of patronage networks belies the menace of factional rivalry. Indeed, factions were important only in unusual political circumstances. Simon Adams emphasizes the stability of the Elizabethan regime up to the 1590s when factional rivalry between Cecil and Essex sprang up.[39] At moments of transition, faction flourished. Thus, at the accession of James I, Sir Walter Raleigh and Sir Henry Cobham fell into conspiracy in the Main Plot. Cecil ascribed their conspiracy to what might be called relative deprivation: "so farr had God blynded theyr eyes, when the king had noe way wronged any of these, by taking from them any matter of profitt or credytt which ever they enjoyed, but it was not enough not to take away, because, he dyd not suddainly geve what they desyred."[40] Cecil claimed that Raleigh had been discontented since James came to the throne even though the king had given him £300 a year for life and had forgiven substantial debts in place of the offices taken away. When major court patrons died, or favorites fell, whether Dunbar, Salisbury, Prince Henry or Somerset, their clients had to scramble for new patrons and connection to new factions.

Early Stuart patronage connections were shaped in the cauldron of late Elizabethan politics. The rivalries between Robert Devereux, the Earl of Essex, and the Cecils, William, Lord Burghley, and his son Robert Cecil, were enhanced by the need not only to secure the continuance of Queen Elizabeth's favor but to ensure the support of her successor. In the late 1590s

Essex and his circle were in contact with King James VI of Scotland. With the death of Essex, Robert Cecil entered into a secret correspondence with James through an intermediary chosen by the king – Henry Howard, later Earl of Northampton. Howard, part of the Essex group, had already been in correspondence with the king. One purpose of the secret correspondence was to convince King James that Cecil and Howard were his principal allies.

During the dominance of Cecil and Buckingham, i.e. between 1603 and 1612, and 1618 and 1628, the impact of factions on policy receded in importance and conflict swirled instead around reward. In the awarding of the Great Farm of the Customs in 1604, for instance, there were three merchant syndicates, each associated with an important councillor: Secretary of State Cecil, the Lord Treasurer Thomas Sackville, Earl of Dorset, and the Lord Privy Seal Northampton. The first two combined and froze out Northampton's syndicate. He continued to challenge their control of the customs each time the farm was renewed. Both Salisbury and the Howards competed to win the favor of the King's favorite, Somerset, and the Howards sealed their triumph with the marriage of Somerset to Frances Howard, Countess of Essex, the daughter of Lord Treasurer Suffolk.

Yet such competition cloaks the co-operation of the Howards and Cecil and the Howards and the Jacobean Scots. Indeed, Cecil and Howard patronage networks were central to court politics up to the emergence of the Duke of Buckingham. With the death of Cecil in 1612, his clients such as Sir Henry Neville, Sir Ralph Winwood and many others turned to Somerset. King James acknowledged this dominance in his letter of complaint to Carr in 1615: "do not all court graces and place come through your office as Chamberlain, and rewards through your father-in-law's that is Treasurer? Do not ye two, as it were, hedge in all the Court with a manner of necessity to depend upon you?"[41] James pointed out that Carr also had placed two of his relations in the royal Households, his nephew in James's Bedchamber and another "who loves not to be idle" in Prince Charles's Bedchamber.

Despite the dominance of Somerset and the Howards, Somerset fell in 1615 as a result of the Overbury scandal, and was replaced by the new favorite, Villiers. Between 1616 and 1628 Buckingham successfully moved to consolidate his control of court patronage. Not since Cardinal Wolsey had one person been "both chief councillor and principal favorite."[42] Although Roger Lockyer argues effectively that Buckingham cast his patronage net wide, including different groupings at court, Richard Cust has pointed out that after 1625 Buckingham narrowed his circle of followers and moved against those who had stood out against his politics in parliament. Kevin Sharpe suggests that Buckingham's clients, particularly those granted Irish and Scottish titles, often had little standing in their localities.[43] The change to Buckingham's monopoly of patronage after the competition of the early Jacobean period did not end the client's continuing problem of access and influence which now focused not on the king but on the favorite. As the Countess of Bedford's letter makes clear, even in 1623 court brokers were uncertain as to the best avenue to gain his support.

The Earl of Arundel and the Earls of Pembroke and Montgomery maintained their own important clientages during Buckingham's dominance. This can be demonstrated by the proxies held by the Lords in the parliaments of 1625 and 1626. In 1625 the Duke of Buckingham held thirteen, Pembroke ten; no other peer came close. In 1626 Buckingham again held thirteen and Pembroke and Arundel each had five. With mounting criticism against the duke, a new rule was introduced in the House of Lords limiting the number of proxies to two, a measure supported by Arundel and opposed, not surprisingly, by Buckingham.[44] In 1628 the duke was reconciled with such opponents as Arundel. Shortly before his departure for La Rochelle and the assassin's knife, the Duke of Buckingham even visited the Earl of Somerset to say farewell.[45]

After Buckingham's death, Charles I had no further favorites. Kevin Sharpe argues that up to 1637 the Caroline court "accommodated . . . many different positions as well as vying personalities."[46] Patronage at court centered around a group of lords who served on the Privy Council and in the Household, including Arundel, Pembroke, Montgomery, Holland and Northumberland. Supporters of Spain included at their center Richard Weston (the Lord Treasurer), along with Sir Francis Cottington (Chancellor of the Exchequer), Thomas Wentworth (Earl of Strafford), Sir Francis Windebank, William Monson (Vice Admiral) and Robert Bertie (Earl of Lindsey and Lord Admiral) as well as the Earl of Arundel.[47] Yet Weston did not lead a faction. According to Clarendon, Weston replaced Buckingham "in the public displeasure and in the malice of his enemies without succeeding him in his credit at court or in the affection of any considerable dependents."[48] Policy and patronage seem to have remained divided, with Household officials like the Marquis of Hamilton and the Earl of Holland affecting the distribution of bounty but not royal policy.[49] With connections to the Household of Queen Henrietta Maria, they leaned toward a French alliance. Although Strafford and Laud took a strong lead in shaping the policy of "Thorough" in the 1630s they did not lead factions. Unlike James, Sharpe argues, Charles did not use factions to check one another, inclining now to one and now the other; instead he remained above the pull of factional politics.[50] "Faction" seems too static a term to describe much of the dynamic search for favor and the nuance of power and reward that court patronage displayed. These can only be captured in practice.

III
The client's search for a patron: the Blundell brothers

Patronage networks could be both carefully constructed, with obligation inherited over a series of generations, and fragile, quickly crumbling as favor shifted at court. The means by which clients gained and kept a patron can be understood by recounting their odyssey. Favor seekers sought access to tangible and intangible resources, to land, office, position, status and economic opportunity; such resources were especially important to a younger son of a landed family who, because of the system of primogeniture, could not look forward to a substantial inheritance. One Jacobean official, Francis Blundell, the second son of an old Bedfordshire family, serves as our guide to the creation of patron–client relationships and profit from court favor. His elder brother George inherited the family property, the manor of Cardington. His younger brother John found employment in the forces of the Low Countries.

Irish administration and land had become tied into the English patronage system by the late sixteenth century and increasing numbers of Englishmen were appointed by the Crown to important positions in the central Irish administration.[51] The Blundell family had ties to Ireland; Francis Blundell's uncle, Richard Cooke, knighted by King James in 1603, served as Secretary of State. His elder brother George became a captain in Ireland in 1600, a profitable position because in addition to wages and allowances the captain was paid a lump sum amounting to more than what it cost him to hire his men. Furthermore, George's service was recognized in 1605 when he was granted the reversion of the custody of Limerick Castle.

Francis began his official career by serving as surveyor of Ireland after receiving his BA from Oxford in 1600 at the age of 21.[52] Because of his good work, in 1610 Blundell was granted the reversion to the office of general surveyor of Ireland and became clerk to the commission for the remedy of defective titles in Ireland in 1612.[53] When Dudley Carleton obtained his first official appointment as one of the secretaries for Ireland, Blundell congratulated him and commended him to his uncle.[54] As his offices increased, Blundell began to build an estate in King's County, Ireland, which he made into the Manor of Blundell and accumulated land in the Wexford plantation. Blundell expressed sympathy for the Irish, arguing for mercy for one of his tenants who had drunkenly threatened to burn his house down. Sir Josias Bodley, who laid out the plantation of Ulster, claimed Blundell as his good friend.[55]

Blundell obtained further advancement at court by becoming secretary to the diplomat turned Secretary of State, Sir Ralph Winwood. Sir Arthur Chichester, Lord Deputy of Ireland, wrote to Winwood describing this client's travels toward the fountain of favor with the same phrase that the Countess of

Bedford had used. Blundell was "an honest and able gentleman and should have found him (the Deputy) ready to give him all befitting employment, but his zeal and hopes of advancement near the well-head, have carried him thither."[56] Like Michael Hickes, secretary to Lord Burghley, or John Daccombe, secretary to Sir Robert Cecil, Blundell was then in a position at court to extend his contacts and his opportunities.[57]

While secretary to Winwood, Blundell sat for Lifford in the Irish parliament of 1613–15 and prepared a report for the Secretary of State. He urged recognition of the Irish willingness to vote subsidies and played an important role in the passage of the subsidy bill.[58] In return King James ordered Chichester to treat him with all kindness and to allow him to enjoy his Irish office with all its accumulated fees.

Secretary Winwood served as patron not only to Francis but also to his brothers, one of whom found a place in the entourage of the Elector Palatine when he came to England to marry the Princess Elizabeth in 1613. Winwood obtained the position of muster master for John Blundell whom he described as "brother to Capten George Blundell, who is well known to your Lordship," from the Lord Lieutenant of Bedfordshire, the Earl of Kent. The exchange at the heart of patronage was obvious when Winwood requested admission to the East India Company for Francis, noting that Blundell might be "good of use hereafter to that societie."[59] Francis himself recommended "his gossip, Captain B.," probably his brother George, to Sir Charles Wilmot, of whom he said his brother was an ancient follower. Blundell asked Wilmot, who served variously as Governor of Kerry, joint Governor of Munster and President of Connaught, to serve as a conduit to the Lord Deputy "that his merits may be remembered ... now in the distribucion of those lands ... as you shall make a purchase of him for ever to be at your disposall, so shall I for him remayne your lordship's faithfull and thankfull servant."[60]

Blundell kept Carleton, now English Ambassador in the Low Countries, apprised of the flux of court politics and Carleton looked after his brothers' interests on the continent. On April 29, 1616, Blundell signalled the great shift in the king's affections. He expressed disbelief in the forthcoming arraignments (presumably those of the Earl and Countess of Somerset for the murder of Sir Thomas Overbury) and noted that the Lords (presumably the Privy Council) were displeased because Sir Oliver St John was nominated Deputy of Ireland through the private influence of Sir George Villiers.[61]

In 1617, Sir Ralph Winwood, Blundell's patron and superior, died. Winwood had been held in high favor, as a sign of which his wife was granted the wardship of their eldest son. But Blundell now needed to find another patron and had the good fortune to become the client of the greatest one of the era. Blundell expressed his perpetual loyalty to Buckingham, acknowledged that he owed him almost everything, and documented the presence of onlookers as an essential part of the patron–client relationship.

By your lookes such is your goodnes as you make your servants happie; for the notice which you have bene pleased to take of me, being observed by men of good qualitie in the Court, hath bene very advantagious unto me ... For this, and your Lordship's many other favors I should render myself more often thankfull, but that I feare to lye in the way of your most noble employments for the good of the Publique, with my empty lines ... I have presumed to adventure, that your lordship may see that the benefits which you have conferred upon me doe not perish. If my service may be any waies usefull to your Lordship, I shall with much comfort receive your commandes.[62]

Blundell cast his thanks and obligation in Senecan terms. Further, as his letter makes clear, once he became the client of Buckingham, whose "goodness hath made me most of what I am," Blundell's status rose rapidly. In 1617, before Winwood's death, he became a patentee for a project that licensed peddlers and in 1618 he was knighted.[63]

The Irish baronetcy was created during Buckingham's ascendancy. Blundell was one of the first of the Irish baronets, who were created with precedence over English knights, according to John Chamberlain, to stir the sales of the title.[64] Indeed, Blundell used his contacts to manage the sale of the title for Buckingham, marketing at least eleven between 1618 and 1622 for amounts ranging from £250 to £500.[65] He sold one to an offspring of an old Bedfordshire neighbor and relation, John Fish, who became a planter in Ulster. Fish had connections through his sister to Michael Boyle, Bishop of Waterford,[66] but he obtained the baronetcy through Blundell and Dudley Carleton, as Francis reported to the Duke:

I have according to your Lordship's command sent a letter to Mr Packer for the making of one Fish a Baronet of Ireland at Mr Carleton's request. I have also sent another to him for the making of one Brown a Baronet for the use of Mr Johnson to whom your Lordship promised the favor whensoever he should send you the name of a sufficient man and your goodness will now come the more seaonably to him, because I think he is poor. These being done, I hope I shall hear of no more suits of that kind until I have made up number for your Lordship, which I am now about. If any man doth move your Lordship about making Sir John Fitz-gerald a viscount, I beseech you take notice of him as a man already presented to your Lordship for yourself. For I am upon terms with him but the nature of the Irish is to use several means, so as your lordship not knowing of my treaty with him, may engage your promise to some other to your own prejudice.[67]

Blundell implied that the Irish use of several court brokers was unseemly. In fact it had been the English practice before Buckingham's ascendancy. The proceeds of the sale of these titles of honor went to the favorite and to other court officials whom the king had trouble paying; such sales taxed the wealthy in the pleasantest way when parliament had refused to vote sufficient subsidies and the king had refused to call it into session.

Blundell served as one of the Lords of the Council in Ireland. In 1620 he was granted in reversion the office of Vice-Treasurer and General Receiver in Ireland, a position he took up in March 1622. Because the post of Treasurer had long been moribund, the post of Vice-Treasurer was, along with the Lord Deputy and Lord Chancellor, one of the three top positions in Irish administration. Just as significantly, Blundell had become a substantial Irish landlord. Granted 1,000 acres in Wexford as part of the plantation in 1618 he received an additional 500 and, in 1620, 200 acres more.[68] He also held land in Lifford and Kings County.

Through the influence of William Knollys, Lord Wallingford, the Comptroller of the Household, Blundell was chosen to represent Oxford in the parliament of 1621, only to be removed during the session as a result of a disputed election.[69] During the same session he was attacked, along with other patentees, for his project for licensing peddlers which he and his associates then surrendered. Blundell maintained his offices and his interests in Ireland until his death in 1625. The courtier, Sir Humphrey May, now Chancellor of the Duchy of Lancaster, who earlier had been the agent for the king's instruction to the Lord Deputy of Ireland, was one of the executors of his will.

Blundell had made a successful career at court and in Ireland through the interest of at least two patrons, Winwood and Buckingham. He was not, therefore, simply the duke's creature. He gained office and built a landed estate before the favorite's ascendancy. None the less, his rise to high office and title was swift once Buckingham became his patron. He used his Irish connections to further the favorite's interests. The duke established a grip on court patronage not seen before and closely integrated his giving of bounty with reciprocal service and payment by the client.

After Lionel Cranfield became Lord Treasurer, he sought, with Buckingham's backing, to bring order to royal finances in the navy and the Household. He also turned his attention to Ireland. In 1621, Cranfield told Blundell that his office of Vice-Treasurer was central to the reform of Irish administration, requested that Blundell provide him with periodic reports, and noted trenchantly that Blundell had not always fulfilled his responsibilities. Alluding perhaps to Blundell's role in selling titles, Cranfield urged him to "put on the mind to do the king's service sincerely, laying aside all other thoughts for the present till the settling of this work." Blundell needed to

> make amends for some slips and errors lately noted to have escaped your hands ... If you run into any other course and either by your under-officers'

negligence or corruption (which are both alike penal to the King's service) shall by misguiding put this goodly work out of frame, you may justly expect his Majesty's displeasure and the transferring of the honour and merit of settling the same to another, who shall and will do that which you leave undone.[70]

Cranfield seemed to suggest that Blundell's concern to organize the duke's Irish patronage might spill over into corruption. Yet the duke's power over the king, the Prince of Wales and royal bounty could not be denied. Because of his ties to Blundell, the duke urged Cranfield to "continue your accustomed favor towards him as a man I take care of."[71]

Both Cranfield and Blundell were the duke's clients and Cranfield served as a broker between the duke and others. When the duke withdrew his favor from Cranfield in 1624, the Lord Treasurer fell to parliamentary impeachment. Afterwards, King James and Prince Charles granted him pardon. Because Buckingham was away, a member of the king's Bedchamber wrote to the duke to explain the pardon apologetically and to send the king's promises to do nothing more for Cranfield without Buckingham's approval.[72]

Patronage, projects, profit and warfare were fused in the career of Sir Francis Blundell's brother George, who was knighted in 1617. Sir George Blundell proposed in 1623 to supply the kingdom with new arms, creating a central storehouse in London to buy up arms made by poor artificers and provision the counties at prices set by the Council. While the project introduced no new technology, it was intended to centralize the provisioning of the trained bands. Blundell asked Secretary Conway to procure for him both the patent and the title of "Captain of the Arms for England and Wales." Blundell had thought out both the political and financial angles: each Lord Lieutenant would compel the trained bands to buy their own arms and not let the purchase be imposed as a tax on the county.[73] To ensure his own profit he requested a monopoly on such sales. Blundell promised to give Conway's son one shilling for each of the first 20,000 arms sold in consideration of Conway's favor. Finally he begged Conway's influence with Buckingham to procure him the Lieutenancy of the Tower if he were able to borrow £1,000 to pay for it.[74]

Hunting for office and projects was only part of Sir George Blundell's career. He served at sea on the expeditions in the 1620s to Cadiz and the Isle of Rhé and his letters to Buckingham and to Secretary Nicholas were filled with complaints about provisioning and requests for favor.[75] In 1627, serving as Sergeant Major in Plymouth, he described the dreadful situation of men, provisions and ships. He went on to say that he had heard that the Lords had settled his allowance at 12 shillings a day. Proclaiming that he would rather serve the king for nothing than receive so base a pay, he begged the duke to put him down for 40 shillings.

Blundell complained that Buckingham made him a packhorse, as he put it, while others lay at court still getting sergeants or baronets to put money in their purses. He did obtain a position for his son on his ship, putting aside a lieutenant with much more service. Such favor had an unfortunate end. Sir George Blundell and his son George were slain at Rhé.[76] But Sir George got his wish: he was entered on the list of the army with pay of 40 shillings a day and the wardship of his grandson was granted to his wife without paying the usual fine to the Crown. As Francis Blundell had promised that Buckingham's benefits to him would not perish, Buckingham's favor to George Blundell lasted beyond the grave.

IV
The competition for office: the Provostship of Eton

The Blundells illustrate the client's successful quest for court favor. The contest for a specific post dramatizes the abundance of suitors who invoked kinship ties and gift-giving along with purchase to gain reward. It demonstrates that the multiplicity of patrons of the earlier period had with Buckingham given way to one. Even the word of the king could not supercede his. And Buckingham used the competition for Eton to satisfy two clients at once.

The provostship of Eton, one of England's oldest and most prestigious schools, was a highly regarded position much sought after both by English ambassadors longing for employment at home and by other court officials. Every time the position appeared to be available during the reign of James I there was a frenzy of eager suitors each applying to one of the great patrons through court brokers currently thought influential.[77]

Sir Dudley Carleton was an inveterate office-seeker. Even as he sought other court positions such as that of Secretary of State, he kept an eye on one particular position, Eton, especially attractive to a well educated connoisseur such as Carleton. Carleton's father-in-law, the famous classical scholar Sir Henry Saville, was the provost. For over ten years, Carleton monitored Saville's health and hotly competed to succeed him. As early as 1614 Carleton confided his hopes to his close friend John Chamberlain. In May 1617, with his father-in-law still in good health, Carleton asked friends at court and at Eton for help. At Eton, his "brother" Richard Harrison said he would do his best for Carleton were Saville to fall ill but worried about the Scots who were waiting for the post to become vacant. He urged Carleton to "make sum worke with your greate frinds at coorte aboute the king, and rest assured of all assistance from your poor country friends, and if your Lordship thinke good to make mee knowen to any of them, I shall by that meanes have the more speedy access to them."[78]

Harrison's language suggests the importance of access to court brokers to link center and locality. But the "poor country" was an artefact of language or a state of mind as much as a place. In the 1620s Carleton successfully approached the Earl of Pembroke to keep Harrison from being named sheriff of Berkshire for two years and Harrison's daughter became a maid in waiting to Queen Henrietta Maria. During negotiations over a lease, Harrison referred to this "unthrifty world we live in ... I shall wish that you make much of that unrighteous mamon, it being theonly frinde of this adge."[79]

At court Carleton's secretary, Edward Sherburn, like Harrison, was blunt: "nothing can be don, in these times without consideration, and it is in vaine to hope (be a [man's] merits never so deserving) that without money anything is to be obtained." Sherburn asked authority to make an offer.[80] Saville himself was agreeable to Carleton's succeeding him, but urged him to obtain the king's promise. Soon after, Saville wrote again that the king had promised the post to one of the Scots, Thomas Murray, and that Sir Henry Wotton had asked for it and been denied.[81]

In the midst of these negotiations, Sir Ralph Winwood fell ill and the jostling for office turned to the position of Secretary of State. Carleton gained the support of the Earl of Arundel through Arundel's cousin, the great miliary commander Sir Horace Vere. Sherburn hoped to be the first to tell Carleton of Winwood's death and thought Arundel a suitable instrument to secure Carleton's promotion.[82] But Arundel was unable to deliver as Buckingham tightened his hold on court patronage.

Sherburn also urged Carleton to write to the Earl of Pembroke. Soon after, Sherburn himself entered Pembroke's service.

> If his favor with his Majesty and the good opinion he hath with the subject decline not, your Lordship cannot address yourself to any (one only excepted) more honorable more powerfull. And therefore I pray your Lordship (though he admit not himself to foreign business but chiefly to domestick) yet be not sparing to advertise his Lordship, as occasion shalbe offered.[83]

It was not the case that Carleton approached *every* court patron. His friend Sir George Gerrard spent a week with the Earls of Southampton, Montgomery and Lord Hay, "but hear of nothing worth writing so farr as your lord-ship."[84]

In March 1619, Saville's health worsened and Carleton's Etonian friend, Richard Harrison, advised him to renew his suit. Although Saville recovered once more, another court contact named Hales told Carleton that Thomas Murray was still promised the provostship. Murray was secretary to Prince Charles; Hales thought that both offices could not be held by the same person and suggested that Carleton might be able to strike a bargain with Murray. Saville lived another three years, but in January 1622 Thomas Locke wrote to

Carleton that Saville was once more dangerously ill. Locke hoped that since Murray was a stranger at court, i.e. a Scot, he would not secure the position. A month later Murray was granted a dispensation to hold the post.[85]

Murray had waited several years to gain the position and had little more than a year to enjoy it. He himself fell fatally ill in 1623. Carleton's nephew (also named Dudley) tried to get the reversion of the provostship for Carleton but wrote that Buckingham had suddenly departed to attend Prince Charles to Spain. Their extraordinary trip to Spain to arrange the Prince's marriage with the Infanta did not, however, end the search for favor.

Several sought the Eton post although none met the requirements of the founder, Henry VI, that the provost be a cleric. But that requirement had been waived for Saville who had used both Essex and Sir Robert Cecil to intercede with Queen Elizabeth for him.[86] The disgraced Francis Bacon, Viscount St Albans, requested the position on the expected demise of Murray in 1623, telling Secretary Conway that the king had promised to have a care for him. In later letters he thanked Conway for the king's willingness to grant it to him if Sir William Becher could be satisfied. The provostship would be most fit, Bacon declared, "in the spent hourglass of his life" because it was both near London and a place of study.[87] Sir William Becher, the clerk of the Privy Council, who had served in diplomatic posts in France and was a client of the Duke of Buckingham, wanted the provostship as did Sir Henry Wotton, the English ambassador to Venice.

One sign of Buckingham's great hold on Jacobean patronage was that the post was not filled while he was away, although obviously the king could make the appointment any time he wanted. The king's views on the provostship were described to the duke by John Williams, Bishop of Lincoln, to whom, according to Eton's statutes, the provost reported:

> Mr Murray the provost of Eaton, is now dead. The place stayed by the fellowes and my selfe until your Lordship's pleasure be known. Whomssoever your Lordship shall name, I shall like of though it be Sir William Becher (though this Provostshipp never descended so lowe). The kinge, named unto me yesterday morning Sir Albertus Morton, Sir Dudley Carleton and Sir [blank] Aton [Sir Robert Ayton], our late Queene's secretarye: but (in my opinion) thoughe he named him last, his Majesty inclin'de to this Aton most. It will rest wholye upon your Lordship to name the man. It is somewhat necessarie he be a good scholler, but more, that he be a good husband and a carefull, provident and stayed man, which no man can be, that is soe much endebted as the Lord of St. Albane's.[88]

Sir Robert Ayton, a Scot who studied civil law in Paris, wrote Latin poetry and was good friends with Ben Jonson, Thomas Hobbes and, according to Aubrey, "acquainted with all the wits of his time in England." He became a Gentleman of James's Bedchamber as well as personal secretary and Master of Requests to Queen Anne. His poetry saluted the king and commemorated the Duke of Buckingham. At the death of Sir Thomas Murray he wrote both an epitaph and some hopeful verses on Eton.[89] Ayton offered to forgo his £500 a year pension in exchange for the provostship in a letter to Buckingham:

> Mr Thomas Murray being dead, there be many suitors for the Provostship of Eton yet none recommended by the dying man but myself; none as I am informed, towards whom his Majesty is more favourably inclined, none so wish'd by those, who wish the good of Mr. Murray's children as myself; and in a word none, that maketh suit for the king's benefit but I; my offer being to surrender to his Majesty my pension of 500 pounds a year in lieu of this place. Yet notwithstanding of all this some rubb there is of a promise pretended to be made by yourself to a man by most men esteemed uncapable of that charge, and therefore opposed by [the] Lord Keeper [the Earl of Pembroke]. Now, my Lord, it is in your power as I hear to strike the stroke.[90]

When Murray died in April, Lady Carleton approached Lord Treasurer Cranfield who told her the naming of a new provost would have to wait until Buckingham's return. The Earl of Arundel urged the king to give Carleton the provostship of Eton both because of his long and able service and because his wife was the daughter of Lady Saville. The king declared his good opinion of Carleton and promised him better preferment in time.[91] When the great patron was absent from court, it was still necessary for the client to gain access to him wherever he was, even if that meant the continent. Letters sped from courtiers and clerics to the Duke in Spain. Henry Rich, later Earl of Holland, who accompanied the retinue to Spain, told Carleton that he had tried his best. Although Buckingham wished to help him, he was engaged to another for Eton; he would favor Carleton in anything else.[92]

It may be remembered that the Countess of Bedford thought in April 1623 that Sir Ralph Freeman would gain Eton. She was wrong, but Freeman had his own interest in the competition, asking that he succeed Sir Henry Wotton if Wotton got Eton and that his place be granted to Sir Albertus Morton.[93] Similarly, Secretary of State Calvert asked that if Sir William Becher were made the provost that Simon Digby might succeed him as Clerk of the Privy Council. In the midst of this free-for-all, Calvert noted somewhat petulantly that the king would be better served if promotions were given in turns as they fell due.[94] No one took no for an answer and with good reason.

When Buckingham returned from Spain, Carleton's nephew went into high gear, presenting the recommendation of Princess Elizabeth, Queen of Bohemia, on behalf of Sir Dudley and moving Sir William Crofts, a member of Prince Charles's Household, to press the prince. Prince Charles, like the king and Buckingham before him, told him that the provostship was out of the question but something else, as good or better should be thought of for Carleton.[95] The duke was bound by honor to Becher but that obligation could be satisfied financially: "he was deeply engaged to

Sir William Becher for the first good thing that should fall, even before Mr Murray dyed, and he had receaved such an obligation from that man, that he should be unworthy, if he made not his promises good, even in the very worst degree of unworthiness." Nonetheless, if Carleton could "finde out any meanes to give Sir William Becher other contentment" the duke assured Carleton that he would "carrie it before any man" and promised to speak with Becher about Carleton's offer.[96]

During these months of negotiation, Buckingham gave Carleton's nephew repeated access to his house and to his chamber and discussed the post even when he was preparing for bed. As the court's greatest patron he gave ear to all requests. While Buckingham clearly had the influence to name the new provost, he claimed to be "cast into such a distraction by the strong reasons that the diverse pretenders produce, every man for himself, that he coulde not resolve to move the king . . . for any body at all." Buckingham had spoken with Becher about Carleton's offer of compensation but Becher responded "that he coulde not esteeme the offer, half so good as the place."[97]

Despite all the jockeying for the position and John Chamberlain's declaration in December that Becher had been granted it, no one was named provost. The position remained vacant to allow Mrs Murray, who had seven children, to enjoy the fruits of her late husband's perquisites as provost. In January court gossip contended that Sir Henry Wotton had secured the job by resigning the reversion of the Mastership of the Rolls to Sir Ralph Freeman who would then resign his Mastership of Requests to Sir William Becher. Six weeks later the gossip was that Sir Robert Ayton would have both Mrs Murray and the post.[98]

Even as money increasingly shaped patron–client relationships, the exchange of favor was still sealed with a gift. In July 1617, in his attempt to gain the provostship of Eton, Dudley Carleton presented Queen Anne with a clock. The protocol of patronage and gift-giving was revealed in a contretemps between two of Carleton's servants, the canny Sherburn and the green Woodward, over how to present it. Sherburn intended to bring it to Queen Anne's lady-in-waiting, "my Lady Roxborough to whom not many daies before his arrivall, I made knowne, what in your former letters to me you commanded concerning this clocke. But I hear that he used for his address Sir John Bennet."[99] Woodward replied that because Sherburn had been "officious" in wishing to go with him to present it to Lady Roxborough, Woodward "presently went and delivered it my self."[100] In short, Woodward "dropped off" Carleton's gift at the palace, thereby threatening the benefits that the proper presentation of such a gift might procure.

At the Jacobean court the collecting of antique and Renaissance art had become increasingly popular and diplomats like Carleton and Wotton shaped the taste of courtiers.[101] At the end of March Dudley Carleton told his uncle that Wotton had presented Buckingham with "many curious pictures" whereby it was thought that he aimed at the provostship. In response, Carleton asked his nephew if this was a good time to offer Buckingham a "gate and chimney of marble?" But he urged him to "use care and discretion, for they are of too great value to be cast away, especially considering my hard estate. Wherefore first weigh with yourself how you find the Duke to continue affected towards me, then what intention he hath or means to favor me." He added that Lady Carleton had gone to Middleburg to see goods that the Dutch had taken from a Spanish prize in order to make Buckingham a wonderful present.[102] Although Carleton's marble chimney appears to have been installed in York House, Buckingham's London mansion, he was unsuccessful in his quest for Eton.

Becher was a diplomat and an educated man but there appears to be a general perception that he was less qualified than others competing for the post, a suspicion probably based on social standing. His grandfather was an alderman of London, his father a merchant with military contracts, and his mother the daughter of a draper.[103] Becher got his position in the household of Sir George Carew in Paris through Robert Cecil's secretary, Sir Michael Hickes.[104] The suspicion arises that Buckingham was actually trying to take care of two clients at once by forcing the successful Eton candidate to satisfy Becher. As it turned out, this is precisely what happened.

In 1613 Sir Henry Wotton had lamented his loss of two great patrons, no doubt referring to Prince Henry and the Earl of Salisbury.[105] After Salisbury's death, Wotton turned to Robert Carr, Earl of Somerset, who supported him for the position of Secretary of State in 1612. In 1614 while on a diplomatic trip to the Hague, Wotton sent Somerset a Dutch painting. Acknowledging "how much I am bound to your Lordship for the late intercession for me with the king . . . when occasion serves I will build uppon your Lordship's mediation and patronage, and in the meanewhile give you some demonstrations of my fidelitie."[106]

By the time Wotton came home from his post in Venice, Somerset had fallen, and he himself was without funds. The king promised him the Mastership of the Rolls after Sir Julius Caesar but when the provostship of Eton became vacant, Buckingham procured the post for him. But Sir William Becher had to be gratified with more than art. Wotton formally transferred to Becher his interest in a Six Clerks position in Chancery which he shared with Sir Julius Caesar, Master of the Rolls, whose profit was based on the sale and revenues of the office and the manipulation of a series of reversions. Wotton acknowledged: "All which I have been moved to doe for your release of a promise which the Duke of Buckingham my noble patron had made you before my last arrival from Venice to procure for you from his Majestie the Provostship of Eaton."[107] The Duke's honor was upheld, two clients were satisfied and contemporaries estimated that Becher made £2,500 from the deal.[108]

V
Women as Court Brokers: Queen Anne's Household

Historians usually talk about patrons, brokers and suitors as if they all were male. Although women's economic and political rights were legally circumscribed in early Stuart England, they played an important role in the economy and, in their social relationships as mothers, daughters, sisters and friends, they bound together kinship groups and patronage networks.[109] In addition, women gave literary commissions to writers and painters for whom they might be both subjects and patrons. Leading aristocrats such as the Countess of Bedford, the Countess of Pembroke and the Dowager Countess of Derby created literary and political salons at their houses at Twickenham, Wilton, and Harefield.[110] Many women were patrons of divines, both Catholic and various shades of Protestant, and some, who held land as heiresses or widows, were patrons of borough elections.[111]

What has remained opaque is the important position women held in early Stuart court patronage. Yet ladies-in-waiting to Queen Anne and Queen Henrietta Maria, especially the Countess of Bedford and Susan Villiers, Countess of Denbigh, and wives of important officials and courtiers, such as Catherine, Countess of Suffolk, and Isabella, Lady Rich, acted as important court brokers.[112] Indeed, the Countess of Bedford and Countess of Denbigh were more important at the courts of James I and Charles I than their husbands, a point rarely noted.[113] Their political role belies the separation between public and private spheres, the latter being the one within which women were expected to act. Their brokerage and connections bridged Household and Privy Council.

Indeed, Queen Anne's Household offers a useful example of the creation of male–female patronage networks crafted from the politics of the 1590s on.[114] Its personnel were members of the major patronage networks at the Jacobean court, followers of Cecil, the Howards and the Jacobean Scots. Officials in Queen Anne's Household who simultaneously held important positions in the central administration included Sir Robert Cecil, Secretary of State, Sir George Carew, Master of the Ordinance, and Sir Roger Wilbraham, Master of Requests. Other members of the Queen's Council were Lord Robert Sidney (Lord Chamberlain), his friend the Earl of Southampton (Master of the Queen's Game), Sir Thomas Somerset (Master of the Queen's Horse), the son of the Earl of Worcester (Master of the Horse to King James), and Sir William Fowler (Secretary and Master of Requests). Fowler was later replaced by Sir Robert Ayton.[115] Queen Anne's Household was dominated by former followers of the Earl of Essex, as Leeds Barroll has described, including Penelope Devereux, Lucy, Countess of Bedford, and Sir Robert Sidney.[116]

Sidney, younger brother of Sir Philip Sidney, and a close associate of Essex, became Chamberlain of Anne's Household and was created Viscount

L'Isle by James. Sidney's inner circle, many of whom later entered Queen Anne's service, were part of the group from which "goships" (godparents) were selected for Sidney's son in 1599. These included Roger Manners, Earl of Rutland, Sir Walter and Lady Raleigh, Sir George Carew, Katherine Carey, the Lady Nottingham, and her sister-in-law Elizabeth Spenser, "the young Lady Hunsdon." The Countess of Bedford was an important friend of the Sidneys.[117] Of these, Lucy Harrington, Countess of Bedford, Sir George Carew, and Audrey, Lady Nottingham, all became important members of Queen Anne's Household and took an influential role in court politics.

In 1605/6 the ladies in the queen's Household were drawn from women related to members of the Privy Council and gentlemen of the king's and prince's Households. These included Katherine, Countess of Suffolk, Keeper of the Queen's Jewels and Lady-in-Waiting. She was the wife of the Lord Treasurer, Thomas Howard, Earl of Suffolk, who brokered important transactions between merchants and other government officials and the Exchequer.[118] Other ladies in the Household were Jane Drummond, later Countess of Roxborough, Audrey Walsingham, Lady Keeper of the Robes, Elizabeth Lady Carey, Keeper of the Sweet Coffers, and five maids of honor, Mistress Anne Carey, Mary Middlemore, Mary Gargrave, Elizabeth Roper and Elizabeth Harcourt.[119] Elizabeth Fortescue was mother of the maids.

As we have seen, King Charles settled a large pension of £1,200 on the Countess of Roxborough for thirty-one years from 1636 in lieu of £5,750 arrearage of her pension granted her by King James. His reason was "her faithful service to his Majesty's late dear Mother, and his Majesty's dearest consort the Queen."[120] The Careys were wife and daughter of Sir Robert Carey, a member of Queen Elizabeth's Household, who announced her death to King James. Elizabeth Carey had charge of Prince Charles and Sir Robert became governor of Prince Charles's Household. Mary Middlemore was the sister of Robert, equerry to King James.[121] Elizabeth Roper married Sir Robert Mansell, Treasurer of the Navy and glass patentee.

The Jacobean Scots and their connections took up their places not only in King James's Bedchamber but also in the Household of Queen Anne. Barbara, Lady Ruthven, was the widow of the Earl of Gowrie. The Gowrie plot to assassinate James had been successfully foiled in 1600 and its anniversary celebrated as a day of deliverance in Scotland much like November 5, 1605, the anniversary of the Gunpowder Plot, in England. Despite her Gowrie connections Lady Ruthven was a friend of Queen Anne; arrangements were made within two months of the accession to bring her to London and she was granted a £200 pension. In 1616 a friend approached the Earl of Arundel, Lady Ruthven and Secretary Winwood to prevail on the king to permit Toby Matthew's return from continental exile. With their help and that of Lord Roos, Lord Villiers, and Sir Francis Bacon, he hoped to gain the favor.[122] She succeeded the Countess of Roxborough as Queen Anne's chief lady in 1617 "though there be much competition."[123] John Murray, later Earl of Annandale, married Elizabeth, daughter of John Shaw who was in the service of Queen Anne. Their son James was baptized in the royal chapel in 1617 and Lady Annandale had a pension for serving Queen Anne.[124]

Fathers and sons served in the queen's Household. Sir George Carew, her Vice Chamberlain, had connections with Essex, Cecil and, later, Buckingham. He helped shape Irish policy and his illegitimate son, Sir Thomas Stafford, one of the gentlemen of the Privy Chamber, served in Ireland.[125] He had close connections with Prince Charles and with Buckingham. After taking part in England's continental campaigns, he became one of the undertakers of the drainage of the fens in Lincolnshire in the 1630s. Stafford served as a member of Henrietta Maria's court in which Lady Thomasizina Carew, another relative, served as Keeper of the Sweet Coffers.[126] In 1635 he was rumored to be about to become Vice Chamberlain of Henrietta Maria's Household, the same position that his father had held in Queen Anne's.[127]

Another son of a prominent courtier was part of the queen's Household. Sir Thomas Somerset, the Queen's Master of the Horse, was the son of Edward, Earl of Worcester, Master of the Horse to the king. Worcester not only held one of the most important Household offices, but was also one of the inner circle of the Jacobean Privy Council centered around Cecil and the Howards. Sir Thomas Tracy, Gentleman of the Privy Chamber, was the brother of Mary, Lady Vere, wife of Sir Horace Vere. She was Secretary of State Conway's sister-in-law; he was the Earl of Arundel's cousin.[128]

The queen's Household was thus a political web from which patronage connections radiated. It was also a mainstay of literary and artistic patronage and not just of court masques; the painter Isaac Oliver and the writers Samuel Daniel and John Florio were members of the Household. Florio had dedicated his Italian–English dictionary to the Earls of Rutland and Southampton, the Countess of Bedford and he left his Italian, French and Spanish books to Pembroke. The Queen was represented at the christening of Florio's child.[129]

Indeed, the Queen served as godmother and matchmaker to the Jacobean court. Her role as godmother was spelled out in court ritual more elaborate than in Scotland in "The Service and Ceremonie to be Performed at a Christening where the Queene's Majestie or her deputie shalbe Present." This ceremony was not "woman's work." Its detail was overseen by the most important officials at the Jacobean court. At the baptizing of the Lord Aubigny's son by the Queen she washed before "she removed from the font by reason the Lord Treasurer and Lord Privy Seale did constantlie affirme it ought to be so."[130] Queen Anne asked to be godparent to the Earl of Arundel's son in 1607, a marked sign of favor, and the Countess of Shrewsbury, the child's grandmother, sent ermine for the occasion.[131]

After the long reign of the virgin queen who begrudged the marriages of her ladies-in-waiting, the reign of James I celebrated uxoriousness. As part of court patronage networks the arranged marriages of aristocratic women cemented connections between different factions. If the king were *pater familias* of the court as Bacon had said, his courtiers strove to become kin. The Earl of Pembroke and the Earl of Arundel, the one a supporter of the godly, the other of English Catholics, were linked through their mother-in-law, the Countess of Shrewsbury, and described by a contemporary as "her two court sonnes."[132]

At the beginning of the reign of James I a flurry of marriages linked Cecils, Howards and relatives and followers of the Earl of Essex. Indeed the great scandal of the reign, the divorce of the third Earl of Essex by Frances Howard in order to marry the king's favorite, Robert Carr, Earl of Somerset, provides two such examples at once. Marriages at court were often celebrated with court masques as was the marriage of Princess Elizabeth to the Elector Palatine. As the same time that the king presented his favorite Somerset in marriage to Frances Howard, Queen Anne presented her lady-in-waiting Jane Drummond to the Earl of Roxborough in ceremonies costing £30,000.

Such politic matches did not always succeed: a projected match between Cecils and Sidneys broke down when the match between Lord Burghley's eldest daughter and Lord Lisle's son was broken off.[133] Yet as Buckingham solidified his hold on political power at court, there were marriages linking the Villiers clan to the Cokes, Cecils and Howards. In April 1623, while the duke was in Spain, the Earl of Suffolk wrote to pay him tribute and to bewail that "an illfate hath a long time led me oute of the way of your Lordship."[134] By the end of the year a younger son of Suffolk's, Sir Edward Howard, had married Buckingham's niece, daughter of Elizabeth Villiers, his half-sister and Sir John Boteler, at York House. The match, Chamberlain reported, was "made chiefly upon hopefull conditions, the Lord of Buckingham professing that he will not only be an uncle but a father unto them: the Prince came thether after supper and lodged there."[135]

John Holles's search for an appropriate wife for his heir provides evidence of the different impulses that drove court marriages. Holles urged his son to choose "a gentlewoman of good blood, good kindred, unblowne, and unacquainted with court conversation, dexterities and entertainments." He rejected the heiress of Sir Edward Gorge, created an Irish baron in 1620, because "by the late death of her brother, she is a great courtier for balls and masques and great meetings ... one of no birth; no kindred, her father a scholar only, besides she hath been in love and will be again by Diogenes rule."[136] Holles, whose great grandfather had been Lord Mayor of London from 1539 to 1540, negotiated with a London Alderman who offered £10,000 to marry his daughter to Holles's son and was prepared to go even higher. But Holles preferred the daughter of Sir Horace Vere, the English

71

commander in the Low Countries, who was his cousin.[137] "If Sir Horace Vere will give £5,000 and state a convenient portion of land, so much prefer I that alliance, my own profit shall give place thereunto."[138] Sir Horace was a great military commander. The Veres were cousins of the Howards and patrons of the godly. Lady Vere's brother, Sir Thomas Tracy, had been a member of Queen Anne's Household and left his estate to her and her children.[139] Court connections remained important to Holles even if court conversation was not.

At the Jacobean court, women served as clients, patrons and brokers. Some, such as Lady Elizabeth Russell, petitioned on their own behalf. Others followed suits for their husbands such as Lady Raleigh who wrote on behalf of Sir Walter to Henry Howard, Earl of Northampton, to protest her husband's imprisonment.[140] Women came to London themselves when their husbands were posted at a distance. In 1588, the wife of Sir Henry Withrington, Knight Marshall of Berwick, followed his suit at court while her husband remained in the north.[141] Archbishop Laud was approached by the sister of his good friend, Sir John Scudamore, to serve as go-between to Buckingham: "Your Sister Mistress Meeke was with mee; Her business was to desier mee to moove my Lord of Buckingham to write his letters in her husband's behalfe, for a place then void about the Inner Temple." Although Laud claimed to be loath to deal with it "yet by her importunity and feare of her husband's going into Ireland for want of meanes, I was mov'd in pitty to doe against my judgment. But the place was suddainly gone and both I and they prevented." Household positions, much coveted for their influence, were closely controlled by the favorite. Hopeful of gaining a Household post, the Meeks "importun'd againe to moove my Lordship to helpe him to a place about the Queen upon the remove of the French, but that was a business too bigg for me and I durst not meddle . . ."[142]

Women served as court brokers beyond the confines of the queen's Privy Chamber even for the post of Secretary of State which included a seat of the Privy Council. In November 1617 Isabella, Lady Rich, told a friend of Carleton's that the ambassador should have applied to the Countess of Bedford who was powerful with Buckingham, Hamilton, and Pembroke about the position of Secretary of State rather than Lady Hatton who had recently fallen out with Buckingham.[143] In this case three different noblewomen played the role of brokers, acting as intermediaries to the royal favorite. Although the Countess of Bedford was both an important friend of Queen Anne and a member of her Household, equally important were her connections to three of the court's leading male officials; her patronage connections spanned council and household.

The death of Queen Anne in 1619 brought the dissolution of her Household, and her servants had to fend for themselves. Caroline Hibbard points out that Sir Robert Carey estimated his extra expense at £1,000 a year now that his family no longer lived at court. After the removal of many of Henrietta Maria's French attendants within a year of her arrival at the English court, her official Household was chiefly English and Scottish although some French servants continued to dabble in politics. Her most important attendant was Susan Villiers, Countess of Denbigh, sister of the favorite, who continued to have access to both the king and the queen independently even after the assassination of Buckingham in 1628. Hibbard argues convincingly that the Countess of Denbigh kept alive the Villiers patronage network in both Privy Council and Household. Her work was made easier by the marriage of her son, Basil, Lord Feilding, to Anne Weston, daughter of the Lord Treasurer, and by the marriage of James, Marquis of Hamilton, to her daughter. Although her husband, the Earl of Denbigh, was Master of the Wardrobe for the king, her preferred intermediary was her son-in-law Hamilton, who was closer to Charles.[144] Thus William Middleton told Basil that he planned to approach "the king by my Lord Marquess and the Countess of Denbigh and by them jointly. My lady has promised me her furtherance and my Lord Marquesses. If they prevail with the King, the business is done, and when it is done, next under God I shall acknowledge your lordship and those noble personages my greatest patrons."[145] The countess herself approached the king on Middleton's behalf. There continued to be a Howard presence in Henrietta Maria's Household: Elizabeth Howard, granddaughter of the Earl of Suffolk, and Sarah Monson whose family were long-time associates of the Howards. Sarah Harrington, a relative of the Countess of Bedford, was a maid of honor, as was Frances Harrison, daughter of Richard Harrison, the friend of Dudley Carleton, now at last Secretary of State and Viscount Dorchester.[146]

Bacon had advised Buckingham not to meddle with the settled but dangerous issue of religion. In the 1620s court connections drew together those of differing religious views. Mary, Lady Vere, was a patron of puritan ministers such as John Davenport. In a squabble in 1624 over the ministry at St Stephen, Coleman Street, London, Davenport, one of the candidates, asked Lady Vere to intervene with Secretary Conway, her brother-in-law. Once again the Countess of Bedford was an important court contact: "The Countess of Bedford wrote me word this day that my Lord of Canterbury doth interpose for a chaplain of his own one Wilson and pretendeth that the said Wilson hath many friends in the parish as I, and that those who stood for me are but a puritanical faction." Denying that, Davenport claimed:

so many as disliked the ceremonies (which are but few about 5 or 6) stood for another. I propose to give the Archbishop notice hereof but, because I am a mean man and unknown to him: if it will please my Lady Vere to acquaint Secretary Conway with these occurrences which happened since my last speech with his Honor God may incline his heart to undertake the satisfying of the Archbishop.[147]

Apparently Lady Vere did intervene; Conway wrote to the Archbishop on Davenport's behalf. Through the Veres Davenport angled for preferment for Robert Herrick, then chaplain to the Duke of Buckingham, told them of his own problems with the Court of High Commission, and became friends with John Holles's son, Lord Haughton, who married the Veres' daughter. In turn Davenport, a member of both the Virginia and Massachusetts Bay Companies, undertook to move the great London merchant Sir Maurice Abbot in business of Lady Mary's. In the 1620s, then, Davenport gained perferment through the brokerage of the Countess of Bedford and the Veres who had connections both in the Privy Council and the Household. By the 1630s, however, he was under attack by Archbishop Laud. He withdrew from his congregation but continued his connection with Lady Mary Vere even after becoming a congregationalist and migrating to Massachusetts.[148]

Unravelling the transactions of patrons and clients dramatizes the ever-present search for favor and lessens the importance of policy differences from the accession of King James to the early 1630s at the least. Factions – which no doubt existed at times of transition and of conflict – fragment when analyzed closely. Courtiers who moved from Essex to Salisbury to Somerset to Buckingham tended to be pleased with the system; those unable to make those transitions in favor tended to discontent, like Raleigh, Holles and many others. Political differences did exist, on foreign policy, religion and taxation but these varying views were represented within the court in the 1620s and beyond. But a further question needs to be asked. How far did court favor extend into the localities? If patronage networks in the sixteenth and eighteenth centuries stretched between center and locality what was the case in the early seventeenth century? There were, for instance, a group of knights appointed to Queen Anne's council, but not in commission, who were officeholders and leading country gentlemen from the counties in which the Queen held land. These included Sir Edwin Sandys, Sir Oliver Cromwell, Sir Richard Verney and Sir Robert Dormer; several later became court critics.[149] The Duke of Buckingham enjoyed virtual hegemony at court. When his brother Kit was made an Earl, James said,"thou was born in a happy hour for all thy kin."[150] His control, however, was not fully extended to the counties. Buckingham's nominees frequently lost elections in the Cinque Ports of which he was Lord Warden and he was not in control of Buckinghamshire of which he was Lord Lieutenant.[151] These vertical ties began to fray, firstly with the monopoly of the Duke in the 1620s, at least so far as those not included, and secondly in the 1630s when many important country cousins found themselves unrelated to the paterfamilias and his court family.

Chapter 4

Court connections
and county associations:
the case of Buckinghamshire

Royal Households were not, of course, the only ones in which extended
kinship, friendship and patronage ties were important; they often found their
mirror image in gentry society. Thus, in a fascinating and unusual document,
"The day of birth of my children," written about 1602, Hester Sandys Temple
recorded the date and time of birth, and sometimes death, of eleven of
her fifteen children along with the names of their thirty-three godparents.[1]
Hester began: "Susan Temple was born the fifth of September 1587 on
Tuesday between the hours of 10 and 11 in the forenoon." Her godfather
was her uncle Edwin Sandys, and her godmothers were her grandmother
Susan Temple, and grandmother-in-law Mary Sandys, "widow before of
Alderman Woodcocke." Hester's first son, Peter, was born Monday October
2, 1592, "being the day that our queen passed through Buckinghamshire."
His godfathers were his grandfathers Sir Miles Sandys and John Temple; his
godmother Elizabeth Sandys, daughter of Lord Sandys. Hester's second son,
John, had as godparents the wealthy sheep farmer, Sir John Spenser and
Erasmus Dryden, a gentleman of Northamptonshire, one of the godly and,
later, a forced loan resister, and Mistress Tyrrell of Thornton, a member
of a politically important Buckinghamshire gentry family. The child died at
two months, "on the New Year's day following presented his soule a sweete
sacrifice to his best father." Hester's memory and affection did not flag. Her
eleventh child, Jane Sibilla Temple, was born August 21, 1602 "betwixt 9
and 10 of the clock in the morning and died the 11th of September next

after." Her godfather was Sir Arthur Throckmorton, a family friend and relation, her godmothers were Jane Sibilla the Lady Grey, daughter-in-law of the second Earl of Bedford and widow of Arthur, Lord Grey, who had succeeded Bedford as Lord Lieutenant of Buckinghamshire, and Mistress Mary Frier of Water Eaton.[2] Prompted by maternal sentiment, family pride, and perhaps by astrology, the list provides important evidence of the kinship and friendship connections of the Temple family.[3]

This chapter explores local connections amongst some of the Buckinghamshire gentry and discusses both formal and informal ties between center and localities. Except for the period between 1616 and 1628 when the Duke of Buckingham was Lord Lieutenant, the Crown appears to have made little use of that important office to aggressively assert its control over the deputy lieutenants and to woo leading gentlemen of the county. Nevertheless, in the late 1620s the Crown demanded that its local governors vigorously impose and collect taxes and raise militia for wars with Spain and France. Several leading Buckinghamshire families enjoyed court office; others of local importance who enjoyed court connections into the 1620s became leaders of the resistance to these royal policies.

In this study of early seventeenth-century politics, it is crucial to see the vertical ties created by court patronage in the context of horizontal connections established by kinship, friendship and religion. Buckinghamshire provided both the king's standard bearer Sir Edmund Verney and John Hampden, the leading ship money resister. County politics revolved around godly gentry especially the Goodwins, the Cheyneys, the Borlases, the Fleetwoods and the Temples and a group with court positions including the Dormers, the Verneys, the Tyrrells, the Tyrringhams, the Pakingtons and the Dentons. Such distinctions, however, belie the ties of friendship and marriage between these networks. Moreover, Buckinghamshire displays the complex interaction between the political elite and the Crown that cannot be captured in separate categories of court and country. It poses two questions for the study of court patronage: the first, did the early Stuarts use the institutions and patronage at their disposal to draw support from all parts of the political elite? the second, were there limits to the efficacy of court patronage in the face of ideological differences over religion and politics? This chapter suggests tentative answers for some of the Buckinghamshire gentry, especially the Temples and those with whom they had connections.

The Temples were a Warwickshire family who had amassed a large estate from sheep raising.[4] In the 1570s Sir John Temple bought Stowe and settled in Buckinghamshire. Over the next decades, Sir John, his son and grandson became prominent in county life and politics. The manuscripts of three generations, Sir John and Susan Temple, Sir Thomas and Hester Sandys Temple, and Sir Peter Temple and his wife Christina Leveson Temple, provide important evidence about kinship, friendship, and patronage ties in Buckinghamshire. While the Temples provide evidence of conflict, child suing parent and husband beating wife, they also show emotional warmth between Sir Thomas and Sir Peter Temple, contradicting the notion of the decline of kinship and the lack of affect attributed to sixteenth and early seventeenth-century families.[5] Moreover, Hester and Christina took an active role in the family's economic, social and political life, handling the estate, transmitting political news and establishing the connections through which these country gentlemen called one another brother.

Hester Temple's naming of her children and their godparents celebrated family and friendship connections in the past, present, and in the future.[6] Godparents, it was hoped, would some day be of use. Even if the nuclear family was entrenched in gentry families in the early modern period, it is still clear that their extensive kinship ties were woven across the county landscape.[7] And such connections continued beyond the horizon of the county community. Their vast cousinage was both instrumental and affective.

Thus Temple godparents ranged from close family members, such as grandparents, aunts and uncles and in-laws, to other gentry friends and connections, whether London aldermen or the nobility. Seventeen of the godparents listed were kin, the rest apparently not. Seven were chosen from the maternal side; ten from the fraternal side. Six of the children were named after godparents; two, Peter and Martha, were perhaps named after saints; two were named after one of the godparents of the previous child. Two children were named John, the first having died. Of the nine godparents of the last three children only one appears to have been a relative.[8] At least twenty of the thirty-three lived in or had come from Buckinghamshire.[9]

How important were such kinship structures? Obviously close family ties had the greatest importance, but extended kinship was always a lever. Its use ranged from introductions to patronage, gifts, economic transactions and the law.[10] The Spensers of Althrop were Temple cousins and Sir John Spenser was godparent to one of the Temple children. In 1597, he noted a Peter Temple sitting on the jury in the case of *Spenser* v. *Willoughby*. At first Spenser thought he was his godson's brother but then discovered, to his evident disappointment, that he was a "mere kinsman." Still he asked Sir John Temple to influence Peter on Spenser's behalf.[11] Kin called each other "cousin" and "friend" and used each other to mutual advantage.

The importance of kinship networks to gentry like the Temples extended beyond godparents even to objects such as books. In 1634, in the next generation, Sir Thomas Temple sent his son Sir Peter a work by Anthony Stafforde entitled *The Guide of Honour*, purchased not so much for its subject matter but for the family's ties to the dedicatee, George, Lord Berkeley: "The like and first cause of kindred to the Carews that caused my son Longueville to buy this book here sent, giveth me some cause to send this treatise to you, being that myself am of blood as nearly linked to the Lord Barkeley by the Spencers as my said son in law was by the Carews."[12] Temple's review of the intricacies of genealogy that linked him to the old nobility suggests the importance of strong kinship ties alongside other connections based on friendship, financial dealings and religion. While this chapter describes such connections as horizontal ties to differentiate them from the vertical ties of patron–client relationships, kinship and patronage relationships were not polar but existed along a spectrum of social ties that were mutually advantageous.

Local studies have made significant contributions to the historiography of sixteenth and seventeenth-century England in the last twenty years transforming not only the landscape of English social history but political history as well. The relationship of the center to localities is essential to the study of early modern Europe in which governments often faced revolt by provinces.[13] If Peter Laslett has argued that most Englishmen never came in contact with anyone of high status, local historians such as Alan Everitt have argued that most gentlemen never came in contact with the court: they married within their counties, socialized within their counties and had little concern or information about events taking place at court or in parliament. John Morrill argued that antagonism to court policy came not from constitutional opposition but from localist resentment against external interference with local affairs.[14] However, recent work by Hassell Smith, Diarmaid MacCulloch, Anthony Fletcher, Ann Hughes, and Clive Holmes, among others, has reintegrated the national and the local, by showing that leading country gentry created important ties outside the county through marriage and political connections and, drawn as to a magnet, focused their attention on the court.[15] Hassell Smith and Diarmaid MacCulloch, especially, have demonstrated the integration and tension between center and localities. The example of Buckinghamshire is instructive.

I

In the late sixteenth century Buckinghamshire was a small, predominantly rural county located near London. Divided between the Vale in the north, which was predominantly pasture land and had been heavily enclosed, and the hilly Chilterns, the county supplied food to London. It had no large towns but Buckingham, Amersham and Aylesbury were the leading boroughs, and the population of the county was about 55,000. In a county society of perhaps 200 gentry families, thirty or forty dominated the bench and even fewer served as members of parliament.[16] Some Buckinghamshire justices were labelled as puritan by contemporaries, and many considered themselves among the "godly."

Thus in the 1580s, when Hester Sandys married into the Temple family, her father Sir Miles Sandys, a Crown official and younger brother to the Archbishop of York, helped Sir John Temple, her father-in-law, achieve a position of political power in Buckinghamshire. In 1584 a group of Buckinghamshire gentlemen, including John Borlase, John Croke, Miles Sandys and Griffith Hampden suggested to the Earl of Bedford that John Temple be made a justice of the peace, citing his education at Lincoln's Inn and "his soundness in true religion (which he hath ever professed even from childhood ... his ability to maintain the charge and countenance thereof without using corruption and likewise for his good inclination to justice and equity." They asked Bedford to recommend Temple to the Lord Chancellor for "the encouragement of such as be godly and sufficient men which possess the gospel in godly and good course."[17]

The Earl of Bedford was a long-time member of the Buckinghamshire bench and a well known patron of reformers in the English church. Those justices of the peace who recommended Temple identified themselves as among the godly. Analyzing wills to identify religious views must be done cautiously because it is often difficult to know whose language one is reading, that of the testator or the notary, yet the wills of Miles Sandys and Griffith Hampden show them to be Calvinists. Hampden, for instance, wrote a long preamble dwelling on the joys of heaven prepared for the elect, eschewing popish rites for his funeral and asking his friends to assemble on that occasion to hear a sermon "by my singular good friend in Christ, Mr Richard Woodcocke, or some other godly learned preacher."[18] Croke and Woodcocke witnessed Hampden's will.[19] John Borlase was labelled "earnest in religion" by his bishop.[20] Sir Francis Goodwin was one of five Buckinghamshire gentlemen to whom Peter Allibond, minister to the Cheyney family, dedicated his translation, *Comfort for an Afflicted Conscience* by the French Calvinist, Jean de l'Espine.[21] Like the Temples, these men and their families continued to be prominent in Buckinghamshire politics from the Elizabethan period to the Civil War.

The Temple correspondence in the 1580s depicts a gentry community vitally interested in marriage, education and finances, quarter sessions, musters and elections. John Temple had a wide acquaintance. Together with John Goodwin, he was attached to Arthur, Lord Grey, the Lord Lieutenant, and maintained links with the Earl of Bedford and Sir Francis Walsingham who were identified with a reforming protestantism. These connections were inclusive rather than exclusive. Temple was friendly too with Sir Robert Dormer who had Catholic leanings. The Temple manuscripts in the 1580s and 1590s also reflect county conflict including disputes between Sir John Goodwin and Thomas Piggott, and Sir John Fortescue and Arthur Lord Grey over property, musters and elections and between Temple and Verney over taxes. These conflicts often had to be resolved by seeking the intervention of a Privy Councillor with connections to local groupings. To this end Temple recorded in his memoranda the names of servants of leading government officials such as the Lord Chamberlain and the Lord Keeper.[22]

Amongst the Temple godparents were Greys and Wottons. Arthur, Lord Grey, and Edward, Lord Wotton, were the noblemen with whom Sir John Temple seems to have had closest association. Grey, the Lord Lieutenant, was a native of Buckinghamshire and had close ties to the Earl of Bedford.[23] Wotton was from Kent. Grey was a puritan, Wotton became a Catholic. This breadth of connection is characteristic of sixteenth-century patronage and continued under James I.

Wotton and Temple had financial dealings. Temple presented Wotton with good cheeses, placed his daughter Katherine in Wotton's household and Wotton used his court contacts to try to get tax relief for them both.[24] These close ties lasted for several decades. In his handwritten will of 1597, Sir John Temple left Wotton his best horse. He asked his heir and executor, Thomas Temple and all his children "to be ever thankful to him and to bear him and his a true loving and faithful heart for that I and my late good father deceased have all my life ... more love, true friendship and benefits at his good father's hands ... and his than ever we found elsewhere in our lives."[25] In 1613 Sir Thomas Temple wrote to Sir Arthur Throckmorton, whose daughter had married Temple's son, of the continuity and constancy of Lord Wotton's favor, calling it an inherent quality as heat to the fire and moisture to water.[26]

The horizons of these country gentlemen reached well beyond the limits of the county to the English court.[27] Richard Cust and Fritz Levy have recently examined the flow of news and information among the English country gentry especially in the seventeenth century.[28] Like English diplomats on the continent, country gentry in Buckinghamshire sought information about the court and foreign affairs. This was not pale gossip but vivid news to country gentlemen who wanted and needed connections to the court. Ralph Sheldon, writing to Sir John Temple in 1581 regarding a suit of his kinsman, reported that "The Master of the Rolls had died, Mr. Attorney most likely to succeed him, Mr. Secretary Wilson is either dead or not like to escape and so many goodly offices and places are like to grow void." Sheldon reported on European courts too, describing the King of Spain's pensions and gifts as "wonderful."[29]

Court politics were of great concern to county elites who followed closely the fortunes of court patrons and favorites. Sir Arthur Throckmorton described in February 1601 the execution and confession of the Earl of Essex.[30] Sir John Lenthall, one of Sir Peter Temple's most faithful correspondents from London, wrote: "in these times you no sooner receive a letter from hence, but you instantly expect to hear of some event of the world's expectation of our unfortunate great ones." In 1616

Lenthall sent Temple "a few verses made upon the unhappy Somerset," commenting:

> as one falleth so another riseth, according to nature's course, Somerset being down Villiers is now up, and hath received that dignity, as never any man of his place and rank had before, he is made Master of the Horse which no man ever had, under the degree of an Earl, but he shall (I believe) before you receive this letter, have a Viscountship or an Earldom made the supporter of this honor, it is not known which, but one of them he is sure of. These times can not want a Phoenix; fortune will have her favorite, and she hath now embarked Monsieur Villiers for the same. We shall have a parliament speedily, it is not known what wilbe done there, only a grant of subsidies.[31]

The compliments and the complements of kinship, friendship and patronage, then, served to link center and locality. Whenever engaged in local conflicts about taxation, musters and elections from the 1570s to the 1620s, many country gentlemen called on leading figures at court to intervene. In 1599, Sir Edward Wotton, who was to become Comptroller of the Household under James I, wrote to Fulke Greville at court to complain about taxes imposed on some of his lands. He invoked both family and friendship in his effort to have the courtier intervene in a local dispute.

> Sir, your brother, Mr Verney hath of late set a very great tax upon my lands in Dassett towards the relief of the poor of a foreign and remote parish. I find the course very hard for many reasons, which the bearer hereof my dear friend Mr Temple will lay open to you ... I could have wished greater discretion to have been observed, than to tax in this peremptory sort, a gentleman dwelling in another countie without making him privy thereunto ... My desire and suit unto you is (because I know you may do much with a brother and he with the other justices that have joined with him) that you will write earnestlie unto him to stay this strange and extraordinary course ... I will hold it for an infallible argument of your love unto me who have ever honored your virtues and will be ready to do you any service I can.[32]

Two days later, Greville wrote to Verney that

> Sir Edward Wotton, my dear and old friend, hath written me a very earnest letter and sent it by Mr Temple. The effect is first to complain of the hard tax laid upon his lands in Dasset, for relief of the poor in the parish of Brayles, the next part is his desire to be heard before you peremptorily conclude against him ... Good Sir both in respect that this demand of his is within that course of proceeding which one gentleman oweth to another. And beside for my sake be pleased thus far to moderate yourself and your fellows.[33]

The evocation of kinship in requests for patronage of course pervaded correspondence among "cousins," as did the use of good offices to soothe disputes between neighbors. Wotton continued to complain to Sir John Temple of the hard measure offered by the justices of Warwickshire, worrying "if the war hold we should hear more of these courses, wherefore I heartily pray for peace."[34] Wotton was to prove prophetic in his fears. When England went to war in the 1620s such issues arose again. What Fulke Greville had described, however, as "that course of proceeding which one gentleman oweth to another," a motto perhaps for early modern local government, was overwhelmed by war and taxation, in the form of billeting and martial law, the forced loan and ship money, and the imposition of Arminian policies amongst the godly Buckinghamshire gentry.

II

There were two sorts of vertical links between the center and localities: the formal orders of the Privy Council to their local agents, the justices of the peace and the deputy lieutenants to ensure order, control musters and monitor recusants; and the informal ties of patronage dispensed by the Crown to the same local elite by which they received favor and resolved their disputes. These tended to go along together, indeed had to go together, for the English system of government to work. Both James and Charles continued to dispense royal patronage to country gentlemen; what needs to be assessed is whether that patronage forestalled or channelled conflict.

There were two important figures in Buckinghamshire who linked center and localities, the Bishop of Lincoln and the Lord Lieutenant. Although Buckinghamshire had a certain notoriety as a puritan county, the Jacobean Bishops of Lincoln were not necessarily sympathetic. Thus William Barlow (1608–13) was attacked by puritans for his published narrative of the Hampton Court Conference which they felt brought them into disrepute. Richard Neile (1614–17) was an Arminian who came under attack by the House of Commons during the Addled Parliament of 1614 for questioning the power of the House. The office of Bishop of Lincoln assumed special importance during the tenure of John Williams; Williams, secretary to Lord Ellesmere, the Lord Chancellor and Lord Lieutenant of the county from 1607 to 1616, was made Lord Keeper in 1621 and a few months later became Bishop of Lincoln. With close ties to the Duke of Buckingham, who became Lord Lieutenant in 1616, Williams acted as a broker for Buckinghamshire gentry. However, Williams was removed from the Lord Keepership in 1625 after angering the Duke by his opposition to war with Spain. When he was replaced as Lord Keeper by Sir Thomas Coventry, Sir John Suckling wrote to the Duke that it was "a due disgrace to one who has been unthankful and unfaithful to his Grace, and may the like misfortune befall all such as tread in his [Williams's] hateful path, and presume to lift their heel against their maker."[35] Although he kept his bishopric, he himself received no further promotion. Moreover, as Arminianism became increasingly important in the English church, Williams found himself the subject of complaint by Sir John Lambe during visitations of the county in the 1630s.[36]

The lord lieutenancy began to emerge in the late sixteenth century as a central hinge between the Crown and the localities.[37] Although chosen for their prominence, social standing and estate, in Buckinghamshire the early Stuart appointees lacked local connections. Arthur, Lord Grey, appointed Lord Lieutenant by Queen Elizabeth in 1586, after his return from commanding the English army in Ireland, served until his death in 1593. No one was appointed Lord Lieutenant and no provision was made for deputy lieutenants until 1607 when Ellesmere was appointed with the right to choose his own.[38] Ellesmere did not have longstanding Buckinghamshire ties but he bought an estate at Harefield, Middlesex, in 1601. When he entertained Queen Elizabeth in 1602, several important Buckinghamshire gentlemen, Sir Francis Goodwin, Mr Tyrrell of Thornton, Mr Darrell, Mr Bowyer of Camerwell, and Sir Thomas Tasborough, brought presents to help him entertain the queen ranging from capons and swans to salmon, partridges, mutton and an ox. After his appointment as Lord Lieutenant, in 1608 Ellesmere named his son Sir John Egerton, Sir Henry Lee, Sir Robert Dormer, Sir Alexander Hampden, Sir Thomas Denton, Sir Anthony Tyrringham and Sir Edmund Ashfield as deputy lieutenants.[39] Ellesmere was also the executor of the will of Robert Dormer, Baron of Wing, the richest gentleman in the county.[40] After Ellesmere's death some Buckinghamshire gentry maintained ties to his son.[41]

In 1616 George Villiers, later Duke of Buckingham, was appointed Lord Lieutenant of the county upon Ellesmere's surrender of the office "of his own desire and voluntary gift" and received the Grey lands in Buckinghamshire. At the same time he served as Lord Lieutenant of three other counties.[42] Within a few months he recommended "my servant" Clement Cotterell as muster master and specifically asked the favor of Sir John Egerton who continued to serve as a deputy lieutenant, "upon whose love for me I most rely." After reciting Cotterell's long and honest service, Buckingham concluded: "I know it needless to use more words, when the least touch of my desire is sufficient with you for using your best means to affect it, and to bind me in all things."[43]

Egerton soon called in this favor. At his father's death in 1617, Egerton angled for the earldom recently bestowed upon Ellesmere, gave 50 pieces in gold to his agent to employ and applied to Buckingham, telling him "how much I ame your Lordships in the true honest affection of my harte." Buckingham asserted that he had done him the best service he could in the matter and would "testify the continuance and constancy of my love which dyeth not with the dead, but descendeth to you as right heyre to all that was due unto him." Such a benefit was also reinforced by £2,000 that Egerton gave to Lady Compton, Buckingham's mother, at the time he received his patent.[44]

Buckingham was also tapped for favor by Buckinghamshire gentlemen. Sir George Croke was appointed Judge of the Court of King's Bench through the duke with Bishop Williams serving as broker.[45] Sir Edmund Verney got the lieutenancy of Whaddon Chase from the Duke of Buckingham who was the Keeper. Sir Richard Graham wrote: "According to your desire I have acquainted my lord of his ingagement unto you. There have been many sutors for the said place to my lorde . . . he . . . grants you the leivetennancy with all his hart."[46] Sir Thomas Piggott got a company in Sir William Leger's regiment when St Leger appealed to the Duke.[47] Sir William Andrewes, Sir Thomas Temple's son-in-law, kept Secretary Conway and Sir John Suckling informed of slanders against Buckingham.[48] But Buckingham could not always assume that his favor would bind his deputies. Thus he criticized the deputy lieutenants for their treatment of another muster master he had recommended to them. Moreover, as Richard Cust points out, Buckingham's connections with the county from which he took his name were uneasy, a matter of no small importance when, in the 1620s, the Crown turned to the deputy lieutenants and the justices of the peace to raise taxes and an army.[49]

After the duke's assassination in 1628, Robert Dormer was appointed Lord Lieutenant. Dormer, grandson of the first Baron Dormer, inherited estates in Buckinghamshire as a child in 1616. Like his grandfather, Dormer served as Master Falconer to the king. Dormer was close to the royal family and court life. He maintained London lodgings, went on the Grand Tour after his marriage and established ties with the Elector Palatine and the king's sister, Princess Elizabeth. Dormer commissioned Inigo Jones to add new apartments to Ascott House, the Dormer residence in Buckinghamshire.[50] Named Lord Lieutenant of Buckinghamshire in his own right in 1641, Dormer died in battle for the king in 1643.[51]

Dormer's wardship had been granted to the Lord Chamberlain, Philip Herbert, Earl of Montgomery, who married Dormer to his daughter Anna Sophia.[52] Dormer was created Earl of Carnarvon in 1628; he was, however, only 18 years old in 1628 and his father-in-law and guardian Montgomery was named Lord Lieutenant during his minority.[53] Montgomery did not hesitate to name his own muster master: "It wilbe expected by our Lord Lieutenant (who is already at all times to do noble service [crossed out] favor to this Country) that you procure for Mr Edward Mole now mustermaster of this countrey the same entertainment and fee which Captain Vaughan the last mustermaster formerly had." He also wished certification from his deputies of those who had neglected the musters. Like Buckingham, Montgomery reprimanded the deputy lieutenants for their "neglect of that service heretofore and that the defaulters are to be sent up to the Council table to abide the order of the

Lords and in some cases to show their defaults supplied in his Majesty's own view."[54]

Although the Dormers were a recusant family, the Herberts educated Dormer at Oxford, where William Herbert, third Earl of Pembroke, and Philip Herbert, Earl of Montgomery and later fourth Earl of Pembroke, were both chancellors. They placed Dormer under the tutelage of the moderate Calvinist theologian John Prideaux who dedicated a Latin sermon to Dormer in the year of the youth's marriage. After the death of Buckingham, in the orbit of the powerful Herberts, Dormer began to cut a figure at court and received dedications of several works including Philip Massinger's *A New Way to Pay Old Debts*. Massinger asked to "shelter this comedy under the wings of your Lordship's favor" declaring "I was born a devoted servant to the thrice noble family of your incomparable Lady."[55]

Clearly, Dormer was being groomed for an important position both in court and country, a role to which William Foster referred in the dedication of *The Means to Keep Sin From Reigning in Our Mortall Body* in 1629. The minister described how he had delivered the sermon before the earl and countess "in a county auditory. Your occasions then carried you elsewhere ... it came from the Country to the City, meeting there with the press, it presumeth to press from the City to the Court, bearing your honour's name on the forehead." Foster lauded King Charles and Dormer's circle. Charles was "so virtuous and pious ... like the Emperor Theodosius the younger ... leaving his princely sports, is an assiduous frequenter of public prayer; and Constantine the great ... is a great and constant hearer of sermons." Dormer himself was surrounded with good precepts and examples: "brought up at the feet of Gamaliel in the University [a reference to Prideaux, Professor of Divinity at Oxford] you have those noble Lords, your uncle and father-in-law, near and bright shining lights" (the Earl of Pembroke, Lord Steward, and the Earl of Montgomery, Lord Chamberlain). Referring to the Bishop of Lincoln, Dr Williams, and others, he noted "You have the daily attendance of such as are able and ready to direct you in both. And you, right noble Lady (as inheritor of your deceased Lady mothers vertues) are ready to join in the practice of such actions as may bring eternal happiness to you both."[56]

Without discord over taxation and religion, it is possible that Dormer would have used the position of Lord Lieutenant to weld court and country. As a patron of the "godly" it is possible that Montgomery had some connections to local gentlemen. But there is little evidence of Montgomery's personal influence on the leading gentlemen of Buckinghamshire. As it turned out an underage Lord Lieutenant represented by an absentee Lord Chamberlain increased the importance of the local country gentlemen who dominated the deputy lieutenancies and the bench.

Between 1616 and 1633 seven or eight country gentlemen usually served as deputy lieutenants. The group shows strong continuity through the 1620s and into the 1630s. In this period fourteen men, drawn from only ten families, dominated these important positions. In the first year of his lieutenancy, Buckingham named as deputies Sir John Egerton, Sir William Clarke, Sir Thomas Tyrringham, Sir Alexander Hampden, Sir Francis Cheyney and Sir Thomas Denton. In 1618 he restructured the list, beginning with Sir Thomas Temple, Sir Francis Fortescue, Sir Thomas Clerke, Sir Thomas Tyrringham, Sir Francis Cheyney, Sir William Borlase and Sir Thomas Denton. Sir Francis Goodwin had been added by 1619 and Sir Francis Fortescue dropped. In 1624, Sir Edward Tyrrell was added,[57] and, in 1625, Sir Edmund Verney.[58] During Dormer's lord lieutenancy, his father-in-law Montgomery appointed the same deputy lieutenants or other members of their families.[59] Indeed, Goodwin continued as deputy lieutenant despite his being called before the Privy Council for his handling of the forced loan. Sir Peter Temple was named deputy lieutenant in 1633.

Of these ten families, some are already familiar. Others, notably the Verneys, held Household positions under James I and Charles I. The Verney family had first received royal patronage from Henry VII. Verneys had served as sheriffs in 1511, 1524, 1540 and 1582, but not thereafter. In all lists of the justices of the peace they ranked below Temple, Goodwin, Fleetwood, Piggott, Borlase. There was no Verney on the bench in 1604, 1608–11, or 1625. Part of this may be accounted for by the career of Francis Verney who served abroad in several military campaigns and to his step-brother Edmund's service at court in the Households of Prince Henry and Prince Charles. That Verney was made lieutenant of Whaddon Chase, Buckinghamshire, a prestigious appointment over which Lord Grey, Sir John Fortescue and the Piggotts had battled in the sixteenth century is a sign of his status at court.

In the early seventeenth century Sir Edmund Verney became a member of Prince Henry's Household and, after his death, Prince Charles's. He was knighted in January 1611 at Whitehall when he came of age and, the next year, at 22, married Margaret Denton. When in 1613 a Household was created for Prince Charles, Verney became one of the Gentlemen of the Privy Chamber. He accompanied the Prince and Buckingham on the trip to Spain to secure the Spanish Infanta and on his return was granted a pension of £400 a year for life; he was named Knight Marshall of the king's palace for life in 1626. Verney became one of the deputy lieutenants for Buckinghamshire along with his father-in-law Sir Thomas Denton and his "cosin" Sir Thomas Tyrringham.[60] Verney's brother-in-law, Dr William Denton, who lived in Covent Garden, became court physician to Charles I in 1636 and attended the king in the Scottish war in 1639.[61] Verney maintained close relationships both with the court and in the country. But though a justice of the peace and a deputy lieutenant, Verney was never knight of the shire. Other Buckinghamshire gentry too held positions in the king's Household. Sir Anthony Tyrringham and Sir Edward Tyrrell were Gentlemen of the Privy Chamber. Sir Timothy

Tyrrell was Keeper of the Buckhounds and on good terms with the Duke of Buckingham.[62] Lady Mary Borlase, wife of Sir William Borlase, attended the Princess Elizabeth and the Elector Palatine.[63]

Thomas Lord Coventry, the Lord Keeper, replaced Bishop Williams as broker for some Buckinghamshire gentlemen. Coventry secured the wardship of Sir John Pakington's grandson and heir who later married his daughter.[64] In the Easter term of 1629 Temple reminded his wife to approach the Earl of Northampton, Buckingham's step-father's brother, to aid him in a law suit and "especially to move my Lord Keeper in this and my greater occasions." In 1624 the Temples angled for a court marriage to a Buckingham relative through Sir Edward Tyrrell and in 1625 Sir Edward included Sir Peter Temple in the negotiations for his wife's jointure, promising in exchange his brother Timothy Tyrrell's favor. In 1625 Secretary Conway was urged to call Sir Francis Goodwin, Sir William Fleetwood, Mr Hampden and others to hear the issue of the debt due to the widow Lancaster that Fleetwood, Sir Robert Banastre, Hampden and others had awarded to her and which Goodwin and others who owed the money opposed. Tyrrell, Temple and Denton dealt with Conway on other county matters.[65] Sir Thomas Temple's son-in-law, Sir William Andrewes, and his son Sir Peter Temple had dealings with the Duke of Lennox.. In the 1630s Sir Thomas tried to get out of the commission of the peace and wrote further remembrances for Hester: "To deale as effectually as you can that he which put you in hope to get me out of the Commission of the Peace if you can not have a better meane, though he have some large gratuity."[66]

Let us take a more general look at the Buckinghamshire political elite. The gentry of Buckinghamshire numbered some fifty-eight families in 1566. By 1634 their numbers had increased to 142.[67] Those local gentlemen who exercised considerable political power in the county were fewer. Between 1585, when the bench numbered thirty-six local gentlemen and 1625, when they numbered forty-five, eleven families served continuously on the bench, many of them familiar: the Crokes, the Lees, the Goodwins, the Fleetwoods, the Pakingtons, the Dormers, the Hampdens, the Darrells, the Tyrringhams, the Borlases and the Bulstrodes. Between 1604 and 1640 the Knights of the Shire from Buckinghamshire were all drawn from these eleven families with three additions: Sir Christopher Piggott and Sir Thomas Denton, both longstanding members of the Buckinghamshire bench, and Sir Edward Coke.

Between 1504 and 1660 twenty-three families held the shrievalty more than once, most gentlemen who owned estates with annual incomes of £1,000 a year.[68] James I knighted a good number of Buckinghamshire gentlemen at the beginning of his reign when on his first progress he visited four leading gentlemen of Buckinghamshire, Sir John Fortescue, Sir Alexander Hampden, Sir John Pakington and Sir William Fleetwood.[69] He continued to knight Buckinghamshire gentry, usually prior to their acting as sheriff.

The introduction of the baronetcy in 1611 provided another mark of court favor (as well as payment). Several prominent gentlemen of Buckinghamshire were willing to buy these titles. Although historians have suggested that the quality of those buying baronetcies declined, that the first creations were dispensed to prominent gentlemen but later creations were wholesaled to upstarts, this is incorrect. Something on the order of 80 per cent of the baronets made between 1611 and 1640 were country gentlemen and their offspring, although often younger sons.[70] If we take a look at the Buckinghamshire baronets a similar pattern emerges but one with interesting political connotations. The first two created baronets in Buckinghamshire were Sir Henry Lee and Sir Thomas Temple, representatives of two of the most prominent families in the county. In 1615, Sir Robert Dormer became a baronet just before buying his barony, thereby moving to the top of the social hierarchy of Buckinghamshire. Anthony Chester, esquire, grandson and heir of a Lord Mayor of London, succeeded to important estates in Chicheley and served as sheriff of Buckinghamshire in 1602/3; John Pakington, son of a Lord Lieutenant of Worcester and grandson of an alderman of London was made a baronet at 20, during the lifetime of his father. All of these families had served on the Buckinghamshire bench, although the Pakingtons had never served as sheriff.

Under Charles I five more gentlemen were created baronet before 1640: Simon Bennett in 1627, John Lawrence in 1628, John Fortescue in 1636, Edward Longueville, a son-in-law of Sir Thomas Temple, in 1638 and Edward Tyrrell in 1637, another in-law of Sir Thomas Temple.[71] All these baronets, then, were well-to-do country gentlemen, but some were not the most politically significant men in the county. Indeed, there were soee significant absences.

None of Buckinghamshire's knights of the shire bought or was given baronetcies or titles. The knights of the shire for Buckinghamshire between 1604 and 1640 were Sir Francis and Arthur Goodwin, Sir William Fleetwood, Christopher Piggott, Sir Anthony Tyrringham, Sir William Borlase, Sir Thomas Denton, Sir Henry Bulstrode, Sir Edward Coke and John Hampden. With the exception of Sir Edward Coke, all were members of families that had served on the Buckinghamshire bench since the 1570s. None of the elections for knight of the shire was contested after 1604. The well known contest in 1604 of Goodwin–Fortescue was resolved by removing both men from county to borough seats. Sir John Fortescue, Queen Elizabeth's Chancellor of the Exchequer, died in 1607 but his son Sir Francis Fortescue remained on the Buckinghamshire bench.

Sir Francis Goodwin was listed amongst the most important gentlemen in the county in the late 1590s.[72] He was repeatedly granted significant local posts by the Crown. He had close ties to the Earl of Essex and his followers. Robert Sidney, Viscount Lisle, had been a close associate of Essex and became Chamberlain of Queen Anne's Household. Sidney and Queen Anne's Council, headed by Sir Robert Cecil, Earl of Salisbury, named Goodwin Surveyor of the queen's lands and profits in Buckinghamshire.[73] Goodwin himself maintained connections with Sir Robert Cecil too and in 1606 asked to be made keeper of Whaddon Chase.[74]

Goodwin maintained connections with his brother-in-law, Thomas, Lord Grey, convicted in 1603 in the Main and Bye plots, and financial connections with the Earl and Countess of Bedford through his mother-in-law, Jane Sibilla, wife consecutively of Edward, Lord Russell, and Arthur, Lord Grey. Goodwin stood surety for a large debt for the third Earl of Bedford and Lucy Harrington, Countess of Bedford.[75] The Earl of Bedford had been High Steward of Buckingham. Goodwin had enough court connections to get a seat at Buckingham through the direct and strong intervention of the Privy Council in 1606.[76] In 1622–3 Goodwin was appointed one of the commissioners to oversee the forest of Barnewood.[77] The death of the powerful Countess of Bedford in 1627 may have removed a strong court contact of Goodwin's but Goodwin continued in contact with Dudley Carleton, Viscount Dorchester, the Secretary of State, who was his cousin. Moreover, the Goodwin and Hampden families were chosen to represent the county in parliament even though they received little or no royal patronage from the Crown under Charles I. Both Goodwin and Hampden were removed from the bench in the 1630s.

Parliamentary elections in Buckinghamshire in the early Stuart period demonstrate the importance of local gentry and the relative lack of interference either in county or borough elections by court and aristocratic patrons. Derek Hirst and Mark Kishlansky have contested the nature of elections in the early Stuart period: did they demonstrate increasing political consciousness and conflict or were selections generally harmonious and consensual?[78] Buckinghamshire provides grist for both.

In the sixteenth and early seventeenth centuries, in addition to its two county seats, Buckinghamshire had three boroughs that sent representatives to parliament, Aylesbury, Buckingham and Chipping Wycombe. The county seats were contested before the poll by country gentlemen testing their political strength, calling in their social and political chits. Between the 1570s and 1604, the Goodwin, Hampden and Grey circle who had attachments to the Earl of Bedford sparred with their neighbors, especially Sir John Fortescue, to secure both county and borough seats. Property disputes, and discontent over musters and taxation spilled over into these elections, and Sir John Fortescue needed to call in Sir Francis Walsingham to tell Arthur, Lord Grey, to cease his opposition to Fortescue in the election of 1588. These local disputes revealed themselves in the contest for the first seat for the county in 1604 in the well-known conflict between Sir Francis Goodwin and Sir John Fortescue. King James and the Privy Council responded to the issue once it was raised by Sir William Fleetwood at the beginning of the 1604 sessions; a second election was held and both men found other seats. Indeed the Council itself asked the borough of Buckingham to choose Goodwin in 1606 after the death of Sir Edward Tyrrell who had held both court and county office. Three decades of local conflicts, which I have described at length elsewhere, subsided in the early Stuart period.[79] John Chamberlain wrote in 1614 "I have not heard of so much contestation for places in parlement, as falles out this time, yet Sir Francis Goodwin and Sir William Burlas have carried yt quietly in Buckinghamshire."[80] And Goodwin and his allies continued to control the county seats until 1640.

Borough elections often provided more abundant pickings for royal and aristocratic patronage in early seventeenth-century England. Thus Aylesbury, of which the Pakingtons were lords of the manor, often returned candidates with court connections. Sir Robert Carr, a Gentleman of the Bedchamber and the former favorite Somerset's cousin, replaced Sir John Pakington and sat for the borough in the parliament of 1625.[81]

In the parliament of 1621 Sir William Fleetwood moved to restore representation to the medieval boroughs of Amersham, Great Marlow and Wendover. The success of that drive in 1624 provided Buckinghamshire gentlemen with six more seats with the result that Buckinghamshire was said to be represented by more burgesses than counties three times the size.[82] The Hampdens dominated Wendover and John Hampden may even have paid for the petition for its restoration. The seat thereafter was served by himself and his extended family, including his cousin, Sir Sampson Darrell, Surveyor of Marine Victuals, his son-in-law Sir Walter Pye and his kin, the Crokes and the Hawtreys.[83] When the Earl of Bedford put Amersham up for sale in 1624 he noted its right to return members of parliament.[84] William Tothill who owned the adjoining manor of Shardeloes bought Amersham and his son-in-law, Sir William Drake, and his heirs represented the borough for the next 200 years. Marlow contained several different manors; Great Marlow belonged to William, Lord Paget, who secured a seat for his son-in-law Sir William Hicks in 1626. Harleyford was owned by Sir Miles Hobart who sat for the borough in 1628. The Borlase family owned Little Marlow and Widmere and obtained seats for themselves and their connections.[85]

Between 1603 and 1640, then, the county and borough seats were occupied primarily by leading Buckinghamshire gentry and local townspeople. As part of his study of aristocratic influence in early Stuart elections, John Gruenfelder analyzed the Buckinghamshire county and borough elections; he suggests that of 108 members of parliament selected between 1604 and 1640, only ten *may* have been influenced by aristocratic patronage, *none* by royal influence. (Although, as we have seen, Goodwin secured the Buckingham seat through the Privy Council's intervention.) Gruenfelder found only two aristocratic patrons in Buckinghamshire in the period: William, Lord Paget, and the Duke of Buckingham who got the Buckingham seat for Richard Oliver in three parliaments of the 1620s; and, perhaps, his follower Sir John Smith.[86] Surprisingly, there appears to be no evidence that Robert Dormer, the Earl of Carnarvon, his father-in-law, the fourth Earl of Pembroke, or the Bishop of Lincoln, John Williams, influenced these elections. The greater Buckinghamshire gentry were able both to expand their number of representatives and control their county's electoral patronage.

At the same time, a crucial change in the court's relationship to local governors came in the 1620s and 1630s. There is evidence that the Duke of Buckingham and Charles I moved purposefully against their political opponents in 1626.[87] In 1637, only four of the eleven families who had served on the Buckinghamshire bench since 1585 were still there. The families had not died out. While political divisions between the Crown and Buckinghamshire gentry kept them off the bench, it did not keep them from political power.

Patronage flowed in two directions: the Crown gave patronage to local governors in order to secure their on-going loyalty and support. The language of deference, so highly developed in the Jacobean period, masked a structure of interdependence necessary to govern. One result was that the Crown was left with a mistaken impression of its supporters. In 1642 when the Royalist Commissions of Array were issued there were nineteen names from Buckinghamshire headed by Robert Dormer and including Peter Temple. Yet fewer than 50 per cent were later shown to be delinquents by parliament, i.e. royalists, and the list did not include families like the Chesters and Darrells who did support the king. A. M. Johnson argues that the king did not know who were his allies in Buckinghamshire. The Commission of Array assumed that the leaders of the county would support the king. Johnson points out that the parliamentary call to arms was more successful; it contained the names of most of the dominant county families, and of their list only four families were later sequestered for delinquency.[88] In March 1642 parliament appointed Lord Paget Lord Lieutenant for Buckinghamshire and, as his deputies, John Hampden, Arthur Goodwin, Richard Grenville and Bulstrode Whitelocke. In April 1642 when parliament asked for contributions for the Irish war, Buckinghamshire offered £6,000. The grand jury of Buckinghamshire responded to Charles I's invitation to address him with their grievances:

None at this time leave so great an impression on the hearts of us your subjects as your Majesty's absence from your parliament, and the fear of civil war, occasioned through the raising of an Army under the title of a guard, a sight terrible to your people, and not conducive to that amicable accommodation so much desired.[89]

When in May the House of Commons passed the Militia Ordinance Buckinghamshire responded. Nevertheless, Sir William Drake probably spoke for most of the county community when he promised to maintain two horses and provide £200 "for the king and parliament conjunctively".[90]

III

Why did the Crown mistake its supporters in Buckinghamshire? Horizontal ties created by kinship, community and religion proved stronger than the vertical ties which bound the elite to the Crown. After 1618, war in Europe presented difficult problems of war and finance which strained relations between center and localities. Moreover, court office granted the Verneys, Tyrrells and Tyrringhams and court connections of the Pakingtons could not overcome resistance to royal policy, especially when the most influential men in the county led that resistance. Grappling with the twin problems of war and finance, Charles and his councillors were emphatic in their desire to bring local government to heel. Previous administrations had tried it.[91] Charles's regime had greater success. In doing so they provoked widespread opposition in which Buckinghamshire gentry took a leading role.

As England prepared for war against Spain and France, the correspondence of these country gentlemen was filled with news of taxes, coat and conduct money, voluntary gifts and forced loans, and musters and billeting of troops. Although the Crown continued to try to sort out local disputes, it insisted that its policies on musters and taxation were of "public consequence."[92] Both taxes and troops divided the political elite and estranged some of its leaders from the court.

In 1625 after parliament voted two subsidies to the Crown and the justices of the peace had collected £3,052 from Buckinghamshire, the Privy Council asked for a privy seal loan "intended onely to the service of the publique". The justices disagreed about assessments. Sir William Borlase, for example, thought John Hampden and his mother too harshly assessed.[93] The Duke of Buckingham wrote that the king took it ill that they had not answered his letter of September and had prepared no book with names and addresses of those fit to give as they had been directed.[94] The deputy lieutenants explained to the Duke of Buckingham that they had used their best endeavors "being somewhat hindered by reason of necessary attendance upon some other of his Majesty's services in this country, as also by your graces' absence out of the kingdom." Moreover, it was not only overwork that burdened them. They were

> importuned at our meetings for subsidies and other payments, that they are unpaid for the coat and conduct money which they have twice laid out this year, amounting unto £437 besides which they have been charged with multiplicity of payments in the levying and maintaining of soldiers, for whose charges the country hath not received full satisfaction from the Council of War, and that in some place for these two years past, in some more, they have received no money from his majesties officers for their composition-wheat and for wood.[95]

This letter had been edited by Goodwin who noted "I approve this letter with the alterations exceedingly well." Although the deputy lieutenants suggested others as collectors, the Privy Council chose Sir Thomas Denton, Sir Thomas Temple's son-in-law, Sir Edmund Verney's brother-in-law and Sir Thomas Tyrringham's "cosin," collector of the privy seal loan. Despite bouts of gout Denton tried diligently to raise the loan urging Temple "not to faile to let me have both the letter and the privy seales certificate subscribed and sent to me tomorrow betimes for I am engaged to send it to Sir Francis Goodwin tomorrow least weebe sent for by a messenger."[96]

In the summer of 1626, amidst preparations for wars against both Spain and France, the Privy Council instructed the Buckinghamshire justices to collect a voluntary gift. Although parliament had voted tentatively for war in 1624, in the first parliamentary sessions of Charles I's reign in 1625 and 1626, they were less willing to finance it. Moreover, they had voted tonnage and poundage for only one year rather than, as was usual, for the lifetime of the new king. In 1626 the Crown decided to ask for a "voluntary offering" from those most able to pay and provided specific instructions to the justices on how to raise the money.

As Lord Lieutenant of the county, in 1620 and 1622 Buckingham had asked for a voluntary contribution for the Palatinate suggesting that leading knights and gentlemen contribute the amount they were rated in the subsidy book. He claimed that some had already given double and treble that sum. Moreover, in 1620 Buckingham advised his deputies "not to call any publique assembley of the countery for that purpose but to deale privately with your friends and such as are well affected to contribute, what every man shall freely and voluntarily dispose himself to give."[97] It is not surprising that the duke and the Privy Council were unhappy with the response of the Buckinghamshire bench. "First the majority of the justices did not assemble for the reading of his Majesty's letters and do not interest themselves in the case ... a great neglect and contempt of his Majesty's commandments." Secondly, where the king had required speed, the justices had delayed the answer. Thirdly, although the Council had directed them to send privately "for such persons as are of ability to give," the Buckinghamshire justices "have required the country to meet again in several places to give a joint answer." Finally they should have been the first to contribute. "We do expect that you should by your own good example first incite others to assist his Majesty in these his great occasions for the security of the kingdom which course hath wrought some good effect in other places."[98]

In extenuation, Temple, Denton and Tyrrell (all relations) blamed Sir Francis Goodwin and Sir William Borlase and some of those who had attended the public meetings. Their explanation is worthy of note because it demonstrates the mutual support of some justices of the peace and the subsidymen of the county.

After receiving the Council's letters, Temple had summoned forty or so members of the bench but only twelve came to the meeting. Of these several were members of families with which we have become familiar: Temple himself, Goodwin, Denton, Sir Edward Tyrrell and Sir Fleetwood Dormer. (Robert Dormer, Baron Wing, was under 20 and at school.) The justices claimed that because they had not yet received the Council's instructions to deal privately with the well-to-do, they decided to call a public meeting, although as we have seen such private meetings had been ordered in 1620. Nevertheless they directed the whole shire to meet in three places in the space of two days.

> to avoid expectation of taking precedents one of another in cause of refusal or suspense. And by cause Sir Francis Goodwin being a deputy lieutenant, knight of the parliament, and held to be a potent man to sway a great part of the shire in the upland of Chiltern where he usually inhabited, it was thought fittest by the other justices ... that he should be present at Beaconsfield for the three hundreds of the Chiltern ... for the more same satisfaction of the county.

When they received the Council's instructions to hold such meetings privately the deputy lieutenants thought it too late to rescind their previous instructions, but decided in the mean time "to prepare as many of the people as they could against the general day." The justices then explained why the meetings had not gone as the Council had desired.

> The remotest parts of the shire meeting at Stony Stratford, Goodwin as a deputy lieutenant or as a justice meets there also and ... making a short speech to the people expressing the tenor of the king's letters, but not reading them, did withal tell the people that the justices did not expect an answer from them at that time because it was harvest, and a busy time. And therefore thought good to give them ... a month and four days longer. To which many people (though privately) answered, they had rather given their answers then, and so not be troubled any more.

Soon after, on August 22, the three hundreds of Chiltern met at Beaconsfield where Sir Francis Goodwin "as the most popular man" was expected but did not appear. As a result Denton declared the king's pleasure, invited his audience to consider the matter and had the king's letters read aloud.

> After which followed a silence for a good space until Mr Pen late sheriff of the shire spake openly. That they came with intent to give unto his Majesty, and that he knew the most part of his hundred were of that mind. Then one Mr Shepwash of Hambledon replied that this was a business of great weight and required a longer time of consideration, which he desired to be granted but Sir Thomas Denton and some others utterly opposed the same as needless. Then Sir William Borlase asked the people what they said to Mr Shepwash his motion to which ... none replied ... Then consideration being had what time was fittest to be given, Mr. Shepwash pressed strongly for 2 October.

Denton and some other justices urged the same September 23 given by Goodwin to the other part of the shire so that the Chilterns "not be farther led by example of the Vale either to second procrastination or refusal, if any such should be," But Mr Shepwash with the consent of Sir William Borlase and some others insisted on October 2. In the mean time the Constable of every parish was to "return in writing what every man will give and who will not give," although the Lords had "directed the justices to mediate particularly with the people the same by this means is put upon the petty constables, who for the most part are poor men from whose mediations there cannot be expected the like good success as if the justices had really undertaken the same."

In the aftermath of the dissolution of the parliament of 1626 in which they sat, both Goodwin and Borlase supported resistance to the King's raising money outside parliament. Their fellow justices dissociated themselves from these tactics and urged the king to

> redouble his command upon the justices to deal particularly with every man in their several divisions according to the last directions of his Council's letters and to return as well the names of the refractory as free givers ... there is no justice of so little in the place where he dwelleth, or with his neighbors in the towns about him, but if he will, he may do his Majesty a real and good service herein. And by that means to disengage and prevent the public assemblies intended where the one half of able persons will not appear as experience hath shewed and yet the residue be in hazard to be drawn by example of a few negative voices to join with them in a public denial, which as by a more private and particular course his Majesty will be better assured of supply, the ill effected discovered, and their factious intentions either wholly prevented or in a great measure suppressed.[99]

The Privy Council acted swiftly. On August 29, 1626, a week after the meeting at Beaconsfield, the Privy Council issued three close warrants directed to Goodwin, Borlase and Robert Shepwash "to make their immediate repair hither in the company of the messenger." Two days later Borlase and Shepwash appeared and were ordered to attend the Board until discharged. Goodwin appeared a few days later. While the Privy Council wrote to the justices of the peace of Derbyshire to congratulate them on their "great care and diligence" regarding the free gift, the Council called the proceedings of the Buckinghamshire justices "illpleasing" and called for "some better demonstration of your affections to the business committed to your care."[100]

Was the response of the Buckinghamshire justices like Goodwin and Borlase due to mere localism? Or did Goodwin and Borlase, both knights of the shire, believe that the Crown's calling together subsidy men for the benevolence was an attempt to get round parliamentary control of taxation? Goodwin explicitly pointed out the fact that subsidy men were being called upon to give.[101] Others who refused to contribute included Sir Fleetwood Dormer, Richard Piggott and Edward Grenville, leading justices of the peace.[102] Because the free gift was not a success, the Crown resorted to the forced loan and encouraged country gentlemen to participate in order to maintain their connections with the court. Bishop Laud wrote to his friend Sir John Scudamore "I would not but you should attend the service of his Majesty in the loan and nourish that good opinion he hath of you."[103] On December 31 Buckingham called the deputy lieutenants to convene at Whitehall on January 3, 1627 for consultations, the lieutenants being those that "best understand the state of that countrie." The Crown made strategic concessions to Buckinghamshire, including repaying the coat and conduct money out of the loans, but Sir Thomas Lee feared that further payments of the loan would fail "except some be made examples, or further cause be taken against them." In May 1627 Denton wrote to Sir Peter Temple to ask him and his father to pay the forced loan as they had previously promised the Duke of Buckingham, saying "we are now called upon to give in the names of such as have payd and such as doe refuse."[104]

Coinciding with the efforts to raise monies outside parliament, billeting of troops raised for the continental wars with France and Spain became an issue between the Crown and local governors. Early in James's reign the Privy Council ordered a viewing of arms, noting that in this "happy time of peace" there was still a need to look after arms.[105] From 1610 to 1620 the Crown increased its efforts at oversight. With the declaration of war in 1621, the issue became a crucial one and 250 men were levied from Buckinghamshire, to restore the Elector and Princess Elizabeth to their inheritance in the Palatine.

The same gentlemen who tried to explain their behavior in regard to the free gift, Temple, Denton and Tyrrell, provided the Council with a list of men pressed.[106] When in January of 1628 the Duke of Buckingham informed the deputy lieutenants that half a regiment was to be placed in Buckinghamshire, there was widespread resistance.[107]

Sir Thomas Temple prepared a list of queries; he included pointed questions about the authority of the deputy lieutenants to press soldiers especially for foreign service, what authority to ask for coat and conduct and impressment money from the county, and "whether new precedents will be dangerous." He also asked "whether the execution of the whole business is to be put to him to whom the letters are first delivered, or hath the place of a baronet in forreign counties ... that I may judge how I am dealt withall."[108]

Sir William Fleetwood was a leading Buckinghamshire justice and member of parliament who had raised the issue of the Goodwin–Fortescue election in the parliament of 1604 and taken the lead in the parliaments of 1621 and 1624 in restoring three Buckingham boroughs whose medieval parliamentary representation had been allowed to lapse. As a result Buckinghamshire was represented by fourteen MPs. Later, Fleetwood had a disagreement over coat and conduct money with Goodwin and other deputy lieutenants.[109] On February 8, 1628, before the meeting of parliament in which the Petition of Right addressed the issues of arbitrary taxation, arbitrary imprisonment, billeting of troops and military law, Fleetwood signified to the Privy Council the importance of these issues. He described a controversy over billeting that he believed threatened "the laws of the land."

On February 5 Richard Biscoe of Chesham, a town three miles away where Captain Read's company was billeted, came to Fleetwood's home in Missenden. He reported that on February 2 Lieutenant Sandelands had come to Biscoe's house accompanied with one of the town constables, to tell him that one of his soldiers was to be billeted in his house.

> Biscoe answered that he did refuse to billet him, whereupon the Lieutenant told him he would break his head, nay he would take his goodes that were in his house and sell them and billet him, nay he would break open his chestes for goods that were therein and by God's wounds and other othes he would cut off his head, which stroke such a terror into him, that for the security of his life he prayed me to grant my warrant for the ... said Lieutenant ... to be bound for the keeping of the peace toward him. I being the next Justice of the Peace to that place, wherein knewing that I was bound by my oath to satisfy his desire, I ministered the oath requisite in that case to Biscoe, and gave him my precept for the bringing of the said lieutenant before me.

Lieutenant Sandelands was brought in by the constables who verified the accusation. The lieutenant was not able to deny it, "it also being proved to me before his face by two woemen upon oath that when the lieutenant was come out of Biscoe's house ... the one of the woemen heard the said lieutenant sweare by God he would fire the house, and the other heard

him swere he would fire it." Fleetwood ordered the lieutenant to the gaol
at Aylesbury. Lieutenant Sandelands asked Fleetwood to punish Biscoe too

> for refusing to billet the kinge's soldier, whereto I answered according to my
> poor skill, that I had never red that word in any of our lawes, and knew not
> what it meant, but if the meaning were that a man should receive the king's
> soldier into his house, against his will and find him meat and drink without
> present payment therefore, I did not know that any of our lawes had ordeined
> it to be an offence for any man to refuse to yield thereto, neither had I any
> authority as a Justice of Peace to punish it who was sworn to do right to all
> men according to the lawes of the land.

After the lieutenant had been sent off with the constables as a prisoner
to Aylesbury, Captain John Read inquired what Fleetwood had done. Read
argued "that his Majesty's soldiers were not subject to the authority of
Justices of Peace but to their superior officers intimating that if he had been
at Chesham when my precept came for his lieutenant it should not have been
obeyed." Captain Read then went to the inn where the lieutenant was being
held and ordered those accompanying the constables to go home. Soldiers
attached to Captain Foxe's company surrounded the house "and swore they
would die before the lieutenant should be carried away to the gaole ... and
so the constables not daring to do otherwise retorned with the captain and the
lieutenant to Chesham." When one of the constables informed the captain that
more of his soldiers were to be brought before Fleetwood upon warrant "the
Captain answered that no Justice of Peace had to do with any of his soldiers for
any default." Fleetwood concluded with a challenge to the Privy Council:

> My Lords if this be so I humbly desire to be discharged of my office of a Justice
> of Peace, seeing the complaint of threats and menaces to break open mens houses
> who shall refuse to billet them and other abuses do daily come to my ears. And I
> know nether that oath can be dispensed with which I took when I became Justice
> of the Peace that I should forebear to do my best to punish offenders complained
> of. If otherwise Justices of Peace shall have authority to punish soldiers as well as
> others, I humbly pray your honours directions what shall be done either touching
> this captain and lieutenant who have thus demeaned themselves or touching any
> other who shall misbehave themselves.[110]

Fleetwood made clear that opposition to the billeting of troops and martial
law went beyond localism to issues of common law and parliamentary power.
Bishop Laud framed the issue in those terms from his proposed reply to the
Remonstrance presented to King Charles on June 17, 1628. "But we doubt
not but our loving people will understand that necessity was then our law.
That course might have been prevented if in the parliament before supplies
had been given in the ordinary way."[111]

Conflicts between Crown and local government extended beyond taxation and militia to religion. Buckinghamshire had a reputation as a puritan county. The vagueness of such a description can be seen in one context where it was used by the chief of the king's carttakers in 1605 to complain about some puritan justices in Buckinghamshire not in the context of religion but of purveyance. We have seen that a cluster of Buckinghamshire justices of the peace certainly identified themselves with the godly in the Elizabethan period. They were identified by their bishops as such and supported reformers in the church. Their wills show that Goodwin and Fleetwood continued to identify with Calvinism into the next reign and even into the 1630s. In his will Fleetwood asked that he be buried without pomp and urged his family not to wear black at his funeral, "seeing that death is a passage unto eternal life the which I do believe that I shall enjoy together with the elect children of God through the passion and death of my lord and savior Jesus Christ."[112]

Goodwin had close connections with Lord Saye and Sele, one of the leading puritan patrons who was also related to the Temples. In the 1625 parliament Goodwin was named to a committee to petition the king for a fast to begin his first parliament; on the day of the fast, the sermons went on for nine hours. He was also named to committees in 1625 to consider an act of punishing of diverse abuses committed on the Sabbath and to repress recusants.[113] In his will Goodwin stated his desire that his granddaughter Jane marry the son of Lord Saye who was his executor.[114] In the end she married another puritan peer, Philip, Lord Wharton. Arthur Goodwin and John Hampden had both been educated at Magdalene College, Oxford, an important center of puritanism in Oxford.[115] J. T. Cliffe identifies Goodwin, Hampden, and Drake as puritan gentry, but does not include Fleetwood, Borlase, Croke or Temple.[116] Nevertheless many of these most important justices too had puritan leanings or ties. Sir William Borlase and his wife Mary, for instance, received dedications of sermons from Calvinist preachers.[117]

In 1634 Archbishop Laud authorized visitation of Buckinghamshire despite the disapproval of John Williams, Bishop of Lincoln. The visitations were undertaken by Sir John Lambe, Dean of Arches, who held visitations in 1635 and 1636 and Robert Neile, half-brother to Richard Neile, Archbishop of York, who as archdeacon visited five parishes in 1637. Amongst those churches in which orders were given to place the communion table at the east end were Newport, Stony Stratford, St Giles and Olney. Residents of the county were described to Laud as "that sort of people that run from their own parishes after affected preachers ... in Buckinghamshire and Bedfordshire ... they find great abetters of this their disorder."[118] The county gentry, "men of some little fortunes are persuaded they may say or do anything against the government or governors (whether ecclesiastic or laic) without control." One clergyman was "so overawed by the justices and lay gentry, that he is wonderful timorous."[119] Although Sir Edmund Verney and John Hampden both apologized for slackness during the visitations in the 1630s, Dr John Andrews complained that the injunctions of Nathaniel Brent, the Vicar-General, were kept "even by the dreadful grandees of our parish for a day or two and they return to their old ways." Efforts to prosecute those who kept musters in the churchyards caused "some of the deputy lieutenants to storm like so many termagants and if they could but learn who it was that did give notice of any muster unto the Court he should want no mischief ... If a person or vicar complain, the whole county cries out upon him, and watches to do him displeasure."[120] Brent struck a more conciliatory note when John Hampden, who had been presented for holding a muster in the churchyard of Beaconsfield and for "going sometimes from his church," assured him of his obedience to the laws of the church hereafter. Brent asked that no presentment be made against him in that visitation without his special direction.[121]

Resistance to the visitations of the 1630s was matched by resistance to ship money in the late 1630s in which leading roles were again played by Buckinghamshire gentlemen, John Hampden and Sir Peter Temple, and Sir George Croke. Ship money, a medieval levy by which coastal towns were assessed for the building of ships, was revived by the Crown in 1634 as the Crown cast around for means to fit out and fund the royal navy. In the absence of parliament the Privy Council made sure that the local governors bent to the task of collecting the levy. Indeed collections were quite large in the early years. Of the £4,500 levied on Buckinghamshire only £188 1*s* 11*d* remained outstanding. This did not compare, perhaps, to the mere £20 deficit left in Cheshire in 1637/8 which did not require as many cajoling letters but it is remarkable nevertheless. This sum was procured only after the Council, circumventing the usual mode of raising taxes, made the sheriff himself, not the justices or the deputy lieutenants, responsible for assessing and collecting ship money.

Sir Peter Temple was ship money sheriff in 1635 and the letters he received from the Privy Council indicate the pressures he faced simultaneously from a central government seeking to enforce its orders and his neighbors used to a more personal and easy-going system. Sir Peter Temple wrote to his mother in 1636 to say that he had to appear before the king himself "to give accompt to him what I have done in the service and as he likes my proceedings, I am to continue in the messenger's hand, or be released, or worse. My life is nothing but toil, and hath been for many years."[122]

Opposition to ship money in Buckinghamshire took different forms. Sir Fleetwood Dormer questioned the assessment, arguing that it was contrary to the levy in 1630 and urged Temple to look to the old levies on the poor as the appropriate rate. An informant claimed that the Earl of Carnarvon's man was assessor for a hundred in which his lord held land, "and so may spare all his master's part and his tenants."[123] The inhabitants of Chesham petitioned Sir Peter Temple that, although he had directed their constables to deliver a list of men of ability, they had instead "imposed great part of the money upon poor tradesmen whereby except your worship relieve them therein they are like to be much burdened."[124] Sir John Denton complained about his assessment for a farm in Buckingham hundred, "more than ever was paid in any payment either to king or church." He asked to be "rated according to equity and former payments (which they to ease themselves) have not done. And my money shall be as ready as any ones."[125] This focus on rates of assessment was not, however, the only form of protest in Buckinghamshire.

Buckingham not only provided the most important ship money refuser, John Hampden, but also the most important ship money judge, Sir George Croke, who denied the legality of ship money. Croke was one of the few judges not impeached by the Long Parliament. When Sir Alexander Denton served as sheriff he did not refuse to collect ship money but wished to wait until the outcome of the Hampden case. Of Denton and other sheriffs it was said that "they privately listen very much to their kindred and friends near to them who to speak very modestly are known to be hollow hearted to the king."[126] In fact Denton was to become a royalist and the Denton family along with the Verneys had been rewarded by the Crown. But the pull of family, friends, and community was strong in Buckinghamshire. It has been suggested that Temple, who presented John Hampden at the top of a list of ship money refusers did so as part of a plan to bring a test case by Providence Island Company members, led conspicuously by his uncle Lord Saye.[127]

By 1637 Buckinghamshire led all counties in ship money arrears, £2,985. In 1639 the county was assessed for £4,500 and paid not a penny. Of the £2,600 in coat and conduct money assessed in May 1640, the county paid only £8 10s. On the eve of the Long Parliament in 1640 the Privy Council released those who had been committed for refusing to pay coat and conduct money. Sir Henry Vane wrote to Windebank, "my Lords of the council have discharged the Buckinghamshire men and the rest that were committed for coat and conduct money . . . that [when] his Majesty comes to the parliament all necessary disputes may be avoided and time husbanded."[128]

In 1640 the county selected its representatives to the Long Parliament; John Hampden and Arthur Goodwin sat for the county; William Drake and William Cheyney, a close relative of the Barringtons of Essex, for Amersham (when Cheyney died he was replaced by Francis Drake); Sir John Pakington, who lived in Worcestershire, and Sir Ralph Verney for Aylesbury; Denton and Temple for Buckingham; Hampden and Robert Croke for Wendover; Edmund Verney and Thomas Lane for High Wycombe. The election in Great Marlow reflected antagonism to those with court connections. The four candidates were Gilbert Hippesley, a Somerset native with court connections nominated by Lord Paget who dominated much of the borough; his step-son, the 21-year-old John Borlase, son of Sir William Borlase and grandson of Sir Francis Popham; Peregrine Hoby, a Berkshireman known locally and identified with parliament; and Bulstrode Whitelocke. Although Sir William Borlase had challenged the taxation of the 1620s his son had recently made a court marriage to Anne, daughter of Chief Justice Bankes, formerly the Attorney-General. Borlase and Hippesley were accused of supplying money and liquor at the election while Whitelocke and Hoby "stood for the liberty of the commons in this election."[129] Arguments over who was eligible to vote and the pricking of Hoby as sheriff were ultimately resolved when Borlase was selected for Corfe Castle, Dorset, and Hoby and Whitelocke were returned for Great Marlow. Hoby served as sheriff before taking part in the Long Parliament.

Most of Buckinghamshire's representatives or their families had sat before: Hampden and Goodwin in 1621, Verney and Pakington in 1624, Drake, Denton and Lane in 1625. All but Thomas Fountain, who replaced Hampden in Wendover, were offspring of the most important county families.[130] Although Verney was to be the king's standard bearer and Denton a royalist, Verney was anti-Laudian and Denton had been less than supportive of ship money in the 1630s.

Of the Buckinghamshire MPs, Hampden, Goodwin and Whitelocke were the most prominent in the House. The Protestation of May 3, 1641, binding the members not to permit the dissolution of parliament without their consent, was taken by almost all the Buckinghamshire MPs: Hampden, Whitelocke, the two Verneys, Fountain, Temple, Goodwin and Sir William Drake. They were joined by Sir John Borlase and Edmund Waller who sat for constituencies outside Buckinghamshire. Sir Alexander Denton took the Protestation on May 8 and Francis Drake on May 12. Only Sir John Pakington and Robert Croke did not take it.[131]

Although the committee community appeared united in 1640, gradually, as elsewhere, this broke down into royalist, parliamentarian and neutral groups. Amongst those who became royalists were Sir Alexander Denton, Sir Edmund Verney, Sir Thomas Tyrringham, Darrell, Croke, Pakington, and Grenville. Between 1642 and 1660, A. M. Johnson argues, the leadership in the county fell to those below the leading gentry families, in part because Goodwin, Hampden, Temple and others were outside the county as members of parliament or officers in the parliamentary army. Within the county there was strong support for the county committee. By the end of 1646 eight of the fourteen Buckinghamshire MPs elected to the Long Parliament no longer sat. Pakington and Edmund Verney had immediately declared for the king as later had Croke and Denton. Ralph Verney refused to take the Covenant and was disabled. Hampden, Goodwin and Fountain died in 1643.[132]

Buckinghamshire's complex relationship to the Crown can be symbolized in different ways. Although Sir Edmund Verney sacrificed himself as standard bearer to the king in 1642, his loyalty to the king did not prevent his unhappiness about the breakdown into civil war in which he and his son found themselves on different sides. Sir Bevil Grenville, who had supported Sir John Eliot in the parliaments of the late 1620s, stood for the king:

> My journey it is fixed. I cannot contain myself within my doors, when the King of England's standard waves in the field upon so just occasion. The cause being such as must make all those that die in it little inferior to martyrs and for mine own I desire to acquire an honest name or an honorable grave. I never loved my life or ease so much as to shun such an occasion which if I should I were unworthy of the profession I have held or to succeed those ancestors of mine who have so many of them in several ages sacrificed their lives for their country.[133]

Another family conflict displays the faltering of kinship and court patronage in the face of parliamentary confrontation in the Long Parliament. In a letter to his wife, Robert Dormer, Earl of Carnarvon, accused her father, the Earl of Pembroke, of misusing the proxy Dormer gave him. Although Pembroke had always said that proxies should be voted the way the lord devising it wished, he used Dormer's proxy against the king. As a result Dormer feared that Pembroke might thereby "hinder much my credit with the king, and lessen my power both to serve him and myself." Dormer had tried to mediate between Pembroke and the king "since that distance that happened between them, and I believe and am confident that if ever there had been a revolution or change in things, it would have been both in my power and will to have served him very considerably towards the king, if I may believe the king's professions to me." But because of the proxy "the king himself takes it very unkindly from me till I cleared myself to him from whom I came yesterday, I mean at my giving my proxy to your father, whom the king does believe to be violent against him in every thing."[134]

IV

In the 1590s Sir Francis Goodwin brought a suit for libel against another justice of the peace, John Darrell, for accusing him of being "the only supporter of all the atheists, anabaptists, Brownists and such like seditious persons ... as also a continual maintainer of all mutinies, factions and quarrels that do daily grow amongst the simple people."[135] There was strong support outside the political elite for John Hampden as there had been for the "popular" Sir Francis Goodwin.

After the king attempted to arrest five members on the floor of the House of Commons (one of them Hampden), he announced that thousands of men were coming from Buckinghamshire to petition against the king's action. In their petition, a large number of freeholders spoke in the name of the county to attack

> a malignant faction of Popish Lords, Bishops and others, and now of late to take from us all that little hope was left of a future reformation, the very being of the Parliament shaken, and by the mischievous practices of most wicked counsellors the privileges thereof broken in an unexampled manner and the members thereof unassured of their lives in whose safety the safety of us and our posterity is involved.[136]

In Buckingham royalist reports claimed that in 1642 Lord Brooke attacked the home of a royalist: "And now the Lord Brooke and his company, being masters of the house, the first thing on which they express their rage, is the King's picture, which they pierce through with their swords in divers places." In 1643 when Prince Rupert and his troops arrived in Buckingham, a royalist newspaper reported that people "confessed how much they had been formerly seduced by the powerful sorceries of Hampden, Goodwin, and the rest of that combination, desired to be restored to his Majesty's favour."[137]

For some, these sorceries went beyond politics to radical religion. In 1648 and 1649 pamphlets appeared entitled *A Light Shining in Buckinghamshire* and *Another Light Shining in Buckinghamshire*, containing Leveller and Digger ideas arguing against enclosure and upholding the rights of the commons. In 1650, another tract portrayed the effort to raise money for the Diggers' work on St George's Hill in Surrey. Among the places supporters passed through were Newport Pagnall, Winslow and Stony Stratford. In fact, Joan Thirsk argues that Leveller ideas influenced the division of this land near Bletchley and Stony Stratford.[138] To the horizontal connections of kinship, friendship, and religion must surely be added communal ties not only amongst the political elite but the community as a whole who combined to oppose Caroline religious and financial policies.

The work of local historians such as Peter Clark, Anthony Fletcher, John Morrill, Ann Hughes and William Hunt over the last two decades confirms the decay of the patronage ties between center and locality in the 1620s and 1630s. In sixteenth-century Buckinghamshire there had been privy councillors and noblemen like Sir Francis Walsingham and the Earl of Bedford, to whom country gentlemen like the Goodwins, Hampdens and Temples could turn. Richard Cust has argued that while the Privy Council was divided on the issue of the forced loan, from 1626 to 1628 the King himself directed a policy focused on forcing his subjects not only to open their pocketbooks but prove their loyalty if they wanted another parliament called.[139] Charles himself monitored appointments to the bench and shrievalty. The ties forged by kinship, friendship and patronage were not in conflict. But by neglecting to use the lord lieutenancy effectively and to bind leading members of the country community to the court with royal favor, Charles I cut himself adrift from those who had to implement his policy.

But could court patronage overcome active resistance from the political elite to royal policy on taxation, arbitrary imprisonment and billeting of troops? In 1628 Sir Francis Nethersole wrote to Elizabeth of Bohemia that the Duke of Buckingham found that he could subdue parliament neither by fear nor favor.[140] One of the strongest supporters of Caroline policy, the Earl of Dorset, said "there was no fear of insurrection in this kingdom as it contained no fortresses, neither could foreign powers foment revolution from lack of large armies."[141] Dorset's analysis suggested a fatal lack of understanding of the informal ties that knit center and localities. These went beyond physical force. Deference to authority and acceptance of governmental legitimacy flowed from court favor and, crucially, convergence of interest and belief between ruler and political elite.

The binding up of wounds took place in Buckinghamshire as elsewhere in the late 1650s where the leading country gentry came back together to reclaim political power. The Temples, the Dentons and the Verneys returned to a dominant position with the Restoration, vying for positions in the Convention parliament. Hospitality, long honored in the breach, gave way to treating. Political patronage linking court and country now took place not so much through positions in the royal Household, such as Sir Edmund Verney had held, but through party positions in parliament. The Temple family was represented not by a godly justice of the peace or ship money sheriff but the trimmer Sir Richard Temple.[142]

This chapter began with the celebration of family by Hester Temple in her naming of her children, their birth dates and godparents. It concludes with the confirmation of the Buckinghamshire gentry community, the 1685 commission by the Earl of Bridgewater, Lord Lieutenant of Buckinghamshire, naming his deputy lieutenants. Of the twenty-one more than half came from families that had served on the early seventeenth-century bench, including Charles, Viscount Cheyney, William Cheyney, Sir Richard Temple, Sir Anthony Chester, Sir William Bowyer, Sir Ralph Verney, Sir Henry Andrewes, Sir William Tyrringham, William Pen, James Tyrrell, Alexander Denton, and William Fleetwood.[143] The county community had, in the aftermath of civil war, reasserted its communal ties and its political connections. To be successful, the Crown had to nest royal patronage within its web. Naming had symbolic and political meaning that extended family unity even to the body politic.

Chapter 5

Corruption and early modern administration: the case of the navy

In 1609 King James travelled to Woolwich accompanied by Prince Henry and the Lord Admiral, the Earl of Nottingham. There on the Thames, James inspected the first new ship built during his reign, a ship which he named the *Prince Royal*.[1] Ten years later, in November 1619, the king, accompanied by Prince Charles and the Lord Admiral, the Duke of Buckingham, travelled to Deptford to see two new ships, "the first that were undertaken by the Commissioners of the Navy." He christened the greater the *Constant Reformation*.[2]

Ritual and symbol existed side by side with efficiency in constructing and using the royal navy in the early Stuart period. These ceremonial launchings made notably different statements about early Stuart administration. Both were completed while royal commissions investigated corrupt practices in naval administration. The first signified the factional triumph of the leading naval officers over the 1608 commission of inquiry; the second, the triumph of the reform commission of 1618 over the naval officers. In the first case Prince Henry had been an important ally of the naval officers and, along with Lord Admiral Nottingham, helped to undermine the year-long investigation of the naval commission.[3] In the second case, Buckingham was a stalwart supporter of the reform commission led by Lionel Cranfield and Sir John Coke.[4] The first ship, while beautifully decorated by Robert Peake and other artists, proved unseaworthy and had to be rebuilt; the latter served in the fleets of the 1620s against Spain and continued in service into the 1650s.

In both cases, administrative change depended on personal connections at court.[5] Patronage helped to create the conditions for corrupt practice; it was also the major instrument of reform.[6] With the speech act of christening, King James signified his support for Buckingham and reform.

In the sixteenth and seventeenth centuries the English navy saw increasing success at sea matched by additional funding and administrative support at home. The early Stuart navy provides a good case study of the incentives to corrupt practices in early modern administration because of the increasing importance of government contracting, expansion of offices, growth in expenditure, diversion of resources from the Crown to its officials and suppliers, and the changing social configuration of naval officeholding. While high-ranking naval officers had often been named from the nobility, lower-ranking officials were not usually gentry. The early Stuart effort to make naval careers befit a gentleman, what might be called the "gentrification" of officeholding, increased officers' retinue and allowances. Efforts to meet demands for realistic salaries, to rationalize funding for the navy and to support England's new strategic role led directly to the imposition of ship money. England was governed by 5–10,000 officials, significantly fewer per capita than France.[7] Nevertheless, corrupt practices in royal administration repeatedly caused political outcry expressed in Crown inquiries and parliamentary debate from 1604 to 1640. Both focused on waste and diversion of supplies from the king, and provisioning and victualling practices whose economic burden fell on the country and the gentry. This chapter examines the incentives to corruption located both in the structure of the early modern state and the specific practices of early Stuart officials, the focus of attacks on corrupt practices and their political impact.

The navy was the largest department of government next to the royal Households above and below stairs. While the character of officeholding showed great continuity from the twelfth century on as great departments of state went out of court, early modern historians agree that between 1530 and 1790 Europe transformed the way in which it waged war with important consequences for administration. John Brewer has recently described the results in *The Sinews of Power*: larger armies and navies, troops more professionally organized, trained and disciplined, financed by increased national taxation and supported by larger state bureaucracies.[8] Changes in technology, strategy and diplomacy shaped military bureaucratic states in France and in England. The success of the English fleet against the Spanish Armada, whether due, as contemporaries thought, to the "Protestant Wind" and the daring of English seamen, or as Geoffrey Parker argues, to more effective gun carriages than the Armada ships that went to the bottom with much of their gunpowder unspent, dramatically changed British military strategy.[9] Instead of ships designed to transport troops to engage in land warfare on the continent, the early Stuart monarchs and their shipwrights like the Pett family recognized the importance of large gunships loaded with heavier guns on a larger number of decks to defend the British Isles, to assert control over shipping and fishing in defiance of the growing power of the Dutch, and to dominate the seas. British doctrine was given specific form in the greatest ship built during the period, the splendid three-decker christened by Charles I *The Sovereign of the Seas* and designed as part of the ship money fleets.[10]

While providing a context spanning several centuries within which to place early Stuart naval administration, this historiographical description of the march to the military state necessarily overlooks the halting policies and flawed practices of the period from 1603 to 1640. The history of the early Stuart navy was as much about the power of sinecures as the sinews of power. The Crown faced great difficulty in redesigning ships to meet newly articulated functions and financing such undertakings. Early Stuart attempts to expand the navy by building more warships rather than relying on merchant marine increased corrupt practices in peacetime. Yet only eight new ships were added to the fleet between 1603 and 1633 for a total of fifty, three fewer than Henry VIII's fleet of 1547.[11] Further difficulties in victualling and supply were revealed in the English continental expeditions of the 1620s and remained chronic problems of early modern government. Charles I's efforts to fund this new naval role in the peaceful 1630s, while initially successful, met increasing recalcitrance. Conrad Russell has pointed out that assemblies, whether in England, Spain or France were reluctant to fund increased expenditures for war at the same time that their monarchs saw national defense as their principal necessity, one which overrode the privileges of these consultative bodies.[12] According to Gerald Aylmer, Gustavus Adolphus and Charles XII of Sweden were able to impose heavy taxes to support their wars because of "the monarchy's prestige and popularity." The early Stuart experience was just the opposite.

To document corruption in the Jacobean navy requires more than evidence of increasing venality. It should also be shown that contemporaries envisioned bureaucratic norms other than those in use and tried to implement them. Contemporary investigations demonstrated that public service and private interest overlapped both in prescription and practice. Thus, by his oath, the Controller of the Navy swore to execute his "office directly to his Majesty's best advantage, and no way particular to your own profit by his Majesty's loss." The oath enjoined him to "proceed to the performance of your duty seriously, justly and uncorruptedly to your best knowledge."[13] On its face, the oath did not limit private profit so long as it did not lead to the king's loss. In 1637 Algernon Percy, Earl of Northumberland, Lord Admiral of the ship money fleet, privately voiced a similar view of his own role. He complained:

to ride in this place at anchor a whole summer together without hope of action, to see daily disorders in the fleet and not to have the means to remedy them, and to be in an employment where a man can neither do service to the state, gain honour to himself nor do curtesies for his friends, is a condition that I think nobody will be ambitious of.[14]

The goals of service, honor and "courtesies" for friends coalesced in contemporary officeholding. At the same time, a more stringent view of the public interest already existed and was increasingly invoked.

On behalf of the naval commission of 1608, led by Henry Howard, Earl of Northampton, Sir Robert Cotton drew up "The True Discipline of the Navy and the Duty of its Officers." Based on Elizabethan models, it prescribed an ideal of bureaucratic behavior that put up a wall between public and private interest:

they worked without encroachments, winking at no man's misdemeanors ... but amending it upon complaint, drawing no unnecessary charge upon your Majesty, employing your ministers, materials and shipping freely only in your service, taking of your own provisions without waste, without gratuities, themselves no purveyors or merchants ... These are all your true and able servants and live so on your salary. They wear not others livery, and are neither by power nor new and needless offices base of those place, whereto they come by merit and not purchase.[15]

As Cotton was well aware, this ideal bore little resemblance to practice either in the navy or other areas of early modern administration.

The intertwining of private and public or royal interest led frequently both to the charge and practice of corruption, especially as venality increased in the early seventeenth century. The structure of the navy, like much of early modern administration, was shaped by its methods of staffing, payment, and procurement as Gerald Aylmer has so ably demonstrated.[16] Appointment to office came through a combination of patronage, family connections, and purchase as well as the movement of the personal servants of officials into public service as deputies. Fees, allowances, traditional perquisites, sinecures and pluralities, not salaries, supported the officeholder.

Furthermore, the Crown's procurement policies helped to shape corrupt practices in the navy. Unlike the judicial system where bribes were given to speed up the process or jump the queue, in the navy bribes were given to gain lucrative contracts, to obtain office or to divert supplies. Procurement and the letting of contracts was shaped by the personal interests of officials who often had close relationships with suppliers or often *were* the contractor. Phineas Pett, the early Stuart shipbuilder, for example, was both government official and government supplier. Efforts to continue or to promote competition in the provision of ordnance foundered on entrenched monopoly.[17]

Overcoming a climate of corruption required more than reining in greedy naval officials. Conscious cost cutting and efficiency sat uneasily next to the mentality of bounty characteristic of the court. Reform revealed the conflict at the heart of early Stuart government. Sir Francis Bacon complained to Buckingham of the reformers' cutbacks, "The number allowed by the commissioners had in my judgement a little of the merchant."[18] When in 1619 the navy captains complained about cuts in the manning of ships, they claimed that honor and specialization aboard ship required those numbers. Nevertheless, the articulation of an ideal of royal service insulated from private profit allowed room for investigation and reform even within the structure of early modern bureaucracy.

"Constant reformation" is an appropriate if unexpected label for the intensive efforts of James and Charles and their officials to rationalize English bureaucracy. While corruption was endemic to early modern administration, Gerald Aylmer quite rightly points out that within that structure, the scope and scale of corrupt practices varied. Joel Hurstfield demonstrated that in the Court of Wards Edwardian laxity was followed by Marian reform, and Aylmer documents the decline of corruption during the Protectorate.[19] There was no necessary correlation in the state mobilized for war and increase in corrupt practices. While warfare helped shape early modern bureaucracy, it was, in fact, a time of peace, roughly 1604 to 1618, that saw the most luxuriant growth of corrupt practices in the early Stuart period. Administrative difficulties which began in the 1590s when the country engaged in a land war in Europe expanded when the country was at peace in the first decade of the seventeenth century. While inadequacies in the navy were revealed by the expeditions to Cadiz and Rhé in 1625–8, the war did not cause them.

The only successful way to overcome the culture of corruption in the early Stuart navy was to win support for reform from the Lord Admiral: Charles Howard, Earl of Nottingham, who served until 1618; the Duke of Buckingham who replaced Nottingham; and Algernon Percy, Earl of Northumberland, named to the post in 1636 after a period of eight years when the office was in commission.[20]

The 1608 naval commission proved successful in locating and analyzing fundamental problems in naval administration. The 1618 commission went further by replacing the Navy Board and running the navy itself until the late 1620s. From 1618 to 1628 the navy was governed by a commission which, under the leadership of Buckingham, successfully reduced corruption during its first five years but faced increasing problems when England went to war in 1625. As a result the commission was replaced by the Navy Board after the death of the Duke.

Attempts to build ships, to provision the navy and to pay adequate salaries to naval officials foundered on the shoals of the Crown's financial exigencies and lack of parliamentary subsidies after 1629. The imposition of ship money began in 1634 as a way of financing the navy systematically after the difficulties of funding the war fleets of the late 1620s. Ship money was as much an attempt to finance the navy without corruption as an implementation of new naval strategy or an illegal tax.

Samuel Pepys, a member of the Navy Board during the Restoration, collected documents for a history of the British navy dating back to the medieval period but focused on the sixteenth and seventeenth centuries. By 1660 England had become one of the two greatest naval powers in Europe. Yet as if in a mirror, Pepys recognized his own administrative problems in those of the early part of the century. He was particularly impressed with the recommendations of the 1618 commission, "they being excellently writ and much to the purpose."[21]

I

The navy expanded in numbers of officials, the size of its budget and its shipbuilding activities after the accession of James I to the English throne.[22] In a time of peace, the navy spent more than it had during the protracted war with Spain. Annual costs of wages, victuals, cordage at home and in sea service had swollen to £53,004. The commission of 1618 estimated that costs could be cut back to £30,000; ordinary wages and victuals could be cut from £19,594 to £8,092 and cordage to as little as a third, from £9,032 to £2,790.[23] Wages paid for little or no work, poor provisions such as the bad cordage for which £18,000 was paid to the Muscovy Company in 1609 alone, exorbitant prices for canvas, line, oil, tar and rosin, light scales and heavy books (both of which worked to the merchant's advantage), recording more than supplied: venality marked naval administration.

> The chief and inward causes of all disorders [were]... the multitude of officers and poverty of wages, and that the chief officers commit all the trust and business to their inferiors and clerks, whereof some have part of their maintenance from the merchants that deliver in the provision that they are trusted to receive. And these men are governed by the chief officers' verbal directions...neither due survey is taken of ought that cometh in nor orderly warrant given for most that goeth out, nor any particular account made nor now possible to be made of any one main work or service that is done.[24]

Venal practices in the Jacobean navy went beyond statutory strictures. The configuration of corrupt incentives in the period had changed first of all, because naval organization allowed, and under the proper circumstances, actually promoted a *lack* of oversight by the head of the department. Secondly, expansion of government contracting was undertaken with obvious conflict of interest. Thirdly, Jacobean naval officials used their patronage and power to create and sell new offices, some of them unnecessary. Finally, in the early years of James I's reign, a culture of corruption was created within the department by which the higher-level officials allowed and even fostered the diversion of supplies, kickbacks and sharing of "dead pays," that is, bogus sailors and ghost ships, by lower-level officials in order to continue their own diversion of profits from government suppliers.

Up to 1546 English naval administration had consisted solely of the Clerk of the Ships who served under the Lord Admiral. In that year Henry VIII established the Navy Board, a recognition of the expansion of the navy in the 1540s.[25] The offices established at that time were Lieutenant of the Admiralty, Treasurer of Marine Causes, Master of Naval Ordnance, Controller of the Navy, Surveyor of the Navy, Clerk of the Ships, and Clerk of the Storehouse. These officials had deputies who increasingly exercised official duties as the country became involved in naval war. Under Mary, in 1557, supervision of naval administration was put in the hands of the Lord Treasurer "with the advice of the Lord Admiral."[26]

In 1558 Lord Burghley crafted ordinances that defined and regulated the duties, administrative records and oversight of the offices especially "that every of our said officers shall see into his fellow's offices."[27] This bureaucratization of the Navy Board was, at the same time, closely combined with personal influence. Burghley placed the navy completely under his own political control; he supervised naval administration, leaving the Lord Admiral to focus on strategy, to represent the navy on the Privy Council and to guard his own perquisites. In addition, Burghley left unfilled the position of Lieutenant of the Admiralty after 1564. The result was to make the Treasurer of the Navy the chief naval administrator. After John Hawkins became Treasurer in 1578, succeeding his father-in-law Benjamin Gonson with Burghley's approval, he clashed with Burghley. Deterioration in naval administration during the war with Spain occurred only after Hawkins departed for active duty in 1588. His deputy, Roger Langford, was left in charge off and on until Hawkins's death in 1595. Langford, who began his career as a clerk in the audit office in 1584, became Navy Treasurer in 1599.[28]

The Elizabethan navy's triumph over the Spanish Armada, accomplished by a fleet made up of a mixture of royal vessels, privateering and merchant ships, marked an important turning point in England's emphasis on sea power. The war with Spain in the Netherlands in the 1590s put the Elizabethan navy on a wartime footing for the first time since Henry VIII's fleets of the 1540s. Costs increased with the dearth and inflation that plagued England in the 1590s. Prices of wheat, malt, beer, casks, beef, stockfish, lings, butter and cheese between 1584 and 1594 showed a sharp increase; by 1597 the price of wheat, malt and salt had doubled.[29] Corrupt practices began to increase in the late Elizabethan and early Stuart period because of the expansion of the navy, its manning and provisioning, during the war with Spain.

James I undertook an extensive building and rebuilding program. The claim that the king neglected the "senior service" is at odds with the money expended on shipbuilding in the early part of the reign and the repeated investigations of naval administrative abuses.[30] As a result of increased expenditure, the Treasurer and the Surveyor had the opportunity to grant more contracts, to make connections with merchants and ship builders, and to serve as suppliers to a larger navy themselves. The Treasurer of the Navy, who received "poundage," three pence for every pound sterling spent on the navy, had no supervision. Lord Admiral Nottingham was willing to focus on his patronage rights and financial perquisites as Lord Admiral, to represent the navy but not to supervise naval administration. Thomas Sackville, Lord Dorset, Lord Treasurer from 1603 to 1608, Robert Cecil, Earl of Salisbury, Lord Treasurer from 1608 to 1612, and Thomas Howard, Earl of Suffolk, Lord Treasurer from 1614 to 1619, did not exercise the sort of oversight that Burghley had. Furthermore, Fulke Greville and John Coke were dismissed at the beginning of the new reign and, on Nottingham's recommendation, the king appointed Sir Robert Mansell and Sir John Trevor as Treasurer and Surveyor of the Navy, courtiers who viewed their offices as market opportunities.[31] That vision was abetted by the actual workings of the Navy Board which insulated officials from inquiry into the corrupt activities of their fellow officers and made possible the conspiracy of these officers to keep any of their fellows from exercising oversight.[32] During the 1608 commission Henry Howard, Earl of Northampton, commented on Sir Henry Palmer's statement that he did not oversee the other offices "lamentable, since his examination and censure might have stayed Trevor's cozening."[33] The Treasury was put into commission from 1612 to 1614. Efforts by Northampton, the leading commissioner, to renew investigation of the navy in 1613 were fruitless.

II
Conflict of interest

The venal practices that early modern naval bureaucracy fostered were conflict of interest, creation and sale of office, overmanning and private use of royal stores. In addition, dead pays, travel allowances or "riding charges" by which officers got double pay, and the use of royal ships for merchant voyages had precedents in the Edwardian and early Marian navy.[34] They were the focus of official concern from the 1580s to the 1630s, from Burghley to Buckingham to Northumberland. Throughout the early Stuart period, efforts were made to use Elizabethan procedures as the bench-mark for reform.

Although it has been suggested that Elizabethan attacks on corrupt practices were mostly personal,[35] Burghley examined closely the structural problems in early modern bureaucracy, especially the problem of conflict of interest, the intermingling of public duty and private gain.

The allocation of contracts for shipbuilding and provisioning the navy provided one major area in which corrupt incentives flourished. Sometime after 1585 Cecil composed "A Memorial of Sundry Public Necessary Things to be Observed in the Marine Causes," in it he included a section entitled "Remembrances of Abuse Past."[36] On this Proustian note he focused on conflict of interest, which occurred when a naval official was also a supplier of goods to the navy, and on the illegal diversion of supplies in the storehouses.[37] These were Burghley's principles for the performance of office in the navy:

> That no officer of the Admiralty be builder of ship nor partner with any others in building of ships. That no officer be a merchant of ... provisions for the Queen's ships. That no officer alone make the prices of the provisions; that no payments be made for any provisions or other charges by the Treasurer without the warrant of the rest of the officers; that all provisions do come first unto her Majesty's storehouse; and that none be issued without warrant from all the officers ... That none that make ships for the Queen should keep timber yards for merchant ships for by color thereof they take up timber.[38]

The problem of conflict of interest, of the naval officer as merchant, supplier, or shipbuilder, continued into the seventeenth century and beyond. Burghley's injunctions, while still in place in the Jacobean navy, were not followed. Sir Robert Mansell, Treasurer of the Navy, was only supposed to make payment for wages or provisions with the agreement of the other three officers. Bills were to provide the merchants' name and the quantity and quality of the provisions. The principal officers were to call the master shipwrights, the purveyors of timber and others for advice and counsel "which they very seldom or never do." Instead they acted on matters in which they "have no judgement at all."[39]

Burghley and Cotton could see the structural problems of early modern administration and the policies necessary to overcome them. Financial resources were, however, lacking. Although Henry VIII had increased salaries, they remained at the levels he set into the next century. Indeed the payment of officers from the highest to the lowest was a major problem. Officials supplemented their fees with pensions, traditional perquisites, travel allowances and gifts. In the 1630s Gerald Aylmer estimates the Comptroller received £258 plus gratuities; the Surveyor, £228 plus gratuities; and the Clerk of the Navy £172 plus gratuities. Because the most important official in the navy, the Treasurer, also received poundage, it was in his financial interest to maintain and even to increase expenses.[40] By the 1630s the Treasurer of the Navy received a fee of £221, with poundage ranging from £200 to £653 in the early 1630s and amounting to perhaps £1,000 by the late 1630s. His total income from office amounted to £1,600 by 1640.[41]

Naval officials increased their income by acting as merchants, middlemen, shipbuilders or suppliers of naval ships and stores which, beyond remunerating the officers, ensured supplies of provisions and monies to the navy. Corrupt practices in provisioning, contracting, extortion and diversion of supplies increased during the Mansell and Trevor regime. Mansell as the Treasurer of the Navy, arranged with Trevor, the Surveyor, to supply the king with all necessary stores. He was later accused of supplying goods of poor quality at high prices.[42] The two combined with merchants to provide supplies of masts, tar, pitch, canvas, to the king at inflated prices, taking as much as 25 per cent or more of the sale price.[43] Merchants had traditionally paid kickbacks to officials for prompt payment of their bills; under the Mansell-Trevor regime, however, they continued to pay kickbacks although their bills remained unpaid.[44] Writing on behalf of the 1608 commission, Cotton urged that supplies be bought "at the cheapest hand, not by factors at great prices to the officers benefit, not wasted idly to bring the purveyors more profit but kept and spent to the properest uses."[45]

The allocating of a victualling contract to one or two suppliers, known as surveyors of navy victualling, went back to the 1540s. Corrupt practices in victualling, including the provision of poor food, the diversion of supplies and kickbacks from suppliers, were a continuing problem into the nineteenth century.[46] While not a principal officer, the victualler served as a middleman between the navy and its contractors.[47] The commission of 1618, drawing on the 1608 inquiries into victualling, was able to eliminate some dead pays and more closely supervise the pursers. It forced contractors found guilty of supplying bad provisions to replace them at their own expense and to answer in Star Chamber. One of its greatest problems was to deal with the large number of contractors; there were fourteen brewers alone. The commission's success was undone with war. In the 1630s the Crown moved systematically to limit its many projectors and contractors.

The victualler of the navy used the large balances on hand from victualling contracts as loans to the navy for ships and stores. From 1625 to 1630 Sir Allen Apsley's personal finances were intertwined with the victualling accounts. In preparing the war fleets he was forced to advance money for the king's service. In 1627 the Crown owed him over £41,000 and granted him land to pay off part of the debt. At his death in 1630 the Crown still owed him money. While contemporaries complained about King James's largesse, his free gift to Buckingham of £30,000 in 1625 went in the main for the funding of the fleet to Cadiz.[48] Sir William Russell, the Treasurer of the Navy, simultaneously held posts as customs farmer and collector of silk duties in the 1620s and 1630s, which provided him with substantial balances on hand to use for navy business.[49]

From the middle of the Elizabethan period on, increasingly large ships, which could be more fully armed and manned, were built. These could ply trading routes and serve as fishing vessels as well as participate in royal war fleets. Because the Crown employed shipwrights who also had private shipyards it helped to underwrite merchant shipping which, in times of war, played an important role in royal war fleets. King James fostered the boom in shipbuilding after making peace with Spain in 1604. Those who served as shipwrights from 1558 to 1640 were increasingly drawn from a few families, the Petts, the Bakers and the Brights and the Chapmans, who held royal patents and had served in the royal shipyards. They retained the right to work elsewhere when their work was not required by the royal shipyard.[50]

Custom was invoked to justify the diversion of stores. Sir John Coke, the leading commissioner of the navy after 1618, questioned expenditure on ordnance, arguing that four of the guns on the *Dreadnought* had been buried in ballast while others were in other ships "and yet spend as much powder, munition and sea-stores as if they were mounted which is an intolerable abuse."[51] At the lower level, where wages were often in arrears, workmen had the traditional perquisite into the eighteenth century of taking away for personal use as many wood chips as they could carry on their shoulders. In the 1630s Henry Yonge, a long-time master gunner in the royal navy, admitted that he had sold three barrels of gunpowder for £7s 10d from one of the king's ships, *The Unicorn*, to William Cobham of Rochester while the ship was at Chatham. He contended that it was customary:

> The powder was the unlading of the guns in *The Unicorn* when she came from her last voyage, and is called scaling powder and has been usually allowed to the master gunner to dispose of at his return from sea. It was sold and sent on shore by him without the privity of the captain ... or other officer of the ship ... It was delivered from aboard the ship about 5 P.M. when daylight was shutting in.[52]

Despite the appeal to custom, the circumstances of the sale and the testimony of a witness suggested that Yonge was selling the king's stores.

III
Sale of office and the culture of corruption

While corrupt incentives were thus inherent in a patrimonial bureaucracy in which public and private interest intermingled, the extent and configuration of corrupt practices increased from the 1590s. The establishment of a culture of corruption in the sale of office, contracting, provisioning, dead pays and diversion of supplies in the Jacobean navy can be documented in detail. First, Burghley's removal of the Lord Admiral from overseeing naval administration, while not a problem in the early Elizabethan period, set the stage for increasing venality in the 1590s and beyond. Complaints about corruption were voiced by Fulke Greville, Treasurer of the Navy and John Coke who served as his assistant in 1602/3. In 1604 Nottingham, who was certainly a patron if not a supervisor, maneuvered Fulke Greville out of office and installed Sir Robert Mansell as Treasurer of the Navy. Despite repeated evidence of Mansell's corrupt practices from two Jacobean commissions, he remained in office from 1604 to 1618 and then, as was customary, was allowed to sell his office before retiring.[53] Nottingham also supported Sir John Trevor in the office of Surveyor despite evidence of his corrupt practices.

Mansell and Trevor, courtiers who held other patents and offices, systematically organized the supplying and hiring of the navy for their own benefit: they created and sold offices, paid double allowances, used royal ships for merchant journeys, allowed the misuse and diversion of naval stores into private hands, increased the kickbacks extracted from suppliers, provided rotten materials and foods, let contracts for extensive and expensive shipbuilding without adequate supervision, placed their dependants in lower offices and farmed work done for the navy to important naval officials.[54] Mansell arranged with Sir John Trevor to supply the king with naval stores; he was later accused of supplying poor goods at high prices. In analyzing Mansell's accounts, the commissioners found that he took too much money from the Treasury by privy seal for supposedly extraordinary expenses, new offices and new storehouses.[55] Under Mansell and Trevor low-level and high-level extraction coexisted. Investigations in 1608 and 1618 provided evidence of the increasing scope and scale of navy corruption. But Mansell and Trevor's patronage ties to the Lord Admiral and, perhaps even more important, to the Prince of Wales, protected them for fifteen years from significant reform.

The sale of office was typical of early modern bureaucracy. Charles V's political testament stated that such sales were preferable to impositions. Sale of office was systematically organized in France for the financial benefit of the Crown with the institution of the *paulette* in 1604. In England, the Treasury Commission of 1612–14 considered such sales as a revenue device, but decided reluctantly that it was politically unwise.[56] Tolerating the sale of offices by its lesser magistrates was a way for the Crown to reward its underpaid bureaucrats.

Royal service provided protection against legal process. In the 1590s Lord Hunsdon, Governor of Berwick-on-Tweed, chastised his Knight Marshall, Sir Henry Withrington, for allowing captains who served under him to place soldiers in the garrison for money "such as being bankrupts here in London and in sundry countries, where for their misdemeanors they dare not show their faces, for 20 Nobles or £10 may buy a soldier's room in Berwick to shroud themselves from all law." He urged Withrington to find out how many had "come in by such corruption, and that they may be presently discharged ... and fitter men to be placed in their rooms, for otherwise the town will become Callis [Callais]." Hunsdon was outspoken. He replied to Withrington's letter on behalf of Roger Case to be a captain "I am sure you did [it] either upon entreaty, or for company as dogs go to church, I should show myself very partial and unskillful in the choice of a captain, if I should appoint him, who I know to be so unfit in all respects." Two years later the problem continued. The queen was informed that "nobody comes into any place there but by bribes ... she is informed that you never come out of your House, but sit there playing at cards or dice ... so that you know not what is done in the town." He ordered Withrington to find out all who had come into office by bribery and turn them out of town, otherwise "it will lie heavily on your neck."[57]

The change introduced by the Mansell-Trevor regime was the systematic creation of new and unnecessary offices for their private profit. A contemporary stressed that maximizing short-term profit from office diverted productive investment to speculation in offices.

> Principal officers purchasing their places at dear rates must strain to cover the same, or live by the loss, seeing they may not only for the Revenues, but the credit, countenance and corruptions which are valued by the sale not only in the certain and just fees, but also in all other usurpations shadow'd under the name of Profit and yet do hazard their money upon uncertainty of life and their time, which might be employed as profitably otherwise and rest only upon the hopes and returns of their places. Wherefore I conceive it no way profitable for his Majesty and the State to permit a Principal officer to purchase or sell his place, but rather to confer it freely upon some man of good estate ... that shall be perfect in accounts, skillful in shipping and faithful to his King and Country whereby he shall be bound to employ his best service and uttermost endeavors truly and faithfully to deserve those favors.[58]

Northampton identified sale of offices and preferment as the root of corrupt practices, "without recovery of some part of those means by filching, which they laid out for the purchases at large, they should famish both themselves and their families."[59] If low wages aggravated venality in the navy, petitions to increase wages threatened the officers' profit from sale of office. In 1608 commissioners heard testimony that "all the boatswains at the king's first coming to Rochester made a purse of £20 to follow the petition to the king for augmentation of wages to keep them true. Sir John Trevor discouraged the man that was the mouth, the reason was because he knew it would overthrow the sales of offices."[60] Boatswains, pursers and cooks paid kickbacks to Sir John and Lady Trevor for wages and places.[61]

The creation of new offices was directly related to their sale. Places were sold at such rates that buyers admitted "they cannot live except they steal."[62] Moreover there were many new and unnecessary allowances including triple allowances for lieutenants and vice-admirals, the Treasurer of the Navy, and the Surveyor of Victuals, for themselves and a number of servants. The principal officers received wages and victuals for a dead pay in each ship and entrusted their duties to inferiors and clerks who often had ties and financial connections with the merchants who supplied the goods. Sir John Trevor sought to sell an office during the 1608 investigation.[63]

The commission of 1618 detailed the creation of new offices under Mansell and Trevor who double-charged the Exchequer and the navy, placed store-keepers where there were no stores and garrisons in castles which had only ceremonial significance. These new offices included first, a Captainship General of the Narrow Seas with 20s per diem, one clerk at 8d and 16 servants at 10s a month, amounting yearly to £481 3s 4d. "Besides he enjoys by pretence hereof [an] other 20s per diem paid by the Treasurer of the Navy and 16 pays under the name of retinue whereof every one amounts to £6-10-3 . . . Both the grant by patent and the title and the allowance are new and not formerly heard of." Second, a Vice-Admiral of the Narrow Seas with 10s per diem and 10s a month to 8 servants of retinue paid twice, once out of the Exchequer and then by the Treasurer of the Navy. "The patent, privy seal and double allowance and dead pays under the name of retinue are all new and unusual." Thirdly, "a patent to one serving in the Narrow Seas with allowance of 10s per diem out of the Exchequer. This has no precedent." Fourthly, a Surveyor of the Tonnage of Merchant Ships with the yearly fee of £18 5s. Under the control of this office the king's charge had risen yearly to £1,888 1s 5d. "This Surveyor and charge now ceaseth. But (as we hear) one Mr Jobson pretends to have a reversion of the patent." Fifthly, a storekeeper at Woolwich. "The office is a new erection and no stores there." Sixthly, to the cleaner of the roads £30: "the pretence of this patent seems to be the removing of lost anchors and other wrecks which . . . might endanger the ships." Seventh, an allowance of twenty soldiers in the Castle of Upnor. "This ever heretofore was ordinarily guarded but with two gunners and extraordinarily with more or fewer, as the times and danger required. In the same there is allowed to a captain £30 per annum payable by the Treasurer of the Navy." Eighth, the keeper of out stores at Deptford, paid £66 13s 4d by the Treasurer of the Navy, was a new and unnecessary office held by the Clerk of the Cheque.[64]

Control of patronage in the navy was closely guarded from the highest official to the lowest. Several rights of appointment had been granted to the Clerk of the Cheque at Deptford, Woolwich and Chatham and to the Principal Masters, which previously had been in the gift of the Lord Admiral and removable for cause.[65] Some of the resentment about new offices came from old officials who worried that their own income would be cut. Nottingham complained in 1600 that a naval clerk had ignored Nottingham's bestowal of a patent on one of his servants, William Delvin, "for the choosing and placing of cooks in the navy." Although Delvin had chosen sufficient and fit men as cooks, John Legatt, Clerk of the Cheque, refused to enter them. The Lord Admiral ordered him to do so hereafter, "so as they be fit and honest" and specifically ordered him to "enter into wages and victuals in the *Defiance* this Bearer Thomas Belme as Cook in the Place of Reignold Pallent."[66] Thus in the midst of the war with Spain, the Lord Admiral spent time worrying about cooks, or more to the point, safeguarding the patronage of his subordinates and himself. Despite the investigation into the navy in 1608, Nottingham's patronage remained powerful. John King, granted the Lord Admiral's favor in 1606, had been made a collector of the king's rents in 1608. Although accused of felonies in 1610, King was granted the reversion of the office of one of the six principal Masters of the royal navy for life.[67] Similarly, in the 1630s the Earl of Lindsey, as acting Lord Admiral, insisted on his right to name the boatswain on the *Reformation*.[68]

The commissioners for the navy, under Buckingham's "authority and protection," specifically linked the new offices created since James came to the throne both to increased expenses and to corrupt practices, claiming "this unnecessary charge to be special causes of the disorders that have happened in the Navy." Focusing their attention on the period from 1613 to 1617, they argued that

> For these five years, the Navy was like an Army of Generals and Colonels without any inferior Centurions or Captains, the Exorbitance whereof will the better appear by the view of former precedents ... these Admirals and Vice-Admirals with their 20 shillings and 10s per diem, together with the allowance of their retinue and other advantages are raised to a condition that enables them to live so contentedly at land that they cannot brook the seas and therefore they begin to get Captains under them in their ships to govern their companies as lieutenants in their absence.[69]

Much of the early Jacobean expansion of the naval bureaucracy in peacetime did not then develop sinews of power but sinecures. For instance, Sir William Monson, Admiral of the Narrow Seas, and Sir Richard Bingley, Surveyor of the Navy and Captain of the Irish Coast, paid their captains 2s 6d per diem, "an innovation of great prejudice to his Majesty we think ought not to be allowed for by this precedent ... every ship in a while will have an Admiral on shore and a captain at sea."[70] Sir Thomas Button, who had allowance in Ireland, also had a patent in England for his wife of 6s 8d per diem and, for his admiral's pay, 20s per diem; in addition he collected £108 16s 7d for his travel in 1616 and £237 in 1617. The commission remarked "we find the charge excessive and the manner of payments irregular and confused." In the 1630s Button served both as provisioner and captain of small ships, called whelps, stationed on the Irish coast while living in Glamorgan, Wales.

In addition to their expansion of sale of office, provisioning and diversion of supplies had become worse under Mansell and Trevor. Increases in the cost of the navy, due to work on large-scale projects in the shipyards, produced unprecedented wage bills in peacetime. Critics claimed that eight new ships at Elizabethan rates could have been built. The dockyards and their great storehouses were plagued by embezzlement and misappropriation which was a constant problem in the seventeenth and eighteenth-century navy.[71] During the 1608 investigation, Northampton established that the cordage supplied was bad, hazarding both ships and men's lives. "The *Rainbow* had lost three cables by that rottenness which a merchant ship would never have done and by the breaking of a rope by rottenness a man was slain which rope the boatswain keeps to show the corruption."[72] The oakum, used for caulking ships seams and stopping leaks, was rotten, the tar full of water. Under-officers claimed that "they dare not complain when they that have to do in the business are favorites to the great officers." Austin Morland, the surveyors' clerk of stores, refused to replace rotten goods and required boatswains to sign for provisions they hadn't seen. Morland even sold the king's provisions to naval officials.

Thomas Buck, an important witness in 1608, urged that ship carpenters not be placed permanently on the royal pay roll, "for private gain of those who took upon them the placing of them." None but the most able should be admitted and

> such as dare become bound for their truth in yielding a true account of their ... expenses both in harbor and at sea which ... will cut off the means which now officers have to put in young men which are of no sufficiency nor experience at the seas which much endanger his Majesty's ships when they shall be occasioned to fight, besides bar them of daily embezzling of his Majesty's provisions which is now so common as four times as much more is required by them as is spent upon the ships which falls out to his Majesty's great loss.

Buck suggested similar qualifications for smiths and pumpmakers.

> There is one George Thorne maintained in pay by Sir Henry Palmer who does yearly charge his Majesty 200 marks besides many abuses daily committed between him and clerk of check in his purveyance of timber ... To cut off this needless charge it will be necessary he be discharged from the ordinary works, especially now in time of peace having very little or nothing at all to do in a whole year altogether of any material or needful business ... There is one Shorter, a joiner, continued likewise in ordinary pay who for the most part works in the officers' houses with his servants by whose continuance his

Majesty is yearly charged needlessly with near £50 in wages, besides stuff; which under color for the kiing''s service he receives out of ttthhe storehouses for other men's uses.[73]

Buck called for inspection of work at the end of a project by the Master Shipwrights in the presence of the principal officers. Buck's description of the connection of workmen with chief officers was reflected in the findings of the commission of 1608 and its prescription for reform.

If war with Spain presented the Elizabethan navy with the problem of officers going off to sea and leaving less competent deputies in their place, the opposite happened under King James. In peacetime, the navy expanded more under its own internal pressures than it had during the war with Spain. At the same time both Jacobean commissions found the actual hands-on experience of the naval officers diminished. The 1618 commission depicted a plethora of admirals who, as gentlemen, no longer went to sea.

To dead weight had to be added the customary problem of dead pays. Captain Duffield confessed to the 1608 commission that "some fourteen persons under strange names that ought not to be paid as ordinaries being officers servants and favorites are borne upon the book of the navy in victuals and pay at the king's charge by favor of the officials." John Legatt, Clerk of the Cheque, had threatened Captain Duffield with

> complaint to my Lord Admiral and hazard of his place for refusing to serve the victuals of 10 men that he found increased upon the sudden in respect that he feared out of the late experiences some fraud ... and yet Thomas Rockwell Master of the Advantage told him that when they were allowed in warrant 67 men they had on board but 36 and 5 gone on shore. Thus it appeared that 26 men were directly increased upon that warrant.[74]

Captain Button required them to agree to take 70 men when the king allowed 100; 'dead pays' numbered 30, and of the 70 only 20 were sufficient to do service in the ship. The boatswains argued that when the labor of 100 was laid on 20 it "drives all from the king's service at sea so as the fleet is in danger." Profits from the "dead pays" were divided between the victualler, the captain and the purser.

The commission of 1618 documented the culture of corruption established by the Jacobean naval officers. The commissioners were instructed by the Privy Council to inquire into provisioning, purveying, the quality of stores required for each ship, to analyze the comparative costs of setting a ship to sea with different burdens and to determine the best size ships for normal use. Under the leadership of Sir John Coke, who had close ties to Buckingham, the commission asked to go far beyond this fact-finding brief, to examine the fundamental structure and practice of the navy. They asked for the power to call witnesses to answer on oath; to inquire into the additional allowances paid to admirals, vice-admirals, and captains since the death of Queen Elizabeth above the rates normal in her reign; and to inquire into "dead pays." The 1608 commission served as one of the guides for the successful 1618 commission: they asked to use Northampton's findings and some of their advisors had served the previous commission.[75] Their other guide was Elizabethan practice to which Coke could personally testify. The commission's stated aim was to view past actions for the better avoidance of future abuse.[76] In making their reports they found the records in decay. Mansell was unable to provide full accounts. Indeed, no dockyard quarter books had been made up since 1615. The king allowed both Mansell and Nottingham to retire from their offices and the Duke of Buckingham was appointed Lord Admiral.

IV
Diagnosis and treatment

The commission diagnosed the lack of appropriate salaries as a major structural cause of the navy's abuses, one which encouraged sale of office, peculation and close connections with merchant suppliers. While recognizing that some officers suffered by serving the king, the commission thought dead pays and sinecures were not the way to reward them. Their prescription to overcome the culture of corruption established by the naval officers was to increase salaries, to rationalize procedure, and to impose severe punishments on offenders in the future. The commissioners also tried to decrease the extraordinary charges for false expenditures, and to remove from the accounts ships that had been broken up, severely damaged or disposed of.[77] They cut back on men, servants to officers and "dead pays," and brought victualling rates more in line with current merchant rates and those due to the good harvest in 1618. To cut wastage and embezzlement they established procedures for the withdrawing of stores.[78]

The 1618 report that Pepys so admired argued that the problems in the navy were due to recent innovations over the last fifteen years, i.e. since the beginning of Mansell's administration.[79] Under Elizabeth the officers had been few and all were in daily attendance. The Mansell–Trevor regime had taken upon itself the power to make regulations which removed rights from subordinate officers, to embark on costly works without warrant and to award allowances and fees. Contemporaries believed that office should be held by those with estates large enough to make it unnecessary for them to steal. The naval officers were accused of placing the trust of their offices in clerks who did everything without giving an accounting and lacked the credit or estate to insure the king against default. The officers created a multitude of new offices, many by patent for life, a growing pattern in seventeenth-century administration. As a result the king was overcharged, the service weakened and the Lord Admiral dishonored because the right to make appointments was his prerogative. Service, honor and courtesy, fundamental to seventeenth-century officeholding, were thereby breached.

In response to the commissioners' prescription in 1619 the navy captains complained about cuts in the manning of ships. "The king's ships have well near one-third of their company that are officers and those that are employed in mean uses as cooks, shifters, swabbers, stewards . . . trumpeters, surgeons, pursers, carpenters and boys all which for honor and use have had entertainment in the king's ships."[80] Thus the *Speedwell* with 36 pieces of ordinance requiring 18 gunners carried a total of 190 men "beside the Captain and his retinue," including 48 men to stand by tackles and port ropes, 50 men to ply the small shot, 50 men to conduct and steer the sails, 4 men in the powder room, 4 carpenters, 3 trumpeters, 3 surgeons and their mates, 4 stewards, 3 cooks and mate, and 3 boys. The officers distinguished the manning of the king's ships from a merchant's ships.

Sir John Coke wittily counterattacked in his response to Buckingham, pointing out that there were few specifics in the captains' discourse but "the indefinite word of undermanning, and the disgraceful name of Merchant ships."

> To judge the better, be pleased to represent to your noble imagination, a present view of such a fight as one of these papers has marshalled before you. First behold 18 gunners standing with flint-stocks in their hands and 48 men looking till they give fire. Then consider 50 men walking on the hatches with their pieces ready charged and 50 more waiting till the Masters whistle to call them to their labors. Next conceive 4 yeomen watching the powder room, 4 carpenters waiting with their tools, 3 Surgeons sitting in the Cabin, 7 cooks and stewards making dinner ready and 2 or 3 boys lurking in the hold. And shall this be called a fight? Is this the face of War? Are they good organists that cannot play without a finger for every key? or be men like dead tools that serve but one use?

Coke argued that real warfare was very different.

> A good man of war no sooner descries his enemy afar off but forthwith he commands every man to his charge, makes ready his fights, ladeth his artillery, quarters his men, puts them in arms, marshals their weapons and encourages every [one] to serve valiantly as a mariner or soldier . . . every man . . . falls to his arms . . . and no man thinks of anything but fight.

The war with Spain had changed English naval strategy. Coke pointed out that up to 1588 soldiers and mariners were divided as the captains had said, "but that and later experience has taught us instead of freshwater soldiers (as they call them) to employ only seamen." At issue was how to make naval administration respond to these new functions.

Coke suggested that the captains revealed "how they served his Majesty when idle Company aboard, idle numbers ashore, idle fighting and idle working are maintained by their pens." While the captains deprecated merchant ships, the latter were better paid and had better men. While the captains boasted that unlike the merchant ships the king's ships sought out pirates, the ships were in fact in home ports. "And their captains happily wait for them at their houses in the country, in London ... where the pirates ... will hardly be found."[81]

Arguing that the Navy Board could not bring about reform, the commission suggested that new offices and patents be suspended, that the Lord Admiral regain his prerogatives and control of patronage in the navy. They asked to carry out their proposals as soon as ratified by the Lord Admiral and to put the navy under his control. They would undertake to discharge both phoney ships and dead pays and, at the same time, undertake to build new ships for the king. When the navy officers refused to administer the navy under these stipulations, Lionel Cranfield offered the service of the commission. The king accepted, the officers were suspended and admonished by the king to meddle no further. Those with patents for life would be paid but at death there would be no renewal and no reversions would be allowed. In the future, the Lord Admiral's nominees would hold office during pleasure. Over the next ten years, the administration of the navy was in the hands of the commission headed by Sir John Coke under the leadership of Buckingham.

In the first five years of its administration the commission significantly cut costs and built ten new ships. In the first year it spent £32,610, £20,000 less than Mansell and Trevor, indeed less than any previous year in the reign, and at the same time it improved the dockyards and began to enlarge the fleet. Although the commissioners could not revoke the new patents, they were able to prevent the granting of further reversions.

Alan McGowan argues that under the commissioners's Treasurer of the Navy, Sir William Russell, "the finances of the navy were probably more efficiently controlled than at any other time between the death of Hawkins and the latter part of the Civil War."[82] Russell monitored accounts closely. In 1627 he gave up his office to a member of Buckingham's household, Sir Sackville Crowe, but returned to the post from 1630 to 1642 during which time he handled ship money efficiently. Navy Treasurers like Russell were able to obtain funds for the navy more easily when Lord Treasurers like Lionel Cranfield and Richard Weston had close connections with navy commissioners.

The success of the commission began to be imperilled in 1624 when the commissioners faced extraordinary expenses for royal expeditions and for war. Charles's return voyage from Spain with Buckingham in 1624 cost £20,719, the transport for Henrietta Maria, made up of eleven of the king's ships and twenty-four merchant ships, cost £35,986; Lord Willoughby's expedition cost £90,283.[83] Seamen from Portsmouth and Chatham demonstrated to demand their pay. The navy's finances continued to be precarious until the levying of ship money on the whole country in 1635.[84]

For the first five or more years of its life, the naval commission successfuly reformed naval administration in peacetime. The failure of the commission came only under the pressure of war in the mid-1620s when it faced the daunting problems of provisioning and victualling ships. The commission was reorganized, and while in its first five years the busiest commissioners had no financial interest in the navy, in the second five years, McGowan argues, all but one had "fortunes inextricably bound up with it."[85] Buckingham was acutely aware of the shortcomings and wrote repeatedly to rebuke the commissioners. When the fleet was driven back to Plymouth after defeat, Buckingham urged a commission of inquiry. It included Jacobean officials such as Sir John Trevor and the shipwright Phineas Pett as well as Sir Robert Cotton, a leading member of the 1608 commission.[86] The expedition to Rhé was a failure too. As a result the navy commission was revoked in April, 1628.[87]

McGowan argues that Buckingham was an effective and conscientious Lord Admiral, greatly absorbed in naval affairs and much more vigorous in its administration than usually thought.[88] In the sixteenth century few of the ten Lord Admirals had service at sea. Before 1628 no Lord Admiral's patent referred to administration. It was not surprising, then, that Nottingham had paid it little attention. Yet without supervision, a naval treasurer like Mansell was in a position to run the navy for his own profit.[89]

In contrast, Buckingham took a close interest and, as the commission had advised in 1619, took personal responsibility for the appointment of all captains and admirals. Subordinate officers were also appointed by the Lord Admiral's warrant issued upon receipt of recommendations from the navy commissioners.[90] Successful recommendations for promotion of subordinate officers were made through Buckingham's secretary, especially after 1624; many of the letters indicated that the writer would show his appreciation to the duke in tangible form.[91] McGowan suggests that another problem the navy faced was that most of its officers in the 1620s had been trained in the period of greatest laxity from 1604 to 1618. But it is equally likely that Buckingham's patronage began to resemble that of Mansell and Trevor. When, at Cadiz, hired merchant ships did not sufficiently support the king's ships, the Privy Council on Buckingham's recommendation ordered that in future expeditions no one could be appointed master of a vessel of which he was in any way part-owner in case he might not be willing to hazard the ship. Buckingham helped develop a new role for the Lord Admiral, showing a surprising grasp of detail, exercise of oversight and use of his own money on the service. The problem in the expeditions for Cadiz, Rhé and La Rochelle lay in lack of funds, technology, and particularly victualling that were not to be solved, McGowan claims, for 200 year.[92]

V

Parliamentary complaint

These issues moved from the dockyards to parliamentary debate at the beginning of the new reign. Amongst the questions Northampton had posed during the 1608 investigation was "Have not you heard that the gentlemen of the country said, it had been better for the country to have given the king freely so much timber as they carried at those rates that formerly were imposed on them?" Corruption in purveyance for the navy was one political irritant that kept King James's subjects from voting him adequate supply.[93] By 1625 the House of Commons had become disenchanted with the Duke. Buckingham, lauded at the time of his return from Spain in 1623 for overcoming faction, was attacked two years later as corrupt. Indeed, one of the major charges raised in 1625 and embodied in the impeachment in 1626 was his conduct as Lord Admiral. When in 1625 the Commons debated supply, Sir John Eliot sought to "clear and vindicate that noble Lord . . . if there has been any abuse in the fleet, it is not his fault . . . the commissioners, if any, faulty."[94] Others were not so generous. Even when put to good use, Buckingham's control of court patronage provoked criticism in the vortex of war and increased taxation of the 1620s.

In debating whether or not to vote subsidies for the king, Sir Edward Coke and Sir Robert Heath, the king's Solicitor General, examined "the leak" that required the Crown to ask aid of its subjects. Coke argued that "no king can subsist in an honorable estate without 3 abilities: 1 to maintain himself against sudden invasions; 2 to aid his allies and confederates; 3 to reward his well-deserving servants."[95] If service and courtesy dwelt together in the bosom of the honorable officeholder, royal bounty existed alongside defence as an important role of the monarch. Yet Coke was deeply critical of early Stuart reward and administration. He called on parliament "to petition the king rather for a logic than a rhetoric hand, a straight than an open hand."

Coke ascribed the king's necessity to improvidence and attacked the operation of the navy:

> It was never heard that Queen Elizabeth's navy did dance a pavan; so many men to be pressed, and lie so long without doing anything. The office of Lord Admiral is the place of greatest trust and experience . . . It will be well when offices are restored to men of sufficiency. If an office be granted to an unexperienced man, it is void . . . The wisdom of ancient times was to put great men into places of great title, but men of parts into such places as require experience. For the most

127

part a tradesman was Master of the Ordnance until 20 H. 8 [the twentieth year of the reign of Henry VIII], and since it was possessed by the nobility was never well executed.[96]

Coke attacked the creation of new offices and new fees, increased household expenses, government mismanagement and fraud. He called for retrenchment of excess annuities.

All the kings since the Conquest have not been so much charged in this kind as the king now is, and by using to be bought and sold they are made perpetual . . . Overmuch bounty in the grant of fee farms and privy seals for money. The King's servants should be rewarded with offices and honors, not with the inheritance of the crown.

Coke urged the reform of the king's household, the pruning of unnecessary officials, their diet and allowances. He went on to make a wide-ranging attack on court patronage:

1. That the officers of court live on their offices without daily begging. 2. That no Lord may have above one office. 3. That all voluntary pensions be cut off. 4. That the courtiers may be rewarded and the king not charged with stipends and pensions. 5. That all fee farms be called in that the king may make the best of his lands, for this is but a damnable course to cozen the king of his land giving him a small chief rent for it . . . That monopolies be taken away.[97]

In response Heath, the Solicitor General, presented the fundamental dilemma of early Stuart politics: "he has two parts to act, one as a private man and the servant of his Majesty; the other as a public man for the public good."[98] He agreed that "the king's estate, like a ship, has a great leak. If a ship be assailed, all must not go to mend the leak, and none to defend her." Heath argued that parliament had committed itself to granting the subsidies for the war, that King James's improvidence should not be attributed to King Charles and that it was not the king's necessity but the kingdom's which was at issue. Further,

there has been something spoken of great offices held by great men which reflects upon the greatest man of the kingdom. Every man knows his great obligation to that great man but that should not make him forget his duty to this place. And when there is time for it, he will be as ready in it as any other.[99]

Another version of Heath's speech reads "If he [Buckingham] deserves blame, let the burden light upon himself, not upon the commonwealth." The issue of supply was foremost.

VI
Ship money

The administration of the navy in the 1630s is only now being fully investigated,[100] but it appears that the worst abuses characteristic of the period up to 1618 did not recur. From 1626 to 1627 a special commission sat to investigate the problems the navy experienced with the voyages to Rhé and Cadiz.[101] The failure of those war fleets led to the replacement of the naval commission by the naval officers once more in 1628. Moreover, with the assassination of Buckingham by an aggrieved soldier, the Admiralty was put into commission. The personnel of the navy board and commissioners of the Admiralty brought back familiar characters such as Phineas Pett and Sir Robert Mansell who had been responsible for much of the corruption of the early Jacobean period. Complaints about the navy continued and Algernon Percy, Earl of Northumberland, prepared a lengthy analysis of abuses when he was appointed Lord Admiral of the ship money fleets in 1636.

Although the navy commission's period of reform had ended, its careful approach towards accounting, procurement and retrenchment continued. The Privy Council – "his Majesty sitting in councell" – ordered the sheriffs and the principal officers and commissioners of the navy to attend the Privy Council armed with prices of provisions.[102] "It highly importeth his Majesty in point of honour and profit to have the services of his Navy and ships to be ordered and arranged with the most advantage for service and with least charge and expense." Attorney-General Bankes was ordered to compare a proposed victualling contract between King Charles and John Crane in the late 1630s with the former contract made with Sir Allen Apsley and Sir Sampson Darell in the 1620s. In the previous contract, the victualler had been granted 8*d* a day for every man serving at sea and 7 1/2*d* on land. In the new proposal this had been raised to 8 1/2*d* a day at sea. Bankes tried to cut back such increases by defining a month as having 28 days. Where Crane wished to have the houses belonging to his office repaired before his entry, the final contract provided that Crane would keep them in as good repair as presently and, were the king to repair them, then Crane would leave them in that better repair.[103] Using this cautious approach, the commissioners did their work well, perhaps too well. In March 1638, Crane gave his one year's notice because costs had risen and he was losing money on every sailor.[104]

The major change in early Stuart naval administration occurred with the countrywide imposition and efficient collection of ship money. Ship money was not, of course, new; it was a medieval levy imposed on maritime towns to supply ships to the Crown. In 1628 ship money was imposed in connection with a Franco–Spanish threat. The systematic imposition began in 1635 when the levy of the previous year was extended to the entire country. Most discussions of ship money treat it as a constitutional issue and revenue device. Collections reached over 90 per cent of their goal between 1634 and 1637 although collection rates differed among counties. But ship money was as much about ships as it was about money.

Charles I justified the imposition of ship money in 1634 by current military and trade problems. Because of continental warfare, the English Channel was crossed by Spanish and French warships; the England and Dutch competed for fishing in the North Sea; and the western coast was beset by pirates.

> the dangers considered which, on every side, in these times of war do hang over our heads, that it behoveth us and our subjects to hasten to the defence of the sea and kingdom ... forasmuch as we, and our progenitors Kings of England, have been always heretofore master of the aforesaid sea, and it would be very irksome unto us if that princely honor in our times should be lost or in any thing diminished.[105]

Charles I wished to establish England's position in Europe and his own control of the Channel: "A great point for the king to be able to put to sea every year a fleet of from forty to fifty large vessels without touching a halfpenny of his revenue. A business of great consequence and reputation, but little to the taste of our neighbours [France and Holland]."[106]

Major figures in Charles's Privy Council, including Richard Weston, Earl of Portland, the Lord Treasurer, and Attorney-General Noy, were directly concerned both with naval policy and naval administration and the imposition of ship money. Noy developed ship money as a regular assessment in the 1630s. On the orders of the Lord Commissioners of the Admiralty he also drew up a "reglement" to preserve the King's sovereignty in the Narrow Seas and secure the nation's trade in February 1634.[107] Weston served on the 1618 naval commission and was one of the navy commissioners from 1619. As Lord Treasurer, he put the paying of sailors' wages on a more systematic basis. It is not unlikely that the attempts in the 1630s to raise salaries for the naval officers were part of a systematic approach to naval reform. Sir John Coke worked closely with Weston as one of the commissioners of the Admiralty and provided the first instructions to the ship money fleets.[108]

Beginning in 1635, the country as a whole was assessed for ships, men, their victuals and wages. Ship money was paid not into the Exchequer but to the Treasurer of the Navy.[109] The funds were kept completely separate from other naval monies and accounted for separately. Excepting the treasurer's poundage, virtually all of the funds were spent on the ship money fleets mounted each year.[110] Indeed, in 1634 when the writs were directed only to the maritime counties, more was spent on the fleets than was collected, with money advanced from the Exchequer. In 1635, almost £195,000 was collected from the whole country and over £180,000 was expended on the ship money fleets.[111] The collection of ship money proved highly successful for the first few years and, with ship money, the Crown had created an effective means to tax and to finance the navy. The king argued in the Short Parliament in 1640 that the monies had been delivered to Sir William Russell and expended "for the good and safety of the nation." Only when it became clear that the ship money fleet would be on the Spanish side in the Thirty Years War did opposition harden in England.[112]

In the 1630s, English administrators tried to avoid the problems faced by the fleets of the later 1620s: lack of wages, poor provisions, mutinous sailors. Beginning in 1635, systematic naval re-armament took place. Charles I had added new ships to the royal navy by 1640, some of them designed to be faster in order to deal with privateers and the Dutch. Fourteen pinnaces were built in the 1620s, and 11 ships between 1632 and 1637. Still the navy never prepared as many ships as the writs called for. In 1635, although the writs called for 47 ships, only 27 were prepared. London was able to provide ships more cheaply and with better provisions and equipment. As in the previous reign there were complaints about some of the ships, in particular, the *Unicorn*. One captain complained "The king's ships are not built as they should be, nor like merchant ships." Kenrick Edisbury, a navy official and servant to Sir William Russell before his appointment as Surveyor of the Navy, attributed the problem to the self-interest of the shipwrights. "I never yet knew any ship built by day-work but the shipwrights have made them of greater burden than their warrants mentioned."[113]

Although the Treasurer of the Navy continued to enjoy poundage, the other naval officers in 1633 argued that reform commissions had so cut back on their perquisites that they were forced back on their fees. These had not been raised since the reign of Henry VIII and, as they pointed out, "a groat then was as valuable as a shilling now . . . In most other offices, both in court and kingdom there are perquisites far exceeding the fees belonging to them, only we are barely to expect those ancient fees with any other the least advantage."[114] In the period from 1633 to 1634 these petitions for increased salaries were accompanied by notes of ancient salaries of principal and subordinate offices of the navy with increases made to them since their first institution under Henry VIII.[115] When Northumberland became Lord Admiral of the ship money fleet in 1636 he presented strong charges against the naval administration and in 1638 was named Lord Admiral of the entire navy.[116] Perhaps as a result of his criticisms, the commissioners forbade reversions in naval appointments. Within the year they had changed the tenure of office from life to the king's pleasure. As a result, in 1638/9 the navy officers were alloted fixed annual expense allowances.[117]

Ship money was developed to systematically fund an expanded navy. But it expressed other important contemporary values. When in 1618 the

131

commissioners had tried to cut down on the manning of ships, they were attacked for thinking too much like merchants. The *Sovereign of the Seas* was an extraordinary three-decker, gorgeously decorated, its size set down by the king himself. Phineas Pett said it would cost under £14,000; it cost over £40,000.[118]

VII

The early Stuart navy graphically illustrates the role of court patronage in shaping both corrupt incentives and administrative reform in early modern government. The culture of corruption crafted by Trevor and Mansell gave way to effective administration between 1618 and 1623–5. Then, under the pressure of war, the administrative machinery proved ineffective in dealing with longstanding problems of provisioning and victualling. Although the most egregious corrupt practices of the Jacobean period diminished after 1618, war and taxation in the 1620s and 1630s made administrative waste in the navy highly visible.

Statutes against corrupt practices did not reach many areas of conflict of interest, payroll padding, sinecures, dead pays or diversion of stores that characterized the navy and early modern government more generally. The contemporary mentality of service and courtesy limited changes in policy and practice. The 1608 commissioners were advised to bring together several lower officials to testify against the principal officers: "for it is the custom of us seamen, if one speaks to good purpose, all the rest will say Amen." Otherwise the "presence of their great Lord will so astonish them as they will not dare confidently utter what they would."[119] But the commission's work foundered on Sir Robert Mansell's indissoluble ties not only to the prince but to the two Howards who had served in the Navy, Lord Admiral Nottingham and Thomas Howard, Earl of Suffolk. Thomas Buck wrote to Sir Robert Cotton during the 1608 investigation that Sir Robert Mansell

> long since feasted diverse young lords and ladies of the court where I heard there was some speech used concerning the business now in hand which was answered by a nobleman that he needed not to care for all was at the highest, which Lord was thought to be my Lord Theophilus [Theophilus Howard, son and heir of the Earl of Suffolk] but of that I am not certain yet thought to give you notice that if you please to acquaint my honorable Lord [Henry Howard, the Earl of Northampton] with it so which I leave to your wise consideration.[120]

Ministerial efforts to rationalize administrative practices were successful when they had the support of the king and his closest advisers. Then, armed with the patronage of the favorite, reform-minded commissioners were able to make some inroads into entrenched venality in the areas of the Household, Ordnance, Crown lands, and fees. From 1618 to 1624 and in the 1630s first the Duke of Buckingham and then King Charles were the great patrons of reform. These efforts, dependent on personal relationships as were the corrupt practices they sought to uproot, lacked administrative infrastructure and tended to run out of steam over time especially when faced with the strictures of war. In addition, Buckingham's monopoly of patronage and financial extraction and Charles I's policies had political costs.

Chapter 6

Corruption and the economy

In a report on corrupt practices in purveyance during King James's first progress in 1604, Robert Fletcher, yeoman of carriages, accused the carttakers (household officials whose duty it was to arrange transport) of making "a very shop of monopoly bribery ... These grievous afflictions laid upon the poor subjects by prowling purveyors and unconscionable carttakers was a just cause of clamor in the Parliament ... crying carttaker, carttaker."[1] The carttakers of London "do some times steal upon an ignorant poor carter who having loaden his cart for Norwich, Yarmouth or place of like distance from London. He is taken by one of the Carttakers, commanded to unload and load a tun of drink and convey the same to the court ... the poor man draweth his purse and payeth £6, £4, 5 marks, etc. to be freed of this carttaker and his broad seal, a naked sword were even as lawful." Corruption had grown in the sixteenth century because of the expansion of administration under Henry VIII. "John Rousley who had been a mayor's officer and that year's carttaker for beer and ale being politick and his hands before polluted with bribes he gave a bribe in court, obtained licence to wear the king's coat or livery and also commission to take up carts ... and here is their first institution."

The Tudor and early Stuart monarchs constructed a new framework for corrupt practices in three ways: firstly by increasing the state's regulation of the economy, secondly by fostering the development of projects to diversify economic activities, and thirdly, as a result of the first two, by increasing the power in the hands of informal agents of the state. This chapter examines each of these in turn. It then turns to the impact of corrupt practices on different segments of the economy. It argues that corruption served to redistribute wealth especially from the merchant community to the gentry and, within the landed elite, to those who had strong court connections. It concludes by examining the provocative issue of whether or not corrupt practices aided economic growth in the early Stuart period.

I

Beginning with Henry VIII the Tudors expanded the role of the state in regulating society and the economy. They used statute and proclamation to control the use of land and capital, to support labor, to control the terms of trade both of imports and exports. Their aim was manifold: to maintain order, to strengthen the Crown, to avoid scarcity and famine, to create a prosperous people, to finance the state through duties and rents, and to cement ties of the localities to the center.[2] They built on fourteenth and fifteenth-century statutes to regulate the poor and rectify decayed housing and took over the church's role in social welfare. The Tudor expansion of the Crown's administration established the conditions for the increased use of office for corrupt purposes. Offices, regarded as private property, were eagerly bought and sold and the expansion of bureaucracy had as much to do with the push from prospective officeholders as from the pull of the state, much as Fletcher described. Tudor economic policy and enforcement expanded the conditions for corrupt practices. In the sixteenth century, the Crown, concerned with employment, economic growth and national pride, established policies simultaneously to discourage imports and to encourage home industries, a policy known today as import substitution. England's main export was woollen cloth as it had been since the time of the twelfth century. Technologically behind the Dutch, the English shipped unfinished wool cloth to Antwerp. Beginning in the 1540s, augmented by the break in wool prices in the 1550s, the Crown turned with energy to the task of diversifying the economy by granting monopolies to new industries. The term "monopoly" denoted a variety of activities, including privileges granted by the sovereign for new inventions and the exclusive trade in some commodity. The latter, "a licence that none shall buy or sell a thing but one alone" came to mean as well the licensing and delegation of the enforcement of economic statutes.[3] From the 1580s on, monopolies were increasingly procured through payoffs and licenses sold.

Whether one sees the Crown as benevolent or predatory, the expansion of government regulation and bureaucracy and the development of monopolies created the conditions for a sizeable increase in corrupt transactions[4] not least because they helped to shape a pattern of behavior known to political economists as "rent-seeking." Rents, which provide profits above costs because of property rights, may be created by government policy. For instance, monopolies confer a surplus profit on the holder above what he might obtain in the free market. Import licensing, permits for industry and control of prices are all examples of government-created rents. Rent-seeking exploits government regulation "as if it were part of the market sphere."[5] Corrupt practices, which grow out of rent-seeking, include bribes to obtain licenses or to avoid the application of established rules such as customs regulations, as well as the corruption of justice and the circumvention of the penal laws.

In the middle ages most outcry against corrupt officials was directed against judges, customs officials, purveyors and local officials such as sheriffs and bailiffs. These were the officials most English people were likely to come in contact with, and those who had the most impact in the areas of the economy the Crown sought to regulate. Complaints about sheriffs and purveyors go back to Henry II's inquest of sheriffs and Magna Carta. The monks of Battle Abbey recorded bribes paid to local officials.[6] In 1376, parliament began to develop the procedure of impeachment to remove Richard Lyons, a leading customs official, from office. To get round regulations, taxes, duties or the misuse of power by officials, the English paid bribes and kickbacks and resorted to smuggling their goods. If medieval administration had its share of corrupt practices, the enlarged state of the Tudors created greater economic opportunity both by increasing state regulations and by extending its administration and its agents. Of 115 penal statutes in force in the middle of James's reign, the great majority had been passed since 1534. In 1604, when the judges compiled a list of statutes to be enforced, they primarily concerned the economy.[7] Where medieval statutes were directed against custom and bullion offenses, the Tudors had extended regulation to many other aspects of the economy, to agriculture, marketing and trade.

II

Policies adopted by the Crown from Elizabeth I to Charles I promoted rent-seeking. Joan Thirsk has argued that the 1540s saw the emergence of projects designed to expand England's economy by establishing new domestic industries to provide work at home and to reduce imports from abroad.[8] This became carefully considered government policy under William, Lord Burghley, who self-consciously pursued a policy of import substitution. In the period from 1540 to 1640 England developed new industries based on consumer demand not just from the elite but from a larger public with an enormous need for pots and pins, stockings and woad.

Thirsk has reversed the view of the projector from the corrupt monopolist of the Jacobean stage to the entrepreneur through whose activities the diversification of English industry took place. The state took an active role in encouraging the introduction of foreign technology by granting patents of monopolies for the mastering of new techniques. Early projects tended to grow quickly into developed industries because of the dispersal of knowledge. Thirsk argues that by 1601 projects had a good record of offering greater work for the poor.[9] In short, the Crown's original aim to provide new employment through import substitution had succeeded.

This successful establishment of new industries at home meant a fall-off in customs duties on goods brought from abroad. As a result the pattern changed in the 1580s when patents of monopoly were granted not only to establish new industries but also to raise monies for the Crown and to reward courtiers. Rich projectors, unlike earlier grantees, were able to take steps to control or dislodge rivals. By 1601 discontent over some monopolies had grown to the point that parliament forced Queen Elizabeth to cancel many patents.

James I at his accession proclaimed all monopolies suspended. In the case of *Darcy* v. *Allen*, the Court of King's Bench declared that monopolies should only be granted

> when any man by his own charge and industry, or by his own wit or invention doth bring any new trade into the realm, or any engine tending to the furtherance of a trade that never was used before; and that for the good of the realm; that in such cases the king may grant to him a monopoly-patent for some reasonable time, until the subjects may learn the same, in consideration of the good that he doth bring by his invention to the commonwealth, otherwise not.[10]

Whether a patent was legal or not was to be determined by common law.

Alongside monopolies arose the privatization of law and order. James I requested the opinion of the judges on the monarch's right to delegate the execution of penal statutes, most of which concerned the economy. The judges expressed concern about allowing the law to be used for private benefit,

> the act, being made ... Parliament, for the general good of the whole realm and of trust committed, to the king, as to the head of justice and of the *weale publique,* the same cannot be prosecuted or executed by his Majesty's grant [other] ... than by the act itself is provided and prescribed. Neither do we find any such grant to any in former ages ... in our experience it maketh the more violent and undue proceedings against the subject to the scandal of justice, and the offence of many. But if by the industry or diligence of any, there accrueth any benefit to his Majesty, after the receipt, such have been rewarded out of the same, at the king's pleasure.[11]

By their last statement, the judges acknowledged the legitimacy of rewarding private individuals for the prosecution of penal statutes after the king had received forfeiture under the law.

By 1604 significant limits had been placed by parliament and the judges on the granting of patents of monopoly and the delegation of the enforcement of penal statutes to private individuals. The king promised in *The Book of Bounty*, drafted in 1608 and published in 1610, not to grant the benefit of penal statutes to individuals. But this was a promise not fully honored. The continuing delegation, indeed privatization, of the enforcement of the law encouraged bribery and extortion.

The Crown, confronted by a lack of resources to administer the law itself and the need to reward its courtiers, began to farm its own judicial functions on a larger scale. Beginning under Elizabeth and increasingly under James, the Crown granted the benefit of penal statutes to a single individual, drawn not from petty tradesmen but from both the gentle and the noble. This is a pattern similar to its grants of monopolies in the same period.

In 1610 the Crown gave Sir Stephen Proctor a patent to pursue those who unlawfully compounded with informers for violation of statutes. Its purpose was to prevent the regulators from conniving with the regulated. In fact, it created one informer where before there had been many. The grant making him "collector of all sums of money payable by reason of any information ... for any forfeiture grounded upon any penal law" since 1558 raised £4,456 in a single term. Proctor's grant came under attack in the parliament of 1610 because "the greatest pressures and grievances to any people in a well governed commonwealth do grow by this: when by colour of authority, show of justice and in direct [execution] of the penal laws the subjects are oppressed and injuriously dealt with."[12] Coke had labelled such activities extortion.

Patents were a form of royal bounty and of indirect taxation since they paid a rent to the Crown. They were an alternative to direct taxation on the landed gentry that parliament had either refused to vote or voted in insufficient amounts. Patents of monopoly, granted in great number under the early Stuarts, were evaluated by a special committee established at the order of the Privy Council. There was an especially large number granted in the period between 1610 and 1620.[13] These patents amounted to an alternative to parliamentary taxation between the failure of the Great Contract, which attempted to create a yearly stipend for the Crown, and the eve of the parliament of 1621. Moreover, in this period, the use of monopolies to support the court and its courtiers had become as crucial to the Crown as the encouragement of native industry.

In 1621 the House of Commons attacked monopolies and monopolists and in 1624 parliament passed the Statute of Monopolies designed to prevent such patents.[14] Sir Edward Coke drafted the original bill. Amended in committee in the House of Commons in 1621 and rejected by the Lords, the bill was reintroduced in 1624 and, with modifications, passed. It presented itself as a petition of right, based on the king's *Book of Bounty* "published in print to the whole Realme and to all Posteritie that all Graunts of [Monapolyes] and of the benefitt of any penal lawes, or of power to dispense with the

Lawe, or to compound for the Forfeiture, are contrary to your Majesties Lawes." The language of the bill was stringent. It barred "all persons, bodies politique or corporate" from using monopolies, defined as "the sole buying, selling, making, working or using any thinge within this Realme," and from compounding for penalties under any law. The validity of patents was to be tried at common law with the penalty triple damages. In committee objections were raised that the bill went too far and would hinder new inventions and possibly invalidate the charters of cities and companies. Provisos added to the bill stated that it would not be prejudicial to the charters and liberties of any city or borough or to grants and letters patents to any company or corporation for any art, occupation or trade. In the end the statute exempted existing grants for terms of years and specific patents such as printing, saltpetre, gunpowder, alum, glassmaking and licensing taverns.[15]

But the history of monopolies does not end there. While the Statute of Monopolies put an end to many projects, it exempted others and left room for judicial and royal interpretation of its clauses, especially over the ten provisos. The grievances presented to King Charles in 1625 during the first parliament of his reign included several patents complained about in 1624 and earlier, including Sir Ferdinando Gorges' monopoly of fishing in New England, Sir John Townshend's patent to inquire into defective land titles, and the patent of surveyorship of Newcastle coal. While the king replied to the grievances by saying that they would be limited or left to the law, Sir Edward Coke and other members were not satisfied, arguing that "when the complaint is that a grievance is against law, it is no answer to say it shall be limited. Therefore in such cases to desire a better answer."[16]

In the 1630s Charles I continued to receive many petitions for projects. The process initiated by James of sending the petitions to advisers continued and the papers of Charles's Attorney-General, Sir John Bankes, are filled with both the petitions and the comments of learned counsel and the king. Rent-seeking behavior continued to characterize both petitioners and the Crown. Charles I asked at times not only if the project were lawful but if it were good for his subjects.[17] His subjects focused on the accumulation of rents.

Petitioners did ask for patents for an array of industrial processes. Industrial patents requested included: the ironworks in the Forest of Dean; the production of iron without charcoal; the making and selling of iron ordnance; the making of sword blades; a new way of heating ovens with coal; the making of latin wire; the alum mines; the glass patent; the draining of the fens; the draining of water from mines; inventions for surveying and navigation; the making of strong waters and vinegar; the erection of snow-houses and the right to sell snow and ice preserved in them; the making of salt from sea water; paper making and making cases for looking-glasses; an engine for cutting timber into thin pieces; a new way to boil great vessels of liquor with less fuel and smoke; and perpetual motion engines.[18]

Patents were also requested for a variety of new agricultural products and techniques. One petition requested a monopoly on the production of a new form of carrot seed which would increase the productivity of the soil, a forerunner of the turnip in English husbandry. The patentee would have the right to discover "corrupt seeds" in return for paying a rent of £20 a year. Others included the curing of rotten sheep; taming and breeding wild fowls; manuring and improving land; a new way of speedily setting corn; the planting of madder; and the production of saffron.[19]

But at least as many projects asked for rights of licensing, to regulate products and behavior, as petitioned for the establishment or reinforcement of new industries and technology. Thomas Jermyn, a member of the king's Household, requested the establishment of an office of surveyors and receivers of the king's fines in all his courts. King Charles rewarded his laundress Agnes Seaton by allowing *her* to grant an office to register and examine bankrupts throughout England and Wales to three others for her long service to the king "ever since his birth and . . . the ease and benefit of his subjects."[20] Other licensing and regulatory projects requested in the 1630s included the enforcement of the assize of bread; the licensing of stairs, ladders and trap-doors on the Thames; the establishment of a commission to inquire into those who have "by color of their places . . . greatly oppressed many subjects by suing in the king's name for debts;" a commission for defective titles; a commission for abuse of receivers; the searching and viewing of silk stockings; the licensing of the export of calfskins and the import of latin wire; the licensing of the transport of remnants of woollen cloth, old shoes, lantern horns, cuttle bone or cuttle shell; the licensing of retail wine sales; and the better planting of brewhouses. One project concerning gold and silver wire was dated, perhaps appropriately, from The Golden Fleece.[21]

Other patents would require merchants to land at Raphe's Quay; establish a commission to look into abuses in gold and silver thread; deliver fines, levied in cases of unjust suits, to the king's servants; establish a duty on beaver hats and require the lease of oyster boats in order to bring down the cost of oysters.

Despite continuing complaints in parliament, petitions were presented for new offices. These included such offices as postmaster; King's Remembrancer; an office to register foreigners; to register and keep the books in all fairs and markets in return for 100 marks a year; a license to print books of fees; a patent for the "sole putting to hire of footcloth horses in order to avoid too many coachers;" an office of registrar to enter sea contracts for ship's freights and men's wages and to arbitrate all differences concerning wages without suit or loss of time. The patentees of fines in the Court of Common

Pleas requested a proclamation to enforce their rights against informers. One month after the Long Parliament began to meet in November 1640, projectors surrendered a patent to compound and grant pardons and licenses to such as had purchased land in mortmain: "being not able to make any advantage by the said grant, they ask that they may surrender it."[22]

During the reign of Charles I, then, projects continued to be proposed and approved despite the Statute of Monopolies of 1624. At the same time the Crown made increased efforts to confront corrupt practices by under-officers by creating patentees to monitor their activities. Thus the Bankes manuscripts show the coincidence of the Crown's efforts to raise money and its attempt to curb abuses by using the delegation of royal rights – often the original cause of the abuses – as its means.[23] The dispensing power, the cause of formidable constitutional conflicts in the later Stuart period, was part and parcel of the Crown's grant of patents of monopoly.

In the later 1630s the Crown began to respond once more, as in 1601 and 1603, with inquiries into abuses in patents of monopoly. A grant made March 14, 1639 to inquire into corrupt practices in suing for royal debts provides a clear contemporary definition of corrupt practices and an explanation to set beside Fletcher's of how they had come about: the movement of private tradesmen into public positions for the purpose of using office as a means of private advantage.

> Divers scriveners, shopkeepers and tradesmen (on purpose to abuse the royal prerogative for their own private profit and unjust ends) have procured themselves to be made farmers, collectors, receivers, bailiffs and accountants to the king; and divers other persons who are not accountants to the king at all have, by colour of their places and employments, greatly oppressed many subjects by suing in the king's name for debts and demands no way appertaining to the king nor applied to his benefit but to themselves and their friends and others whom, either for friendship or lucre, they were pleased to favour.[24]

In return for money and brokage, they had made "deputies and substitutes in great number to enable them to commit the like abuses, who, by colour of such deputations, have in like manner oppressed many subjects ... by which means trade and commerce have been hindered."

To remedy these abuses of under-officers, the Attorney-General was authorized to draw up a commission "to find out all offenses concerning the premises and all such as have in any sort offended ... either as actors and parties or as procurers, to the end that ... they may be brought to justice and severely and condignly punished." So far so good. But the warrant went on to give this commission the power to compound with offenders "for pardons to be passed under the great seal for the offences and all things thereon depending." Those who were found refractory to summonses to appear would be named to the Privy Council. To deal with corrupt practices, the Crown adopted means that resembled those for compounding for the violation of forest laws and distraint of knighthood, which were primarily revenue devices for the Crown. Charles's war on corruption was part of the 1630s policy of "Thorough."

Although the 1630s witnessed a tightening up of administrative procedures, rent-seeking behavior by both Crown and patentees continued. Certain types of licenses were long lived, surviving calumny in one reign to be resurrected in another. One good example is provided by alehouses, a frequent source of concern to government in the sixteenth and seventeenth centuries as centers of disorderly behavior.[25] James I granted a patent of monopoly for their inspection to his courtier Charles Howard, the Earl of Nottingham, who sublet it to Sir Giles Mompesson. The alehouse patent was one of the most notorious of those challenged by parliament in 1621. Yet in 1637 a petitioner asked for a patent to search for illegal wine casks. Basing his argument on statutes of Henry VIII, Elizabeth and James I, the petitioner argued that illegal wine casks were putting out of work the coopers who were supposed to gauge barrels, and that a good yearly revenue might be added to the Crown "by an advised restraining to an orderly number the use of wine cask in every alehouse-keeper's and victualler's house." The patent would prohibit innholders, cooks, tipplers and victuallers from drawing any beer in or out of any great cask without a special license. The patentee argued such licensing was not against the statute of monopolies: it "does not impeach common trade but advances it, does not engross by way of monopoly a public benefit, but restrains a public harm ... and reforms the corruption of the present time and reduces it to ancient use according to the meaning of the laws of the land in that case." Once granted, the patentee promised,

> the sin of drunkenness would not abound as it does; idleness would be suppressed and men of trade would resort to their occupations and bring up apprentices to it; Justices of Peace eased of their travail for suppressing of tipplers; the peace better preserved and the laws less offended; rents of houses not so enhanced; his Majesty better furnished with cask for home and foreign business; the merchants and owners of ships in like sort, and no such voyages overthrown as now be; the price of corn kept more reasonable for the good of his majesty's subjects; people kept and preserved to do his majesty's service in time of need; and a revenue answered to his majesty's coffer yearly, and all good subjects well pleased without prejudice to any.

With such benefits, Sir Anthony Dyet judged the suit commodious and therefore convenient and necessary. Attorney-General Bankes advised the Privy Council not to enrich a private person but to create a royal commission to dispense licenses for wine casks. He found that it had been proposed twenty-two years earlier in 1615. The then Attorney-General certified upon reference from King James "that he held a reformation thereof most necessary, but to be put in execution in his majesty's name and not in the name of any private person." Therefore, Bankes thought "the fittest way" was a proclamation "to inhibit the same to be used by any after a convenient time prefixed other than such as shall be licensed by his majesty or such as shall be by him authorized." A proclamation was accordingly issued and a commission established to issue licenses and pay the king a yearly revenue of £2,000.[26]

From the middle of the sixteenth century, the Crown fostered monopolies as a means of diversifying the economy. In addition, in the 1570s and 1580s it began to grant monopolies for rewards and for revenue. These policies continued in the early Stuart period. With the Crown's decreasing income from its own estate and from parliamentary subsidies, patents and their rents became increasingly important. The status of the patentees changed from low-level producers to courtiers or their clients, as informers changed from petty traders to gentry. Despite parliamentary action against monopolies in 1621 and 1624 and a tightening up of the bureaucracy in the 1630s, the Crown and its subjects continued their rent-seeking behavior. The Crown was forced in 1601, 1603 and 1639 to rescind most of its grants of monopoly because of parliamentary opposition or the fear of it.

III

If the Crown's social and economic policies fostered rent-seeking, legal procedures in the sixteenth and seventeenth centuries relied on private agents to provide information especially about illegal practices under the economic statutes. Because it lacked a paid local bureaucracy, the Crown was forced to rely on informal agents to enforce its laws. Corrupt practices are carried out by the agents of the state and those with whom they interact. The agent of the state in sixteenth and seventeenth-century England operated in both formal and informal guises. Some agents were members of the central and local administration, others were informal agents of the court such as courtiers who served as middlemen in transactions and private individuals who served as informers in court actions. Put another way, the parties to these transactions ranged from courtiers and great merchants on the highest level to under-officials, such as purveyors, searchers, and informers and local merchants, tradesmen and peasants on the lower level, a reflection of the early modern enforcement of law and policy by public officials and private individuals in their own as well as the Crown's interest.

Maurice P. Beresford has argued that informers were "the chief instruments for the enforcement of economic legislation" from the late 1530s to 1624. Informations in customs and foreign trade were predominant up until 1551;

143

between 1551 and 1624 they made up only one-quarter to one-third of the informations laid; after the reforms of 1624, the former returned to their dominance.[27] In the mid-sixteenth century informers were seen as a positive means of prosecuting "rent-raisers, oppressors of the poor, extortioners, bribers, usurers."[28] But while efforts were made in 1552 to encourage informers, there was criticism of those motivated "partly for their own singular gain, partly for malice, corruption and other devilish affection."[29] Not all informers were corrupt, of course, but accusations of corrupt practices among informers were prevalent in contemporary complaint literature. In the thirtieth year of Elizabeth's reign one John Crapnall was committed to the Fleet for exhibiting seventy informations in King's Bench, only one of which was brought to trial.[30] Such evidence is reinforced by the number of informations laid in the Court of Exchequer, the chief forum of the informer. Most were not followed up beyond the original laying of the information. This has led historians to the suspicion that informers often made informal compositions with those they accused.[31]

Most informers used

> the laying of informations as a means of supplementing income as petty tradesmen and artisans. When corrupt, their extortion was usually modest, ranging from 5*s* to 10*s* to the £200 reported from Wiltshire tradesmen in the 1630s. One Elizabethan informer collected 20*s* for each instance in which he did not inform, another required £3 down with an installment of 13*s* 4*d* and a lifetime annuity of 20*s*.[32]

Informers were an accepted if disliked part of the judicial machinery both in economic regulation and penal law. Informations waxed and waned. The informer was thus not just a Jacobean figure; the 1560s witnessed totals close to those of 1610–20. Even in the midst of parliamentary debate in 1621, Sir Edward Coke, a long-time opponent of informers, said that "informers must not be quite taken away but regulated."[33]

As they had moved against high-level officials, the Crown and parliament tried during James I's reign to curb the abuses of informers, "ever odious, commonly varlets."[34] The Crown responded to the continuing outcry against informers and to the reduction in Crown income from out-of-court settlements. In 1604 a bill was introduced into parliament to reform the abuses of informers. The Privy Council began to take action against corrupt practices among informers beginning in 1617 shortly after the informations laid in the Exchequer reached their peak. It called on justices of the peace to collect evidence of abuses and summoned those cited. In addition, it ordered the Barons of the Exchequer to stay informations under certain regulations, such as wool-dealing, the retaining of butter and cheese, importation of playing cards and the East India Company, all of which had contributed to the boom in informing. These actions were successful. Informations in the Exchequer fell off drastically. In addition, parliament in 1624 passed three statutes to decrease corrupt practices: the Statute of Monopolies, the Repeal of Penal Laws, which cancelled fifty concerned with economic crimes, and a bill for the easement of the subject, which required most informations to be laid in the localities. The threat of an Exchequer action posed by informers and the time and distance it imposed on a defendant had been decisively removed.

The Crown remained concerned about informers. In the case of Joseph Sutton who was fined in Star Chamber in 1635, Sir John Bankes noted that he was "not brought hither because he is an informer but for his abuse." His abuse lay in taking up informing as a trade over a five-year period. He

> intrudes himself into all public business, intermeddles in matters of state, informs in all courts for all manner of offences against the common law, statute laws, and proclamations, and pretends himself to be a public minister to put the laws and edicts in execution, and that in public business which no way concerns himself, not in zeal to the public but for private ends ... He confesseth that in divers suits ... he never put in a bill; in others he hath put in bills but took out no process of contempt

receiving composition instead from his victims.

In language common to Crown, parliament and pulpit, Bankes denounced

> these perverters of justice, these prevaricators, the vermin and caterpillars of a republic, who inform merely for themselves and for their private ends and not for the king nor for the commonwealth, I wish that by your lordships' sentence, not only this delinquent at the bar but by his example all other common traders in this kind might be rooted out of this kingdom.

Sutton was fined £1,000; he was to stand upon the pillory bedecked with papers and disabled from further informing.[35] Nevertheless, of the statutes that remained actionable at Westminster, most were economic.[36] Indeed by the 1630s the investigation of informers had itself become the subject of patents of monopoly, a case of the parasite feeding on itself.[37]

The large number of informations actually laid in the Court of the Exchequer in the period may argue against simple extortion, but does support Christopher Clay's notion that "craftsmen and traders could not carry on their ordinary livelihood without being technically in breach of the law ... ultimately the fines had to be paid by consumers in the form of higher prices."[38] Beresford labels the penal statutes "a political irritant ... a means of private profit and lawyers' fees, and an irregular charge on manufacturers and trade." The Crown's method of enforcing economic regulations and the rent-seeking behavior of its subjects had an unlooked-for effect on the English economy.

IV

The English economy in the early seventeenth century was shaped by striking population growth and the inflation of prices. At the end of the sixteenth century "grain prices were about six times, meat livestock and animal products between three and a half and four and a half times and industrial products rather less than two and a half times what they had been a hundred years before," according to Christopher Clay.[39] Wages had doubled but the cost of living for the building worker, for instance, was close to five times that of 1500. Agricultural prices continued to rise, although more slowly, in the early seventeenth century. It should be noted that the cost of living then, as now, must be scaled according to status group. For well-to-do merchants and landed aristocracy the basic stuffs of life formed only a small part of their expenditure. But the late sixteenth century saw some changed forms of spending: the taste for new luxury goods imported from the east and the new fashion of a town house in London in addition to a house in the country. This was of crucial significance to the increasing prevalence and price of corrupt practices.

Corrupt practices had differing impact in each of the sectors of agriculture, manufacturing, internal and external trade and finance. England was predominantly agrarian in the seventeenth century. At least 80 per cent of the population was engaged in agriculture. In the late sixteenth century, the pull of population increased trade in agricultural products. Commercial farming increased. London, in particular, served as the locus of demand. Landowners seeking to increase their incomes during an inflationary period helped to increase commercialized farming, which generated a high rate of return in the sixteenth and early seventeenth centuries and provided a surplus for reinvestment. Landlords increased their investments in their estates as testified by the open fields newly enclosed and the efforts to reclaim land from waste. But, in general, investment in agriculture remained low. Given surplus funds, landowners preferred to buy more land or lend money at high interest rates of 8 to 10 per cent in the early seventeenth century. Landowners with surplus to spare invested in mining and trade.[40] Rent-seeking behavior was more likely as a result. If most English people were involved in land, whether as landlords, yeomen or peasants, they were not necessarily solely employed in farming. Peasants made additional money as industries spread out to rural areas in the sixteenth and seventeenth centuries.

Agriculture offered room for corrupt practices because of the extensive Tudor regulations governing land usage. The agrarian statutes developed by the Tudors dealt with four sorts of issues: the cutting of wood, enclosure and engrossing, the size of flocks of sheep and the balance of milk cows to sheep. Since informers were part of the enforcement procedures, their role might lead to corruption either by bribing to get round statutes or extortion by Crown agents.

Statutes against depopulating enclosure and engrossing had been enacted in the fifteenth century. With the dearth of grain in the 1590s such laws were revived.[41] In 1607 the Midland revolt, an uprising against enclosure, broke out in three counties. As a result, the government initiated a commission of inquiry followed by prosecutions and fines in Star Chamber. But the Crown was beginning to see the benefits of enclosure and in 1618 appointed a commission to grant exemptions from tillage statutes. The rationale was that corn was in good supply and that informers had acted unlawfully. "Some great offenders were spared by connivance of the informer, and others that were innocent were vexed without end."[42] In 1624 the tillage statute of 1563 was repealed, and thereafter that of 1597 went unenforced.

The act against enclosure (keeping excessive number of sheep) of 25 Henry VIII, c. 13, passed in 1534, provided an equal division of the money penalties between the Crown and informers. Yet of the 25,000 or so informations examined by Beresford, only 4 per cent dealt with strictly agrarian offenses, which is remarkable in view of agriculture's dominance of the economy. Moreover the peak year for the laying of informations under agrarian statutes was 1584. These statistics suggest that landowners did not suffer from corrupt practices in informing as much as did traders and manufacturers. Marketing offenses, however, made up 43 per cent of the informations laid in the Exchequer. These offenses included engrossing of grain and other stuffs, the illegal sale of animals, sale outside a market or fair, forestalling, regrating (that is, buying up and reselling grain in the same or nearby market) and other illegal sales. The agricultural sector of the economy was more likely, then, to suffer corrupt practices in the enforcement of statutes regulating the market rather than land usage in the early Stuart period. Indeed the peak year for marketing offenses was 1613.[43] In the 1630s the Caroline government used these statutes to raise taxes by establishing another commission to investigate enclosure, which "condoned as much as it condemned."[44]

If tillage statutes affected primarily the well-to-do landowners, corruption in purveyance affected all those engaged in agriculture, especially those living in the southern counties.[45] Purveyance, the king's ancient prerogative to take foodstuffs and carts at a price below the market to enable the court to travel around the countryside, had long been the subject of complaint. Neither the Crown's effort to levy composition on counties in lieu of purveyance under Elizabeth, nor parliamentary statutes against the corrupt practices of the purveyors, such as taking carts at harvest or extorting money not to take carts or foodstuffs, proved effective. After the issue was raised in the first parliament of James I, his privy councillors made new efforts to deal with the problem. The victims of these corrupt practices were the poor; their oppressors yeomen, merchants, even gentlemen who bought their commission. Corrupt practices in purveyance were also as old as the court itself; its abuses were attacked in clauses 28 and 30 of Magna Carta. If the tillage statutes went unenforced, purveyance was enforced with a will after the failure of the Great Contract in the parliament of 1610. It remained a source of discontent and was finally abolished in 1660. It became a potent political issue but it is arguable that its impact on land usage was minimal.

It was in trade, especially foreign trade, that corrupt practices had their greatest impact on the English economy. Collusive transactions between merchants and customs officials took the form of smuggling and the paying of bribes to courtiers for the enormously valuable monopoly rights to trade in certain commodities. Smuggling existed on a giant scale by the beginning of the eighteenth century.[46] By 1733 it was estimated that one-third of all goods traded between England, Holland and France was smuggled. G. D. Ramsay argues that large-scale smuggling began in the late sixteenth century. The causes were several: the break in the Antwerp woollen market which changed the control of trade by the Merchant Adventurers; the steep rise in prices in the sixteenth century; the increasing imports of luxury goods; and the growing exports of other items. The sale of offices and the low level of fees, characteristic of early modern administration, made customs officials and those who named them vulnerable to bribery. The Duke of Norfolk, for instance, took pride in the fact "that he had never taken bribes for the appointment of customs officials though all his predecessors had."[47]

The Crown's augmentation of the Book of Rates in 1558 to increase its income helped to make collusion, extraction and smuggling a very profitable business, especially since many customs officers were themselves merchants.[48] Smugglers were selective; they tended to smuggle goods of high value, packaged in small units. David Sacks had pointed out that in Bristol, one of the main English ports and centers of smuggling, wine, tobacco and currants were especially favored illicit cargo.

Trade was hampered not only by increased rates but by legal and financial regulations. Tax collection interfered with trade and made it important for the merchant to have friends both in the customs and the Exchequer. The costs of smuggling, Sacks suggests, compared favorably to the sixteenth and seventeenth-century customs.[49] In the 1550s the government was notified of thousands of fabrics smuggled to Antwerp. It responded by passing in the first year of Elizabeth's reign the Act of Frauds which cited the evasion of customs duties by "many greedy and covetous persons respecting more their private gain and commodity than their duty and allegiance or the common profit of the realm." The act attacked both merchants who conveyed their wares from places where no customs official resided and officials who through "negligence or corruption … as by diverse other fraudulent undue and subtle practices and devises, allowed them to convey good without paying customs."[50] The act forbade landing or loading goods except at places which had a resident customs officer and during daylight. In 1566 parliament passed an act calling for the forfeiture of all goods, a year's imprisonment, and the cutting off of the left hand for smuggling sheep or lamb overseas.[51] In addition to statutes, Lord Burghley began to try to strengthen the customs administration by building a new customs house and monitoring customs officials.

Collusion between officials and merchants was an important form of corrupt practice in trade. Ties between city merchants and customs officials were close throughout England. One contemporary accusation about the export of Norfolk corn said that "if it be without licence and all stolen out, ye may be sure the customers and other that sort of officers be privy to it." In the 1550s merchants accused customs officers of trading though third parties and showed how they had gained great wealth "within eleven or twelve years worth thousands" while their clerks "were not able to have … so much as a pair of hosen to their loins."[52] To handle such accusations the Elizabethan administration removed and fined dishonest officers in the 1560s, but by the 1570s the web of customers, merchants and loans to the government had become too important to Crown finance. Regarding the customs officials, the queen herself wrote to Lord Treasurer Winchester of "the decept of some, the corruption of others and the negligence of the rest."[53]

William Byrde was the collector of the petty duties, a member of the Mercers' company and part of a group making short-term loans to the government. In 1572, he was found guilty in Queen's Bench of customs violations but the Privy Council took up the case and fined him merely for the negligent oversight of his clerk who was said to have entered mistaken entries. Byrde's case coincided with the government's turning to the farming of the customs as an alternative to its direct administration. This policy tacitly admitted the likelihood that the customers would make out well. By farming the customs, the Crown received an annual rent which could be increased and others administered the customs. The assumption was that the customers would deal with the merchant community of which they themselves were a part and provide the Crown not only with rent but also short-term loans. The Elizabethans did not wholeheartedly embrace the farming of the customs and in the 1590s returned to direct administration while food and ordnance continued to be smuggled to the Spanish even in the midst of war.

With the accession of James I, Crown policy changed and the customs were systematically farmed. The king received an annual rent, his kingdom was provided with a customs service manned by leading merchants and the king's officials accepted bribes to ensure that "their merchants" retained the farms. The Crown now received most of its permanent revenue from the customs rather than from the Crown lands. Rent-seeking is seen most clearly in the close connection of leading merchants, aristocratic patrons, and the Crown which depended on short-term loans.[54] Leading officials such as the Earl of Salisbury and the Earl of Nottingham often had personal interests in trade and were often in debt to leading merchants.[55] The growing importance of the customs to the Crown's annual revenues helps to explain the Crown's increasing focus on customs rates, impositions and tonnage and poundage. The rates were raised in 1604. In addition, impositions were levied on top of the standard 5 per cent on many goods.[56] Indeed, impositions and tonnage and poundage became important political issues in the early Stuart period.

If we turn from trade to industry, corrupt practices appear in bribery to gain monopoly rights, corrupt dealings by projectors in their handling of their projects, collusive activity with government officials and the investment of corrupt gains by officeholders in manufacturing projects.

New and larger-scale forms of industries emerged in the sixteenth and seventeenth centuries, especially in mining, metal and manufacturing finished goods such as paper, gunpowder and wire-making.[57] Nevertheless, technology did not improve greatly in the period, and many branches of industry were carried on as they had been in 1500, in the homes of the workers or in small workshops using inexpensive modes of production. Large-scale capital was not necessary for most industry; what was available often came from three sources: the savings of peasants doing industrial work on the side; urban merchants; and successful craftsmen reinvesting their profits. In mining, landlords frequently provided the capital for industries on their own lands.

Merchants involved in overseas commerce played a limited role in investment in manufacturing. Most of what they lent was spent by aristocratic clients on conspicuous consumption.[58] Some were involved, alongside courtiers, in patents of monopoly granted in the late sixteenth and early seventeenth centuries, which brought new techniques to older industries and produced new goods at home.[59] Sir Robert Mansell's participation in the glass industry provides one example.

Sir Robert Mansell, the younger son of a Welsh gentry family, received preferment through the favor of his cousin, Charles Howard, Earl of Nottingham and Lord Admiral, and served as Treasurer of the Navy under James I. Although different investigations of the navy, as we have seen, had accused him of corrupt practices, Mansell remained in office, perhaps with the support of the Prince of Wales, and sold his office in 1619. After serving on the board of the Virginia Company and participating in the East India Company, Mansell secured the patent for the making of glass. Mansell's process, which used coal instead of wood, brought down the price of glass and produced various kind of glassware not made in England before. The glass patent was excepted from the Statute of Monopolies and, until 1635, there was no evidence of graft or bribery in connection with the glass patents granted for the coal process. Mansell apparently fulfilled his promise to furnish England "with good glass of all sorts at moderate prices."[60] The Crown's granting of the patent to change from wood to coal in the Elizabethan period brought "cheap fuel, improved technology and a climate of opinion congenial to experimentation. What had been in 1560 a luxury item had now been made a general consumer item in windows and bottles."[61] Mansell provides an important example of the investment of gains from corrupt practices, in his case from the navy, to developing industry.

Transfer payments were the means of corrupt practices and redistribution of wealth the result. We have seen that in agriculture, purveyance generally transferred monies from the poor or the landed to petty officials; customs offenses on the lower level transferred monies from traders and merchants to petty officials. On the higher level, leading merchants paid off courtiers drawn primarily from the nobility and gentry. From another point of view, these practices were collusive. In a "second best" situation, merchants contrived with their noble patrons to share the benefits obtained from getting round state controls. This helps to explain the political outrage in the 1630s when Charles I tried to establish a more efficient and indeed more honest bureaucracy.

The issue of profits from office has been much explored by English historians with the consensus that such profits were not substantial enough to found many new fortunes. In reality, office often imposed expenditures beyond the income received.[62] The difference between three to four years' purchase for office (ie. the price of office, usually three to four times its annual income) and fifteen to twenty years' purchase for land (the price of land, fifteen to twenty times its annual income) reflects not only the greater insecurity of office and life expectancy and the greater prestige of land but also perhaps some notion of the limits of the profits available from office. Still, profit from corrupt practices such as bribery and extortion provided additional income to many officeholders. As a result, brokers and rent-seekers frequently transferred money from commerce to land or to conspicuous consumption. Indeed even in the early nineteenth century at the time of the Industrial Revolution the largest fortunes were those not of manufacturers or entrepreneurs, but the old administrative classes.[63] As we shall see, transfer payments within the landed elite were one of the most important results of corrupt practices.[64] These transfers occurred through the extraction practised by court officials from those who used their services.

V

Since the 1960s economists, political scientists and sociologists have asserted the close connection of corruption and modernization and the efficacy of corrupt practices in promoting political integration and economic development in the Third World. While focusing on developing nations, the most prominent theorists including Professors Samuel Huntington and James C. Scott have cited early modern England to provide evidence of these assertions.[65] "Modernization" is an attractive catch-all explanation because it is not explicit about when or just exactly what is occurring. While Professor Huntington has argued for the conjuncture of corrupt practices and the industrial revolution, Professor Scott has focused on early Stuart England, arguing that the corrupt practices much complained of in the period can be directly linked to new wealth elites who had to circumvent the abundance of Tudor–Stuart economic regulations.[66] By their evasion these commercial groups helped promote English economic growth. Many examples in this chapter support some part of this argument.

The hypothesis of a nexus of economic growth and corrupt practices is three pronged. First, the argument goes that in an economy controlled by a top-heavy bureaucracy burdened with red tape, the market operates so that the most efficient entrepreneur is able to pay the largest bribe and thereby secure the contract. Nathaniel Leff has argued that "with competition forcing prices up, the favors will tend to be allocated to those who can pay the highest prices. In the long run the favors will go to the most efficient producers."[67] Bribery, then, acts as a way of weeding out the inefficient. Second, the bribed official uses his graft so as to promote economic growth by investing in trade or in new forms of production. Third, financial and commercial interests, closed off from political power in traditional societies or developing nations, obtain access to benefits informally. As a result their ability to engage in economic activities is enhanced, and they play a larger economic role in what was previously a closed system. If the link made between corrupt practices and economic growth is correct, we should find substantial evidence of it in the careers of the leading merchants and the richest and most powerful officials in early Stuart England.

We need to distinguish between trade and manufacturing. During the sixteenth and early seventeenth centuries, there was significant growth in England's overseas trade. This trade was often controlled by the great chartered companies such as the Merchant Adventurers, the Levant Company, and the East India Company. Members of these companies had close connections with the Crown.[68] In the case of the Merchant Adventurers, their livelihood depended on the Crown's issue of licenses to export unfinished cloth in spite of parliamentary statutes against the practice. There is little doubt that by paying bribes for such favorable treatment the Merchant Adventurers contributed to the expansion of English trade. Moreover, Robert Ashton has closely analyzed the relationship of the import–export traders and Crown concessionaires. The foremost among these were the syndicates that farmed the king's customs. The Great Farm, organized in 1604, was granted by King James to a group led by Sir William Garway and Francis Jones, clients of the Lord Treasurer, Thomas Sackville, Earl of Dorset, and Robert Cecil, Earl of Salisbury, to whom they paid substantial sums to obtain the concession. In the absence of financial institutions, these customs farmers soon became the leading and continuing source of loans to the Crown and to their patrons. Who were they? Francis Jones and another member of the syndicate, John Wolstonholme, were customs officials. Sir William Garway was a founding member of the East India Company and, along with his partner in the Great Farm, Nicholas Salter, a prominent Levant merchant. Garway's son Henry, who continued to be active in the Great Farm, also became governor of the Levant Company, the East India Company and the Greenland and Russia Companies. Many customs farmers were involved in various aspects of international trade at the same time as they were government concessionaires. Ashton points out that "capital from orthodox commerce flowed into customs farms ... patents and other concessions and the fruits of this investment in turned flowed back into commerce."[69] Rent-seeking behavior coexisted with production and trade for the free market.

The connection between corrupt practices, especially the bribes paid to gain such concessions, and economic growth is plain in the careers of the customs farmers. But one or two additional points must be made. First, the Garway syndicate retained its hold on the customs despite better offers from other merchants, such as Sir John Swinnerton in 1608 and in 1612–13. Repeated efforts to dislodge them failed because of their stranglehold on the king's officials and favorites who were overwhelmingly in their debt.[70] Secondly, some of the great merchants of Jacobean London did not participate in these farms. Others, like Lionel Cranfield, divested themselves of their commercial ties as they moved into customs farming and government service.[71] If investment in trade was replaced by investment in office, or in land, the positive impact on economic growth may be questioned. Finally, with so much attention focused on the glamorous export trade, merchants who invested in domestic trade have tended to be overlooked. These were not the country cousins from the outports but other London merchants whose major investments were in internal trade in textiles, food and fuel. Of the 140 London merchants who served as aldermen between 1600 and 1625 fewer than half had their primary investment in overseas trade.[72] The rest invested primarily in domestic trade where the need to pay bribes to secure licenses or to get round regulations was not so important. In short, even if in this economic version of the survival of the fittest some of the most wealthy productive entrepreneurs did secure government favors, others, often as wealthy, did not bother. Rent-seeking behavior was not characteristic of all early Stuart merchants.

In manufacturing, it is not at all clear that the largest bribes were paid by the most successful entrepreneurs for manufacturing rights, as two examples,

Alderman Cockayne's project and the alum business, will show. Arguing for a finishing industry at home, in order to jolt the Merchant Adventurers from their accustomed place in the marketing of English cloth, Alderman Cockayne was rumored to have paid bribes particularly to Thomas Howard, Earl of Suffolk (the Lord Treasurer) and Robert Carr, Earl of Somerset, the king's favorite. But the result of bribery in this case was to replace the experienced company with a syndicate lacking the infrastructure, the financing and the trading connections to make good on its promise to develop a new export industry in finished cloth. In three years it had brought about a sharp decline in the traditional English cloth trade which had just reached its peak in 1614, the year Cockayne received his patent. By 1617 the Crown had once again granted to the Merchant Adventurers their traditional privileges, although at the cost of another bribe to Lord Treasurer Suffolk.[73] It is hard to find any connection between the Cockayne project and economic growth although it is easy to document the transfer payments from merchants to officials.

The situation is somewhat similar in the production of alum, a mineral used in dying cloth. Queen Elizabeth had begun to encourage the home industry, and when alum was discovered in Yorkshire in 1607, King James subsidized a variety of syndicates to provide the material to the home market at reasonable rates. A succession of farmers tried unsuccessfully to meet this objective in which the king had invested perhaps as much as £100,000, some of it appropriated by agents. Although the mines ultimately began to pay back some of the royal investment, the project remained parlous. One farmer wrote to another in 1619:

> I go in fear of the workmen, who clamor for pay ... it being a lamentable thing to see a multitude of poor snakes tattered and naked and ready to starve for want of food and clothes, not finding any credit for bread and drink because they are unpaid for three months and some four ... and some of them this day arrested and carried to prison for their diet.

If the creation of an above-subsistence wage scale is requisite to consumer demand, the alum business was a disaster. Did its projectors at least profit? Not so if one goes by this same letter, for the farmer wrote: "I am undone by this business, and so will you be if you cannot work yourself out of it."[74]

It might be argued that thesse manufactures would ultimately make their mark. By 1750 the finishing industry and the alum industry had become domesticated. The policy of diversifying the English economy ultimately proved successful after 1650; its foundation was laid under Elizabeth.[75] But instead of being an aid to such manufactures, corrupt practices may rather have constituted a hiccup. Indeed, they were much the same sort of bottleneck that technological backwardness was in the diversification of

English industry between 1500 and 1750. During the Jacobean period, corrupt practices proved a hindrance to manufacturers, not an aid, but were tolerated in hopes that in the long term they would prove profitable.

If entrepreneurs who bribed officials were not always or even usually the most efficient producers or traders, what about the theorists' second point, the productive investment of these funds by corrupt officeholders? Three obvious cases of bribery among the king's highest officials permit an examination of how these proceeds from office were invested. All three had close connections to the customs farmers. If there is an ideal type of the modernizing bureaucrat in early Stuart England, it is Robert Cecil, son of Elizabeth's minister Lord Burghley, Secretary of State to Elizabeth and James and, between 1608 and 1612, Lord Treasurer. He was one of the handful of privy councillors to analyze and to try to change the archaic way in which the Crown was funded.[76] From office, from payoffs, from customs farmers, from Spanish pensions, Salisbury amassed a gigantic income. Lawrence Stone has estimated that his income from office, patents and gratuities was double his landed income.[77] How did he spend it? Much of it went to the upkeep of his family and his household; £11,000 more went to the repayment of loans (often his creditors were the same merchants to whom he had granted the Crown's lucrative customs farms). About £26,500 went equally into buying land and into building. Indeed, Stone suggests that it was the building of Hatfield House that raised the level of extraction that Salisbury required.[78] There is little question that in putting together these lands, in building his country house and city palace, Salisbury laid the basis for the long-term inheritance of the Cecils. Whether that aided England's economic growth in the early Stuart period or merely concentrated landed property in the hands of the Cecils remains doubtful. While the building of such palaces might set the underemployed to work, it might also have a deleterious effect on its neighborhood by taking labor away from productive manufacturing or trade.[79]

In one important area Salisbury did make a substantial commercial investment. In the creation of the New Exchange and in his part in the urban development of the Strand and St Martin's Lane, Salisbury created, indeed promoted, an important real estate venture to cater to aristocrats, officeholders and lawyers ensconced in London's newly developing West End. Called "Britain's Bourse" by King James, Salisbury's New Exchange was a combination stock exchange, real estate agency, and Burlington arcade. Salisbury paid almost £12,000 for the New Exchange in land and building costs and he leased its management to a syndicate of customs farmers. This ambitious venture proved a successful investment from 1611 to 1617 and again in the 1630s, but earned its greatest profits after the Restoration from 1661 to 1681. Thereafter it slowly declined and was torn down in 1737. But the reasons why Salisbury built this ambitious complex illustrate the values of his era. He consulted Inigo Jones on its façade, adorned it with marble sculpture and pillars and celebrated its opening with an entertainment for King James composed by Ben Jonson. Culture is not, of course, incompatible with money-making, but Salisbury seems as much like a seventeenth-century connoisseur as a twentieth-century shopping mall magnate. Even so, this extraordinary commercial venture did not equal his expenditure on Hatfield House which amounted to almost £40,000.[80] There were other peers who invested in business ventures, but it may be significant that many of them remained outside the golden circle of royal reward. Salisbury's career undeniably shows the massive transfer of the profits of trade from the customs farmers who were his clients away from such trading ventures and into land, both rural and urban, for an estate that has lasted until the present.

If Salisbury was the dominant political figure of the early Jacobean period, George Villiers, Duke of Buckingham, dominated the court from 1618 until 1628 when he was assassinated. Roger Lockyer documents how rapidly Buckingham made his fortune.[81] In 1619 Buckingham received £5,000 in landed income, £4,000 from office, £4,500 from sale of office and honors and almost £3,000 from customs farms as well as a £1,000 pension. The total, Lockyer reckons, was about £18,000. As to Buckingham's expenditure, most went on building, display, hospitality and land purchases. He even loaned funds to the English war effort in the 1620s, paying the expenses of the fleet of which he was admiral. Warfare, of course, had an important impact on the economy of early modern states. Such loans might have some effect on production for military equipment. But this is "trickle down" theory indeed.

The third great magnate for analysis is Thomas Howard, Earl of Suffolk. His profits from office came from his control of court favor which he shared with the king's favorite, Robert Carr, Earl of Somerset, who had married his daughter Frances. Suffolk had long-term dealings with concessionaires. He had farmed the currants farm in the early years of James's reign through Sir Arthur Ingram, one of several merchants who became the well-paid middlemen between courtiers and the great merchants and built up their own landed estates out of the profits. Suffolk was greatly in debt to his own clients. Like Salisbury and Buckingham, Suffolk had close ties to the Great Customs farmers to whom he owed a debt of £10,000. After tough negotiation with them, "to avoid the Earl's displeasure and such inconveniences as they might fall into" the farmers agreed to pay him £1,500 a year for seven years to be set against his debt – so long as he remained Lord Treasurer and they the farmers of the customs. A supporter of the Cockayne project, when the Merchant Adventurers were once again granted their customary privileges by the king in 1617, Suffolk was paid £3,300 in gold "for his favor and to the intent that he should not oppose against them."[82] Suffolk's is a familiar story.

Again, like Salisbury and Buckingham, he wound up in great debt because of his building activities at Charing Cross, Newmarket and especially at Audley End, the largest palace constructed in that extravagant era.

By focusing on corrupt practices involving wealthy merchants and efforts to get round economic controls, scholars have missed other types of corrupt practices prevalent in this period. Suffolk, his wife Katherine and Sir John Bingley, his agent, made it a habit to use Exchequer funds for themselves and to extort kickbacks from other government officials. In particular, they were accustomed to use money appointed for Irish services for themselves, so that the army in Ireland went unpaid. To secure these revenues Crown officials in Ireland agreed to kickback £1,000 a year to Suffolk and £200 to Bingley. After paying six months' worth of bribes they still went unpaid. Among the Suffolks' victims were Sir Miles Fleetwood, Sir David Murray and Thomas, Lord Ridgeway, Treasurer at War in Ireland, all government officers. Sir Allen Apsley, for instance, "within six years last past hath given Sir John Bingley six hundred and sixty pounds besides an usual New Year's gift to obtain payment of money due for victualling his Majesty's navy."[83] Payments were demanded not only by Suffolk, his wife and Bingley, but even his son. Perhaps the scale of corruption varied not only with building projects but also the size of kinship networks.

Analyses which focus on merchants bribing officials for economic gain omit a whole range of payoffs at the early Stuart court, including kickbacks by one officeholder to another and misappropriation of funds. If the landed gentry were the principal officeholders in this period, those who paid off were usually landed gentlemen too. Corruption in these latter cases had as much to do with political power and economic transfers within the political elite as with merchants buying economic privilege.

It may be useful to look at the economy more generally. The principal choice for investment in England in the early seventeenth century was land, because it conferred status and because other forms of investment were lacking. The return on land waxed and waned with changing cereal and wool prices. In fact, England's yield on cereal grains in the first half of the seventeenth century was less than that of France, Italy and Spain in the first half of the sixteenth century. Improved yields only occurred after 1650. The prosperity of the landowner in the period is now thought to have depended less upon his social origins or the origins of his capital and more upon the nature of his land and "its sensitivity to economic change."[84] In other areas of investment such as the cloth trade and shipping, the statistics are equally revealing: there was a serious depression in the cloth trade in the 1620s and 1630s. In shipping there was an increase of a third between 1609 and 1660. What is striking is that while foreign trade makes up the largest portion of tonnage in 1582 and again in 1702, in the first half of the seventeenth century collier trade was the most important component;

indeed, it doubled in this period.[85] Commercial interests were certainly important in England by the early seventeenth century, but they did not strike a bargain with the Crown at the expense of the aristocracy, contrary to Scott's suggestion.[86] Rather they gained access to economic privileges through and with aristocratic courtiers who were their patrons. Much of the bribery at the early Stuart court was of the gentry, for the gentry, by the gentry.

Of course, courtiers were interested in profits. One telling example is the Scottish courtier, Sir John Seton, who resented the efforts of Thomas Wentworth, Earl of Strafford, to oversee the Irish plantation. In particular, Seton was unhappy with Strafford's insistence that Irish planters guarantee royal rents, hold land by knight service, and even reside in Ireland. Seton complained that "he has made so harsh conditions as a man that has little money can hardly embrace them ... a man that will have 1000 acres must have £1300 in his pocket, for the which cause I will bid Ireland adieu and visit the fens of Lincolnshire."[87] Early Stuart courtiers did not lack a capitalist mentality; what they lacked in the main were investment opportunities. While most of their profits went into land, without detailed study it would be impossible to suppose that all corrupt officeholders were also improving landlords. Indeed, most officeholders made too little from their offices to invest large amounts in land.[88] And those who paid for corruption included the king and the poor as well as the bourgeoisie.

To see the productive investment of profits both in agriculture and manufacturing, attention should turn from City financiers, royal favorites, and crown servants, toward people like the Lowther family of Cumberland who came to dominate the coal trade. Sir John Lowther wrote in 1636: "I care not for honar, whitch now in England is tituler and the shaddow of what was, and without power, nor for pleasure as an enemie to health, nor for wealth, whitch is not got nor kept without danger and am resolved, in a faire prudent way to husband our fortunes."[89]

The theory connecting corruption and economic growth reflects the view that large sums of capital for investment were required to bring about the industrial revolution. In casting about for such sums in the seventeenth century, it is not surprising that one would be struck by the payoffs made by important merchants to early Stuart magnates. Jan de Vries has pointed out, however, that esoteric sources of capital were not central to this transformation. What was necessary was the preservation and productivity of the capital stock already in existence. In that sense the major weakness of early modern Europe was not inadequacy of capital but misinvestment and dissipation.[90]

To conclude, between the sixteenth and eighteenth centuries in England, corrupt practices actually functioned as the normal means by which the Crown and the aristocracy maintained their traditional political and economic control, indeed, how they ensured the status quo.[91] While corruption also allowed commercial elites access to political and economic power, such access was usually in association with their aristocratic patrons. There is little evidence to show that corruption aided capital formation for investment in growth industries or consistently allocated rewards to the most enterprising. It was neither the key to nor an important part of England's economic growth. In fact at times such as the Jacobean period, corrupt practices may have acted to retard economic growth by levying too high an invisible tax on production and trade.

Where modernization theory fails to explain the relationship of politics to the economy, "rent-seeking" theory is perhaps more successful.[92] The Elizabethan policy of diversifying the economy has unintended effects. It not only encouraged entrepreneurs and inventors, it also produced vested interests of rent-seekers, both those in old monopolies who wanted to limit entrants and those who sought new monopolies through an appeal to the Crown's wish for more industries. By the 1620s such licenses could only be provided through the patronage of aristocratic brokers.

The turning point in the Crown's policy on projects, which now included not only new trades and inventions but also monopolies of government functions and government offices, came in the challenge posed by parliament. Beginning in 1601 and culminating in the Statute of Monopolies in 1624 parliament consistently sought to limit royal monopolies.[93] This challenge came not from doctrines of free trade but from the opposition of the outports, who were losing business to London, and older trading companies in conflict with new created monopolies such as the Spanish and French companies.[94] In addition, the corrupt practices of monopolists such as the licensers of alehouses caused the revival of the procedure of impeachment in 1621 which was then used against royal ministers such as Francis Bacon, the Lord Chancellor, Lionel Cranfield, the Lord Treasurer, and the royal favorite, the Duke of Buckingham.[95] While the Statute of Monopolies had enough loopholes to allow projects to continue in the 1630s as we have seen, corrupt practices in general fell off in the 1630s and the 1640s. It was at this point and in the second half of the century that projects such as the draining of the fens, begun 100 years before, came to fruition.[96]

English policies of regulation sought two ends, order and economic growth. Their policies had unintended effects in the creation of vested interests of rent-seekers who undermined both the political and the economic goals proposed. The underdevelopment of administration caused monopolies to be granted to officeholders in lieu of salaries thereby creating a vested interest whose goals differed from those of the Crown. The Crown lacked a form of financing that would put it beyond the control of vested interests. In 1640 Charles I was forced to call parliament into session because he could no longer borrow money from the customs farmers. Even vested interests and rent-seekers inside and outside the administration refused to support the king in his religious war with Scotland.

Corrupt transactions were embedded in the English economy. However, they had another meaning at least as significant, especially in the early seventeenth century, and that was political. The discourse of corruption was a powerful mode in which to criticize the court.

Chapter 7

Corruption and political ideology

In a trial held by the Crown in Star Chamber in 1619 corruption was defined as the use of "monies designed for the public service for private ends" and "monies taken corruptly for rewards and gratuities and private gain from public service."[1] This was the definition put forward explicitly by the prosecution and accepted implicitly by the defendants. Contemporary evidence contradicts those historians who have argued that a sense of public and private existed only sketchily in the early modern period.[2] Within the English polity, structured by personal relationships, existed a rhetoric which emphasized service to the public and commonwealth. Accusations of corruption usually thought the hallmark of "country" ideology were levied by the Crown against its own officials. "Court" and "country" shared elements of a common language on corruption. This shared discourse drew on indigenous tradition as well as classical sources, especially Cicero. Law, administration, religion and politics had separate if similar "scripts" about corruption.[3]

The language of corruption was a staple of English political discourse. Corruption had figured as a legal and political issue in England at least from the late Anglo-Saxon period and recurred periodically. Complaints escalated in the late sixteenth and early seventeenth centuries, spilling over into sermons, Star Chamber and administrative investigations and parliamentary impeachments. It became a matter of such intense focus in the first three decades of the seventeenth century that corruption occupied a central place in contemporary political ideology.

Scholars have tended to separate the concept of corruption as specific venal practices from corruption as the sense of the moral decay of the political system.[4] Yet the earliest definitions of corruption included the corporeal and referred to the decay of the body; when applied to the body politic, from the late fourteenth century on, the concept signified both corrupt practices *and* the corruption of the political system.[5] By analyzing the language of corruption in a variety of texts and the political context in which they were embedded, this chapter demonstrates how the traditional themes took on a changed and, indeed, a charged meaning in the early seventeenth century. Linking political discourse with political action illuminates how corrupt practices and the concept of corruption intersected in the early seventeenth century to create an ideology used in the 1640s to attack the court and the monarchy itself.

Fundamental to the study of corruption in English political ideology is the continuing tension in English law and administration around the associated ideas of office and of gift. From late Anglo-Saxon times, the essential role of the king was to guarantee justice, a function performed through his officials. Because the earliest offices in the English state were quasi-judicial, the earliest notions of political corruption were attached to judicial office. Whether justices or administrators, English officials presided over courts and took on the aspect of judges, roles demanding impartiality.[6] Yet rooted in medieval law at the same time was the notion that office was the property of the officeholder as if it were a piece of land, including the right to its income and to its sale. For royal administrators, the sale of office sometimes appeared a more acceptable practice than impositions or taxes in order to pay for government salaries.[7] While judges held their offices at the king's pleasure and not as freeholds, like other royal officials they could supplement their royal salaries with fees. The taking of fees and the sale of offices in royal administration by government officials, however, tended to conflict with the judicial meaning of office.

The notion of the gift was equally problematic. In archaic societies, in ancient Rome and medieval and Renaissance England, gifts took the form of free offerings even if factually that was social pretence. In the thirteenth century Bracton's treatise on law defined a gift as "a disposition arising from pure liberality." The requirements of a valid gift were that "it must be complete and absolute, free and uncoerced, extorted neither by fear nor through force. Let money or service play no part, lest it fall into the category of purchase and sale."[8] Gifts also signified the position of great men and the private ties that allied them with their followers. For judges and other officials, however, gifts had an equivocal meaning, raising the issues of partiality and injustice.

The tension around these principal foci of political corruption, office and gift, remained over the centuries in uneasy balance. That tension was increased by new social and economic conditions in the sixteenth century. The confluence of increasing commercialization of the economy, growth of trade and inflation, the lavish style of the Renaissance and Baroque court that made office-holding an expensive luxury,[9] and the pressure of a larger landed elite on royal bounty, established the context for corrupt practices and increased the scale of extraction. A greater number of officials demanded larger amounts of money from those with whom they did business. In response to the growth in official venality, the types of practices labelled corrupt were extended beyond those spelled out in statute, and bribery was defined more narrowly. The results were mounting numbers of investigations by the Crown, increasing numbers of prosecutions of under-officers, the revival of impeachment by parliament and the introduction of new statutes on bribery and sale of office. The Crown made continuing efforts to prevent corruption in the legal system including attacks on "pocket" or "basket" judges.[10] The language of the Crown's strongly worded assize charges, characteristic of the Elizabethan and early Stuart period,[11] overlapped with assize sermons we will examine. Nevertheless, the language of corruption became a discourse of conflict capable of undermining governmental legitimacy, especially when it became tied to other critical issues such as foreign policy, justice, taxation, honor and fundamental law.

To understand the meaning and force of the concept of corruption in seventeenth-century politics we need to examine the vocabularies of law, religion and politics that helped to make corruption a vital political issue in the early seventeenth century as both Crown and parliament mounted powerful attacks on monopolists, judges and officials. In the 1640s, long after many of the abuses denounced in the 1610s and 1620s had been remedied, the concept of corruption remained central to political discourse.

I

The contradiction of office and gift shaped the problem of corruption throughout the medieval and early modern period during which influence and hospitality characterized social relationships. *The Dialogue of the Exchequer*, written in the late twelfth century, justified offering a sum to the king to obtain justice in terms that were still debated in the seventeenth century:

> not of course, to ensure justice being done – so you must not lose your temper with us and say the King sells justice – but to have it done without delay. Note also that the King does not accept all such offers, even though you may think him to overstep his limit. To some he does full justice for nothing, in consideration of their past services or out of mere goodness of heart; but to others (and it is only human nature) he will not give way either for love or for money ... sometimes because the demandants have done nothing to deserve it, being charged with offences against the reallm or the King in person ... But owing to the King's kindness, those who lose their cases after promising money are usually more

gently treated, lest they should suffer twice over, both by disappointment of their hope, and by spending their wealth to no advantage.[12]

By the middle of the thirteenth century both magnates and monasteries were paying judges regular pensions and thereby making them their retainers. Yet from the emergence of a professional bench in the twelfth and thirteenth centuries, judges were periodically accused of partiality and bribery in contemporary complaint literature. John of Salisbury in the twelfth century accused judges of corruption "as is proved by their love of gifts and rewards, exercising the power which they have in the service of avarice or advancing the fortunes of their own flesh and blood." The Provisions of Oxford in 1258 stated that "justices shall accept no gifts except presents of bread, wine and the like – that is, such food and drink as is customarily brought to the tables of important men." The Provisions called for the payment of salaries to the justices "so that they shall have no need to accept anything from anyone else."[13] Such rhetoric and reforms were to be repeated up until the nineteenth century.

The usual reason for removing cases from the county courts in medieval England was supposed bias by the undersheriff deriving primarily either from family ties with the litigant or from payment.[14] In the judicial scandals under Edward I, most of the professional judges were found guilty of crimes including bribery and extortion, tampering with evidence, forgery, embezzlement and sorcery. Complaint literature linked attacks on ambition to the judge's servile origins.[15] The complaints of bribery and partiality were traditional and the charge of sorcery, although much diminished, still found its place in seventeenth-century complaint literature. Twelfth-century promises of future payments to the king to ensure justice, condemned in Magna Carta, were, however, no longer acceptable in theory.

In practice, in the mid-fifteenth century during Cade's rebellion the corruption of justice had been decried: "the law serveth of nought else in these days but for to do wrong, for nothing is sped almost but ... for mede, drede [dread] and favor."[16] Complaints of corrupt practices in the sixteenth century continued to focus on corruption in the local administration of justice. In 1538 Sir Anthony Fitzherbert's *The New Boke of Justices of the Peas* noted "The greatest offence nexte unto felony as it semyth is Extorcion done by shyreffes and other officers ... And Extorcion is nothyng els but spoyle and robborie done by colour of offyce." William Lambarde in his *Archeion* described the corruption of juries and sheriffs.[17] The Elizabethan and early Stuart period saw repeated reference to the corruption of under-officers in assize charges.[18]

In legal discourse, early Stuart prescriptive notions of corruption found stringent expression in a charge to the jury by Sir Edward Coke, newly appointed Chief Justice of the King's Bench in 1606. In addressing the

Norfolk bench in a speech entitled "A Discovery of the Abuses and Corruption of Officers," Coke forthrightly stated the contradictions of office and gift especially those facing a judge in a society which placed a high value on kinship and patron–client ties. He detailed the corrupt practices found throughout the judicial system and offered as its resolution the insulation of the judge from all influence except his own conscience. Moreover, Coke saw systemic corruption growing out of an accumulation of individual acts of venality. As a result, Coke argued, corruption caused the decay of the state. For the significance of those evils went beyond individual corrupt practices, he wrote, "to deface, ruin and utterly subvert the Honor of our ancient name and our now Great Britain's Monarchy."[19] Coke's prescriptive tract may not have reflected the reality of behavior in the early seventeenth century; it did set out a rhetorical ideal of public service that had important political significance. Indeed, it was increasingly invoked by Coke and others in language and practice over the next two decades.

Coke began his charge with a story of a Roman youth. "The Senate without any means of his, was pleased freely to bestow upon him" the office of judge. The young man refused. Because he had many friends, kinsfolk and allies, some of high rank, in the government, he feared that he might by his decisions lose friends or attract suspicion of partiality. When the Senate refused to reconsider, however, the young man consulted a noble friend who advised him to accept the office with these words: "He that is a judge . . . ceaseth to be a friend: for in the manner of judgement, no acquaintance, no griefs, no friends, no remembrance . . . or hope of future friendship must direct the thoughts of him that is a judge . . . in thy love to Rome's Commonwealth dedicate thy labors to her public benefit."[20] Accepting the office, the young man then prepared a feast for his friends and kinsfolk as if he were departing the country. He took leave of them all by saying he would hereafter "be a stranger to my dearest friends, and nearest allies: I must forget all former friendships and my most familiar acquaintance . . . in the seat of Justice . . . to keep my conscience clear, I must with equity and uprightness, justly administer justice unto you all." Coke then suddenly shifted into the present tense and brought home the point to the audience made up of his Norfolk neighbors.

And this is my cause, by the love and favor of my greatest master King James . . . I am . . . without price or request, freely called unto this great office . . . I am thus sent to be a judge amongst my kinsfolk and familiar friends, even in the bosom of my native country. I must therefore as the young Roman did, take leave of all former acquaintance and do that which is just unto all estates and degrees without partiality.

The two evils to which justices might be prone were bribery and partiality. Coke argued that once a judge was known to take a bribe or found partial, he left no actions free from suspicion. "A judge that for a bribe will speak, and but once execute a justice purchased, all his words and actions for ever after may justly be suspected." Furthermore, Coke extended his discussion to corruption practiced by officers lower down in the bureaucracy, to the escheater, the clerk of the market, the purveyor, the concealer, the informer, and the monopolist. Coke's homily signified the tensions, even contradictions, between law and politics, between justice and friendship. Coke drew on classical sources for his admonitory talk to reinforce the laws of England which were his touchstone, thereby combining humanist and jurisprudential concepts of office and duty. While exalting the position of the judge in the commonwealth, Coke reminded his audience that the role of the judge and of the justices of the peace came from the king who at his coronation was sworn to do justice unto all his subjects. His call for reform of corrupt practices came from within the court. "The dignity of his Majesty's prerogative Royal is not used to enforce his subjects to endure wrong. But the rust being scoured off, which abused time hath cast upon it, then will the glory thereof shine in the perfection of an uncorrupted brightness."[21] Coke suggested that corruption cast a pall over the royal prerogative, indeed seemed to mark its limits.

Coke's stringent standards for office in a society in which gift-giving, appointment to office through patronage and sale were widespread, seem far removed from political reality. Yet such rhetoric from Coke and others, if not their behavior, reflected the concerns shared by Crown and parliament alike in the next decades: in 1613 the Crown forbade the judges from riding circuit in their home counties and in 1621 parliament revived impeachment, dormant for 150 years, to remove the Crown's officials on charges of corruption.[22]

Coke's view of corruption can be supplemented by a tract written a year before, in 1605, which describes in detail contemporary corrupt practices. It sets out a specifically English language of corruption, reflecting a native tradition of complaint literature. As we have seen, Robert Fletcher, yeomen purveyor of carriages, wrote a tract on ways to reform purveyance.[23] Fletcher defined corruption as officials handling the king's service "for their own private gain," and believed the sale of office was crucial to corrupt practices.[24]

The problems of abuses in royal purveyance were first attacked as early as 1215. In the first parliament of James I (1604–11), the issues of wardship and purveyance were central to negotiations over the Great Contract, the effort by royal officials and members of parliament to trade the king's feudal revenues for a regular yearly income.[25] But Fletcher's anatomy of abuses included new categories as well as old. He attacked bribery, oppression of the subject, sale and proliferation of unnecessary offices, conflict of interest and monopoly. The first two, bribery and oppression of the subject by royal officials, were legal offenses proscribed by common law and statute. Certain sales of office were illegal. But like many of his contemporaries, Fletcher extended the meaning of corruption to include monopolies, conflict of interest and proliferation of offices. These were by no means illegal in seventeenth-century England.

If Coke painted the picture of the good judge, Fletcher magnified the warts of individual carttakers who commandeered carts on behalf of the king when he went on progress. For instance, "the most abominable, execrable, wretched briber that ever the carttakers had amongst them" was an aide hired for royal progresses, John Bremell. Bremell was "a bowling alley mate, a common gamester, cunning cheater ... his briberies ... continual and his shifts in taking of bribes so artificial as an honest man would wonder at his folly." Summing up his associates, Fletcher wrote "for, as the Emperor said of physicians that too many of them had killed the Emperor, even so I of carttakers that too many of them dishonor the king by abusing his subjects and are worse than the devouring beasts and vermin of the Commonwealth." Fletcher's image recalled Sir Thomas More's vision in *Utopia* of sheep devouring the commonwealth. Court and country shared this vision of purveyors. "These are the carttakers of whom preachers in their pulpits do exclaim," said Fletcher, citing sermons preached at the Elizabethan court in 1585 and 1603.

Significantly, Fletcher did not exclude profit from office, but profit, he maintained, should come not from extortion of the subject but from the king's gift. Such bounty, freely given, was not corrupt. Indeed it prevented corruption. Like the boatswains who wanted to petition the king for higher wages "to keep them true," at James's accession Fletcher had told the other carttakers "we are now sworn the servants of a sacred king; if we do keep our hands pure from bribery and corruption his majesty will give us more forth of his princely liberality in [an] hour than we have or can attain unto by bribery in all our lives how long soever." But on the king's first progress, while Fletcher was ill, the "carttakers having no consciences therefore no overseer to control them bribed and abused the countries round ... as that grievous was it to hear the general complaints but all was smoothed up and passed over, a second bribe in court answering for sundry ones inflicted upon the country."[26] These bribes did not, he noted ruefully, smooth over parliamentary outrage.

Writing in the first decade of the seventeenth century, Coke and Fletcher illustrated the tensions in the contemporary language and practice of office. In presenting vivid pictures of the righteous judge and corrupt under-officials, they delineated the ideals of office, royal justice and royal bounty undermined by corrupt practices some of which were medieval in origin, some attributable to the expansion of administration under Henry VIII, some to Elizabethan policy and practice. For court officials, corruption was a significant cause of discord between the king and his subjects.

167

II

Religion provided another language in which the vocabulary of office and gift were important. The liberality that Coke and Fletcher referred to as coming from the state or the king came, in religious terms, from God. Protestant theology emphasized the free gift of divine grace and salvation without works. Both Luther and Calvin had emphasized the separation of the individual and office in their attack on the proprietary church, a separation similar to the legal language of Coke who stressed that the official should not be influenced by private concerns either of blood or money, family or friends. Conscience was important to both. The separate scripts overlapped, providing a language in which both the secular and the divine resonated. God, not the king or the law, was the touchstone, the goal salvation, but in the ideal of the godly magistrate and commonwealth different traditions of discourse converged.

A series of sermons, tracts and administrative investigations between 1615 and 1621 looked at the contradictions of covetousness and gift-giving, the "immoderate desire of riches ... opposed to liberality,"[27] from which they came to a newly rigorous definition of a bribe and the sale of office.

Covetousness, a vice traditionally complained about in sermons, was usually viewed as the sin of the merchant or tradesman. It was dubbed "The Churl's Sickness" by Thomas Pestell who argued that covetousness marked the decay of all Christian virtues including liberality, justice, and charity.[28] Separate traditions in law and religion converged when Pestell and other ministers urged contemporaries not to be like the wicked judges in the Bible. "For a covetous judge is but a blind guide; For a reward puts out his eyes ... Remember that you are here ... in Gods stead ... For he that walks in justice ... shaking his hands from taking of gifts, stopping his ears from hearing of blood, and shutting his eyes from seeing of evil, he shall dwell on high."[29] Pestell urged the judges not to give "the people cause to take up the complaint of the Prophet: Judgement is turned backward, and Justice stands far off, Truth is fallen in the streets, and equity cannot enter."[30]

Justice was as central to the language of religion as to the language of law and politics. Indeed, religion, law and politics were overtly combined in sermons preached at the meeting of the assizes before the justices of the peace. The preachers upheld the notion of the god-like king and the hierarchy of society while maintaining the important position of the godly magistrate. At the assizes at Hertford in 1616, John Squire stressed that it was "the sword of the potent Magistrate, not the word of the poore Minister which must ... blow away the contentious grasse-hoppers of this corrupt generation." Nevertheless he admonished the judges to "take heed for with the Lord there is neyther respect of persons, nor receiving of rewards." Squire attacked the bribe-taking of bailiffs, undersheriffs, juries and judges' servants who could only "see through a paire of silver spectacles."[31] In another assize sermon, Samual Burton called for an end to the contemporary proverb that opined "as a man is friended, so his case is ended."[32] While family and patronage provided important bonds in early Stuart England, ministers repeatedly stressed that justice was guaranteed to all not just by English law but by God.

In a sermon dedicated to Sir Francis Bacon in 1619 William Pemberton too attacked bribery and partiality urging people to "bribe no judges, lawyers, nor ministers of justice lest the fear of the Lord be upon you." He charged the judges to judge not for man but for the Lord, "for there is no inequity with the Lord our God, nor respect of persons, nor taking of gifts."[33] These were not just individual corrupt practices but portended the corruption of the commonwealth. "When Rulers and Magistrates do swerve in government, growing careless and negligent, ungodly and unjust . . . all things in Church and Common-wealth grow disordered and confused and finally fall."[34]

If justice and liberality were terms of discourse in law, politics and religion, so too was conscience. Religious and legal notions of conscience overlapped as one contemporary sermon made explicit. Using the images of legal rolls and historical records Anthony Cade vividly pictured conscience as a "living book annexed to the soule." It had two parts:

> One is a Law booke, wherein are set downe principles of Trueth and Equity, the grounds of the Law of Nature . . . A Schoolemaster ever accompaning the soule . . . the other part of the Booke is a Chronicle, or Register, Roll or Record, where this Embassadour sets downe all the . . . thoughts, words and actions, be they good or evill: that it may bee a manifest, and authenticke witnesse with God his master, either against the man or with him.[35]

Although the book seemed "clasped up for a time," conscience continued to record. When the devil saw man "plunged in sin, and past al hope of recovery, then he awakes the sleeping conscience, and opens the woefull booke and compels the sinner to reade it: . . . and he cannot withdraw his thoughts from it, but may say with David . . . my sin is ever before me." This religious vision of conscience rested on the law of God and the law of nature metaphorically expressed in the documents of English law.

To understand early seventeenth-century notions of the corrupt official, it may be useful to examine a contemporary view of the good judge. Robert Bolton's "Funeral notes upon my patron, Sir Augustine Nicolls" of 1616, paints an idealized portrait of the godly magistrate and contrasts it with contemporary practices. Bolton's religious vocabulary coincided with Coke's legal and classical concepts of office, gift and conscience although he eschewed secular writers both ancient and modern, especially Machiavelli, in favor of scripture.[36] In his portrait of Nicolls, Bolton combined the prescriptive notion of office with the practice necessary to fulfil that ideal.

Nicolls had been a sergeant-at-law to Queen Elizabeth and to Prince Henry, Judge of the Court of Common Pleas and Chancellor to Prince Charles. What ennobled Nicolls' memory was that "he had and held all these places ... he neither begged them, nor bought them, nor gave so much as a New-yeare's gift for them." When he was presented to a place of honor about the prince the king called him the judge that would give no money. Like the young Roman described by Coke and Coke's own description of himself, Nicolls had been granted the position freely. Because the sale of office encouraged extortion, Nicolls insisted that subordinates "come in clearehanded, that they might deale honestly in their places," and he asked under-officers not to bring petitions to him so that he might be secured even from the appearance of corruption. Nicolls even refused gratuities after giving judgement.[37] In contrast, Bolton lamented contemporary practices "when men ... follow the execution of their places, and administration of justice, onely as a trade, with an unquenchable and unconscionable thirst of gaine." Bolton strongly emphasized the contradictions of office and gift, of justice and trade. To fail to distinguish them led to the moral decay of the state.

Virtue and commerce were not antithetical. But what was virtuous in one sphere was not in another. Covetousness, merchandizing, retailing, regard for money, described in pejorative terms in these and many other sermons and often ascribed to the merchant and shopkeeper, contrasted with the justice and liberality ascribed to the monarch and his officials. Corruption was the bane of all honest government; the godly magistrate its backbone. Bolton urged all magistrates

> with all noblenesse of a free spirit, and clearenesse of a good conscience, [to] take their places of justice to heart; be active, conscionable, resolute; not onely formall and cyphers ... that they would abominate even all appearance of bribery and partiality to the pit of hell ... otherwise, howsoever they may please themselves with the common applause: it were better the common-wealth had never knowne them.[38]

Theoretically there were important differences between exchange based on duty, obedience and justice on the one hand and the notion of unlimited royal bounty, mercy and the circulation of benefits on the other.[39] For if obedience, duty or gift were enjoined it could no longer be freely given, an action central to the contemporary understanding of gift and bounty. The notion of the king as unlimited giver of bounty paralleled the vision of God but raised problems for the notion of the mutual duties between king and subject embodied in some contemporary understandings of the king's coronation oath. As tension rose over foreign policy, religion, and venal

170

practices, the differences between the two systems of organizing obligation became clearer.

Robert Bolton, the prominent puritan minister, preached two sermons on the same theme, that "when the righteous are in authority, the people rejoyce; but when the wicked beareth rule, the people mourne." Like Coke, he included in "the guilt of bribery" not only "money, gold and silver, or presents, as they call them ... [but also] exorbitant affection, which swayes a man aside, from the impartial execution of Justice."[40] There was an intrinsic contradiction between contemporary ideals of doing justice and doing one's duty and the equally persuasive notions of unlimited bounty and the circulation of benefits.[41] In denouncing the gangrene of gaining office through corruption, he described the corporeal decay of the body politic.

In 1620 Anthony Cade preached a sermon at the Leicester Assizes, which drew on Cicero and St Augustine to set forth the ideal of the commonwealth and its present decay.

> Our Age receiving the common wealth as a stately picture that by long keeping was much decayed, now not onely neglecteth to renue it with the Colours it had, but careth not so much as to preserve the forme and utmost lineaments thereof ... Good laws are perished for want of good men to preserve them in life. Thus Tully. For the life of the common wealth is the Law: the life of the Law is the good execution ... So the Roman Common wealth expired (with Tully) not for want of good Lawes but of good men to keepe life in them.[42]

As humanists had argued, virtuous rulers were necessary to maintain the commonwealth. Fundamental to virtuous rule "Lawes and Justice are the very bonds and sinewes of the commonwealth, yea the life and soule of humane society." Cade cited St Augustine: "Take away justice and what are great kingdoms, but great thieveries?"

Corruption was not merely attacked as a series of evil practices but as undermining the entire political system. This theme now became increasingly important. In 1621 Samuel Ward preached a sermon at the Suffolk assizes entitled "Jethro's Justice of the Peace"[43] which attacked the intrusion of the market into government. Ward argued that the sale of the offices of justice was the root of all evil in the church and commonwealth. Proffering a cynical vision of office, Ward imagined Moses advised by a Jacobean:

> A beaten Politician of our times, learned in the wisdome of newer state, and acquainted with the mysteries of the market, that knowes how to improove things to the best, for his owne time and turne, and to let the common body shift for it selfe, would have projected Moses a farre more commodious plot, after this or the like manner: Now you have offices to bestow, a faire opportunity in your hand, to make your selfe for ever, to raise your house, to pleasure your friends, either proclaime it openly or secretly, set it abroach by some meanes

or other, see who bids fairest, waigh the sacrifices, chuse the men of the best and greatest gifts.

Ward's *double entendre* presented succinctly the contemporary conflict over gifts and bribes, of public office and personal gain. Accepting gifts undermined justice for "he that will admit them for Justice shall soon take them for unjustice ... Judges that judge for reward [are] ... such as the Country calls Capon-justices." Attacking the loopholes in the statutes prohibiting sale of office, Ward questioned distinctions between judicial and other offices. "Oh gall of bitternesse! oh root of all evill to Church and Commonwealth, when authorities and offices of Justice shall be bought and solde ... Civill and Ecclesiastical courts will soone proove dens of theeves. Whose soul bleedes not to see mens soules bought and solde, like sheep at the market to every Butcher." The price of offices, he claimed, was now almost equal the price of land. Ward asked "are they not all offices of Justice? Doe they not prepare to judicature, and lies it not in them to guide or misguide, to hasten or delay Justice, etc. which how can they freely give, which buy dearely ... Offices are not livings and salaries; but charges and duties: not preferments for favourites; but rewards of deserts."[44] Corruption was not new; Augustine had seen it in his own time. When places were sought not to provide for the welfare of others but for private interest it produced "muck wormes of the world."[45]

Duty not bounty should be the basis of holding office. In religious language that recalled Pestell's sermon in 1615, Ward dramatized the interior monologue of the good judge.

> When an unlawfull suit is commenced by power or by friendship, his heart answers ... with Job: How shall I doe this, and answer God when hee comes to judgement. As for bribes, hee dares not looke on them, lest they blinde his eyes before he be aware ... when he comes in court, he fixeth his eye, neither before him on that person, nor about him on the beholders, nor behind him for bribes, but upward on God.[46]

Officials should not be chosen by family connection or alliance for office was not an honor, a commodity or a sword, but service.

> But what doe I making my selfe ridiculous to this olde doting covetous age of the world ... And so doe they serve all our caveats against covetousnesse, applauding themselves and laughing in their sleeves, when they behold their bags in the chest, and their lands from off their Turrets, saying to themselves, What is a man but his wealth? What is an office but the fees?[47]

Like Cade, Ward emphasized that the legitimacy of office rested on the virtue of the officeholder. "Complete magistrates" were

men of courage, men of religion, men of truth, hating covetousnesse ... if all
were ... as eminent for them as for their place: and did (as the great Dictator of
reason speakes in his Politicks) as far exceede the vulgar sort in those heroycal
vertues, as the *statues* of the gods, the *statues* of men: then would people
become voluntary subjects, put the scepters into their hands, and the law of
commanding and obeying become easie, things thought irreparable would easily
be reformed.[48]

Although he might be accused of conjuring a Utopia, Ward asked

Was there ever more neede of courage then now, when sin is so audacious?
... The onely way to repaire these ruines of the dying world is to renew
government to the primitive beauty of it: the face whereof I have now shewed
in this excellent Mirrour or Looking-Glass: so you goe not away, and forget both
the comelinesse and spots it hath shewed you, but wash and bee cleane.[49]

Samuel Ward's accusations were to be repeated in the language of the
impeachments brought against the man to whom he dedicated his sermon, the Lord Chancellor, Sir Francis Bacon. Assize sermons that attacked
corruption and questioned the virtue of rulers uncovered the fundamental contradictions in early Stuart political thought between duty and benefits. Most important, they provided a language in which criticism of the
Crown might be expressed within a political system that emphasized consensus. Indeed some of that criticism came from within the court itself.

III

It has been suggested by anthropologist Pierre Bourdieu that in pre-capitalist
societies the "great" are those who can least afford to take liberties with the
official norms, and that the price they must pay for the status accorded
them is outstanding conformity to the values of the group, the source of
symbolic value.[50] Much the same can be said of early modern society. The
increasing emphasis on corruption in Jacobean England came in part from
the falling away of some of "the great," officers and favorites, from official
norms at the same time that those norms were being more stringently
defined. Indeed we have seen this notion repeatedly in the rhetoric of
contemporary sermons. Virtue, which Bourdieu names "symbolic capital,"
legitimizes modes of domination. When that virtue fails, the legitimate basis
for the exercise of authority fails with it.

To the discourses of law and religion should be added the discourse
of the court and the courtier. If the language of law and religion emphasized responsibility to the public commonwealth, writings on the courtier
stressed his or her private relationship to the king. Renaissance humanism

emphasized the importance of the courtier as royal adviser. Within the discourse on the courtier, too, there were corrupt practices: the use of private positions at court without providing service to the king. Emphasizing the courtier's personal qualities which allowed him to rise, such literature built on Anglo-Saxon notions of the comitatus and feudal ties between lord and vassal. An indigenous English literature from the fourteenth century on described the attractions and the dangers of the court. The image of the wheel of fortune portrayed the rise and fall of those who depended on the court and *The Mirror for Magistrates* reflected the vices and virtues of late medieval and Tudor politics. Castiglione's *The Courtier*, translated into English in the mid-sixteenth century, presented the model of the courtier.

The Elizabethan period illustrated the strong tensions in this tradition: at one and the same time it saw the celebration of Gloriana in literature and art and the danger of court service as in Raleigh's "The Lie," Spenser's "Mother Hubbard's Tale" and the anguished letter written from the Tower by England's highest ranking nobleman, Thomas Howard, fourth Duke of Norfolk, warning his young children to beware the lure of the court.[51] Such views cannot be labeled specifically Jacobean, however sycophantic or dark were the pictures of court life painted by Jacobean playwrights such as Marston, Middleton or Webster.[52] The influence of the neo-Stoics and Tacitus helped shape a more sinister vision of court life at the end of the sixteenth century.[53]

The complex contemporary view of the court is illustrated in several tracts from 1614 to 1619. In 1614 William Camden added some new chapters to his *Remaines*. In one he called his contemporaries "foolishly proud in apparel ... exceedingly crafty in legal contracts ... compared to the plainness of their ancestors." Yet Camden, the great historian of the era, did not think the Jacobean era singularly bad. Rather, citing Tacitus and Seneca, he wrote:

> All things run round, and as the seasons of the year, so men's manners have their revolutions ... Our age is not only faulty, our ancestors have complained, we complain, and our posterity will complain, that manners are corrupted, that naughtiness reigneth, and all things wax worse and worse ... In one age there will be more adulterers, in an other time there will be excessive riot in banqueting ... In an other age cruelty and fury of civil war will flash out, and sometimes carousing and drunkenness will be counted a bravery. So vices do ruffle among themselves, and usurp one another. As for us we may say always of ourselves: We are evil, there have bin evil, and evil there will be. There will always be tyrants, murderers, thieves, adulterers, extortioners, church-robbers, traitors and others of the same rablement.[54]

While Camden reminded his readers that vices were inherent in man, only changing their appearance in different times, a year later one of the greatest scandals of the century was uncovered. Deceit, arbitrary imprisonment, murder existed not only in the fictional world of Webster's Italian revenge dramas but in the reality of the intrigue leading to Sir Thomas Overbury's death in the Tower and the conviction of the king's favorite, Robert Carr, Earl of Somerset, for his murder. Overbury, a close friend of Carr's, opposed the latter's marriage to Frances Howard, Countess of Essex, who had procured a divorce from her husband from a special panel of bishops convened by the king. Overbury was sent to the Tower by the connivance of Frances's uncle, Henry Howard, Earl of Northampton and the favorite. While there, Frances tried to poison him. His death in the Tower was not questioned until the appearance of a new favorite on the scene, George Villiers, Duke of Buckingham. Then the rumors about Overbury's death, the odd state of the body, and the hasty burial became not just gossip but the basis for a series of trials in which the Somersets and their accomplices were found guilty. While there is real doubt as to whether Northampton and Somerset participated in the murder plot, Sir Edward Coke vigorously led the Crown's prosecution of them. All were found guilty and only the Somersets were spared death.[55]

The scandal encompassed the lurid circumstances of the divorce as well as the murder. When the bishops refused to confirm Frances's claim that her marriage should be annulled on the basis of her husband's impotence, the king had named two more with connections to the Howards to bring in the desired verdict.[56] The news spread throughout the kingdom. Salacious lyrics were recorded in a gentleman's notebook as far away as Chester.[57] It evoked a number of tracts that focused on the evils of the court and the great and linked moral corruption to political corruption. At the same time such tracts seemed to exempt James I from the corruption of his favorites. Dedicated to or favored by court officials, these narratives held in somewhat precarious balance the notions of the evil of the court with the glory of the monarchy.

Most striking is that of Richard Niccols, whose "Sir Thomas Overburies Vision" was published in 1616. Niccols was the editor and reviser of *The Mirror for Magistrates* and his tract drew on classical sources, medieval and sixteenth-century precedents. Niccols focused on the murder not just as scandal but more systematically as the outcome of court politics. Invoking the notion of the Norman yoke, i.e. that the Normans had conquered the English thereby snuffing out Anglo-Saxon liberties,[58] he pointed out that Overbury's murder in the Tower was by no means the first. "Thou sad monument of *Norman* yoke, / whose great foundation hee whose conquering stroke / . . . our neckes to *Norman* rule first laid."[59] Following Tudor tradition Niccols referred to Richard III as "that bloody beast" and cited his previous murders of the Duke of Clarence and of the princes in the Tower. But Niccols then went on to name Tudor martyrs who had died there: "famous *Essex* woefull fall was seene; [/] Where guiltie *Suffolk's* guiltlesse daughter *Jane* / The scaffold with her noble blood did staine: [/] where royall *Anne* her life to death resignd."[60] In so doing, Niccols explicitly went beyond the notion of Overbury's death as a moral crime to view it as a political one.

As in legal and religious writings, gold and love of friends were the keys to corrupt practices. In addition, conscience wrestled with ambition. Echoing late Elizabethan critiques, Niccols attacked those who attached themselves to the great and those who hoped to rise at court.

> Ye servile sycophants, whose hopes depend / On great mens wills; what is the utmost end / At which ye aime? why doe ye like base curres, / Upon your Patron fawne? why like his spurres, Will ye be ever ready at his heeles, / With pleasing words to clawe him, where he feels / The humour itch? or why, will ye so waite / As to lie down and kisse the feete of state? / And oft expose yourselves to wretched ends, / Loosing your soules to make great men your friends?

Gervase Helwys was the Lieutenant of the Tower who discovered the plot but feared to reveal it. In Niccols's presentation, as in Helwys's own confession, fear of the great contended with conscience. "Feare said that if the same I did disclose, / The countenance of greatnes I should lose, / And be thrust out of office and of place; / But conscience said that I should lose that grace / And favour, which my God to me had given, / And be perhaps thrust ever out of heaven." Niccols's language was reminiscent of contemporary assize sermons. "T'is good to feare great men, but yet 'tis better / Ever to feare God more, since God is greater."[61] Like the Duke of Norfolk, Helwys's father had warned him against the court. Like so many contemporaries Helwys suffered the contradictions of the pleasures of the simple life and the attraction of the court. But

> Ambitious mist did blind my weaker eyes,
> I thought by this preferment I should rise;
> Yet no desert but gold did gaine me grace,
> Mine owne corruption purchas'd me that place:
> For brib'rie in the soule a blemish makes
> Of him that gives, As well as him that takes,
> And bribing hands that give, must guilty be . . .
> whose golden fingers, as in sport,
> Like lime-twigges catch at offices in Court,
> In which obtain'd ye ever after live
> Corrupt in minde, to gaine what ye did give.[62]

As we have seen, contemporary critics, whether clergymen or court reformers, recognized the sale of office as an important source of corrupt practices. In Niccols's tract this accepted part of contemporary political practice was an evil which could lead to death. Yet such a pious suggestion was belied by Niccols's patrons, Charles Howard, Earl of Nottingham, and James Hay, Earl of Carlisle. Both were leading courtiers; Hay, in fact, became the symbol of the extravagance of the age. If they took a personal interest in sponsoring Niccols's tract, it probably stemmed from factional struggles at court at the time and personal satisfaction in the fall of Somerset.

Niccols's strong attack on court corruption drew a significant line between the monarch and his favorites. Urging the ghost of Helwys to rest easy, the poet said "Thy foes decline, proud *Gaveston* is downe, / No wanton *Edward* weares our Englands crowne." Invoking the precedent of the fourteenth century, the poet not only saw the recurrent problem of favorites, but distinguished his own monarch from the ill-fated Edward II. While overtly the poet held the king himself blameless, by equating Somerset with Gaveston the poet also suggested dangerous similarities between the two monarchs who both had male favorites.[63] A series of ideas are held in tension in Niccols's tract: the Norman yoke, the dangers of the court, and the apotheosis of the king, ideas that were ultimately in the 1640s seen to be in contradiction. While it was possible for Niccols to juggle all these in 1616, the language he used was also available for a more critical stance toward the monarchy.

Another tract on the Overbury murder, *The Bloody Downfall of Adultery, Murder, Ambition* examined "the customes of this age." Focusing on ambition, "catching at nothing but starres, climing only for Greatnesse," the author attacked the discrepancy between inner reality and outward appearance, portraying the evil of the courtiers who were "comely without, but within, nothing but rotten bones, and corrupt practises."[64]

The recipe for climbing was to creep "into the favour of some great Peersonage" and make an advantageous marriage, thereby achieving notice at court. "Then begins hee with guifts to winne hearts ... by offices of friendship, to bind his equalls, by cunning insinuations to worke his superiours, by which meanes hee is held to be worthely a Statesman ... if any cross him, look for poyson in his cuppe or conspiracy in his walkes." Such language conjures up *Othello*, *The Duchess of Malfi* or *The White Devil*. "If the nature of the Nobleman whom hee envieth be gentle, hee bringeth him in feare, either of his servants in his household, or his familiars ... or else some mislike betwixt his Prince and him, sworne and confirmed by flatteries and intelligences, till the noble looseth either his land, authoritie, or place, and hee attaine both his stile and promotion." His aides were witches and charmers, "excellent at poysons, to kill lingringly like the Italian ... to the Ambitious man, there is commonly belonging a rustic troup of flatters, bauds, adulterers, soothers, that hating all virtue makes sin seem pleasing."[65]

While attacking Frances Howard and the king's favorite, Somerset, the author implicitly criticized the king for raising the young man to great heights too quickly. "Where Honors have a true beginning, a ground of vertue springing up by noble deserts, continued by Wisedom and maintayned with Care, there cannot choose but follow a fruitfull harvest ... contrariwise to obtaine sodaine Honors begets Pride and Vaineglory ... Brittle is that greatnes that fadeth in a moment." Similar criticism would be voiced of Buckingham who was also accused of poisoning James I. Sorcery was part of the thirteenth and fourteenth-century package of complaints against corrupt officials and it lingered into the seventeenth.

The language and the life of the courtier contrasted with that of the godly. According to the author, one of the accomplices, Mistress Turner, prayed the night before her death: "With Mary Magdalene I kneele (O Jesus) at thy feete ... and how (for a golden bribe) have I sold that love of thine, and my owne salvation." The writer concluded: "If the feare of God had shined in their hearts, it would have been a light to have led them from all darke practices ... that for the favors of Greatnes, will dip their hands in the blood of Innocents."[66] Religious and courtly discourse about corruption were here interwoven.

The cynicism about the court evoked by the Overbury scandal found outlet in *The Court of King James* published in 1619. Claiming to teach men not to love or loath either "court" or "cart," the uncertain tone of the tract reflects the uncertain center of Jacobean court life. The tract was dedicated to the Duke of Buckingham, who had replaced Carr as royal favorite. Although most courtiers were rushing to ingratiate themselves with the favorite in 1619, the writer, amidst his praise, insinuated an underlying suggestion of satire that raised questions about royal bounty. Citing Buckingham's "lineage, the great and most grave wisdom, which doth inhabit in so green and young a breast, your modesty and affability and great humanity," the author goes on:

> A figg for envious Criticks ... the judgement of the most judicious and just judges may give both mee and all good men full content, principally the great love and favour of our most potent and prudent King, who hath graciously elected and made choice of your Honour, as a man most excellent most accomplisht: on whom (many others being neglected) he might conferre, yea accumulate the favourable effects of his Princly benevolence, bounty, and benignity. This your Honours lovely lot and felicity, no doubt may bite to the quicke, and even (as it were) boyle the harts of the malicious ...[67]

On the one hand the author evoked the traditional vicissitudes of the court and on the other set out the limitations of private life. Like many other contemporaries he cited Cicero's *De Officiis* to emphasize the importance of duty to the public and commonwealth.

> Let us never suppose, that true Fame or Felicitie, doth consist, in a private or retyred life ... true glory, reputation, and renowne consisteth in Vertue, which also is especially illustrated and made famous by worthie and meritorious actions and imployments in a Common-Wealth.

How then could an aspiring courtier live a virtuous life "amongst manie fawn-
ing smooth-boots, false hearted flatterers, and crooked perverse minds?"[68]
The author, known only as A. D. B., implicitly reversed Thomas Wyatt's cynical
sixteenth-century definition of the nature of the courtier: "rather then to be,
owtewerdly to seme."[69] He urged "let this be thy sweete and soveraigne Anti-
dote, that with grave Cato, you be of an honest and uncorrupted life . . . that
with invincible Vertue . . . to be good in deed, rather than seeme so to be."[70]

He urged the courtier to seek the court of a powerful prince for "to live
under a most wise and mightie Monarch is not thraldome and servilitie, but
freedom and libertie."[71] Playing with this vocabulary, the author referred not
to the free-born Englishman but to "the free borne courtier" whom he defined
as one who "either by his owne power and industrie, or by some especiall
and singular grace and favour of his Prince hath floated aloft."[72]

The issues of justice, equity and gift-giving were as central to the language
of courtiership as they were to law and religion. Like King James, he used
Senecan language to describe the exchange of benefits. "To take or receive is
the sweetest thing of all" he wrote, quoting Seneca. Gift-giving was a positive
good: "the sores and swellings of a Court, must of necessitie be mollified
and softned with those like poultesies, and healing plaisters, whereby we
may asswage and mitigate the wicked and perverse qualities and conditions
of men, and the most vicious and pernicious customes and practises of this
our Age." The author urged the courtier to use liberality towards those whom
he had offended. "If there be any hammar or wedge wherewith to pierce, penetrate, or cleave in sunder the most obdurate . . . heart of man, tis this, namely
Gifts or Rewards." These "silver streams" of court life returned to the courtier
himself. The courtier might accept gifts under certain circumstances.

> Neither may he take all things, nor at all times, nor from all men, but each of
> these discreetly and wisely; For as in all other matters, two extreames are to
> be avoided, namely Excess and Defect, even so it is here, for the extremitie
> of defect, is, not to receive ought from any man, which were very inhumane
> and uncivill; and the extremitie of excesse, is, alwayes to receive all whatsoever
> is proffered, which is most vile and avaritious.

Courtiers might accept freely the bounty of the monarch and take small
rewards, sparingly, from the poor on issues concerning justice.

> But those Courtiers are contrariwise most worthy detestation and bitter execration,
> which doe sell Justice and Truth for gold and gaine. Let the Courtier therefore
> thinke upon that, which that most wise Oratour and Philosopher Cicero makes
> mention of in the second Booke of his Offices . . . The Basis or Foundation
> of eternal Fame and Commendations is Justice, without which nothing can by
> any meanes, be prayseworthy . . . Let not therefore any gaine, any gifts, though
> never so sweete, never so sumptuous, no pleasant enticements or inducements

of honour, favour or affection, move the honest and conscionable courtier from the love and true delight of Justice and equity.[73]

In practice, Jacobean and Caroline courtiers moved within the constraints of the early modern state in which corrupt practices were endemic and within a mental world in which service to the king and courtesy to the one's friends overlapped. Corrupt practices were tolerated by those who benefited and by some administrators who saw no other way to administer the realm. Courtiers differed on the label of corruption and the level of extraction. In transactions with businessmen and ambassadors, kickbacks appear to have been somewhere between 5 per cent and 15 per cent. The Earl of Northampton told Lionel Cranfield that he should double his gift to the Earl of Somerset for the farm of the sweet wines from 1,000 to 2,000 marks because of Cranfield's projected profit.[74]

As an outcome of the peace with Spain in 1604, Spanish pensions amounting to £9,125 a year were paid to English officials including several of the most important members of the Privy Council. Some English officials termed the Spanish pensions "ordinary courtesies."[75] Thomas Studder, English agent in Brussels, complained to Northampton that he had tried "to procure me payment of such money as the King of Spain is behind with me which are ordinary courtesies amongst them to those they affect. If I knew how to have my suit preferred again unto him so as it might take effect, I should be the more able and would employ it in the service of my sovereign and your lordship." Such distiinctions went up in smoke when the pensions became public knowledge, printed in tracts and published from the pulpit. Sir John Digby, Cornwallis's successor as English ambassador in Spain, was amazed too discover pensions paid by the Spanish to English privy councillors. To the king, he quoted the Spanish ambassador's aassessment that "they are to be bought and sold withal, as he wouldd do with shop-keepers ... that as nothing is to be had of them without money, so for money he thinketh they would sell their souls to hell."[76] Digby tried to explain Salisbury's actions by suggesting that the promotion of peace and the Spanish marriage fitted in with English interests and that when English and Spanish interests diverged, Salisbury withdrew his support but allowed the pension to continue. Digby concluded, nonetheless, that "no circumstance can make his proceedings excusable or free from the name of falsehood and treachery unless he freely acquainted your Majesty with all that passed, and that your Majesty were contented not to be displeased that the Spaniards should be cozened."[77] James made no direct reply. But he received lists of Spanish pensioners and for several years was able to read all of the Spanish ambassador's secret correspondence. He neither demanded an explanation from his councillors nor took any action to prevent such payoffs. While taking pensions from foreign governments, France, the Netherlands as well as Spain, his agents appear nonetheless to have carried out his policies.

Anti-Spanish feelings had run strong among the English since the Armada. Many identified Spain with popery and the anti-Christ. In 1620, as King James considered a Spanish bride for Prince Charles, war broke out in the Palatinate, threatening the position of his daughter Princess Elizabeth and her husband the Elector Palatine. The king's unpopular foreign policy was attacked in a series of tracts which questioned his commitment to the international Protestant cause which, as the embodiment of the godly prince, he was to lead. Spain, popery and corruption became linked when the Spanish pensioners became known, leading to attacks on corrupt courtiers who "gaped wide for Spanish gold."[78] Even at Paul's Cross, often used by the government to present its point of view, preachers spoke out against the marriage of Prince Charles and the Spanish Infanta.[79] The issue continued to provoke outcry. In 1622 a tract claimed that Gondomar, the Spanish Ambassador,

> knows your secrets before the greatest part and most faithful of your council; and which is worse, they say your Majesty knows it and therefore suspect that yourself is bribed against yourself. Otherwise they think not the devil himself could so abuse the times we live, as to make things pass in that fashion as they do, contrary to all sense and conscience and reason of state.[80]

Such tracts began to ask the dangerous question whether the king himself, and not just his courtiers, could be corrupt.

IV

Justice was central to a variety of discourses in early seventeenth-century England whether they focused on law, religion or the court, Moreover, office, gift and conscience were important concepts in those discourses. Such rhetoric helped shape political behavior. Defining office and the proper giving of a gift became central to the trial in Star Chamber of the Lord Treasurer on charges of corruption in 1619.

For all these pejoratives associated with complaint literature were now applied by Crown officials themselves to the highest official in the land, Lord Treasurer Thomas Howard, Earl of Suffolk. Suffolk, the father of Frances, Countess of Somerset, had dominated the court with his son-in-law, the favorite, Somerset, since 1614. The king himself had acknowledged their hegemony. Somerset's fall undermined Suffolk's political power. Factional rivalry, then, made the trial possible. Extensive evidence of corruption made it necessary. In 1619 charges of corruption were filed in Star Chamber against the Lord Treasurer, his wife and an Exchequer official, Sir John Bingley.

The Suffolks and Bingley were accused of "bargaining, delaying, persuading, threatening etc. saying no door could be opened without a golden key."[81] The countess esteemed "no friends but money" and made "my Lord's house a snare for the subject."[82] The Countess took a central role in the arrangement of the kickbacks, complaining that Sir Arthur Ingram "could procure her but five in the hundred, when ... Bingley could bring her to far better bargains." The Countess of Suffolk and Bingley required merchants, customs farmers, courtiers, and citizens granted pensions or favors from the king to kickback to them between 5 per cent and 15 per cent of the value of the grant. If 5–10 per cent was the usual douceur, 15 per cent must have seemed avaricious. The specific practices of which Suffolk stood accused included falsifying the books in the Ordnance office and Exchequer, misemploying the king's treasure, withholding of funds intended for the king's service in Ireland, and pervasive extortion.

The Suffolks defended themselves in several ways. First, the earl claimed it was not supposed that someone of his rank would closely oversee the books in the Ordnance and Exchequer: his "eminent quality might exempt him from such mean inquisitions and duties." Secondly, he had erred "not of wilfulness but of too much credulity, much less of corruption."[83] He claimed not to know of his wife's importuning for kickbacks and had returned the money when he found out about it. Finally, he portrayed other payments as gifts. As a result of this claim, the court was moved to distinguish gifts from kickbacks.

Suffolk admitted taking gifts both in plate and cash. Thus Sir Allen Apsley testified that he gave Suffolk £100 or plate of that value every year "but with no contract," i.e. as a free gift. Suffolk argued that the same was true of monies taken from Sir Miles Fleetwood, William Ashton and Arnold Spencer, that is, "the said gratuity was given freely without any contract."[84] Accused of taking £300, a cup of gold worth £100 and other rewards "for favors to be done" Suffolk replied that he had received no monies but confessed he had accepted a cup of gold as a New Year's gift.[85] It is worth noting that these were definitions of a gift even as Bracton had defined it. His judges, however, did not accept this label saying "which offenses, if they would not have them termed extortions but gratuities, it was but to clothe a hare in a fox's skin, and that they were but cloaks lined with bribery." Of the £10,000 loan from the customs farmers, Suffolk claimed that

it was agreed between him and the said farmers that £1500 yearly should be paid as a New Year's gift unto him ... and the said £1500 was to be defaulted

out of the foresaid sum of £10,000 borrowed and this was done by the free
and voluntary act of the farmers without any coercion or compulsion on his
part either by himself or any other for him.[86]

What Suffolk omitted to say was that the £1,500 a year was to last only so
long as he was Lord Treasurer, that is only so long as he was in a position
to maintain the custom farmers' monopoly.

While the countess had taken a leading role in these economic transactions,
she was defended on the grounds that she had acted as the wife of the earl,
not the wife of the Lord Treasurer and so not by color of office. Her acts,
therefore, did not fall under the legal definition of extortion. Indeed she was
deemed a good wife.[87] Finally, Suffolk's attorney argued that the number of
persons from whom he was supposed to have extorted money was seventeen,
the sum £3,000, over four years, "a light burden among so many and not worth
the speaking of."

Summing up the case for the Crown, the Attorney-General used language
reminiscent of those texts we have examined. He called Suffolk "a great star
fallen out of their own firmament; . . . great men stand not by their greatness
but by their goodness, he concluded with a mitigating wish that his Majesty
would be pleased to remember my Lord's service and his quality, and after
God's imitation whose representant he was, look upon him rather with the
eyes of mercy than of severity of justice."[88]

The judges found the Suffolks guilty of corrupt practices. They differed
only as to the fine and as to their understanding of the nature of the crime.
Sir Edward Coke's judgement used harsh language to describe the corruption
of great courtiers. He argued that there were

> three loud speaking relaters that stood up against the defendants, the common
> weal, the voice of the oppressed and the cry of the labourer robbed of his
> hire. That the king's treasure was the soul of the commonwealth, so as who
> destroyed this was guilty of civil murder, that great men should not be called
> to that court for petty offenses, but since the corruption of the greatest and best
> was the worst and this was no petty offence . . . he would not give sentence out
> of his own opinion but out of records . . . Hereupon he cited from Henry III's
> time to these days what several treasurers and great officers entrusted with the
> king's money had incurred severe punishments for deceit of trust, oppression
> of the people, consuming of the treasure, taking of bribes, compounding unduly
> for the king's debts.

Coke called for a fine of £100,000 on the earl and countess. Although Lord
Hubbard "held it an unlucky thing that bribery should be found so ancient
and so quick in return during the reign of so many kings as Sir Edward Coke
had proved it," he was less harsh. Of Katherine he said "she was a better wife
than woman." He found Suffolk not to offend in corruption but in frailty. Since

his fault might have been worse,"he should be loth to fine him so as his estate should crack for it." Hubbard urged a fine of £30,000 and imprisonment in the Tower during pleasure. Most others agreed with Hubbard, excusing Suffolk for loving his friends too much, certainly an important value of the period but a quality, as we have seen, that Coke urged officials to throw off, or yielding to the temptation of his place. While the Archbishop of Canterbury compared extorting officers to ill shepherds and the countess to Eve provoking Adam to the Fall, he said that "none should be more forward than he to mediate with his Majesty for extenuation of their punishment."[89]

It was left to the highest-ranking judge in England, Lord Chancellor Francis Bacon, to conclude and to make the connection between the corruption of the great and the market-place. Bacon compared Suffolk, the son of the fourth Duke of Norfolk, to a shopkeeper. "My Lady kept the shop, Bingley was the prentice that cried 'what do you lack,' but all went into my Lord's cash."[90] To the claim of the Suffolks that they might take gifts, Bacon replied "new years gifts did not last all the year."[91]

By 1619, then, in sermon and in investigation, in short in prescription and in practice, the definition of corruption as the use of public office for certain if not all private ends was not only established but was repeatedly and increasingly invoked in the Jacobean period. Moreover, corrupt practices included not only bribery and extortion both directly and indirectly but was extended to conflict of interest and monopoly. In addition, the definition of the gift had been narrowed, through increasing attacks on exchange of money whether in traditional attacks on covetousness or contemporary indictments of the sale of office, gratuities and New Year's gifts. Indeed, the stringent notion put forward by Coke in 1606 of the function of the judge was about to be applied in practice to Francis Bacon himself.

Chapter 8

The language of corruption:
a discourse of political conflict

The metaphor of the fountain, used so frequently to describe the justice and bounty of God and the king, was invoked in parliament in 1621 to describe the pollution caused by corruption. In presenting the report of the committee on abuses in the Courts of Justice Sir Robert Phelips put the issue this way: "The principal thing ... was whether at the time of giving those gifts to the Lord Chancellor there was any suit depending before him." Those concerned were not only immediate parties to the suit but all of the king's subjects who were wronged by corruption. Phelips concluded with "It's a cause of great weight. It concerns every man here. For if the fountains be muddy, what will the streams be? If the great dispenser of the king's conscience be corrupt, who can have any courage to plead before him?"[1]

I

In 1621 James I called parliament into session for the first time in seven years against the backdrop of a trade depression and war on the continent. The previous session in 1614 had been dubbed the "addled parliament" because it had passed no statutes and had been dissolved after two months. Parliaments were an occasion for the redress of grievances. In 1621, the list of grievances presented to parliament and the king focused primarily on monopolies.

The procedure of impeachment originated in the late fourteenth century and, after fifty years of use by parliament to remove royal officials, lay dormant for 150 years until its revival in the 1620s.[2] But from 1621 to 1628 parliament repeatedly turned to impeachment to challenge government policy and to indict and remove government officials on the grounds of abuse of office. That abuse was almost invariably on the grounds of corruption.

185

Traditionally, historians have argued that members of parliament mounted these attacks to defend the liberty and property of the subject; more recently, revisionists have argued that impeachment reflected factional politics at court. While factionalism may explain both victims and timing, it is not sufficient to explain the expansion of the definition of corruption, the revival of procedures of parliamentary judicature to remove government officials from office, and the extension of such attacks to others in addition to the initial victim. The process developed a life of its own once parliament began to investigate corrupt activities.

In these proceedings charges of corruption were extended to activities beyond the sixteenth-century statutory definitions to include certain kinds of gift-giving, the sale of non-judicial office and monopoly. Their scope and language paralleled the drumbeat of sermons in the middle Jacobean period. While those impeached initially were monopolists, the House of Commons moved on to those who had approved the grants of monopolies, including Sir Francis Bacon, who as Attorney-General had approved many. James I held out some protection to the referees by urging the Commons "not to condemn men for error in opinion if there were no corruption."[3] But the charges against Bacon extended beyond his approval of monopolies to include his role as Lord Chancellor in which he was, like many other officials, both administrator and judge. Bacon was accused of taking gifts from litigants. "The luxuriant authority" of Chancery was attacked. One member of parliament called it "an inextricable labyrinth, wherein resideth such a monster as gormandizeth the liberty of all subjects whatsoever."[4] Sir Edward Coke now had the opportunity not only to implement his prescriptive view of the good judge but also to vanquish a long-time rival. Bacon's case brought into focus the tensions around the concepts of office and gifts, of the spheres of public and private. One witness was described as "struggling with himself betwixt gratitude and honesty. But public and private goods meeting together, he preferred the public."[5]

In conference with the Lords, the House of Commons presented its accusations against Bacon; these centered on the fundamental attributes of royal justice.

> The incomparable good parts of the Lord Chancellor were highly commended, the place he holds magnified, from whence bounty, justice and mercy were to be distributed to the subjects, with which he was solely trusted . . . the Lord Chancellor was accused of great Bribery and Corruption committed by him in this eminent place.[6]

Bacon made submission to the House of Lords, saying that he was a man of his times and "hereafter the greatness of a judge or a Magistrate shall be no sanctuary or protection of guiltiness . . . after this example it is like that judges will fly from anything that is in the likeness of corruption (though it were at great distance)." Although he did not defend himself, he claimed that "a defence might in diverse things extenuate the offence in respect of the time or the manner of the gift."[7] Time and manner, which served to contextualize transactions and distinguish between gifts and bribes, had increasingly been renounced in contemporary prescriptive literature and now were disregarded in political action.

The king himself shared the discourse of the preachers and members of parliament. On March 26, 1621 James addressed the House of Commons in language which recalls contemporary sermons.

The State he compared to his own Coppices, the outside well grown and making a good show, But inwardly eaten and spoiled ... His government seemed to be well fenced with laws, judges and other magistrates. And yet his people, by secret corruptions, projecture, bills of conformity and such like courses, had been more grieved and vexed than if they had given diverse subsidies.[8]

Bacon was not the only judge attacked in the 1621 session, for once the process had been set in motion, the House of Commons moved against others. Sir John Bennett, Judge of the Prerogative Court of Canterbury, was impeached for taking excessive fees and for bribery in the probate of wills and granting of letters of administration. There were as many as thirty cases alleged against him. Walter Yonge wrote in his diary, no doubt hyperbolically, "there was found in his custody two hundred thousand pounds in coin. He was as corrupt a judge as any in England, for he would not only take bribes of both parties ... but many times shamefully begged them."[9] Bacon later claimed that to compare him to Bennett was to compare white to black or, at the least, gray to black. Others said that "Sir John Bennett hath made my Lord Chancellor an honest man."[10] In his defence Bennett argued that having served for nineteen years, "proof cannot be produced of £4000 which is not above £200 per annum, since I was a judge; whereof if I cannot give good account, I will beg my bread all my life."[11]

Coke led the charge against Bennett too, saying "nothing is of so much moment as the taking away of corrupt judges."[12] "All his excuses are turned against himself ... Now bribery stands in his face, he wisheth he had never been a judge .. This is a thing that concerns the whole land. If fountains be corrupted, look for no health in anything that comes from them."[13]

Because the civil judges sat alone, opportunities for payoffs were greater and they incurred greater opprobrium. From the point of view of the litigant, such payoffs may have been necessary to expedite cases caught in red tape. Bribes were required not so much to procure a favorable judgement as to prevent an unfavourable one. Sir Francis Mitchell, the Clerkenwell Justice of the Peace, was accused of "exacting bonds from London merchants and extorting money from alehouse keepers;" Dr Theophilus Field, Bishop of Llandaff, of acting as Bacon's broker in taking a bribe; Alexander Harris of extorting larger fees from prisoners. In addition, the House began to prepare charges against two ecclesiastical chancellors, Dr John Lambe and Dr John Craddock, for taking bribes and selling letters of administration.[14] The attack on these judges grew out of the groundswell of grievances, especially about monopoly, and reached Bennett and the others not through faction but through the opening up of the issue of judicial corruption by parliament.

The House of Commons drew up a bill against bribery in the same session. The issue arose on April 27 during a discussion of the workings of Chancery. Edward Alford, who linked prosperity with public interest, argued "that we may see the reason why we decay and the Low Countries flourish, vizt because we look to the private, they to the public, ergo strictness against bribery by some sharp law."[15] One crucial question addressed in debate was whether or not those who offered bribes should be punished along with the judges. Alford argued that "men are compelled to give bribes because justice will not come else. Nay, counsel tells their clients that they must give because the other side have given." Sir Samuel Sandys framed the issue in terms of disease in the body politic:

> We suffer aspersions to be cast upon judges, we suffer the whole kingdom to be scandalized. Here is a disease that needs an Aesculapius to remedy it. We punish the takers of bribes but let the givers alone, not imitating the God of justice, who, when Adam had sinned, not only punished him but those that tempted him ... Let the bribe giver and taker both be touched. Stop the fountain and the rivers will be dry ... The wound will fester if a man search not the bottom.[16]

Sir William Cope too invoked the corporeal image of corruption. "As physicians that look to the bodies of men by considering how the disease came can give rules to prevent the like, so I desire that this committee out of these enormities of bribery may consider of the causes thereof and make some law to prevent bribery in all courts for the future."[17]

A committee was named to consider a bill concerned with problems in the legal system from bribery to legal fees. Reflecting the debate, the bill sought to punish both givers and takers of bribes but distinguished between bribes given voluntarily and bribes given involuntarily "many times ... of necesssity," meaning that the giver had no choice. Further, the bill punished "bribery and affection by letters and messages;" the partiality of judges on behalf of their sons, favorites and cousins'; "the liberty which lawyers take to use opprobrious and disgraceful speeches and scandalous phrases in bills;" excessive fees of lawyers and their taking fees from both sides.[18] Although the bill was not passed it was reintroduced at the next parliament in 1624.

Satirical prints of Sir Giles Mompesson, the alehouse patentee, circulated after his impeachment in 1621 and contemporary tracts attacked official venality. Thomas Scott published *The Projector* in 1623. In theological language Scott attacked the Jacobean practice of selling honors and office in church and state.

> Again, have we not married sin and honor together? Consider if honor be not bought and sold: Nay consider if all honorable officers either in Church or Commonwealth be not exposed to sale, and set upon the market hill with this word of Judas in their mouths ... what will you give me? what will you give me and you shalbe a knight, a Lord, an Earl? what will you give me, and you shalbe a justice of peace, a serjeant, a judge? Nay what will you give me, and you shalbe a Parson, a Dean, a Bishop? This I think is sin: for the law ... calls it sin, calls it bribery, corruption, simony, abomination, though our practice calls it, wisdom, policy and justice. Yet how hard is honor got without this hook? And what preferment need that man despair of, who hath this bait, and knows how to lay it? And must not the buyer sell? I appeal to your consciences whether it were not injustice to deny him that liberty.[19]

Jacobeans did not merely repeat the traditional denunciations of Edwardian corruption by Latimer in the 1550s. To show that his accusations described contemporary practice one quoted the statements of King James and Sir Francis Bacon on corruption from the impeachment proceedings in the parliament of 1621.[20]

If the 1621 impeachments grew from a groundswell of grievance pent up for a decade, the impeachment of the Lord Treasurer, Lionel Cranfield, in 1624 was more overtly political, inspired by the animus of the Duke of Buckingham and Prince Charles. Buckingham suspected that Cranfield had tried to insinuate Sir Arthur Brett in the king's affections and knew that Cranfield refused to support war with Spain, the policy that Prince Charles and the Duke embraced after the failure of their extraordinary journey to secure the Spanish Infanta. The animosity of the Prince and the Duke was shared by court officials who had suffered from Cranfield's reform of court administration. He was accused both of bribery and of introducing new procedures in the Court of Wards designed to defraud the subject. The latter upon examination appeared to be rather paltry.[21] More important, members of the House of Commons such as Sir Edwin Sandys and Sir Robert Phelips held the Lord Treasurer responsible for impositions, royal customs duties that were placed on imports without parliamentary sanction but upheld by the judges in 1606 in Bate's case. In order to make their argument, however, Cranfield had to be isolated both from the king and Robert Cecil, Earl of Salisbury, who had inaugurated the policy of impositions. Cranfield was also accused of taking bribes from the farmers of the Great Customs, one of the charges that had brought down the Earl of Suffolk.

Cranfield's impeachment, a political coup, showed the utility of the charges and the language of corruption even against the reign's most important administrative reformer. The procedure of impeachment had first been used in 1376 to attack Sir Richard Lyons, Richard's II's customs official, and much was made of the parallels. Sir Edward Coke once again expatiated on the evils of extortion. Unlike Bacon, Cranfield defended himself and, in so doing, shifted the grounds for such a defense in a significant way. He did not describe payments from the farmers of the Great Customs as New Year's gifts as Suffolk had, but payment for shares in the farm that he himself owned. Nevertheless, with few supporters in parliament, Cranfield was removed from office and heavily fined. While King James supported him against most charges, the king held him responsible for the diversion of £30,000 in the Court of Wards and upheld the sentence passed by parliament.

In Cranfield's case, although there was some effort to raise the issue of justice, the language of corruption was tied most closely to the evocative issue of taxation. When the Prince and the Earl of Southampton argued that Cranfield's abuses were worse than Bacon's, Lord Keeper Williams disagreed, claiming that extortion was not as serious as the bribing of a judge. He returned to the traditional themes of justice and bribery which had been re-emphasized in the session of 1621. He stressed "the Lord St. Alban's fault [Bacon] as great as any. For bribery; yea, by contract, which destroyed the formality of his place. No such proved against the Treasurer for his judicature. Faulty for extortion, whereby he destroyed also the formality of his place. No fault can be greater than a judge to be corrupt."[22]

In 1626 Buckingham himself was attacked in parliament. Attitudes toward Buckingham throughout his period of dominance from 1618 to 1628 varied. His reputation was closely linked to other crucial issues of foreign policy, religion and taxation. The Jacobean tilt toward Spain in foreign policy and the public discovery of the Spanish pensions had helped make the issue of corruption, long a staple of English political debate, central to criticism of court practice. Such criticism issued from the press and stage in the 1620s in, among other texts, Thomas Scott's *Vox Populi, parts I and II*, and Thomas Middleton's *A Game at Chess*. *A Game at Chess* attacked the Spanish and the Jesuits, daringly put living personages on stage and satirized the sale of offices in the royal Household. Attended by courtiers and court watchers like John Holles, who said it was the first play he had seen in ten years, the play's extended run led contemporaries to believe that it had backing within the court. Although Prince Charles's wish to marry the Infanta had led to his reckless trip to Spain in 1623, by 1624 Prince Charles and the Duke of Buckingham were enraged at the Spanish, and one observer said they "laughed heartily" at the play.[23] While *The Court of King James* (1619) raised questions about a new favorite in the wake of Somerset, Thomas

Scot's *Vox Dei* (1623) lauded the favorite for his anti-Spanish policy. Scott described Buckingham as

> long time held to be the child of fortune only, but now is found to be the favorite of virtue also. Whilst he shot up suddenly, who did not take him for a gourd, and expect his more sudden withering again ... But now who doth not look upon him, as upon an oak or cedar sound at the heart, like to last long, and be profitable for the upholding of the church and state ... the first honors he had, were freely given, this last faithfully earned.

This positive view carried over to the Duke's control of patronage. The frontispiece of *Vox Dei* portrays faction and bribery on the ground and an accompanying panel explains: "the Duke kills bribery (bane of commonweals) / With firebrand Faction and so truly deals / For king and kingdom, as a man that knows / Upon one root, their equal welfare grows."[24] By 1626, however, some members of parliament were unhappy both with the conduct of the war and with Buckingham's control of patronage.

Buckingham faced thirteen articles of impeachment.[25] The majority concerned corrupt practices including sale of office and extortion. Buckingham's judicial functions as Lord Admiral, although tangential to most of the articles, were brought forward and allusions to "absolute authority" were invoked, which would be heard again in 1641 in the attack on Thomas Wentworth, Earl of Strafford and William Laud, Archbishop of Canterbury. Buckingham, who had backed the most thorough-going investigation of the navy and presided over the commission that successfully ran the navy until the campaigns of the 1620s, was charged with dereliction of duty and extorting money from those who had business before the Admiralty court.

John Selden presented a learned discourse on the office of Lord Admiral and England's claim to sovereignty of the seas of England and Ireland based on his *Mare Clausem*. By his patent as Lord Admiral the seas of England and Ireland, part of the possessions of the Crown of England, were committed to Buckingham "not as if he should thereby have jurisdiction only as in cases of the Admirals of France and Spain." Though hypothetically barred by law from retaining the offices of Lord Admiral and Lord Warden of the Cinque Ports because he had bought them, Selden argued that Buckingham was bound justly to execute them, so long as *de facto* he held them. Buckingham had not certified numbers and complement of royal and merchant ships, had not overseen provisioning, and had not personally attended on "the service of guarding the seas." To the objection that money was wanting to perform these tasks Selden replied "his power hath been so great in procuring vast sums, both in the revenue of the Crown and of whole sums in gross (as appears in a following article) that he might also, for this purpose, which so properly belonged to his office, have done the like."[26]

By his patent, the Lord Admiral was judge of all maritime causes. Buckingham had detained the *St Peter* of New Haven and a great part of its goods to his own use. Not only did this affect merchants and foreign trade but also served as "an example that may ... hereafter ... justify all Absolute authority in the Admiral without law or legal course over the ships and goods of all merchants whatsoever."[27]

Furthermore, Buckingham was accused of extorting £10,000 from the East India Company for a heavily freighted vessel they had seized from the Portuguese, based on his judicial rights in Admiralty Court. That King James had undertaken to wring even more money from the company was an embarrassment but the Commons members who presented the charges to the Lords at a committee meeting on May 8 and 9 repeatedly indicated that they were not blaming King James or his son.[28] Nevertheless in his defence Buckingham identified himself with the king and his authority.

John Pym presented the articles of impeachment which accused the duke of ennobling his family and misappropriating the royal revenue. Pym argued that Buckingham's offence was "a great grievance to the commonwealth." Yet how could the king's liberality to his favorite and his favorite's family be a charge against Buckingham?[29] Although complaint literature from the late sixteenth century had attacked the granting of arms to the unworthy, there were statutes neither against the sale of titles nor the king's unwise dispensation of bounty. Pym admitted as much, "It is prejudicial to the king, not that it can disable him from giving honor (for that is in a power inseparable) but by making honor ordinary it becomes an incompetent reward for extraordinary vertue." There were no statutes against such bounty but Pym argued some laws were

> coessential and conatural with government which being broken all things run into confusion, such is that rule observed in all states of suppressing vice by apt punishments and encouraging vertue by rewards. And this is the fittest law to insist upon in a court of parliament where the proceedings are not limited either by civil or common laws, but matters are judged according as they stand in opposition or conformity with that which is *suprema lex, salus populi*. By this law whoever moves the king to bestow honor (which is the greatest reward) upon any man, binds himself to make good a double proportion of merit in that party ... there ought to be in the first root of this honor some such active merit in the service of the commonwealth as might transmit a vigorous example to his successors whereby they may be raised to an imitation of the like.

The duke's liability was even greater because in the midst of "weakness and consumption of the commonwealth he hath not been content alone to consume the public commonwealth treasure, which is the blood and nourishment of the state, but hath brought in others to help in this work of destruction."

192

The twelfth article accused Buckingham of "misemploying the king's revenue." Pym divided this in two, crown lands and "money in pensions, gifts and other kinds of profit." Although others had benefitted from the grant of Crown lands, Buckingham had benefitted most. Pym claimed it "a great grievance that in a time of such necessity so much land should be conveyed from the Crown to a private man." Because of the way that Buckingham had the grants drawn up they were greater than the king intended. (Of course King James was as much the author of these practices as was the favorite, as his order to Cranfield to convey estates to Buckingham as quickly as possible demonstrates.) Using agents to contract for lands for his own use and phoney tallies struck in the Exchequer, Buckingham was false to the king and to parliament because "the grants seem to have the face of valuable purchases whereas they were indeed free gifts." As a result, the king was not left "minister of his own liberality."[30]

Pym claimed that Buckingham had received £162,995 in ten years in addition to £3,000 per annum of customs duties from the levy of three pence in the pound on strangers' goods plus the moitie of £7,000 out of the customs of Ireland. Buckingham had served himself "before his duty and before the service of the State." But whose fault was that, king or favorite?

> If we look upon the time past, never so much came into any one private man's hands out of the public purse. If we respect the time present the king never had so much want, never so much foreign occasions, both important and expensive; the subjects have never given greater supplies, and yet those supplies are unable to furnish these expenses.

To find laws which reached to these grievances Pym turned to civil laws which carried the punishment of death but claimed to do so only to note "that in the wisest states the public treasure was held in the same reputation with that which was dedicated to God and religion."[31] As a sign of his guilt, Buckingham hid the king's bounty and concealed his actions under the "disguise of public service." There was "so great a mixture and confusion betwixt the king's estate and his own," they could not be distinguished in the records. From the sale of honors and offices, and "projects hurtful to the state both of England and Ireland," Buckingham made a tremendous gain. "All those gifts and other ways of profit notwithstanding, he [Buckingham] confessed before both houses of parliament that he was indebted £100,000. If this be true, how can we hope to satisfy his prodigality? If false, how can we hope to satisfy his covetousness."[32]

Buckingham was accused of selling offices including the Lord Wardenship of the Cinque Ports and the Lord Treasurership.[33] The language of the impeachment sounded much like the discourse in contemporary sermon literature. The charges made it clear that justice was at the heart of almost every office, much as Samuel Ward had argued, and that justices ought to "be magistrates not merchants of justice." "Because the merchants' trade consists wholly in buying and selling ... it is feared they would even in places of judicature walk in the same ways they did when they were merchants and sell justice." Like the navy commissioners, contemporaries believed that those who bought their offices were more likely to take payoffs. Pym said in committee "when men are called to high estate and have not livlihood to support it, it enduceth great poverty and causeth extortions, embraceries and maintenançe."[34] Extraction by their patrons and themselves increased because of the uncertain costs of such transactions.

Those that have the best purses, though the worst causes, shall find the best measure in the courts of justice ... The great men that sell places and offices to others must and will maintain the undue exactions .... of those whom they have so raised, both because they are their creatures as also for that the more the gain is threatened, the great fineer must be paid to the next vacation by the following successor.[35]

Sale of titles and honors had predated Buckingham's eminence. Buckingham extended such sales to titles of nobility, marketed Scottish and, especially, Irish titles and systematized the business. Members of both houses attacked "the introduction of this new trade and commerce of honor." They argued that such sales of honors and titles were illegal even though there were no statutes that dealt with the matter. Rhetoric rose to a fever pitch. "There was never any nation so barbarous as to assess a certain price for titles of honor." Before Buckingham's rise "honor was a virgin and undeflowered." Such hyperbole could not stand when it was recalled that the duke was only 19 when the title of baronet was introduced by the Jacobean Privy Council in 1611, so the speaker continued, "at least not so publicly prostituted before the times of this man who makes account all things, all persons would stoop and subject themselves to his loose desires and vain fancies."

The purpose of royal bounty was undone by such policies. Christopher Sherland presented the charges on "honor and justice; two great flowers of the Crowne ... titles of honor of the kingdom were not to be put upon such as are rich, but upon such industrious persons as should merit them by their services ... the Duke hath not only perverted the honorable and ancient way, but (for gain) hath forced some ... to receive honors."[36] As in the debate over bribing judges, the Commons was anxious to excuse those who had offered, they claimed, unwillingly.

Honor, Sherland posited, was a "beam of virtue, and can be no more fixed upon an undeserving person for money, than fire can be struck out of a stick."[37] Honor was spiritual, sublime, transcendent, sacred and divine,

194

money earthly and base. "Honor is a public thing: it is the reward of public deserts." The sale of titles

> extremely deflowers the flowers of the crowne; for it maketh them cheap to all the beholders ... It taketh away from the crown one fair and frugal reward of deserving servants; for where honor cometh to be at so mean a rate as to be sold, there is no great or deserving man will look after it, if this evil be suffered to grow on ... It is the way to make men more studious of lucre and gain than of virtue and sufficiency when they know they shalbe preferred to titles of honor according to the heaviness of their purses and not for the weightiness of their merit.[38]

Describing the sale of honors as "a prodigious scandal to this nation," Sherland said there were no precedents. "But certainly it is now a fit time to make a precedent of this ... great Duke, that hath been lately raised to this transcendent height in our Sphere, that thinketh he cannot shine enough, unless he dims your Lordships honor in making it contemptible through the sale and commoness of it."[39]

Buckingham's response to these charges, delivered on June 8, 1626, argued that the proceeds from the sales of titles and offices had been put to uses directed by the king and that the ennobling of his relatives reflected values of family and kinship that he shared with his accusers. Pleading both "the law of nature and the king's royal favor," he believed "he were to be condemned in the opinion of all generous minds, if, being in such favor ... he had minded only his own advancement and had neglected those who were nearest unto him."[40] Most of all he relied on royal bounty and authority as justification.

> He may, without blame, receive and retain that which the liberal and bountiful hand of his master has freely conferred on him; and it is not without precedents both in ancient and modern times that one man, eminent in the esteem of his sovereign, has at one time held as great and as many offices. But when it shall be discerned that he shall falsify or corruptly use those places ... or that the public shall suffer thereby ... he will readily lay down at his royal feet not only his places and offices but his whole fortunes and his life to do him service.[41]

Charles I dissolved parliament before it could proceed further. "His Majesty cannot believe that the aim is at the Duke of Buckingham but ... your proceedings do expressly wound the honor and government of himself and of his father."[42] One observer wrote "some think that my Lord of Buckingham's cause is so involved with his Majesty's that it will hazard the parliament, and if thes [sic], we are hopeless of ever seeing more."[43]

The tension between office and gift was not completely resolved by Bacon's and Buckingham's impeachments. But in the process parliament delineated a newly stringent definition, shaped in part by the prescriptive literature that we have been examining. Henry Sherfield, an M.P. who helped to develop the case against Buckingham, recorded in his diary during the impeachment proceedings his own guilt and regret at having accepted a gift.[44]

In 1628 parliament met in the shadow of England's war with Spain and the forced loan to which King Charles had resorted to pay for it. The King had refused to let the House of Lords judge Buckingham's impeachment in 1626 and now threatened to dissolve the session if the charges were renewed. At the same time that parliament wrestled with the Petition of Right, which challenged arbitrary taxation, arbitrary imprisonment, billeting of troops and martial law, it also brought forward charges against Dr Roger Mainwaring, one of the king's chaplains, who was accused not of corrupt practices but of upholding the king's right to levy forced loans without parliamentary consent, of undermining parliamentary authority and dividing the king and parliament.[45] Mainwaring had delivered a sermon before Charles in which he argued that "as Justice … intercedes not between God and Man," neither does it intercede "between the Prince, being a Father; and the People, as Children."[46] The king as God-like judge could not be judged by his people. Such a formulation, the Commons claimed, undermined the king's fundamental obligation set forth in his coronation oath to uphold the law. Mainwaring was found guilty by the Lords. Buckingham's impeachment proceedings marked the major threshold of the language of corruption in the early Stuart period. Thereafter, accusations of corrupt practices accompanied charges of undermining fundamental law in articles of impeachment against royal officials.

Beginning in 1621, the House of Commons named a Committee of the Whole House on the ecclesiastical and royal courts to meet weekly.[47] In 1626 and 1628 Committees of the Whole House on the ecclesiastical and secular courts were appointed early in the session and called Grand Committees. In the sessions of 1621, 1625, 1626 and 1628 bills were introduced against bribery and the buying and selling of judicial offices. And in debating judicial bribery, members of the Commons echoed contemporary sermon literature going beyond the payment of money to "the bribery of affection, that judges be not solicited by letters, messages, or speeches from great men … and against favorites in all courts."

In the first week of the parliament of 1628, on March 22, 1628, a bill was introduced entitled "an act against the procuring judicial places for money, or other rewards, and against giving and taking of bribes." It was read immediately before "An act concerning liberties of parliament." The bill, presented by Sir John Danvers, went beyond previous legislation to create harsher penalties for buying offices and accepting bribes. Furthermore, it required this new oath to be taken by anyone coming into a judicial office: "I do swear that neither I, nor any by my consents or procurements, have given or will give directly or indirectly any money or gratuities, etc. And if he shall receive any reward, etc. except meat and drink that he shall therefore forfeit an hundred times as much."[48] Finally, it would vacate judgments by anyone who bought a judicial office.

> If any person shall give, or it shall be proved that any do give a bribe or reward for any place of judicature, or office of justice, [he] shall be disabled of the place, and shall pay ten times so much as he gave or promised for the place; and he shall take an oath to that purpose. If any judge, having any suit depending before him, shall receive any bribe or reward, he shall forfeit 100 times so much, and be disabled to hold that place, and shall be fined at the king's pleasure. If any servant or clerk of his shall receive, or any person shall give any money, they shall forfeit 20 times so much, and be imprisoned for a year, and pay £20 for a fine. And no act that the judge shall make shall be effectual.

These provisions not only created much more severe punishments for bribery but also, by vacating acts done by the judge, went beyond statutes that had provided that the acts of those who bought office remained valid. Another version provided a *praemunire* against any judge who received such rewards. The committee appointed to examine the bill on judicial bribery included Sir William Fleetwood, who had raised the issue of the Buckinghamshire election case in 1604, John Hampden, William Noy, an opponent of the forced loan, later Charles's Attorney-General and designer of the ship money writ, and Sir Robert Cotton, the antiquary who by the late 1620s often supplied precedents to the Commons and whose library was sequestered in 1629. The issue seemed of such importance that it was the first item raised at the beginning of the Oxford session even before the establishment of the committee for privileges.[49] The prominence of the issue and of those to whom the bill was committed suggests the close connection of corrupt practices to issues of overriding political and constitutional concern in 1628–9.

II

Between 1629 and 1640 the king called no further parliaments. Through proclamation and Star Chamber, both James and Charles had attempted to dampen the enthusiasm of some who complained of government. Charles was later blamed in the Grand Remonstrance for listening to court sermons which exalted the royal prerogative. "The most publick and solemn Sermons before his Majesty, were either to advance Prerogative above Law, and decry the Property of the Subject, or full of such kind of invectives." While many sermons did exalt royal authority, others expanded many of the themes already examined, although few seem as overtly critical as those of James's reign. In 1634 Edward Reynolds preached "The Shields of the Earth" in which he examined the role of the justice. Emphasizing the honor, power and great duty of the office, Reynolds contrasted, as Coke had done, the rule of law with the rule of favor.[50]

In assize sermons the emphasis on corruption seems to have receded but did not disappear. Attacks on judicial misconduct continued, even as concern turned to the judges' role in upholding the forced loan in the Five Knights Case in 1627 and the legality of ship money in the 1630s. In his diary John Rous recorded charges of judicial corruption in sermons preached at assizes. Thus in March 1630,

> Mr. Ramsay, whom Sir Roger Townsend, high sheriffe, had preferred to an impropriation in him appropriated (as is said), preached before the judges at Thetford … I heard but the latter ende, which was wondrous pithy; full of all good wordes and all learning. He had many touches upon the corruptions of judges and councellors. A similitude he had of the head receiving all the nourishment, and causing the other members to faile and the whole man to die, which he applied to the commonwealth, where all is sucked upwards and the commons left without nourishment. Also of a fish that first putrifies at the heade, so some commonwealth.… He apologized (*ut dicitur*) before and after, saying that judges and all must learne at the lips of the priest. Sale of offices and simony he pithily set out, etc.

The next summer Rous recorded two more sermons on similar topics and a justice's anger at charges of corruption.

> Summer assises at Bury had one Mr. Scot, of Ipswich, that preached before the judges, who made a sore sermon in discovery of corruptions of judges and others. At Norwich Mr. Greene was more plain, insomuch that Judge Harvy, in his charge, brake out thus—"It seemes by the sermon that we are corrupt, but know that we can use conscience in our places, as well as the best clergie man of all."[51]

In 1631 *The Just Lawyer his Conscionable Complaint* appeared, republished as *The Courts of Justice Corrected and Amended* in 1641, although written, according to the preface, many years before. Its author was described as a lawyer

> moved with the corrupt courses used, and the excessive bribery affected in those days by his brethren learned in the laws … and the continual condescending or proclivity of the judges … to the private and undue solicitations of their own menials, besides their friends and favorites at large … whereby many a client in his just cause hath suffered wreck and perished contrary to law, all equity and good conscience.[52]

This tract continues themes from Coke's 1606 charge to the jury, the assize sermons we have examined and Bacon's impeachment in 1621. The language in which the attack on the judges is couched also conjures up the charges against the favorites and "great men" of the early Stuart monarchs.

> The Counsellor ... having ... become inward with the Judge by the benefit of kindred, alliance recommendations of great persons, former education and acquaintance ... shall be followed with a cloud of clients and waged treble more than men of better merit; and if he ... can bring the Judge to be his fee-man (or pensioner under color of a yearly new year's gift,) or may find the means to possess the Judge with the loan of some hundreds of pounds, without taking any interest therefore, then shall ... no door be kept against him, then shall he be a guest at the judge's table, and shall be admitted private both in the closet and also in the bedchamber ... The culling and cherishing of favorites, draweth the favorer into suspicion of corrupt partiality.

The author attacked the judge's servants who were "so miraculous Machia-vellious, that they are able to express two sundry liquors out of one same vessel, making their own profit, by both the parties, to one same suit and controversy." The remedy for all these evils lay in the judge himself, who may "with a lofty look take it unkindly at the hands of his better, equal or inferior friends; blaming them with the touch of his credit for their so unadvised tampering with him in matter of his judicial and sworn duty." The ideal judge was that pictured by Robert Bolton in his panegyric on Augustine Nicolls; otherwise "the scale of Justice suffereth reproach."[53]

It would be a mistake to assume an irrevocable split between court and country. Preachers critical of the court still maintained their connections to courtiers in the early 1630s. Robert Bolton had emphasized the importance of the godly prince to prevent "a very hell upon earth."[54] Although in 1630 Bolton preached an assize sermon arguing that "great men are seldom good," a year later he dedicated his "Instructions for a Right Comforting Afflicted Consciences with Special Antidotes against Some Grievous Temptations" to Sir Robert Carr, Gentleman of the King's Bedchamber. Similarly, Thomas Scot dedicated his sermon of 1631 "Of God and the King," in which he cited Cicero's familiar injunction that "he deprives himself of the office of a friend who takes upon himself the person of a judge," to Sir Thomas Jermyn, Vice Chamberlain of his Majesty's Household. The traditional complaints about the great, however strong, remained within a discourse shared by court and country. The powerful Earl of Pembroke referred to great ones in parliamentary debate about the Duke of Buckingham.[55]

Sir Robert Carr, a cousin of the Earl of Somerset, accompanied Prince Charles to Spain in 1623 as Gentleman of his Bedchamber, later became the Keeper of the Privy Purse and was made first Earl of Ancram. A cultivated man, Carr was connected to some of the important literary figures of the times. In addition to Bolton, David Lindsay, the presbyterian Scottish divine, and Henry Tozer also dedicated sermons to him as did another Scottish divine, John Weemes, reprimanded for not carrying out ritual. Carr did not share in the Arminian attitudes which were coming to dominate the court. He praised the work of a well-known puritan divine but also showed support for some Catholics. Thus he wrote to the Earl of Carlisle on behalf of one Dr Echelin, whose father had been "one of the last men that stuck to Queen Mary, and was loved and esteemed for it all his life by King James ... [who] has no fault but that he is a papist, but such a one as will be in Heaven as soon as he is dead."[56] During the Civil War his son the Earl of Lothian took the covenant, while he himself remained a royalist.

It was to this man that the puritan Robert Bolton dedicated his tract both because Carr had applauded his earlier work and for the edification of those around the king.[57] At a time when Arminianism dominated the English hierarchy and found a supporter in Charles I, Bolton thought perhaps that Carr provided an avenue of resistance. Bolton focused on the traditional theme of the problem of great men who were subject to great temptations. There was "too much gazing upon the outward illustrious splendor, which is wont to glister in the Court of great princes." Bolton did not shun the use of influence around the king; instead he wanted that influence used on behalf of godliness not self-serving ambition. A godly man in a high place could do a world of good. Adopting the language of the courtier, Bolton wrote:

> he may also by observing the calmness of a royal countenance, and openness of a princely ear unto him, wisely and humbly suggest some things, and speak those words for the public good and good relation, whereby not only a kingdom but the whole Christian world may fare the better. Upon these ... grounds, I hold it an high happiness and great honor to have an hand in working spiritual good upon those excellent spirits which hold high rooms, or stand in near attendance unto mighty Princes.

Bolton's millenarianism heaped up the dangers of the court.

> You stand in a slippery place ... For although Satan be most solicitous and stirring in all places, and now more than ever (the long day of Mankind drawing fast towards an evening, and the world's troubles, and time near at an end) to do all the mischief he can possibly; yet you may be assured, he reserves his most desperate services, ambushments, surprises, practices, and Powder-plots, for kings' courts: because he finds there, an extraordinary confluence of greatness ...

Self-serving courtiers would desert the king in bad times, while those driven not by gain but by grace would remain loyal. In millenial terms Bolton painted a picture of the state's decay coinciding with approaching apocalypse.

Wherefore let Great Men, without grace, profess and pretend what they will; and protest the impossibility of any such thing ... yet ordinarily (I know not what some one moral puritan amongst a million might do) in such tumultuous times, and of universal confusion, for the securing of their temporal happiness ... they would fly from the declining state, and downfall of their old Master; though formerly the mightiest Monarch upon earth, as from the ruins of a falling house. And it can be no otherwise; for they have no internal principle.

The godly would prove more loyal to the king than the worldly. "For conscience, that poor neglected thing, nay, in these last and looser times, even laughed at by men of the world; yet a stronger tie of subjects hearts unto their sovereigns than man or devil is able to dissolve."[58]

While Bolton worried about Satan invading the precincts of the court, court masques were a genre designed to exhibit the godlike position of the king who interceded between heaven and the earth-bound world. The anti-masque is supposed to have become a formal part of the masque as a result of Jonson's response to Queen Anne's request for "some dance, or shew, that might precede hers and have the place of a foyle, or false Masque."[59] In its structure the masque presented the triumph of virtue over the discord of the anti-masque and, especially in its Caroline form, presented the king as the embodiment of virtue and harmony overcoming the forces of discord.[60] Kevin Sharpe has demonstrated the importance of the anti-masque not only in Jacobean but Caroline productions and the possibility within the genre to make critical comment on the court, and Leah Marcus has argued the importance of "present occasions" to the construction of the masque.[61]

In James Shirley's *The Triumph of Peace*, a masque sponsored by the four Inns of Court, the central emblems of Charles I's rule, Peace, Law and Justice, were presented, but projectors, at once ridiculous and familiar, were attacked both in the procession to the Banqueting House and the anti-masque. Although Fancy was a major character in *The Triumph of Peace*, these amusing figures of patentees and the poverty that followed them were not fanciful. Bulstrode Whitelocke, who had a hand in planning the entertainment, described them beginning with

a Projector who begged a patent that none in the kingdom might ride their horses, but with such bits as they should buy of him. Then came another fellow with a bunch of carrots upon his head ... describing a projector who begged a patent of monopoly, as the first inventor of the art to feed capons fat with carrots, and that none but himself might make use of that invention, and have the privilege for fourteen years, according to the statute. Several other Projectors were in like manner personated in this Antimasque; and it pleased the spectators the more, because by it an information was covertly given to the King of the unfitness and ridiculousness of these projects against the law: and

the Attorney General Noy, who had most knowledge of them, had a great hand
in this Antimasque of the Projectors.[62]

The projectors' anti-masque followed a scene in a tavern in which a
gentleman presented charity to four crippled beggars who then threw
away their crutches and danced. Opinion commented "I am glad they are
off: Are these effects of peace? Corruption rather." Fancy responded that if
these beggars were too noisome he could present some who were more
clean. "What think you of projectors?" Now entered each of the projectors,
the jockey who proposed a hollow bridle containing a vapor to cool the
horse; the country-fellow whose wheel could thresh corn without the aid
of hands; the philosophical projector who had studied for twenty years to
find a "lamp, which plac'd beneath a furnace, shall boil beef so thoroughly,
that the very steam of the first vessel shall alone be able to make another pot
above seethe over;" the fourth who had developed a case with which to walk
underwater and find gold and jewels in the sea; the fifth who had found
"a new way to fatten poultry with scrapings of a carrot, a great benefit to
th'commonwealth;" the sixth, "a kind of sea gull, too that will compose a ship
to sail against the winds; He'll undertake to build a most strong castle on
Goodwin Sands, to melt huge rocks to jelly, and cut'em out like sweetmeat
with his keel."[63]

However exaggerated, these very sorts of projects can be found in
the papers of Noy's successor, Attorney-General Bankes.[64] As we have
seen, although monopolies had been limited in 1624, the statute allowed
exceptions for new inventions and corporations. Throughout the 1630s
proposals for new projects and monopolies were agreed to by the Crown,
even after *The Triumph of Peace* was used to convince the king of their
"unfitness." Indeed, in 1639 King Charles issued a proclamation suspending
monopolies as had his father in 1604 and Queen Elizabeth in 1601.

Coelum Britanicum, with Thomas Carew's text and Inigo Jones's spectacle,
was put on at court in February 1634. If the usual conceit in early Stuart
masques was that the king was the intermediary between the gods and the
earth, this masque presented Charles and Henrietta Maria as a virtuous
pattern to the gods themselves. "Your exemplar life / Hath not alone
transfus'd a zealous heat / Of imitation through your vertuous court, /
By whose bright blaze your pallace is become the envy'd patterne of this
underworld. / But the aspiring flame hath kindled heaven."[65] (lines 62–7)
In a dialogue Mercury, Ambassador from Jove, and Momus, a "freeborne
god" and "Protnotarie of abuses," debate the virtues and vices of heaven
and earth.[66] The structure of the gods' government with councils and star
chamber, and stringent household ordinances and proclamations ordering
hospitality, resemble those of Charles I. Even a crowd of suitors throngs
(lines 838–9). In a series of anti-masques with riches, poverty, fortune, and

pleasure, Mercury argues that "the gods keep their thrones to enstall Vertue, not her Enemies" (lines 547–8). Rejecting both riches and poverty, Mercury lays out the virtues of the Caroline court. Royal bounty overflowing alongside justice is the Renaissance and Baroque king's most important work.

> we advance
> Such vertues onely as admit excesse,
> Brave bounteous Acts, Regall Magnificence,
> All-seeing Prudence, Magnanimity
> That knowes no bound, and that Heroicke vertue
> For which Antiquity hath left no name,
> But patternes onely, such as *Hercules,*
> *Achilles, Theseus*
>
> (lines 659–66)

In the following scene England, Scotland and Ireland appear and in the distance a young man "representing the Genius of these kingdoms" who holds in his hand "a Cornucopia fill'd with corne and fruits," the image of royal bounty (lines 892–6). The masque ends with the appearance of two clouds with emblematic figures expressing the values of the Caroline court: Religion, Truth, Wisdom, Concord, Government and Reputation. The virtue of Charles and Henrietta Maria raise them to constellations in the firmament.

III

It has been argued that there was no language of opposition in early Stuart England, indeed that the system, based on consensus, was incapable of it.[67] But the rhetoric of corruption, which connected venal practices with the decay of the state, provided such a language. The charge of corruption clothed attacks on diplomatic, religious and financial policies of James I and Charles I. Arminianism, ship money and other financial innovations were issues as crucial to the Caroline political elite as Spanish pensions, the sale of titles and monopolies had been during his father's reign. To respond to these issues, parliament revived its authority to impeach and remove royal officials.

From its opening days, members of the Long Parliament attacked evil counsellors who had undermined the fundamental laws and tried to establish arbitrary government. On behalf of Dorset's freeholders, George, Lord Digby, presented these grievances: ship money, the pressing of troops and illegal raising of monies for that purpose: "the multitude of monopolists;" and the new canons and oaths. Digby called for the removal of "such unjust judges, such pernicious counsellours, and such discontent divines as have of late years, by their wicked practices, provoked aspersions upon the government of the graciousest and best of kings" and the drafting of a Remonstrance "as may be a faithful and lively representation unto his Majesty of the deplorable estate of this his kingdom."[68]

It would be hard for an historian to argue that the financial, religious and diplomatic policies adopted during the personal rule were intended to divert public revenue for private benefit. Yet leaders of the Long Parliament who aimed to dismantle Laudian religious pollicy, remove illegal taxes and reverse pro-Spanish foreign policy, used charges of corruption to denigrate the Archbishop of Canterbury William Laud, Thomas Wentworth, Earl of Strafford, and other Caroline officials.

According to the articles of impeachment, Laud had "traitorously laboured to subvert the fundamental laws and government of the kingdome." He was accused of trying to introduce civil law, of saying "that the king might at his owne pleasure take away without law, and make it warrantable by God's law," and of maintaining "his unlimited and absolute power, wherein the power of the Parliament is denied, and the Bishops power of prelacie set up." Amongst the fourteen charges, the fourth claimed that Laud "hath taken bribes, and sold justice in the high commission Court, as Archbishop, and hath not only corrupted the Judges there, but hath also sold Judicious places to be corrupted."[69]

Attacked within the first week of the Long Parliament, Strafford was accused similarly of having "traitorously endeavoured to subvert the fundamental lawes and government of the realmes of England and Ireland, and instead thereof to introduce an arbitrary and tyrannical government against law." In addition the charges stated that

> the better to enrich and enable himself to go through with his traitorous designes, he hath detained a great part of his Majesty's revenue, without giving legall account, and hath taken great sums out of the Exchequer, converting them to his own use, when his Majesty was necessitated for his own urgent occasions, and his army had beene a long time unpaid.

The charges of venality against Strafford included farming the customs of Ireland to his own use, retaining the licensing of exports in his own hands, and controlling the monopoly on tobacco and flax trade into Ireland.[70]

John Pym, who had been one of the leaders of the impeachment proceedings against Buckingham in 1626, directed the assault on evil councillors in the Long Parliament. On April 12, 1641 he laid out the issues of high treason against Strafford.

> It cannot be for the honour of a king that his sacred authority should be … applyed to patronage such horrid crimes, as have been represented in evidence against the Earle of Strafford … when the judges do justice, it is the king's justice, and this is for his honour, because he is the fountaine of justice: but when they

doe injustice, the offence is their owne: But those officers and ministers of the king, who are most officious in the exercise of this arbitrary power, they do it commonly for their own advantage, and when they are questioned for it, they fly to the king's interest … this is a very unequal distribution for the king, that the dishonour of evil courses should be cast upon him.[71]

As part of his declaration Pym argued that there were two pacts between the king and his people, a legal and a personal union confirmed by oath on both sides. A fourteenth-century bribery case provided Pym with the precedent for Strafford's impeachment.

The king and his people are obliged to one another in the neerest relations; he is a father … he is the husband of the commonwealth, they have the same interests, they are inseparable in their condition be it good or evill; He is the head, they are the body; there is such an incorporation as cannot be dissolved with the destruction of both. When Justice Thorpe, in Edward the Third's time was by the Parliament condemned to death for Bribery, the reason of that judgement is given, because he had broken the king's oath, not that he had broken his own oath … the king's oath, that solemn and great obligation, which is the security of the whole kingdom: If for a judge to take a small sum in a private cause, was adjudged Capital, how much greater was this offense, whereby the Earl of Strafford hath broken the king's oath in the whole course of his Government in Ireland, to the prejudice of so many of his Majesty's subjects, in their lives, liberties, and estates.

In 1640, at the beginning of the sessions of both the Short and Long Parliaments, Grand Committees on courts of justice were appointed. Lord Keeper Finch, who had served as Chief Justice of the Court of Common Pleas and strongly supported the king on the enforcement of ship money and the forest laws, was impeached for endeavouring "to subvert the fundamental laws." But two charges dealt with judicial corruption: "that he, being lord-chief-justice of the court of Common-pleas, did take the general practice of that court to his private chamber;" and that "for his private benefit, endamage and ruined the estates of very many of his Majesty's subjects, contrary to his oath and knowledge."[72]

Corrupt judges were satirized on stage in the late 1630s and early 1640s. In 1641 Richard Braithwaite's *Mercurius Britannicus*, set in the Roman Senate, depicted the impeachments of the ship money judges.[73] While Braithwaite repeated parliament's accusations that the judges acted against "the peace of the Commonwealth and the liberty of the subject," he omitted reference to their subversion of fundamental law, such as Magna Carta and the Petition of Right, and parliamentary authority. As Martin Butler points out, his satire focused instead on personal abuse, denouncing the judges for corruption, avarice, and pride.

The Long Parliament impeached those judges who had upheld the royal prerogative in the cases of ship money. One, Justice Berkeley, was arrested while sitting in court. Not only did parliament impeach seven judges, it also changed their tenure from during the king's pleasure to during good behavior.[74] In addition to accusations of violating fundamental laws of the kingdom, contemporary tracts continued to accuse the judges of partiality and taking bribes. Stuart judges were tainted not only with the abuse of power but with corruption.

The Long Parliament brought forward a variety of grievances. S. R. Gardiner wrote that early in the session it looked as though monopolies were coming to the forefront. The king's proclamation in 1639 suspending them did not obliterate the sense of grievance. On November 9, six days into the session, the House of Commons ordered the exclusion of all monopolists. Said one member,

> These men ... like the frogs of Egypt have gotten possession of our dwellings, and we have scarce a room free from them. They sup in our cup, they dip in our dish, they sit by our fire; we find them in the dye-vat, wash-bowl, and powdering tub; they share with the butler in his box, they have marked and sealed us from head to foot ... They have a vizard, to hide the brand made by that good law in the last Parliament of King James; they shelter themselves under the name of a corporation; they make bye-laws which serve their turns to squeeze us and fill their purses.[75]

The House of Commons directly attacked sale of office, resolving "that the buying and selling of judicial places is one cause of the evils of this kingdom." John Pym was ordered to draw up a clause about the sale of judicial office and other offices of trust to be inserted in the Grand Remonstrance "among the causes and remedies of the evils of this kingdom."[76]

The Grand Remonstrance attacked "councilors and courtiers" who, "for private ends," had engaged themselves to work for the interests of foreign princes or states to the prejudice of his Majesty; monopolies; purveyors; and the sale of offices and honors.

> Titles of Honour, Judicial places, Sergeant-ships at Law, and other Offices have been sold for great Sums of Money; whereby the Common Justice of the Kingdom hath been much endangered, not only by opening a way of employment, in places of great trust, and advantage to men of weak parts; but also by giving occasion to Bribery, Extortion, Partiality; it seldome hapning that places ill gotten are well used.

The language of corruption was applied to issues ranging from religion to the prerogative courts, from evil councillors to ship money and other prerogative revenues. The Long Parliament had undertaken to suppress monopolies including some that cost the king's subjects over £1,000,000 a year; it considered "the regulating of Courts of Justice, and abridging both the Delays and Charges of Law-suits." The Grand Remonstrance disqualified as royal councillors those who favored papists and "such as are Factors or Agents for any Foreign Prince, of another Religion; such are justly suspected to get Counsellors' places or any other of Trust, concerning publick Imployment for Money."[77]

In the Grand Remonstrance parliament claimed that its work was to reform the corruption of Charles's reign. It asked the king

> to remove from your Counsel all such as persist to favour and promote any of those pressures [oppressions] and corruptions wherewith your People have been grieved, and that for the future, your Majesty will vouchsafe to Imploy such persons in your great and publick Affairs, and to take such to be near you in Places of Trust, as your Parliament may have cause to confide in.[78]

The language of corruption pointed toward reform and the reassertion of harmony after a cleansing of the body politic. Nevertheless it contained within it the seeds of violence and purge.

Conclusion

It has been vigorously argued by several English historians that "everyone spoke the same language," that the political thought of king, parliament and justices coincided and that the conflict and breakdown of government in the 1640s was over the practical operation of the constitution.[1] Johann Sommerville has argued persuasively, however, that profoundly different theories of politics coexisted in early Stuart England. Even if we accept the notion of a single political language, or what is more likely, that ideas about politics existed along a spectrum, overlapping and shading into one another, we need to explain how seventeenth-century English people were able to justify to themselves not only presenting grievances and attacking evil counsellors but purging the body politic by transforming its political institutions and killing the king. Let me suggest that the ideology of royal bounty and corruption provided such a language and justification for violent overthrow of a monarchy celebrated as free and absolute.[2]

The pervasive image of the fountain, used by contemporaries to describe, on the one hand, the bounty, justice and mercy of seventeenth century monarchy and, on the other, its corruption and pollution, drew on classical writers, especially Plutarch, and humanists, such as Sir Thomas Eliot.[3] More generally, contemporary analysis of benefits was Senecan, of office Ciceronian and of patron–client relationships in general, Roman. At the same time, discussion of the body politic also transferred somatic language of health and disease from the natural body to the body politic. The way the English thought about the circulation of benefits and pollutioon structured their political and social worrld both macroscopically and microscopically; they applied images from the body to the body politic, to the universe, to politics, to theology, and to commerce.

Whiile the language of patronage was classical and humanist, the Protestant English continued to describe patron–client relationships in a religious vocabulary borrowed from Roman Catholicism, to emphasize the patron or broker as the intercessor with the king, much like the saints or the Virgin

Mary in Catholic theology. According to Catholic doctrine, intercession is a form of prayer by one who has standing before God to obtain mercy or divine benefits for another.[4] Similarly, the Calvinist King James gave his bounty freely as God granted salvation, but man did not have to rely upon grace alone for redemption; good works, the right "saint," or in John Prideaux's metaphor, Jesus as the greatest Master of Requests, provided access both to salvation and advancement. The individual submerged his or her interest in that of the patron in order to gain access to both symbolic and material resources. "Men (who never saw the Sea, yet desire to behold that regiment of waters,) choose some eminent River, to guide them thither."[5] Underlying such a conception theologically was the virtue both of the intercessor and of God.

Society was conceived of as an extended family. Members of that society were all connected, as in a body with a single head, much like the Great Chain of Being which linked all beings in the universe from the animals to man, the saints to God. But in the seventeenth century, these connections were not static but dynamic. Benefits circulated swiftly; "a continual suppeditation of benefits," as Chichester had described the commonwealth, echoed the circulation of money in the economy and, even, new notions about the circulation of the blood in the body.

The contemporary debate over economics in the 1620s between Malynes, Misselden and Mun, used language about the circle of commerce that resonated remarkably with the language we have examined about patronage and corruption:

> Let not your heroical virtues for the public good be blemished with private centers of commerce . . . let the procuring of bullion be your first study . . . For money of itself (be it more or less) in whose hands so ever, without bullion to supply, is but water in a cistern taken from a spring, that by use becomes exhausted, or being let alone, consumes itself to nothing . . . So coin becomes but medals, out of use or out of fashion. For bullion being the Fountain, money is but the water, and exchange the river that serves all private turns . . . To be short, Bullion is the very body and blood of kings, money is but the medium between subjects and their kings, exchange the heavenly mystery that joins them both together.[6]

If the king was the fountain of bounty and justice, he was also the head of the body politic. That contemporary political notion was reflected in analogies between the body and the body politic. The flow of vital fluids was essential to both.

> The other substance which most commonly is found culpable of this disease, is nature or *sperma*: which besides the suspicion of superfluitie in some persons may also receive diverse sorts of alteration, and likewise of corruption, able to work most strange and grievous accidents in our bodies. For as it is a substance of greatest perfection & purity so long as it retaineth his native integrity: So

being depraved or corrupted, it passeth all the humors of our body, in venom and malignity. For it must needs be a vehement and an impure cause that shall corrupt so pure a substance, which would easily resist any weak assault: and a substance so pure and full of spirits as this is, must needs prove most malicious unto the body when it is corrupted.[7]

This hierarchical and patriarchical image of the body resonated with contemporary theories of monarchy and, as we shall see, the powerful critiques of monarchical practice levelled at the beginning of the Long Parliament. Because of flattering sycophants and evil counsellors, Webster declaimed in *The Dutchesse of Malfy*, "Death and diseases through the whole land spread."[8]

Amongst the most potent weapons in the seventeenth-century arsenal against disease were bleeding and the purge.[9] The answer to disease in the body politic, as in the natural body, was to purge the humor or the fever, removing the offending malignancy, whether through attacks on evil counsellors, or the impeachment of court officials. After their fall from power, Sir Francis Bacon and the Earl of Somerset were prevented from coming near the court not just because of the pragmatic fear that they might regain influence over the king or be a nuisance, but also because the favorite or the fallen minister was a malignant humor whose entrance into the body politic represented a threat to its health.

I

Early Stuart court patronage was transformed with the accession of James I in 1603 and by the invasion of what was perceived to be a foreign body, the group of Scots who came south with the king. England was a much richer country than Scotland with a more formal court and a larger bureaucracy. Desire for court office among the nobility and gentry, pent up throughout Elizabeth's reign, burst out with the accession of the new monarch. His bounty was claimed by a larger elite than that of Elizabeth, bolstered by population growth and the expanding numbers of those considered gentle. Recognizing his obligation to reward his subjects, James I expanded the numbers of honors, titles, offices, pension and annuities to his new people. He named English noblemen to the Privy Council in larger numbers than Elizabeth. Yet English courtiers like John Holles felt deprived and attacked the Scots who stood between the "beam of royal virtue" and his English subjects.

The royal bounty bestowed by the early Stuarts was greater than that of their glorified predecessor Elizabeth. In accordance with Renaissance and Baroque values of liberality and magnificence, James rewarded his followers more lavishly and Charles I made the court a center of greater grandeur. Yet their subjects' return of loyalty and support wavered and ultimately faltered. Although prominent noblemen and councillors did retain independent connections, contemporaries thought access to increasing royal bounty was constricted first by the Scots who took up places in the king's Household and especially in the Bedchamber, and later by the favorites, Robert Carr, Earl of Somerset, and especially George Villiers, Duke of Buckingham, whom the king allowed, even perhaps required, to handle all of his patronage. Moreover, connections between the court and localities frayed in the 1620s over issues of taxation, billeting and martial law and unpopular diplomatic and religious policies of alliance with Spain and Arminianism. Royal patronage proved neither the tie nor the salve it was intended to be.

Corrupt practices were endemic to English government, as were periodic efforts to root out abuses. Economically, the period was one of inflation, a greater orientation toward market relationships and the creation of monopolies to diversify the economy and reward the political elite. Venality in government increased as government took on new social and economic responsibilities in the sixteenth century and inflation flared from the 1590s. Although there were statutes designed to deal with corrupt practices such as extortion, kickbacks and favoritism in the judicial system, they did not extend to the sale of titles, monopolies and conflict of interest. The growth in government contracting, as in the navy, created incentives to corruption because of the structure of early modern administration in which public and private interest were difficult to disentangle. The increasing privatization of royal rights transferred wealth to those who had access to royal favor from those who did not.

As a result the issue of corruption, a staple of the languages of humanism, law and religion, assumed greater significance, prompting increasingly strident callls for the return to traditional practices and the enforcement of more stringent rules of behavior among "the great."

As we have seen,, the court itself began to investigate corrupt practices in 1603. Nevertheless, in 1610 and 1614 parliament began to attack corruption, especially monopolies, sale of titles and offices and bribery of judges, and in 1621 revived impeachment to remove corrupt officials. The charge of corruption could easily move from defining individual acts to denying governmental legitimacy.

The Jacobean policy of inventing new titles of honor for sale, although a rational response to the need for ready cash, infuriated members of parliament, even those willing to pay. During the Addled Parliament of 1614, the House of Commons attacked impositions and "undertaking," the charge that the Crown coordinated a policy of influencing Commons elections and directing Commons business. Furthermore, a petition was presented against the order of baronets created three years before. Sir John Holles attacked the creation and marketing of the baronetcy calling it, as Sir Edwin Sandys did, "temporal simony." [10] The king's power to grant titles of honor to whomever he wished was part of his prerogative. How then could it be simony, the illegal sale of church benefices? Holles placed his attack on the baronets in the wider context of the expansion of the royal prerogative, taxation and what he took to be contemporary contempt for the common law limitations on the monarch.

> Seeing according to the modern Aphorisme, the people is to supply their Kings wants, without questioning, or accounting with them their mispendings, the questions is only de Modo: whether by... prerogative, whose interpretation for the most part lodgeth in the havers brests, and wills, or by a generall consent of all the Estates of the Kingdom assembled by the Kings writt and warrant. The prerogative (without looking back to Fortescu, Bracton and other doting worme eaten fathers of our Common law) ... dilateth itself into many branches, tending cheefly to the encreas of the Kings power, and the augmentation of his revenues which beeng rather a byway, and unbeaten by antiquity, is for the most part succesless, allwaies distastefull and sumtimes dangerous as it appeareth by many examples enrolled in the scriptures, antient, and modern histories as well at home as abroad ... The branches of the Prerogative be impositions, either uppon inheritances, and commodities, or uppon our humors, and sumtimes vanities, which latter according to the new ... denomination is termed a Project. The first I send back to the Parlement, which hath disputed it largely, and endeavoured to conclude it, and I will betake my self to projects ... Of which litter is the late invention of Baronets, which besyds the scandall in forrein parts for selling honor, as ware (which from all beginnings hath usually been the prize of vertue, and therefore sequestered like the shew bread from common hands) which the greatest Princes have so muche respected.

Such sales of titles injured descendants of noble houses and the king's ability to reward and motivate his troops. Holles argued

> Knighthood which heerofore was our Civica and Muralis Corona, is no less abased, then that of St Michels was in France, when those of that order hung their Ensines about their lackies necks: For ... a beggars brat, whose father ... had scantely swads ennough to fill his panche before his death, and who perhaps at fuller age may be made a prentise, or whose father had lately scrambled together, from sum base and mechanicall course of life, some heap of pelphe, this mans chyld so descended ... without meritt, or any other inducement soever, shall in the Court and Cuntrie, in all assemblies aboute the Princes person, in warr ... ceremonies, at board, in conversation, in appellation, word and writing, be both presently and futurely preferred.

To distinguish the useful servant, the king would be forced to create new titles and new distinctions with estates to go with them. The wisdom of former times demonstrated that men were more satisfied with glory than with wealth. If the Princes abased their honors

> by transferring it uppon unworthines, or by communicating it without too many (as the sunn shineth generally, and without respect of persons) or by making it merkitable, which ... was not unaptly termed a temporall Simonie; they can not avoide the former inconveniences, which if the first founder of this Baroneticall disorder had discovered, or foreseen, he would I suppose rather have cutt his own throat, than have given aire, or milke to suche a Monster.

Despite claims that the baronets would all be gentlemen and have estates of at least £1,000 per annum,

> this age knoweth, and the future will be no more therwith deceaved, then the Indians of later times were with the vaste magnitude and stature of Alexanders souldiors, notwithstanding the gyantly armes, swords, targetts, spurrs and horsbitts, which he caused to be dispersedly buried, and sowne all over the cuntrie. That therfore it would pleas his Majestie, as he is the fountaine, from whence all honor floweth and in that measure, as all light from the sunn, so in Justice to himself, and subjects [to reduce the baronetcies to term of life.] Those of them, who lying so under their dets can not with their liberty crawle into the streets, whose lands allso sould, and brought to extreame povertie, must soone after either begg, steal with bankreroute Cateline turne against their King, and Cuntrie, or enslave themselves to suche services as they can, horseheelrubbers, tapsters, or worse and their ospring peradventure prentises, or artificers.[11]

Holles urged that attention be turned "from the extension of the praerogative whereof this is a branche, to aides by common consent." Holles's violent and strained language did not accurately describe the buyers of baronetcies and indeed, as we have seen, he bought a barony and earldom himself. But many agreed with him that the use of the prerogative to raise money outside parliament by the sale of titles threatened political stability and social hierarchy.

The increasing intrusion of the market into the court and government worried contemporaries. In the margin of one of his books Gabriel Harvey wrote: "prince's court, the only mart of preferment, and honour. A Gulf of gain."[12] Such comments were not reserved for the study. In April 1617 King James raised a loan from his people in the absence of parliament. Three weeks later Sir Henry Saville reported to Carleton that "of the £100,000 which was so unwillingly lent £70,000 was very willingly given away."[13] On April 19, John Chamberlain wrote to Carleton, as the king made his way north to visit Scotland,

> But I marvayle how we shall do hereafter, when upon such a flush we are alredy come to so lowe an ebbe but new gifts and dayly warrants under the privie signet do alter the course of orderly payments and disorder all ... One Drope

of Magdalen College in Oxford is called in question for a sermon at Paules Crosse on Sonday was fortnight, wherein out of the Proverbes among other things he wold prove that kinges might steale as well as meaner men both by borrowing and not payeng and by layeng unreasonable and undue impositions upon theyre subjects.[14]

The Duke of Buckingham established a monopoly of royal favor, closely integgrated the patronage of England and Ireland, continued and expanded the massive infusion of money into the exchange between patron and client and systematized the sale of titles. The traditional language of patronage continued. Raleigh asked the favorite to "vouchsafe to become my intercessor" and thereby "bind an hundred gentlemen of my kindred to honour your memory." John Hoskins described Buckingham as a "sweet conduit of the king's mercy."[15] But these metaphors referring to the royal fountain of bounty and of religious intercession came under attack, as we have seen, with the attempt to impeach the duke in 1626, in which he was accused of undermining royal virtue and honor.

At his elevation to the position of Lord President of the North in 1628 Thomas Wentworth described the reciprocal obligations on the king to support the subject's liberties, and on the subject to support the royal prerogative. "These are those mutual intelligences of love and protection descending, and loyalty ascending, which should pass ... between a king and his people. Their faithful servants must look equally on both ... labour to preserve each ... and by running in the worn, wonted channels ... cut off early all disputes."[16] By 1640 the interlocking issues of bounty and taxation, and the interruption of the circulation of benefits now not by Scots, but by evil counsellors who stood between the king and his subjects, found strong expression in the speech of George Digby in the opening week of the Long Parliament.

It hath been a metaphor frequent in parliament, that what money kings raised from their subjects, they were as vapors drawn up from the Earth by the sun, to be distilled upon it again in fructifying showers: The comparison Mr. Speaker, hath held of late years in this kingdome too unluckily: what hath bin raised from the subject by those virulent attractions, hath been formed, it is true, into Clouds, but how? to darken the Sun's own lustre, and hath fallen again upon the land only in Hailstones and Mildews, to barter and prostrate still more and more our liberties, to blast and wither our affections; had the latter of these [not] been still kept alive by our king's own personal virtues, which will ever preserve him in spite of all evil Counsellors, a sacred object both of our admiration and loves.

Mr Speaker, it hath been often said in this House, and I think can never be too often repeated, that the Kings of England can do no wrong; but though they could Mr Speaker yet Princes have no part in the ill of those actions which their judges assure them to be Just, their Counsellors that they are prudent, and their divines that they are conscientious.[17]

Digby himself ultimately became a royalist; but using charges of undermining fundamental law and corruption, the Long Parliament impeached and executed Strafford and Laud, impeached the ship money judges, abolished the prerogative courts and ultimately accused, tried and executed Charles I.

Such violence requires explanation that goes beyond practical debate. I suggest that it lies embedded in contemporary ideology and corporal analogy. Sir Arthur Throckmorton had described the plot of the Earl of Essex to his Buckinghamshire friend, Sir Thomas Temple, "He was confronted by his own councillors. He confessed he meant to surprise the Queen in her court ... that he would have altered the state of government, called a parliament. And I know not what ... It seems the state was sick. I hope this letting blood will do it good." Digby focused on the purge:

Let me acquaint you Mr Speaker, with an aphorism, in Hippocrates, no less Authentic (I think) in the body politick than in the natural. Thus it is, Mr Speaker, bodies to be thoroughly and effectually purged must have their humors first made fluid and moveable. The Humors that I understand to have caused all the desperate maladies of this nation are the ill ministers. To purge them away clearly, they must first be loosened unsettled, and extenuated.[18]

Throckmorton's and Digby's somatic imagery of bleeding, purgation and evacuation provided part of the justification for political upheaval.

II

On the eve of the Restoration, William Cavendish, Marquis of Newcastle, wrote a letter of advice to the future Charles II. Cavendish, Charles II's tutor and privy councillor, remembered the political conflicts of the early seventeenth century and determined to help Charles avoid the problems of his father and grandfather. Newcastle brought to the task a vision of Queen Elizabeth's as a golden age and perceptions of errors made by James I and Charles I. These perceptions were shared by contemporaries and strengthened by the experience of civil war. Royalists in the 1650s, for instance, regretted the sale of titles. Reflecting the evidence of the signet books that I have examined, Newcastle thought allowing Household officers to strongly influence court patronage and politics a mistake. He urged

no courtier that is not a privy councillor, to meddle with state affairs ... nor no grooms of the Bedchamber, to make with petitions and business, more than belongs to himself, for your Majesty has Masters of Requests for all petitions, and so every man keep within his own circle, of his office and place. For I assure you sire their meddling did much disorder the Commonwealth for their particular gain.[19]

Like the 1626 attack on the Duke of Buckingham, Newcastle argued that favorites and sales of office were other areas in which Stuart policy was at fault. Using his idealized vision of Elizabethan practice Newcastle described court service frequently given to younger sons of gentlemen who had attended university, the Inns of Court and then served as ambassadors abroad. After thirty years' hard work the son might hope to be clerk of the signet or the council. "But when great favorites came in, they jostled out this breed of statesmen, whoseover would give a thousand more for the place, he had it, so the gentry seeing that, disposed of their sons otherwise ... and so our race of statesmen was at an end."[20]

Like Seyssel and Holles, Newcastle argued that royal bounty should be granted primarily to the nobility and gentry who served the king in court and country, not to favorites, whom he considered mean men.

> One of the things that brought these woeful times upon us, to make much of mean men ... Those men to be respected, that could not raise a man but only live of the king, and the others that lived of themselves and could raise thousands, to be despised, because they could not make le bon reverance and could not dance a serebon with castenetts of their fingers.[21]

It may be recalled that Coke had attacked Buckingham as Lord Admiral in the parliament of 1626, by saying sarcastically that the navy requires more than dancing a pavan.

Newcastle spelled out the benefits to king and country of patron–client relationships when he recalled the old Earl of Shrewsbury. At a Saint George's feast, well-to-do gentry willingly acknowledged themselves his servants by wearing his livery. Yet the next day they sat next to him at his table and he addressed them familiarly as cousins.

> Thus they did oblige my Lord, to be their servant all the year after with his power to serve them both in court and Westminster Hall and to be their solicitor, and again my Lord had no business in the country but they did it for him and the king had an easy business for whatsoever business his Majesty had in any county in England, or in all England, it was but speaking to Shrewsbury, or Derby and such great men and it was done ... and what does it cost your Majesty, a blue ribbon, a privy councillorship or such offices as your Majesty cannot bestow better, than upon such great men. For the people do not envy great men, as they do meaner men and then all their kindred, friends, dependences, servants, tenants are well pleased and your Majesty safe, but now the pride of the times are such as if very mean men be not made of your Majesty's Bedchamber, they presently rebel and grow discontented.[22]

Great men in Newcastle's vocabulary meant the great nobility, the king's natural counsellors; great men in the 1610s and 1620s were royal favorites.

By rewarding the nobility and gentry the king supported his own monarchy. Newcastle's golden vision of Elizabethan court patronage carried out through great nobles may not have reflected the reality of the decline of hospitality in the late sixteenth century complained about by contemporaries and documented by Felicity Heal.[23] His text looks backward and creates a fiction that combines both old baronial language and classical language of patronage. But the context of political patronage changed dramatically in the late seventeenth and early eighteenth centuries, because of the changed role of parliament, the rise of parties and the shift in the focus of the Crown's patronage to building a majority in the House of Commons.

III

J. G. A. Pocock in his important book, *The Machiavellian Moment: Florentine Political Thought and the Atlantic Republican Tradition*, constructed a striking paradigm for the intellectual history of early modern Europe, England and America.[24] It has been especially potent in explaining the Anglo–American political tradition, so much so that a recent issue of the *American Scholar* edited by Joyce Appleby traced Pocock's paradigm of republicanism in the historiography of the United States from the founding fathers to the progressive era.[25] The "Machiavellian Moment" in the hands of enthusiasts now lasts some 600 years.

Pocock deals extensively in *The Machiavellian Moment* with the concept of corruption, arguing that it was central to efforts by Florentine political thinkers, especially Machiavelli, to explain the decay of republics. He goes on to argue that Florentine republican notions, specifically the necessity for an active and even armed citizenry to restore and maintain the virtue of the republic in the face of corruption, had radical political implications in the 1640s and 1650s during the English Civil Wars and the Commonwealth period.[26]

The pivotal link between the first and second part of Pocock's title is the reception of Florentine political thought in England in the seventeenth century. Pocock generally examines "modes of civic consciousness" in England in order to establish the context for the reception of Florentine republicanism especially in the writing of the mid-century figure James Harrington.

But he gives surprisingly little attention to the early Stuart period, moving quickly from Sir Walter Raleigh and Sir Francis Bacon to 1640 with just a nod at John Pym. It may not be necessary, however, to import the *deus ex machina* of Florentine republicanism to explain the strength of corruption as a political issue under the early Stuarts and during the Civil War.[27] It may be that Machiavelli and Florentine republicanism found a home in what Pocock acknowledges as England's overtly unreceptive climate during the Commonwealth period, 1649–53, because corruption had *already* become a central political issue. The texts that we have examined, whether tracts, sermons, parliamentary debate or private letters, did indeed draw on classical sources, including Plato, Aristotle, Tacitus and Seneca, but it was Cicero, especially his emphasis on justice and his treatment of office, who was most influential.

Blair Worden has pointed out that the influence of the classics contained many different political lessons, suggesting that "Machiavellian" is too narrow an adjective to convey the influence of the two authors on whose works Hobbes especially blamed the collapse of the early Stuart monarchy, Aristotle and Cicero.[28] In *Vox Dei* Thomas Scot wrote that "bodies politic are best seen in bodies natural ... Cicero is a member, a servant, a child of the Commonwealth, yet is he truly what he is, called the father of the Commonwealth."[29] Cicero's work had remained popular throughout the Middle Ages. John of Salisbury owned copies of *De Officiis* and *De Oratore* which he bequeathed to Chartres. While Cicero's view of office and duty was complex, his injunction, in Book III of *De Officiis*, that "he lays aside the role of friend when he assumes that of judge" was repeatedly invoked in the political discourse of the period.[30] It may be of more than passing interest to note that the same Book III stated that no duty was due to, indeed it was morally right to kill, a tyrant. The Roman people held it to be glorious, a most noble deed. "For as certain members are amputated, if they show signs themselves of being bloodless and virtually lifeless and thus jeopardize the health of the other parts of the body, so these fierce and savage monsters in human form should be cut off from what may be called the common body of humanity."[31]

If such violence seems far removed from the Caroline court masque with its celebration of monarchical virtue and order, it found an echo in the language of contemporaries. During the parliament of 1628, a member of the House of Commons, using the metaphor of monopoly, imagined a coup d'etat by the Duke of Buckingham. William Cox said that a leading monopolist, Philip Burlamachi, "hath had licence to convey out ordnance, and to bring in ordnance to kill us."[32] The real financial problems of the state which resulted in forms of indirect taxation including ship money were merged in the public mind with contemporary condemnation of corrupt practices at the early Stuart court. In 1639 charges were brought against John Glascocke for saying that

he did not love the king, that he was not bound to love him more than another man, that he had as good blood in him as the king had, that the money which the king pretended to be ship money was but counterfeit and not just and of necessity but for the caterpillars of the court, that he had read kings had been deposed, that he had not paid nor would pay any money towards the shipping business, and that the king should not have the ship money.[33]

Glascocke was pardoned by a merciful monarch for being distempered with drink. But the discourse of corruption was central to early seventeenth-century politics and proved crucial to the undermining of the early Stuart monarchy.

IV

By the late seventeenth century politics had been transformed with the introduction of parties, annual parliaments, the government's successful waging of war through increased taxation and expansion of government bureaucracy. The quest for office focused on the Crown's need, especially under William III, to gain the support of enough Commons men to obtain money for his wars with France. This change is reflected in the financing of the royal Household which had expanded under James I and now, under Anne and George I, steeply declined.[34] The pensions list of Charles II reached £180,000; Anne's £70,000. The role of the Household changed in the Age of Party and indeed by 1703 sales were no longer allowed.

In 1711 Henry St. John, a Tory, described the locus of contemporary politics in language different from that of the earlier period.

It made me melancholy to observe the eagerness with which places were solicited for; and through interest has at all times been the principal spring of action, yet I never saw men so openly claim their hire, or offer themselves to sale. You see the effects of frequent Parliaments, and of long wars, of departing from our old constitution, and from our true interest.[35]

After the Restoration, candidates for parliamentary seats obtained them by "building an interest," through local ties, treating, contributions to local social institutions, even bribery. The cost of elections grew enormously.[36]

In the early seventeenth century it was taken for granted that court officials would sit in parliament. Successful efforts beginning in 1694 excluded some officials, commissioners of customs and excise and salt duty, from the Commons. The Act of Settlement of 1701 aimed to prevent any person "who has an office or place of profit under the King or receives a pension from the Crown" from serving as a member of the House of

Commons but it was modified in 1706 and 1708. Country members repeatedly introduced bills to prevent placemen from taking seats in the House of Commons. Brought forward repeatedly between 1702 and 1716, they failed each time.[37] They were directed against more than 100 office-holders and pensioners in the Commons, whose numbers had burgeoned due to the wars with France and the War of the Spanish Succession. Their purpose was to "secure the freedom of Parliaments" from the Crown's influence.

English politics in the era of Walpole were completely different from those a century before. Political patronage was organized to maintain support for the Crown in parliament through extensive grants of royal pensions, sinecures, licenses. What the early seventeenth-century parliamentarians labelled "undertaking" became the normal way the Crown ruled.[38] Few in the early seventeenth century had spoken for "influence" and "interest;" reference instead was to "royal bounty" and "liberality." But the newspapers allied to Walpole in the 1730s were outspoken in the righteousness of the Whigs' control of office and property to support the revolutionary settlement and the Hanoverian succession.[39] *The Case of the Opposition Stated Between the Craftsmen and the People* of 1731 argued that "the Tory interest grows weak and the Whigs powerful by the disposition of favors and employments ... the prevailing party, by continuing in employments of profit, must become able to purchase all the lands in the kingdom." Furthermore to preserve the balanced constitution, to weigh sufficiently in the balance against the House of Commons, the king needed to dispense places of honor and trust. Such views were repeated by Hume who argued that the Crown's influence in parliament was "inseparable from the very nature of the Constitution."[40]

The political discourse of early Stuart England expressed in prescriptive literature and practice helped to make "Old Corruption"[41] central to the political ideology of early modern England and America. Crafted in the cauldron of early Stuart politics, it found its most comfortable home in the American colonies where its fundamental distrust of government and monopolies found its way into the politics of the Revolution. The early Stuart kings were by no means the most corrupt of English monarchs; late seventeenth and eighteenth-century politics were more venal. But the Stuarts' political misjudgments made corruption a potent weapon with which to kill even the king. In another way, theirs was the Machiavellian moment, for Machiavelli had cogently described their dilemma in *The Prince*.[42] In his chapter "Generosity (in Italian, *liberalita*) and Meanness," Machiavelli pointed out the value of royal liberality and its political pitfalls.

It would be desirable to be considered generous; nevertheless, if generosity is practised in such a way that you will be considered generous, it will harm you.

If it is practised virtuously, and as it should be, it will not be known about, and you will not avoid acquiring a bad reputation for the opposite vice. Therefore, if one wants to keep up a reputation for being generous, one must spend lavishly and ostentatiously. The inevitable outcome of acting in such ways is that the ruler will consume all his resources in sumptuous display; and if he wants to continue to be thought generous, he will eventually be compelled to become rapacious, to tax the people very heavily, and raise money by all possible means. Thus, he will begin to be hated by his subjects and, because he is impoverished, he will be held in little regard. Since this generosity of his has harmed many people and benefitted few, he will feel the effects of any discontent, and the first real threat to his power will involve him in grave difficulties. When he realizes this, and changes his ways, he will very soon acquire a bad reputation for being miserly.[43]

Machiavelli's vivid description comes close to the reality of Stuart rule.

In *The Dutchesse of Malfy*, Webster had described the judicious monarch who brought order to both his state and people by ridding "his Royall Pallace of flattring Sicophants" and listening to "a most provident Councell." As John Guy points out, counsel and council were not completely differentiated in the sixteenth century, or even the early seventeenth.[44] Listening to provident counsel or council might denote taking the advice of the Privy Council, of the nobility who claimed to be the king's natural councillors, of humanist advisers or of parliament. Despite the alarm expressed by all of these, the failure of the early Stuart monarchs to listen to counsel helped, as Webster put it so vividly, "poyson't neere the head."

Notes

Introduction
The fountain of favor

1   John Webster, *The Dutchesse of Malfy* (London, 1623), I,i; the passage centers on the importance of the court and of the king's ridding it of flatterers. Antonio asked how he liked France, says

> I admire it;
> In seeking to reduce both State and People
> To a fix'd Order, there juditious King
> Begins at home: Quits first his Royal Palace
> Of flattring Sicophants of dissolute,
> And infamous persons, which he sweetely termes
> His Masters Master's-peece (the worke of Heaven)

   The 1623 edition places quotation marks at the beginning of the line "'Death and diseases through the whole land spread" to underline its importance.
2   See Elisabeth B. MacDougall and Naomi Miller, *Fons Sapientiae, Garden Fountains in Illustrated Books, Sixteenth–Eighteenth Centuries* (Washington, D.C., 1977), ix–xii, p. 32, "Fons Justitiae;" Naomi Miller, *French Renaissance Gardens* (New York, 1977), pp. 17–20, 286–93; Donald R. Dickson, *The Fountain of Living Waters* (Columbia, Mo., 1987). The image of the fountain is used in contemporary literature and letters such as Sir Francis Bacon's dedication of the *Advancement of Learning* to the king.
3   John Stoughton, "The Magistrates Commission," in *Choice Sermons Preached Upon Selected Occasions* (London, 1640), p. 9.
4   See K. B. MacFarlane, *The Nobility of Later Medieval England* (Oxford, 1973) and *England in the Fifteenth Century* (London, 1981); Lewis Namier, *England in the Age of the American Revolution* (2nd edn, New York, 1961); Roland Mousnier, *La Venalité des offices en France sous Henry IV et Louis XIII* (Rouen, 1945), and *Les Hierarches sociales de 1450 à nos jours* (Paris, 1966); Conrad Russell, *Parliaments and English Politics, 1621–1629* (Oxford, 1979); Kevin Sharpe, *Faction and Parliament* (Oxford, 1978); David Starkey, "From Feud to Faction: English Politics Circa 1450–1550," *History Today*, vol. 32 (1982),

16–21; Simon Adams, "Faction, Clientage and Party, English Politics, 1550–1603," *History Today*, vol. 32 (December 1982), 33–9; Kevin Sharpe, "Faction at the Early Stuart Court," *History Today*, vol. 33 (1983), 39–46; David Starkey, "The King's Privy Chamber, 1485–1547," (PhD thesis University of Cambridge, 1973); and William Tighe, "The Gentlemen Pensioners in Elizabethan Politics and Government," (PhD thesis, University of Cambridge, 1983).

5 John Guy, *Tudor England* (Oxford, 1988), pp. 165–73; C. Given-Wilson, *The Royal Household and the King's Affinity: Service, Politics and Finance in England, 1360–1413* (New Haven, 1986), pp. 203–57.

6 BL Add. Mss 38139, f. 104v: Sir Edwin Sandys, Sir Roger Dallison, Sir Richard Verney, Sir [William] Walgrave, Sir Oliver Cromwell, Sir Rowland Lytton, Sir Henry Maynard, Sir Robert Dormer, Sir John Scott, Sir Maurice Berkeley, Sir Thomas Ridgeway, Sir Thomas Conigsby.

7 For a discussion of the Tudor–Stuart patronage system see Geoffrey Elton, "The Points of Contract" in *Studies in Tudor and Stuart Politics and Government* (3 vols; Cambridge, 1974–83), especially Part III: The Court, pp. 38–57; Wallace MacCaffrey, "Place and Patronage in Elizabethan Politics" in S. T. Bindoff, J. Hurstfield and C. H. Williams (eds) *Elizabethan Government and Society* (London, 1961), pp. 95–126; J. E. Neale, "The Elizabethan Political Scene," in *Essays in Elizabethan History* (London, 1958), pp. 59–84; G. E. Aylmer, *The King's Servants* (London, 1961); Linda Levy Peck, *Northampton: Patronage and Policy at the Court of James I* (London, 1982); Linda Levy Peck, "'For a King not to be bountiful were a fault' Perspectives on Court Patronage in Early Stuart England," *Journal of British Studies*, vol. 25 (1986), pp. 31–61; Starkey (ed.), *The English Court* (London, 1987). For an important sociological analysis of patronage see S. N. Eisenstadt and Louis Roniger, "Patron–Client Relations as a Model of Structuring Social Exchange," *Comparative Studies in Society and History*, vol. 22 (1980), pp. 42–77 and "The Study of Patron–Client Relations and Recent Developments in Sociological Theory," in S. N. Eisenstadt and Rene Lemarchand (eds), *Political Clientalism, Patronage and Development* (London, 1981), pp. 271–329.

8 Robert Braddock, "The Rewards of Office Holding in Tudor England," *Journal of British Studies*, vol. 14 (1975), pp. 29–47.

9 See for example "Truth Brought to Light," *Somers Tracts* (2nd edn, London 1809); Anthony Weldon, *The Court and Character of King James* (London, 1650); Arthur Wilson, *The History of Great Britain Being the Life and Reign of King James I* (London, 1653); Francis Osborne, *Traditional Memoirs in the Reign of King James I* (London, 1658); Sir Walter Scott, *Secret History of the Court of James the First* (2 vols; Edinburgh, 1811); George Smeeton (ed.), *Historical and Biographical Tracts* (2 vols; Westminster, 1820); John H. Jesse, *Memoirs of the Court of England* (4 vols; London, 1840); D. H. Willson, *King James VI and I* (London, 1956).

10 Joel Hurstfield, *Freedom, Corruption and Government in Elizabethan England* (Cambridge, Mass., 1973), p. 154; Gerald Aylmer, *The King's Servants*, pp. 178–81; *The State's Servants* (London, 1973), pp. 139–67.

11 See Natalie Davis, *From Alms to Bribes* (University of Wisconsin Press, forthcoming).

12 *Statutes of the Realm* (London, 1810), Vol. I, p. 33, Statute of Westminster I, 3 Edward I, c. 26; Vol. I, p. 93, Statute of Westminster II, 13 Edward I, c. 44. According to Coke, *1 Institutes*, p. 368, later statutes permitted

them to take fees in some cases, "by color thereof, the king's officers and ministers as sheriffs, coroners, escheaters, feodaries, gaolers and the like do offend in most cases; and seeing this act yet standeth in force, they cannot take anything but where, and so far as latter statutes have allowed unto them."

13 *Statutes of the Realm*, Vol. I, pp. 235–6.
14 1 Henry IV, c. 11 (1399), "if any sheriff from henceforth do any extortion to the people, and be thereof attainted, he shall be duely punished for the same extortion at the king's will." *Statutes of the Realm*, Vol. II, p. 115.
15 *Statutes of the Realm*, Vol. II, 579–80, 11 Henry VII, c. 15, addressed the "greate extortion . . . yerely used . . . by the subtile and untrue demeanour of sherifs undershirefs shire clerkis" and other officers. It gave justices of the peace the authority to examine the sheriff, convict and attaint him without further process; 3 Henry VIII, c. 12, attacked extortion and oppression in composing panels of juries, *Statutes of the Realm*, Vol. III, 32; 29 Elizabeth, c. 4, dealt with extortion by sheriffs, *Statutes of the Realm*, Vol. IV, p. 769. Informations for champerty or extortion might be laid in any county according to 31 Elizabeth, c. 5. *Statutes of the Realm*, Vol. IV, pp. 801–2.
16 *Statutes of the Realm*, Vol. II, p. 55. Those who appointed officers in the courts were to be sworn to appoint sufficient men according to a statute of 2 Henry VI, c. 13, *Statutes of the Realm*, Vol. II, p. 222.
17 *Statutes of the Realm*, Vol. IV, p. 152.
18 *Les Reportes du Treserudite Edmund Anderson . . . Seigniour Chief Justice del Common-Bank* (London, 1664), pp. 152–8.
19 William Holdsworth, *A History of English Law* (Boston, 1923), Vol. I, p. 19, noted that "The idea that governmental rights and offices and privileges are property to be dealt in . . . has died hard." Such rights limited the monarch himself. Blackstone, writing in the eighteenth century, stated, "offices, which are a right to exercise a public or private employment, and the fees and emoluments thereunto belonging are incorporeal hereditaments."
20 Holdsworth, *A History of English Law*, Vol. I, pp. 246–64. For a discussion of the sale of office in early modern Europe see K. W. Swart, *The Sale of Offices in the Seventeenth Century* (The Hague, 1949) and Mousnier, *La Venalité des offices en France sous Henry IV et Louis XIII*.
21 J. S. Nye in Arnold Heidenheimer, *Political Corruption* (2nd edn, New Brunswick, 1989), p. 966; J. C. Scott has provided the term "proto-corruption" for practices in patrimonial bureaucracies. *Comparative Political Corruption* (Englewood Cliffs, N.J., 1972).
22 Arnold Heidenheimer, *Political Corruption*, (1st edn, New York, 1970), p. 54.
23 Hurstfield, *Freedom, Corruption and Government*, pp. 137–62.
24 Robert O. Tilson, "Emergence of Black-Market: Administration, Development and Corruption in the New States" in M. U. Ekpo (ed.), *Bureaucratic Corruption in Sub-Saharan Africa*, (Washington, D.C., 1979), p. 347.
25 Susan Rose-Ackerman, *Corruption* (New York, 1978), p. 6.
26 Rose-Ackerman, *Corruption*, p. 8. Rose-Ackerman challenges those who argue for a cost-benefit analysis of corruption or relate corrupt practices simply to the size of government. "Corrupt incentives are the nearly inevitable consequence of *all* government attempts to control market forces . . . since some level of corruption will be associated with every mix of market and

democratic mechanisms, its existence cannot be taken as an indictment of any particular system."

27 Rose-Ackerman, *Corruption*, p. 92n; pp. 85–8, 110–11. Such a distinction was incorporated into American law when corporate bribery overseas was made illegal. While service provided by a single official in which he enjoyed monopoly power, such as a Civil Court judge in early Stuart England, provided corrupt incentives, the alternative case in which several different officials performed similar functions, as in the case of low-level officials such as purveyors, did not always reduce corrupt payments.

28 Sir Robert Naunton, *Fragmenta Regalia*, edited by J. S. Cerovski (Washington, D.C., 1985).

29 *Dive* v. *Manningham* (1551), Plowden's *Commentaries*, ff. 61–9.

30 Coke, 1 *Institutes* lib. 3, cap. 13, sect. 701, p. 368; *Sherley* v. *Packer*, King's Bench, 1 Rolle, 313, *English Reports* (Edinburgh, 1908), vol. 81, pp. 509–10, Hilary term, 13 James I.

31 Coke, 1 *Institutes*, p. 368.

32 See Chapters 7 and 8.

33 J. S. Cockburn, *A History of English Assizes, 1558–1714* (Cambridge, 1972); T. G. Barnes, *Somerset 1625–1640: a county's government during the "Personal Rule"* (Oxford, 1961); J. A. Sharpe, *Crime in Early Modern England, 1550–1750* (London, 1984), pp. 31–2.

34 See M. J. Ingram, "Communities and Courts: Law and Disorder in Early Seventeenth Century Wiltshire," in J. S. Cockburn (ed.), *Crime in England, 1550–1800* (London, 1977), pp. 123–5.

35 Thomas G. Barnes, *List and Index to the Proceedings in Star Chamber for the Reign of James I* (3 vols; Chicago, 1975).

36 PRO STAC 8/4/03; STAC 8/4/9.

37 Rose-Ackerman, *Corruption*, p. 113.

38 On the Queen Caroline tracts see Thomas Laqueur, "The Queen Caroline Affair: Politics as Art in the Reign of George IV," *Journal of Modern History*, vol. 54 (1982), pp. 417–66.

Chapter 1:
The language of patronage:
a discourse of connection

1 Malcolm Rogers, *William Dobson, 1611–1646* (London, 1983), p. 32, color pl. 2. C. H. McIlwain (ed.), *The Political Works of James I* (New York, 1965), pp. 53–70.

2 Seneca, *On Benefits* in Thomas Lodge, trans. *The Workes of Lucius Annaeas Seneca, Both Morrall and Naturall* (London, 1614), p. 6, Book I, Chapter 4, p. 6.

> because that he who is obliged to acknowlege a good turne, requiteth not the same, except his remuneration exceede the givers merit ... Teach thou mee somewhat that may make mee more forward to doe good unto all men, and more thankfull unto those that have done me good offices ... so as the benefactors keepe no account or memorie of their good deedes, and those that shall receive the same, put them not in oblivion, but perpetualy remember them.

See John Salmon, "Stoicism and Roman Example: Seneca and Tacitus in Jacobean England," *Journal of the History of Ideas*, vol. 50 (1989), pp. 199–225. An earlier English translation of the work was A. Golding, trans. *The woorke of . . . Seneca concerning Benefyting* (London, 1578).

3 See John Wallace, "*Timon of Athens* and the Three Graces: Shakespeare's Senecan Study," *Modern Philology*, vol. 83, no 4 (May 1986), pp. 349–63 and Louis Montrose, "Gifts and Reasons: The Contexts of Peele's *Araygnement of Paris*," *ELH*, vol. 47 (1980), pp. 433–61. I am grateful to John Wallace for a discussion of the influence of Senecan ideas of benefits. See Natalie Davis's forthcoming book *From Alms to Bribes*; I am grateful to Natalie Davis for permission to cite her work before publication.

4 "Letterbook of Sir Arthur Chichester, 1612–1614," *Analecta Hibernica*, no 8, p. 56, Chichester to the Archbishop of Canterbury, October 23, 1612.

5 For the traditional assessment of James I see Anthony Weldon, *The Court and Character of King James* (London, 1650); Arthur Wilson, *The History of Great Britain Being the Life and Reign of King James I* (London, 1653); Francis Osborne, *Traditional Memoirs of the Reign of King James I* (London, 1658); D. H. Willson, *King James VI and I* (London, 1956); but see Godfrey Goodman, *The Court of James I*, ed. J. S. Brewer (2 vols; London, 1839) and Jenny Wormald, "James VI and I: Two Kings or One?," *History*, vol. 68 (1983), pp. 187–209.

6 Elizabeth Read Foster (ed.), *Proceedings in Parliament, 1610* (2 vols; New Haven, 1966), Vol. I, p. 6.

7 See, for instance, Quentin Skinner, "Ambrogio Lorenzetti: The Artist as Political Philosopher," in *Proceedings of the British Academy*, vol. 72 (1986), pp. 1–56.

8 Desiderius Erasmus, *Apophthegmes*, trans. Nicholas Udall (London, 1542; reprint, Amsterdam, 1969), p. 168.

9 Marcel Mauss, *The Gift: Forms and Functions of Exchange in Archaic Societies*, trans. Ian Cunnisan (Glencoe, Ill., 1954), pp. 34–5.

10 See Margaret Judson, *The Crisis of the Constitution* (New York, 1964), pp. 27–8.

11 C. H. McIlwain (ed.), *The Political Works of James I* (New York, 1965), p. 53.

12 Foster (ed.), *Proceedings in Parliament, 1610*, vol. I, p. 6.

13 Claude de Seyssel, *The Monarchy of France*, trans. J. H. Hexter, ed. D. R. Kelley (New Haven, Conn., 1981), pp. 95–6. Seyssel did go on to argue against rewarding inadequate noblemen.

14 C. H. McIlwain (ed.), *The Political Works of James I*, pp. 25–6, 42, 52.

15 See Frank Whigham, *Ambition and Privilege, The Social Tropes of Elizabethan Courtesy Theory* (Berkeley, 1984).

16 Angel Day, *The English Secretorie* (London, 1592), p. 108; *The Mirrour of Complements* (London, 1635), A4, pp. 1–7.

17 BL Additional Mss 48150, Yelverton Mss 161 part 2.

18 BL Egerton Mss 860, ff. 65v–72. These included a letter to protect a servant in the time of parliament, a proxy for parliament, a dispensation from the parliament for some days without leaving a proxy, the return of a writ for the election of a burgess from a town; a *congé d'élire* for a bishop, the letter to go with the *congé de'élire*, the royal assent, the homage and oath of a bishop, the restoration of temporalities, the installment of first fruits, the warrant for a chaplain, the presentation to a church

living from a private patron and licenses of wood sales granted by the Lord Duke as justice in eyre south of Trent. Buckingham granted two of the latter to the Lord Mountjoy and the Earl of Warwick in Rockingham, Northamptonshire.

19 See R. P. Saller, *Personal Patronage under the Early Empire* (Cambridge, 1981).
20 *OED*, "Patron," "Client."
21 *OED*; Robert Cawdry, *A Table Alphabeticall* (London, 1604), denoted "patronage" as a French word meaning "defence," "protection;" "client" as "he that is defended," and defined "vassal" as "slave" or "client." The volume was dedicated to five noble women: Lady Hastings, Lady Dudley, Lady Mountague, Lady Wingfield and Lady Leigh, "his Christian friends."
22 The Earl of Northampton to Charles Cornwallis, April 10, 1607, Oxford, Bodleian Library, Tanner Mss 75.
23 See S. N. Eisenstadt and L. Roniger, "Patron–Client Relations as a Model of Structuring Social Exchange," *Comparative Studies in Society and History*, vol. 22 (1980), pp. 42–77.
24 HMC *Portland*, Vol. 9, p. 154.
25 Oxford, Bodl. Tanner Mss. 75, Northampton to Cornwallis, April 10, 1607.
26 B. L. Cotton Mss Vespasian Cx, f. 96, May 29, 1607.
27 Marcel Mauss, *The Gift*, pp. 34–5; Felicity Heal, "The Idea of Hospitality in Early Modern England," *Past and Present*, no. 102 (February 1984), pp. 66–93; Eisenstadt and Roniger, "Patron–Client Relations as a Model of Structuring Social Exchange," p. 71.
28 Eisenstadt and Roniger, "Patron–Client Relations as a Model of Structuring Social Exchange," p. 71.
29 I am grateful to Natalie Davis for sharing with me her paper "The Gift in Sixteenth Century France."
30 For royal New Year's gifts see John Nicols, *The Progresses ... of Elizabeth I* (4 vols; London, 1828); and Folger Shakespeare Library, Loseley Mss for references to New Year's gifts from the 1560s to the 1630s.
31 Folger Shakespeare Library Mss Xd 428, Cavendish Talbot Mss nos 120, 127, 128, 130, 131.
32 PRO SO 3/5, December, 1610.
33 PRO C 115, N5 8628–69, James Palmer to Scudamore, December 24, 1625.
34 HMC *Thirteenth Report*, part IV, Rye Mss, p. 134.
35 Nathaniel Brent, *A Discourse Consisting of Motives for Englargement and Freedom of Trade*, April 11, 1645, in *Tracts on Wool, 1613–99*, BL 712.g.16, Wing D 1591. I am grateful to the late Ellen Goldwater for this reference.
36 OED, "briber;" see also John Noonan, *Bribery* (New York, 1984), p. 314.
37 Noonan, *Bribery*, pp. 315–16.
38 Lawrence Stone, "Terrible Times," *The New Republic*, May 5, 1982, pp. 32–4.
39 See William Roper, *The Life of Sir Thomas More* (London, 1822), pp. 61–2. I am grateful to John Guy for this reference.
40 Quoted in Penry Williams, *The Tudor Regime* (Oxford, 1979), p. 106.
41 *Calendar of the Talbot Papers*, vol. II, p. 227.
42 See Pierre Bourdieu, *Outline of a Theory of Practice* (Cambridge, 1977); Susan Rose-Ackerman, *Corruption* (New York, 1978), and Mauss, *The Gift*.
43 For the use of money as a major form of exchange in court patronage, see Aylmer, *The King's Servants*, pp. 86–96, 219, 225–40, 274; Neale, "The

Elizabethan Political Scene," pp. 59–84; Roger Lockyer, *Buckingham* (New York, 1981), pp. 39–41, 61, 67–8; for the political impact of money on patronage, see James C. Scott, "Proto-corruption in Early Stuart England," *Comparative Political Corruption* (Englewood Cliffs, N.J., 1972), pp. 12, 54; Peck, "'For a King not to be Bountiful were a Fault': Perspectives on Court Patronage in Early Stuart England," *Journal of British Studies*, vol. 25 (1986), pp. 31–61.

44 Peck, *Northampton*, p. 71.

45 Sir John Holles to Lord Norris, June 17, 1617, *Letters of John Holles*, ed. Peter Seddon, Thoroton Society Record Series, (3 vols; Nottingham, 1975–86), Vol. II, p. 167.

46 See Seddon's introduction to his edition of Holles's letters. Alexander Thomson, "John Holles," *Journal of Modern History*, vol. 8 (1936), 145–72.

47 HMC *Portland*, Vol. 9, p. 6. Perez Zagorin, *The Court and the Country* (New York, 1970), p. 45, points out that his advice is borrowed from Lord Burghley.

48 See, for instance, "The Emperor Charles V's Political Instructions to his son Phillip II," translated by Henry Howard, BL, Lansdowne Mss 792; and Sir John Temple's advice to his son Thomas, Henry E. Huntington Library, Stowe Mss, Temple Correspondence, STT 1943 [1567–1603].

49 John Holles to his father Denzil Holles, August 7, 1587, Seddon (ed.), *Letters of John Holles*, Vol. I, p. 1.

50 HMC *Portland*, Vol. 9, p. 141.

51 ibid.

52 ibid., p. 33.

53 ibid., pp. 102–3.

54 See Russell, *Crisis of Parliaments*, pp. 216, 218, 269, 285, 302–3, 327, 373–4, 391; and Lockyer, *Buckingham*, pp. 150–1, 160–1, 276, 321, 333, for a discussion of the attack on Digby, now Earl of Bristol, by Buckingham.

55 HMC *Portland*, Vol. 9, pp. 129, 14–15.

56 David Starkey, "The King's Privy Chamber, 1485–1547," PhD thesis, Cambridge University, 1973.

57 See HMC *Portland*, Vol. 9, pp. 113, 14–15. See Neal Cuddy, "The Revival of the Entourage: The Bedchamber of James I, 1603–1625," in David Starkey (ed.), *The English Court* (London, 1987), pp. 173–225.

58 HMC *Portland*, Vol. 9, p. 113; others who raised the issues of the court Scots in parliament were John Hoskyns in 1610 and Sir Charles Cornwallis in 1614. See Foster (ed.), *Proceedings in Parliament, 1610*, vol. 2, pp. 344–5 and n.; Peck, *Northampton*, pp. 209, 256, n.97. The effort to control the monarch's Household appointments reached its peak in the Nineteen Propositions.

59 HMC *Portland*, Vol. 9, pp. 14–15, 28–9, Holles to the Earl of Somerset, March 4, 1615, Seddon (ed.), *Letters of John Holles*, Vol. 1, pp. 61–2.

60 Seddon (ed.), *Letters of John Holles*, Vol. 1, pp. xli–xliv. See Beatrice White, *A Cast of Ravens* (New York, 1965).

61 Holles to Lord Norris, July 1, 1617, Seddon (ed.), *Letters of John Holles*, Vol. 2, pp. 171–2; Holles to the Earl of Somerset, September 16, 1623, pp. 282–3; July 5, 1624, pp. 285–6; August 11, 1624, pp. 288–90; September 2, 1624, pp. 292–3; September 20, 1624, pp. 294–5; September 24, 1624, p. 296; October 20, 1624, pp. 296–7; March 2, 1625, pp. 298–300; August 2, 1627, pp. 359–61; and Holles for the Earl of Somerset to the Earl of Dorset, August 12, 1627, p. 364.

62 Holles to the Earl of Somerset, September 26, 1630, Nottingham University Library (NUL), Newcastle Mss NEC 15404, and NEC 15405, Holles Letters, no. 163, pp. 239–41. I am grateful to the Yale Center for Parliamentary History for use of their microfilm of these manuscripts.

63 Holles to Lord Norris, July 1, 1617, Seddon (ed.), *Letters of John Holles*, Vol. 2, pp. 171–2; Holles suggested that this rule is "all the religion, and state discipline in this age: as our nabors of Spain, and France, especially in the murther of Marques d'Ancre do tell us."

64 Holles to Sir Thomas Lake, July 26, 1617, Seddon (ed.), *Letters of John Holles*, Vol. 2, pp. 180–1.

65 Holles to the Earl of Somerset, July 18, 1617, *Letters of John Holles*, Vol. 2, p. 174.

66 Holles to the Earl of Somerset, July 18, 1617, *Letters of John Holles*, Vol. 2, pp. 174–5.

67 HMC *Portland*, Vol. 9, p. 61.

68 ibid., p. 140. For a discussion of monetary awards in use during the same period in France, see Robert Harding, "Corruption and the Moral Boundaries of Patronage in the Renaissance," in Guy Lytle and Stephen Orgel (eds), *Patronage in the Renaissance* (Princeton, 1981), pp. 47–64.

69 Holles to the Earl of Somerset, March 4, 1615, Seddon (ed.), *Letters of John Holles*, Vol. 1, pp. 61–2.

70 Holles to the Duke of Buckingham, July 17, 1617, Seddon (ed.), *Letters of John Holles*, Vol. 2, p. 173.

71 Holles to the Duke of Lennox, July 25, 1617, Seddon (ed.), *Letters of John Holles*, Vol. 2, pp. 178–9.

72. HMC *Portland*, Vol. 9, pp. 41–2. Holles discussed Sir Arthur Ingram's appointment as Cofferer of the Household through payment, and the complaints made by the officers of the Household that the king had promised to promote according to merit and seniority. The king responded that he had been told they agreed to Ingram's appointment. "Leapfrogg" Ingram, as Holles called him, was removed from the office. Holles to Lord Norris [March, 1615], Seddon (ed.), *Letters of John Holles*, Vol. 1, pp. 63–5.

73 Stephen Orgel, *The Illusion of Power* (Berkeley, 1975); Sir Roy Strong, *Art and Power* (Berkeley, 1984), pp. 153–70.

74 Per Palme, *Triumph of Peace* (London, 1957), p. 258.

75 Sir Roy Strong, *Brittania Triumphans, Inigo Jones, Rubens and Whitehall Palace* (London, 1980), pp. 46–7. Palme, *Triumph of Peace*, pp. 241–5, calls this "Abundance overcoming avarice." Strong shows Inigo Jones's use of figures of liberality from a contemporary emblem book. A printed key to the ceiling, dating from 1820 if not earlier, calls it "Royal Bounty pouring from a Cornucopia Crowns Medals and Trampling Avarice Underfoot."

76 Strong, *Brittania Triumphans*, pp. 46–7.

77 Ben Jonson, *The Golden Age Restored* (1615) quoted in Strong, *Brittania Triumphans*, p. 49. In the coronation ceremony of James I, the presentation of the ring requested blessing from God as "the fountain of spiritual grace." Cf. Legge (ed.), *The Coronation Order of James I* (London, 1902), p. 32.

78 Seneca, *On Benefits* trans. Lodge (London, 1614), p. 235.

79 PRO C 115, M24, no. 7750.

80 Quoted in S. R. Gardiner, *History of England from the Accession of James I to the Outbreak of the Civil War* (10 vols; London, 1883–4), Vol. III, p. 98,

from a letter of the Spanish Ambassador Gondodmar to the Archduke Albert,
October 2/12, 161?, Madrid Palace Library.

81 Linda Levy Peck, "Benefits, Brokers and Beneficiaries: Reading Buckingham's
Patronage".

82 John Prideaux, *Twenty Sermons* (Oxford, 1636), p. 27.

Chapter 2:
The structures of patronage and corruption:
access and allocation

1 PRO SP 14/61/41, January 1611.

2 See, for example, W. H. Dunham, *Lord Hastings' Indentured Retainers,
1461–1483* (Hamden, Conn., 1970); Ian Rowney, "The Hastings Affinity in
Staffordshire and the Honour of Tutbury," *BIHR* 57 (1984), 35–45; Charles Ross
(ed.), *Patronage, Pedigree and Power in Later Medieval England* (Totowa,
N.J., 1979); C. J. Given-Wilson, *The Royal Household and the King's Affinity*
(New Haven, 1986); D. A. L. Morgan, "The House of Policy," in David Starkey
(ed.), *The English Court* (London, 1987).

3 For a discussion of the Tudor–Stuart patronage system see works listed in
Introduction, note 4 above.

4 See Christopher Clay, *Economic Expansion and Social Change: England
1500–1700* (Cambridge, 1984), Vol. 1, p. 2.

5 Clay, *Economic Expansion and Social Change*, Vol. 1, pp. 142–58. L. Stone,
The Crisis of the Aristocracy (Oxford, 1965); J. P. Cooper, *Land, Men and
Beliefs: Studies in Early Modern History*, ed., G. E. Aylmer and J. S. Morrill
(London, 1983), pp. 17–42. Keith Wrightson, *English Society, 1580–1680*
(London, 1982).

6 Joyce Youings, *Sixteenth Century England*, (London, 1984), pp. 66–87, 110–29;
Robert Ashton, *The City and Court* (Cambridge, 1979).

7 MacCaffrey, "Place and Patronage in Elizabethan Politics," pp. 59–84, emphasizes the importance of these symbolic grants. In February 1614, Robert
Carr, Viscount Rochester, the king's favorite, stayed the grant of a keepership of a park that had already gained the king's signature. PRO SO
3/5.

8 Stone, *The Crisis of Aristocracy*, pp. 71–81.

9 ibid., pp. 82–97.

10 ibid., p. 104.

11 Anthony Fletcher, *Reform in the Provinces, The Government of Stuart England*
(New Haven, 1986), pp. 5–11.

12 Wallace Notestein, Frances Helen Relf and Hartley Simpson (eds), *Commons
Debates, 1621* (New Haven, 1935), Vol. VII, xi–xiv, Appendix B. Elizabeth
Read Foster, "The Procedure of the House of Commons Against Patents and
Monopolies, 1621–1624," in W. A. Aiken and B. D. Henning (eds), *Conflict
in Stuart England* (New York, 1960), pp. 59–85.

13 See Joan Thirsk, *Economic Policy and Projects* (Oxford, 1978), p. 100.

14 James F. Larkin and Paul L. Hughes (eds), *Stuart Royal Proclamations* (2
vols; Oxford, 1973), Vol. II, no. 283, pp. 673–6.

15 Magdalene College Cambridge, Pepys Mss 2870, pp. 57–9.

16 F. C. Dietz "The Receipts and Issues of the Exchequer during the Reigns of
James I and Charles I," *Smith College Studies in History*, Vol. XIII, no. 4 (July

1928), pp. 158–71. While these numbers do not represent all the monies disbursed by the Crown, they clearly indicate the increase in expenditure from 1603–40. The amounts have been rounded off.

17 Seddon, "Household Reforms in the Reign of James I," *BIHR*, vol. 53 (1980), pp. 49, 55.

18 G. E. Aylmer, *The King's Servants*, p. 349.

19 PRO LC 5/183, f.118, January 23, 1632.

20 Aylmer, *The King's Servants*, pp. 74–5, 165, 167; see, for example, PRO SO 3/5 February 1613. A warrant to the Exchequer to pay Sir David Murray, Master of Robes to the late Prince Henry, £19,024 9s 5d as surplusage upon his account for the robes, wardrobe, stable and privy purse of the said Prince to be taken out of the first monies to come to the king out of lands that reverted to his highness by death of the prince, was stayed at the signet. Four years later, Thomas Murray wrote to Secretary Lake, recommending Sir David Murray, reminding him that Murray had been a most trusted servant of the late Prince and almost the only one neglected. *CSPD 1611–1618*, p. 456, April 1, 1617.

21 PRO SP 16/180/16–18.

22 The largest of these was £2,000 to the king's daughter Elizabeth, Queen of Bohemia, but there were several of £1,000. Charles I paid out of the Exchequer and the privy seal pensions of over £35,000 in addition to his father's grants of over £40,000 a year for a subtotal of £76,247 14s 3d. Another £23,000 was allocated to the King and Queen of Bohemia and Prince Charles, later to be Charles II, for a total of £99,247 14s 3d a year. In addition there were annuities, granted out of customs farms, amounting to another £48,678 5s 5 1/2d; and yet another group of fees to officeholders not listed in the pension book, amounting to almost £15,000.

23 Magdalene College Cambridge, Pepys Mss 2870, pp. 85–7, October 1, 1614.

24 For the attack on the Jacobean Scots see Peck, " 'For a King not to be bountiful were a Fault': Perspectives on court patronage in early Stuart England", *JBS*, vol. 25 (1986), pp. 31–61; see also Neal Cuddy, "The Revival of the Entourage: The Bedchamber of James I, 1603–1625," and Kevin Sharpe, "The Image of Virtue: The Court and Household of Charles I, 1625–1642", in Starkey (ed.), *The English Court*, pp. 173–225 and pp. 226–60; *A Calendar of the Talbot Papers*, vol. II, p. 226.

25 PRO SP 16/180/18f.57ff.

26 There are difficulties with using PRO SP 16/180/18 because under Charles many of the pensions became linked to customs farms so that it is difficult to ascertain whether they are new or repayments of outstanding pensions.

27 Aylmer, *The King's Servants*, pp. 249, 170.

28 ibid., pp. 246–52.

29 *A Declaration of His Majesty's royal pleasure, in what sort he thinketh fit to enlarge, or reserve himself in matter of bountie* (London, 1610).

30 See Maurice Lee, *The Road to Revolution* (Urbana, 1985), pp. 10–12, 16, 21–2. I am grateful to John Guy for discussion of this point and to John Morrill for this reference.

31 Magdalene College Cambridge, Pepys Mss 2870, p. 547, June 28, 1588.

32 See Gerald Aylmer, "Attempts at Administrative Reform, 1625–40," *English Historical Review*, vol. 72 (1957), pp. 229–59; Peck, *Northampton*, pp. 146–67; Menna Prestwich, *Cranfield: Politics and Profits under the Early Stuarts* (Oxford, 1966), pp. 199–252; Michael Young, *Service and Servility* (Woodbridge, Suffolk, 1986), pp. 45–58, 73–92.

33 *The Acts of the Parliaments of Scotland*, ed. T. Thomson (Edinburgh, 1966), III, 563, c. 41. I am grateful to Jenny Wormald for the reference.

34 Larkin and Hughes (eds), *Stuart Royal Proclamations* vol. I, no. 6, pp. 11–14; see Peck, *Northampton*, p. 28.

35 PRO SP 14/37/72–76, November 1608. David Thomas, "Financial and Administrative Developments," in Howard Tomlinson, *Before the English Civil War* (London, 1983), pp. 107–8, 111, notes the attempt to restrict the granting of leases in reversion in the *Book of Bounty*.

36 BL Cotton Mss Titus B VII, ff. 428–9v. Such procedure might have validated the actions of officials who refused to seal grants such as Henry Howard, Earl of Northampton, who stopped forty-six grants from passing the Privy Seal from 1608 to 1614. See Peck, *Northampton*, pp. 48, 151–2.

37 Larkin and Hughes (eds), *Stuart Royal Proclamations*, vol. II, no. 283, p. 674.

38 See Pierre Bourdieu, *Outline of a Theory of Practice* (Cambridge, 1977), Rose-Ackerman, *Corruption* (New York, 1978) and Marcel Mauss, *The Gift* (Glencoe, Ill., 1952).

39 Father A. J. Loomie, *Ceremonies of Charles I* (New York, 1987), p. 320. Expenditures in 1628 were £5,700; in 1633, £2,360; in 1636, £1,400; in 1637, £5,820; in 1639–41, £5,720.

40 Loomie, *Ceremonies of Charles I*, p. 37. PRO SO 3/5 July 1611, Warrant to the Exchequer "for sums for chains and other awards given to the ministers of certain princes which have been sent to His Majesty and of others who have visited . . . under the hand of the Lord Chamberlain not exceeding the sum of £300."

41 Loomie, *Ceremonies of Charles I*, p. 38.

42 *CSPD 1611–1618*, pp. 510–11; Aylmer, *The King's Servants*, p. 91.

43 Charles Carter, *The Secret Diplomacy of the Hapsburgs, 1598–1625* (New York, 1964), pp. 120–33; Garrett Mattingly, *Renaissance Diplomacy* (Baltimore, 1964) PRO SP 31/12/34, 35.

44 Magdalene College Cambridge, Pepys Mss 2425, pp. 229–31, February 14, 1604. This letter is not in PRO SP 78, which contains most of the correspondence between Cecil and Parry in the years 1602 to 1605. Pepys Mss 2425 contains other letters between Cecil and Parry not found in SP 78.

45 *A Calendar of the Talbot Papers*, p. 234, February 2, 1604.

46 For a later example see A. J. Loomie, "The Spanish Faction at the Court of Charles I, 1630–8," *BIHR*, vol. 59 (1986), pp. 37–49.

47 "Tom Tell-Troath," *Somers Tracts* (13 vols; London, 1809–15), Vol. II, p. 473.

48 Magdalene College Cambridge, Pepys Mss 2425, p. 218, Cecil to Parry, January 24, 1604.

49 See for instance, A. G. R. Smith, *Servant of the Cecils: The Life of Michael Hickes, 1543–1612* (London, 1977).

50 M. S. Guiseppi, *Guide to the Contents of the Public Record Office*, I, 258–9. Several of the grants recorded in the signet book are not listed in the *Calendar of the State Papers Domestic*. Thus Thomas Leighton's office as captain and governor of Guernsey in reversion granted to Sir George Carew for life in May is not listed, nor is his appointment of April 25, 1603, to offices in Ireland.

51 BL Add. Mss 12497, f. 143, "Sir John Fortescue's means of gaine by Sir Richard Thekstin, knight, told me, 26 November 1608."

52 One of the few books dealing with this is Starkey (ed.), *The English Court*, especially the essays by Cuddy, "The Revival of the Entourage," pp. 173–225 and Sharpe, "The Image of Virtue," pp. 226–60.

53   BL Add. Mss 35832, f. 154.
54   See Cuddy, "The Revival of the Entourage."
55   PRO SO 3/5, December 1610.
56   PRO SO 3/2; PRO SO 3/5.
57   PRO SO 3/5; PRO SO 3/5, July 1611. A note added to a warrant to the Exchequer about chains for ambassadors called for the Exchequer and Privy Purse to pay two Frenchmen who were servants to the Duke of York. Windebank, a clerk of the signet, wrote "This addition of £70 and £40 was made to the bill signed by express commandment from my Lord Treasurer's own mouth to my self Windebank." The same volume of the signet book had a marginal note from Windebank, "These letters following neither passed in my month of July, neither was I ever acquainted with the entring of them here and therefore I make no accompt of them nor of my money Windebank."
58   For a discussion of Northampton's stopping of grants at the privy seal between 1612 and 1614 see Peck, *Northampton*, pp. 48, 151–2.
59   PRO SO 3/5, December 1611. In 1604, Cecil appears briefly to have stayed a grant of incorporation to the Minstrel's Company with authority to govern all minstrels.
60   PRO SO 3/5, November 1611.
61   PRO SO 3/5, March 1612.
62   PRO SO 3/5, February 1612.
63   PRO SO 3/6, first page. This caveat also had a line through it.
64   PRO SO 3/5, September 1612; see T. W. Moody, F. X. Martin, and F. J. Byrne (eds), *The New History of Ireland* (Oxford, 1976) PRO SO 3/5 lists a series of five letters to the Lord Deputy in October 1612, procured by May. Most concerned patronage, one dealing with ecclesiastical patronage by order of the Archbishop of Canterbury, another by the Lords of the Council. In August 1611 King James authorized Salisbury as Lord Treasurer to employ Humphrey May in dispatches between the Lord Deputy and "this State" and to employ him in drawing all bills and warrants relating to Ireland. *Calendar of State Papers, Ireland 1611–1614*, p. 92. May thus was the instrument of the King and Cecil.
65   PRO SO 3/5, October, November, December 1612, February 1614.
66   PRO SO 3/5, February 1614. Other stays of grants at the signet included these in PRO SO 3/6: the office of His Majesty's chief joiner to two men for life; a prebend in Bristol subscribed by the Bishop of Landaff and procured by Mr Livingston; a grant of licenses to several persons to sell wines in various towns. A reversion of a Welsh receivership, although subscribed by the Attorney-General, was stayed. The Treasury Commissioners, 1612–14, signified grants concerning land and projects, but an effort to obtain a grant by two men (one was the king's footman) of £110 in land "as the lords commissioners for the Treasury shall assess" was stayed at the privy seal.
67   PRO SO 3/5, September 1612.
68   PRO SO 3/5. One stay that appears not to have been overridden was a grant of a poor knight's room in Windsor subscribed by the Earl of Nottingham and other knights of the garter.
69   PRO SO 3/5. December 1612. Northampton sought the pardon of James Ingram, William Bostock, and John Waller of all fines and imprisonments imposed upon them by decree of the Star Chamber for "slanderous speeches divulged by them against the said Lord Privy Seal and others of His Majesty's council."

70 PRO SO 3/8, April 1624.
71 PRO SO 3/8, April 1624. Mr Livingston procured a warrant for the Earl of Holderness to choose lands from the Duchy of Lancaster to make up £200 of the £500 granted to him by the king.
72 Oxford, Bodleian, Bankes Mss; see Chapter 6.
73 PRO SO 3/11, July 1635.
74 PRO SO 3/11, November 1635. This bill was cancelled and passed again with an alteration, that of a £500 annuity for the same purpose.
75 PRO SO 3/8, April 1624. Secretary Calvert wrote to Secretary Conway in February 1623 that Sir Henry Holcroft's plea of ignorance on Irish matters was false. *CSPD 1619–1623*, p. 499. In 1627, Holcroft subscribed and procured a letter to the Lord Deputy of Ireland in favor of James Lesly, the king's servant.
76 *CSPD 1625–1626*, p. 526.
77 PRO SO 3/8, April 1627.
78 PRO SO 3/11, 1634–1638. For instance, December 1634: warrant to pay Richard Crockford £65 arrear of pension of £10/yr granted by his late Majesty, "signified to be his Majesty's pleasure by Sir Ralph Freeman (Master of Requests) entered by Mr. Maxwell."
79 *CSPD 1627–1628*, p. 87, March 10, 1627. See PRO SO 3/8, July 1624. Warrant under the signet to William Murray, one of the grooms of his Majesty's Bedchamber for preservation of his Majesty's game of hares, pheasants, partridges and other wild fowl between Richmond and Kingston upon Thames. Subscribed on signification of H.M.'s pleasure by Mr. Pitcairne, Master of His Majesty's hawks and procured by him.
80 PRO SO 3/10, August 1630. There is a marginal note: "the bill signed of this grant was delivered to be cancelled in regard of some alteration made in it, and passed again in June 1631."
81 PRO SO 3/11, April 1637. The payment was to be made quarterly by the receiver of that revenue out of the first monies to arise to the king. Should she not receive the £5,750 arrears from the gold and silver threads, she was to be paid out of the Exchequer. Annuity holders realized the need to have a fall-back in order to ensure payments.
82 PRO SO 3/10, August 1630. Occasionally grants were premature: in May 1635 a gunner's room in the Tower with wages of 6*d* a day granted to John Babbington in place of John Kidd, deceased, subscribed by the Earl of Newport, Master of the Ordnance and procured by Secretary Coke was stayed because "Kidd was living."
83 PRO SO 3/11, October 1637.
84 PRO SO 3/11, January 1638. A Warrant to the Exchequer to pay to George Kirke, Esquire, Gentleman of His Majesty's Robes or assignees £250 without account for provision of St George's robes for the king and the prince and for fur to line the coat was stayed even after the king's pleasure was signified by Mr. Kirke and by him procured. But the bill for this privy seal was cancelled only so that the king could increase the amount to £330.
85 PRO SO 3/11, May 17, 1636; July 1636; May 1638.

Chapter 3:
Court patronage networks

1   PRO SP 14/143/63.
2   *Cabala, Sive Scrinia Sacra* (1691), 111; Theophilus Field, Bishop of Llandaff to the Duke of Buckingham.
3   For circulation of court news see Richard Cust, "News and Politics in Early Seventeenth Century England." *Past and Present*, no. 112 (1986), pp. 60–90; F. J. Levy, "How Information Spread Among the Gentry, 1550–1640," *Journal of British Studies*, vol. 21 (1982), pp. 11–34.
4   Thus Lord Hastings's affinity in the late fifteenth century was drawn primarily from his stronghold. Ian Rowney, "The Hastings Affinity in Staffordshire and the Honour of Tutbury," *BIHR*, vol. 57 (1984), pp. 35–45. See also Barbara Harrisss, *Edward Stafford, Third Duke of Buckingham* (Stanford, 19866); Carol Rawcliffe, *The Staffords, Earls of Stafford and Dukes of Buckingham, 1394–1521* (Cambridge, 1978).
5   Trial of Northumberland in Star Chamber, *Les Reports del Cases in Camera Stellata, 1593 to 1609* (London, 1894), p. 297.
6   *CSPD 1603–1610*, p. 12; PRO SP 14/1/108. In 1604 the Earl of Suffolk, the Lord Chamberlain, tried to mollify him by giving him the lodging next to his own room risking, he suggested, the complaint of the Scottish surgeon, PRO SP 14/9/85.
7   John Bruce (ed.), *Correspondence of King James VI of Scotland with Sir Robert Cecil and Others in England*, Camden Society, o.s. vol. 78 (1861), p. 59. For James's attitudes toward the nobility see *Basilikon Doron*, in C. H. McIlwain (ed.), *The Political Works of James I* (New York, 1965), pp. 24–5.
8   See for instance Sir Henry Wotton's verses on the fall of the Earl of Somerset, *Reliquiae Wottonianae* (London, 1651), p. 522. See Robert Shepherd, "Royal Favorites in the Political Discourse of Tudor and Stuart England" (PhD thesis, Claremont, 1985).
9   James Spedding (ed.), *The Letters and the Life of Francis Bacon* (7 vols; London, 1861–1874), Vol. 6, p. 14. Bacon's letter of advice to Villiers exists in ms. at Trinity College Cambridge and was published in the 1660s. Spedding publishes two versions and analyzes their date of composition and relationship, Vol. 6, pp. 9–56.
10 Quoted in Richard Cust, *The Forced Loan* (Oxford, 1987), p. 21.
11 Quoted in Lockyer, *Buckingham*, p. 19.
12 ibid., pp. 20–2, 34, 43.
13 ibid., p. 55.
14 Lockyer, *Buckingham*, p. 28.
15 Spedding, *The Letters and the Life of Sir Francis Bacon*, Vol. 6, p. 13.
16 Lockyer, *Buckingham*, p. 113.
17 Spedding, *The Letters and the Life of Sir Francis Bacon*, Vol. 6, p. 15.
18 ibid., pp. 16–17.
19 See Peck, *Northampton*, pp. 27–9. Indeed it had been recommended by Fortescue; see John Guy, *Tudor England* (Oxford, 1988), p. 6.
20 PRO SP 14/78/62, November 1614. Lord Treasurer Suffolk and Lord Chancellor Ellesmere considered objections against a proposed patent for Sir Henry Neville, a client of Carr's, for prosecuting offenders who spoiled the king's woods. After considering Neville's answers they saw no reason that the grant should not pass.

21 Spedding, *The Letters and the Life of Sir Francis Bacon*, Vol. 6, pp. 18–20; moreover in important matters "persons of great judgement and known experience" should be chosen and young men joined with the elder to learn diplomacy. The elementary nature of Bacon's advice to the favorite appears in his etymological aside, "the truth of Religion, professed and protested by the church of England (whence we are called Protestants)."

22 See Roy Schreiber, *The First Carlisle, Sir James Hay, First Earl of Carlisle as Courtier, Diplomat and Entrepreneur, 1580–1636*, Transactions of the American Philosophical Society, Vol. 74, Part 7 (1984).

23 Spedding, *The Letters and the Life of Sir Francis Bacon*, Vol. 6, p. 24.

24 Quoted in Lockyer, *Buckingham*, p. 169.

25 ibid., p. 202. (Trinity Mss. 18.128).

26 Linda Levy Peck, "Benefits, Brokers and Beneficiaries: Reading Buckingham's Patronage," forthcoming.

27 B. Dew Roberts, *Mitre & Musket, John Williams, Lord Keeper, Archbishop of York, 1582–1650* (Oxford, 1938), p. 110. Westminster January 7, 1625: "If I were guiltye of any unworthye unfaithfulness for the time past, or not guiltye of a resolution to doe your Grace all service for the time to com, all consideration under Heaven could not force me to begge it soe earnestlye, or to professe myselfe as I doe before God and you."

28 Lockyer, *Buckingham*, pp. 39–41.

29 Quoted in Lockyer, *Buckingham*, pp. 45–6.

30 ibid., p. 41.

31 BL Harl. 6987, ff.1v–2, received January 22 1621, "I neede saye no more, if he once runne in arrear he will ever go bakkwarde ... And so I conclude, ather now or never, god blesse your labours."

32 See David Starkey, "From Feud to Faction," *History Today*, vol. 32 (November 1982), pp. 16–22; Simon Adams, "Faction, Clientage and Party, English Politics, 1550–1603," *History Today*, vol. 32 (December 1982), pp. 33–9; Kevin Sharpe, "Faction at the Early Stuart Court," *History Today*, vol. 33 (October 1983), pp. 39–46.

33 Quoted by Starkey, "From Feud to Faction," p. 16.

34 Magdalene College Cambridge, Pepys Ms. 2425, p. 143. Cecil to Parry, October 22, 1603 st. antiq. Although the English sought to make use of friendly French officials such as the Lord Chancellor and M. Villeroy, Parry wrote that "manye tymes the courses of justice are subject to the commandments of the court in favour of men that the king entertaineth in service", p. 132, Parry to Cecil, September 30, 1603.

35 Adams, "Faction, Clientage and Party," pp. 33–9.

36 See, for example, Louis Knafla, *Law and Politics in Jacobean England* (Cambridge, 1977).

37 Peck, *Northampton*, pp. 26–7, 70–1, 223 n.18.

38 See PRO 31/12/35, January 25, 1614, Gondomar to Duke of Lerma.

39 Adams, "Factions, Clientage and Party," p. 39.

40 Magdalene College Cambridge, Pepys Ms. 2425, pp. 103–7, August 4, 1603.

41 G. P. V. Akrigg, *Letters of James I*, pp. 339–40 [early 1615].

42 Starkey, "From Feud to Faction," p. 18.

43 Sharpe, "Faction at the Early Stuart Court," p. 43.

44 In 1625 Buckingham held proxies from: the Earls of Bath, Cumberland, Exeter, Northumberland, Rutland, and Salisbury; Viscounts Colchester, Mansfield, and Tunbridge; Lords Carew, St. John, Teynham, and Noel. Pembroke held those of

the Earls of Bedford, Bristol, Derby, and Huntingdon; and from Lords Darcy, Deincourt, Sheffield, Stanhope of Shelford, Wotton, and Zouche. Jansson and Bidwell (eds), *Parliament of 1625* (New Haven, 1987), pp. 590–1, HLRO proxies for 1626.

45 Sharpe, "Faction at the Early Stuart Court," p. 43. Holles, *Letters*, Vol. 2, p. 387; I am grateful to Albert R. Braunmuller for drawing this to my attention.

46 Sharpe, "Faction at the Early Stuart Court," p. 46.

47 A. J. Loomie, "The Spanish Faction at the Court of Charles I, 1630–8," *BIHR* vol. 49 (May 1986), pp. 37–49. Sharpe points out that some thought Weston favored France, an indication that designations such as "Spanish faction" and "French faction" should be handled gingerly. See Sharpe, "Faction at the Early Stuart Court," p. 44.

48 Quoted in Michael Van Cleave Alexander, *Charles I's Lord Treasurer* (Chapel Hill, 1975), p. 173.

49 See Barbara Donagan, "A Courtier's Progress: Greed and Consistency in the Life of the Earl of Holland," *Historical Journal*, vol. 19 (1976), pp. 317–53. We await detailed studies by Caroline Hibbard and Kevin Sharpe on court politics in the 1630s. In 1637 a contemporary commented on Hamilton, "I know he is strong in the King's favor ... none more." HMC *Denbigh*, Vol. V, p. 51, September 1, 1637, William Middleton to Lord Feilding.

50 See Malcolm Smuts, "The Puritan Followers of Henrietta Maria," *English Historical Review*, vol. 93 (1978), pp. 26–45; Sharpe, "Faction at the Early Stuart Court," pp. 44–5.

51 See R. D. Edwards and Mary O'Dowd, *Sources for Early Modern Irish History, 1534–1641* (Cambridge, 1985), pp. 9–10.

52 *CSP Ireland 1600–1601*, p. 412; *1601–1603*, pp. 113, 200, 351, 488, 526, 534; *1603–1605*, p. 265; *1608–1610*, p. 321.

53 *A Repertory of the Inrolments of the Patent Rolls of Chancery in Ireland Commencing with the Reign of King James I*, I, pt. 2, p. 751.

54 *CSP Ireland 1608–1610*, p. 373.

55 *CSP Ireland 1615–1625*, p. 15; Bodley wrote to Winwood that he had entrusted a suit to his good friend Mr Blundell to solicit for him.

56 *CSP Ireland 1615–1625*, p. 13.

57 See A. G. R. Smith, *Servant of the Cecils*. Winwood himself had become a client of Somerset's after the death of Cecil.

58 *CSP Ireland 1615–1625*, pp. 50–1; *CSP Ireland 1611–1614*, p. 513.

59 Folger Shakespeare Library Mss., GB 10, ff. 58v, 69v.

60 Folger Shakespeare Library Mss., GB 10, f. 69v, no date.

61 PRO SP 14/86/157, April 29, 1616, Blundell to Carleton.

62 Folger Shakespeare Library Mss., GB 10, f. 70.

63 *CSPD 1611–18*, p. 451. Warrant to erect an office for licensing peddlers and petty chapmen, on producing certificates of good behavior and putting in good security, appointing Abraham Williams, Francis Blundell, Rowland Wynn and others as licensees, and reserving a rent to the king of 1,000 marks after the first year.

64 N. E. McClure (ed.), *The Letters of John Chamberlain* (2 vols; Philadelphia, 1939), Vol. II, p. 316.

65 Lawrence Stone, *The Crisis of the Aristocracy* (Oxford, 1965), p. 96.

66 *Complete Baronetage* (Exeter, 1900), Vol. I, 236.

67 PRO SP 14/124/29, December 11, 1624, Blundell to Buckingham.

68 Richard Bagwell, *Ireland Under the Stuarts* (London, 1909), Vol. I, pp. 158–9.

As Vice-Treasurer he had a pension of 8s per diem. *CSP Ireland 1615–1625,* pp. 187, 303.

69 See W. Notestein, H. Simpson and F. Relf (eds), *Commons Debates 1621,* vol. 5, p. 444; Mark Kishlansky, *Parliamentary Selection* (Cambridge, 1986), p. 41.

70 Quoted in Menna Prestwich, *Cranfield: Politics and Profits under the Early Stuarts* (Oxford, 1966), p. 348, March 14, 1623. Blundell provided reports on the plantations and, according to Prestwich, Cranfield relied on Norton and Blundell for implementing strategies of reform. Cranfield told Buckingham that he would save £20,000 in Ireland, and Blundell's reports claimed he had stopped the council from granting petitions which cut down on the profits of justice and that he had reformed the system of paying the army. Prestwich argues that Blundell's account was too good to be true (pp. 355–6).

71 Quoted in Notestein, Simpson and Relf (eds), *Commons Debates 1621,* II, 49 n.14, January 15, 1622.

72 Cranfield was listed as among Buckingham's kindred in "A schedule of the gifts and grants bestowed upon the Duke of Buckingham and his kindred." BL Add. Mss. 5832. Although this list may have been prepared for the proceedings against the duke in the Parliament of 1626, such lists of grants to major officials were also prepared for Sir John Fortescue (BL Add. Mss. 12497, f. 43, November 26, 1608), and George Hume, Earl of Dunbar (PRO SP 14/61/41, January 1611). In August 1621 the Earl of Arundel asked Cranfield to write to the Lord Admiral on behalf of a kinsman of his. HMC *4th Report, Appendix,* p. 299.

73 PRO SP 14/155/47, 48 and 48 I. December 1623. Old arms would be disposed of to able men outside the trained bands and no one admitted into those bands but those able to buy arms for themselves.

74 PRO SP 14/180/7. Claiming that he would procure arms of good quality at the lowest rates, Blundell asked for allowances to cover the expenses of providing an armory and attendants and for sending the arms into the country. Blundell feared that James Maxwell, a member of the Privy Chamber, supported by John Murray, Lord Annandale, long a member of James I's Scottish retinue, might get half the profits on the arms project. Blundell may have had connections with the Duke of Lennox because after the death of Esme Stuart, he wrote to an unnamed Lord, to ask despatch of his suit for £500 or £1,000 saying that he kept a son of the duke who had no other means to live. This was perhaps Sir Henry Lennox, who in 1625 was granted a pension. Sir George Blundell claimed the right as part-holder of the barony of Bedford to serve as Almoner at Charles I's coronation.

75 In 1626 Blundell asked for the command of a new regiment, offering in exchange to forgo his pay of 20 shillings a day as Quartermaster General. He also presented a project for raising money for the king's service by the coinage of £100,000 in farthings.

76 *CSPD 1625–6,* pp. 142, 343, 350; *CSPD 1627–1628,* pp. 148, 154, 159, 166, 171, 293, 348.

77 See H. C. Maxwell-Lyte, *A History of Eton College, 1440–1910,* (London, 1911).

78 PRO SP 14/92/49, May 28, 1617.

79 ibid.

80 PRO SP 14/92/43, May 25, 1617. Sherburn acknowledged receiving Carleton's packet of letters and distributing them. Carleton raised the issue of Eton with several people at this time. See John J. Barcroft, "Carleton and Buckingham: The Quest for Office," in Howard S. Reinmuth (ed.), *Early Stuart Studies* (Minneapolis, 1970), pp. 122–36.

81 *CSPD 1611–1618*, pp. 232, 484.
82 PRO SP 14/93/137, 147, 152, 153, 155, October 1617.
83 PRO SP 14/92/86, July 5, 1617, Sherburn to Carleton.
84 PRO SP 14/92/101, July 22, 1617, George Gerrard to Carleton.
85 *CSPD 1619–23*, pp. 22, 58, 339, 350.
86 Maxwell-Lyte, *Eton*, pp. 182–4, 577–8.
87 *CSPD 1623–5*, pp. 538, 542.
88 BL Stowe Mss. 743, f. 52, April 11, 1623.
89 *DNB*; McClure (ed.), *The Letters of John Chamberlain*, May 17, 1623.
90 BL Add. Mss. 4107, f. 68, April 10, 1623.
91 *CSPD 1619–23*, pp. 494, 542, 559, 574, 580.
92 *CSPD 1623–5*, p. 22, July 19, 1623.
93 *CSPD 1623–5*, pp. 22, 70.
94 *CSPD 1623–5*, p. 559.
95 PRO SP 14/153/32, October 10, 1623; SP 14/14/2, November 1, 1623.
96 PRO SP 14/153/32, October 10, 1623.
97 PRO SP 14/153/99, October 25, 1623; Becher thought it would weaken his pretension if he lent "an ear to any proposition." Carleton's friends, such as Rich and Sir George Goring, did not give up all hope and thought Buckingham distracted between Carleton and Becher.
98 McClure (ed.), *The Letters of John Chamberlain*, vol. II, p. 532, December 6, 1623; PRO SP 14/158/172; SP 14/160/58.
99 PRO SP 14/92/103.
100 PRO SP 14/92/106, July 24, 1617. Because he had to wait upon Prince Charles at Richmond, Woodward wrote, he "wold not make two labors and two charges of that which I might doe by one, I took the Queene's clock alonge with me, and delivered it the same day at Nonsuch, with your Lordship's letter to Hir Majesty and that to the Lady of Roxburrowe who hath commanded me to attend upon the Queene againe upon Sunday or Monday next, at Oatlands where I shall know hir Majesties liking of the clocke, and receive a letter from her to your Lordship."
101 The subject of Jacobean collecting remains to be fully explored. See David Howarth, *The Earl of Arundel and his Circle* (Yale, 1985); A. R. Braunmuller, "The Earl of Somerset as Collector and Patron," in Linda Levy Peck (ed.), *The Mental World of the Jacobean Court* (Cambridge, forthcoming).
102 Lockyer, *Buckingham*, p. 215.
103 J. P. Ferris (ed.), *The House of Commons, 1604–1629* (forthcoming). I am grateful to the History of Parliament Trust for permission to read their biography of Sir William Becher. My thanks too to Sabrina Alcorn Baron. Sir William signed his will Becher.
104 See also J. W. Stoye, *English Travellers Abroad, 1604–1667* (London, 1952), pp. 47–8.
105 PRO SP 14/72/43, February 25, 1613, Wotton to Carleton.
106 Folger Shakespeare Library Mss. GB 10, f. 87v. This manuscript contains copies of Sir Ralph Winwood's correspondence especially with English ambassadors. Although the sender is cited as WH, the copyist has transposed the initials of other writers. The recipient is "the right honorable my very good Lord the E. Of S. Lord Chamberlain."

> I am bould by this gentleman to intertaine your Lordship with a piece of perspective which is a very busie kinde of worke, and therefore thease patient and phlegmatique hands doe commonly more excel therein then Italians who rather affect draughts

of spirit and action: but this piece which I now send hath a little life more than ordinary by the addition of the personages which made me make choice of it for your better delectation. The king hath given me leave to come home when this publique businesse shall draw to some issue one way or other which I hope wilbe within 2 months or such ... And then I will take Antwerpe in my returne for the search of some good pieces: And if I cannot serve your Lordship with judgement yet I will doe it with zeal. Mr. Dowrick hath made me know besides my other obligations how much I am bound to your Lordship for the late intercession for me with the king: wherein the trouble was your Lordship's, and the misfortune mine own ... My comfort is now that though His Majesty's memory did faile him as might easily among so infinit sutors, and after so long time of silence in it, yet his goodnes will never faile him.

107 BL Egerton Mss. 860, f. 113v, Sir Henry Wotton to Sir William Becher, "dated at my lodging in Kings Street this 8 of November 1624." King James ratified the agreement, f. 113.

108 McClure (ed.) *Letters of John Chamberlain*, Vol. II, pp. 572–3 and 573n.

109 See Lawrence Stone, *Family, Sex and Marriage*; Barbara J. Harris, "Gender and Politics," *Historical Journal* (forthcoming); Carole Rawcliffe, "The Politics of Marriage in Later Medieval England: William, Lord Botreaux, and the Hungerfords," *Huntington Library Quarterly*, vol. 51 (Summer 1988), pp. 161–75.

110 Barbara J. Lewalski, "Lucy, Countess of Bedford: Images of a Jacobean Courtier and Patroness," in Sharpe and Zwicker (eds), *The Politics of Discourse* (Los Angeles, 1987), p. 54. See also Malcolm Smuts "Cultural Diversity and Cultural Change in the Court of James I," in L. L. Peck (ed.) *The Mental World of the Jacobean Court* (Cambridge, forthcoming).

111 The discourse of queenship in political theory has been discussed by Constance Jordan, "Woman's Rule in Sixteenth-Century British Political Thought," *Renaissance Quarterly*, vol. 40 (1987), pp. 421–51. On women as literary patrons see for example French Fogle, "Such a Rural Queen: The Countess Dowager of Derby as Patron," in F. Fogle and L. Knafla (eds), *Patronage in Late Renaissance England* (Los Angeles, 1983). Most recent work on women in seventeenth-century England has focused on their social and legal position. See for example Sara H. Mendelson, *The Mental World of Stuart Women* (Brighton, 1987) and Susan Amussen, *An Ordered Society: Gender and Class in Early Modern England* (Oxford, 1988). Recent work has begun to focus on their political role as well. See Lois Schwoerer, *Lady Rachel Russell* (Baltimore, 1988); Harris, "Gender and Politics," *Historical Journal* (forthcoming).

112 Barbara J. Lewalski, "Lucy, Countess of Bedford," p. 52. On the Countess of Bedford see also Leeds Barroll, "The Literary Patronage of the court of Queen Anne," in L. L. Peck (ed.), *The Mental World of the Jacobean Court* (Cambridge, forthcoming). I am grateful to Caroline Hibbard for allowing me to read before publication her article "The Court and Household of a Queen Consort: Henrietta Maria, 1625–1642," in Ronald G. Asch and Adolph M. Birke (eds), *Princes, Patronage and the Nobility: The Court at the Beginning of the Modern Age* (Oxford, forthcoming) which addresses the general issue of the role of women at the early modern court and in particular focuses on the role of Susan Villiers, Countess of Denbigh. Hibbard's book on the Household of Henrietta Maria will address these issues further.

113 Hibbard, "Aristocratic Women at Court," paper given at the Berkshire Conference, June, 1987, p. 13.

114 See also Malcolm Smuts, *Court Culture and the Origins of a Royalist Tradition in Early Stuart England* (Philadelphia, 1987); Roy Strong, *Henry, Prince of Wales and England's Lost Renaissance* (New York, 1986). Historians are just beginning to examine the importance of royal Households other than the king's as centers of political power and cultural influence.

115 BL Add. Mss 27404, ff. 35–41v. "The accompt of Sir George Carew, knight, Lord Carew, Baron of Clopton, Receiver General to the most excellent Princesse Queen Anne, for one whole yere ended in the feast of St. Michel the Archangell." September 29, 1605 to September 29, 1606. By 1605–6 Queen Anne's learned counsel included Sir Robert Hitcham, who had ties to the Earl of Suffolk, Sir Edward Coke and Sir John Dodderidge; ff. 43–44v, Letter from the Earl of Worcester to the auditors in the counties in which Queen Anne held land. BL Add. Mss 38139, f. 1v, "Officers of our Council appointed by us to be in commission for the ordering of our Revenue and of other our affairs of importance." For the oath taken by Queen Anne's servants see BL Stowe 574, f. 64. For accounts concerning Queen Anne see PRO E 315/107, 138, 470.

116 See Leeds Barroll, "The Literary Patronage of the Court of Queen Anne" in Peck (ed.), *The Mental World of the Jacobean Court* (Cambridge, forthcoming).

117 HMC *De L'Isle and Dudley*, Vol. 2, p. 419, Rowland Whyte to Sir Robert Sydney, November 29, 1599.

118 See Chapter 8.

119 BL Add. Mss 27404, f. 37. Mary Gargrave had an annual fee of £50. Later she was granted a £200 pension during her life plus £1,000 toward the payment of her debts.

120 PRO SO 3/11, April 1637.

121 McClure, *The Letters of John Chamberlain*, I, 296, January 23, 1610. Mary Middlemore was in the middle of a quarrel between Sir Edward Herbert and one Boghvan [Buchan?] a Scot (gentleman-usher to the Queen) "about a riban or favor taken as yt were by force from Mistris Middlemore;" the matter was taken up by the Privy Council.

122 PRO SP 14/88/73, September 6, 1616.

123 *CSPD 1611–18*, pp. 464–5, 484, 598. *CSPD 1603–1610*, p. 9, May 17, 1603, warrant to pay to Sir George Hume, Keeper of the Privy Purse, £1,000 for the king's use; and £200 to such person as the king shall nominate for relief and transportation for Lady Barbara Ruthven; p. 43, September 1603, grant of £200 per annum to Lady Barbara Ruthven in commiseration of her distress; because though family is hateful on account of the abominable attempt against the king, she has shown no malicious disposition. *CSPD 1619–1623*, p. 110; CSPD 1623–5, p. 548. December 1614 Greenwich, Barbara Lady Ruthven to Carleton: The Queen is willing to see the hangings and wishes him to visit her next week; she is too poorly at present to see anyone.

124 HMC *Fourth Report Appendix*, p. 299.

125 BL Royal Mss 136, ff 503–508v. "Les noms et les gages des officiers et serviteurs domestiques de la feu Reine d'Angleterre." This list is placed in a volume relating to the marriage of Henrietta Maria to Prince Charles. Although undated, it may have been prepared for negotiations over the Household of the French princess and have reflected the shape of the Household at the end of Queen Anne's life.

126 *CSPD 1635–6*, p. 28, *1637–8*, pp. 151, 540, *CSPD 1638–9*, pp. 201, 489, 573, Caroline Hibbard, "Aristocratic Women at Court," pp. 5–6, 6n. Hibbard

points out that Carews had held Household positions going back to the Tudors; p. 10.

127 HMC *Hastings* Vol. II, p. 76, E. R. to ——, February 14, 1635: Carew served as Master of the Ordnance. He used Stafford to convey his "woeful estimate" of the king's munitions as preparations were made for the expedition for Rhé and his disagreements with Buckingham on supplies. "As the Duke is like to be the principal actor and commander in martial affairs, prays him to take care that they be not taken unprovided." *CSPD 1629–1631*, pp. 507, 557; pp. 4, 19. Stafford as his deputy executed his office during Carew's disability and continued to serve as deputy under the next master Sir Horace Vere. Stafford ran into problems with Sir John Heydon who claimed that as Lieutenant of the Ordnance he should serve as deputy in Vere's absence and Stafford sued for back pay which he hoped would be granted in the form of a pension in Ireland.

128 One of nine patentees for making glass with seacoal, Tracy left his interest in the project to Lady Mary Vere's children. Lady Mary sought to prevent Sir Robert Mansell from engrossing the whole project without compensation. Sir Edward Conway, Secretary of State, married to her sister, recommended her petition to the Earl of Arundel, her husband's Howard kinsman.

129 BL Add. Mss 27404, ff. 38v–40; J. Florio, *A World of Words* (London, 1598); the dedicatees are described as "Patrons of vertue, Patterns of Honor," a3.

130 BL Stowe Ms. 574, f. 62. BL Add. Mss 48150, Yelverton 161, part 2, f. 111: "warrants extraordinary at christenings," includes the charges of Sir Thomas Cheyney sent in 1546 to "christen the dolphins daughter in France."

131 Folger Shakespeare Library, Cavendish Talbot Ms. xd 428, (2), (118).

132 PRO SP 14/92/15, George Gerrard to Carleton, May 9, 1617,

> The widowe Countes of Shrewsbury, hath by degrees since her englargement and her husbands death, growne into so ill a disposition of mind, near to madness, that her two court sonnes, the Lord Chamberlayne and the Erle of Arundel, have desyr'd of the king, the protection of her estate; and the fruits thereof they will enjoy, if she mend not. That which chiefly works her to thys, is an apprehension that she shall be poisoned.

Caroline Hibbard makes an important point of the family unit at court and the centrality of intermarriage to it in "Aristocratic Women at Court," paper delivered at the Berkshire Conference, 1987, p. 14.

133 McClure (ed.), *The Letters of John Chamberlain*, vol. I, p. 512, John Chamberlain to [Alice Carleton], February 17, 1614.

134 BL Stowe Mss 743, f. 46, April 9, 1623.

135 McClure (ed.), *The Letters of John Chamberlain*, vol. II, p. 533, December 20, 1623.

136 Seddon (ed.) *The Letters of John Holles*, vol. II, p. 314, c. 1625.

137 See C. R. Markham, *The Fighting Veres* (London, 1878), pp. 433–4. At the death of Holles's younger brother George, who had served in the continental wars, Holles, now Earl of Clare, and Lord Vere were the chief mourners. Cloaked as a Roman soldier, the statue of Sir George Holles overlooks the tomb of Sir Francis Vere in Westminster Abbey.

138 Seddon (ed.), *The Letters of Sir John Holles*, vol. II, p. 315, 333. The match was made and Holles in August 1626 sent his "best affection and service to them, being really theirs, not only by this ligament my Cousin their daughter (all my fortune, and part of theirs in one bottom stowed and

coupled together) but by my own inclination ever purchased by their merit."

139 McClure (ed.), *The Letters of John Chamberlain*, vol. II, p. 75, May 10, 1617; vol II, p. 375, May 19, 1621.

140 See Peck, Northampton, p. 21.

141 Magdalene College Cambridge, Pepys Mss 2870, p. 547, June 28, 1588.

142 PRO C 115/M24, no. 7759 Laud to Scudamore, August 26, 1626. Laud claimed that had he handled the first matter his own way, he would have come closer to success. I am grateful to Esther Cope for drawing my attention to these letters.

143 *CSPD 1611–1618*, p. 598, November 28, 1617. John Proy to Carleton.

144 Hibbard, "Aristocratic Women at Court," pp. 7–8. Hibbard notes the marriage of maids of honor to men in the king's entourage, one to Patrick Maule, who served both James and Charles, and Anne Killigrew, who married George Kirke, p. 10. Michael Alexander, *Charles I's Lord Treasurer*, (Chapel Hill, 1975) p. 167, 173.

145 HMC *Denbigh*, Vol. 5, pp. 50–1, July 13, 1637, William Middleton to Lord Feilding.

146 Hibbard, "Aristocratic Women at Court," p. 11.

147 Isabel MacBeath Calder (ed.), *Letters of John Davenport, Puritan Divine* (New Haven, 1937), p. 19, *c.* October 1624.

148 Calder (ed.), *Letters of John Davenport*, pp. 18, 19, 27–33, 38–40, 56–65, 75–7, 81–3.

149 BL Add. Mss 38139, f. 104v. These represented Buckinghamshire, Bedfordshire and Berkshire.

150 Quoted in Lockyer, *Buckingham*, pp. 153–4.

151 See Chapter 5.

Chapter 4:
Court connections and county associations:
the case of Buckinghamshire

1 Henry E. Huntington Library, Stowe Collection, Temple Mss, STT Personal, Box 5, no. 7, 1600–03.

2 Water Eaton was a hamlet held by Arthur, Lord Grey, and in 1615 devised by the Crown to Lady Jane Sibilla Grey. After her death all the Grey lands were granted to George Villiers, Duke of Buckingham. George Lipscomb, *The History and Antiquities of the County of Buckingham* (4 vols; London, 1847), Vol. IV, pp. 15–17.

3 HEH STT Literature (12), "To my right worthy my very loving brother Sir John Lenthall at Stowe" [horoscope for son William?], seventeenth century.

4 Edwin F. Gay, "The Rise of an English Country Family: Peter and John Temple to 1603," *Huntington Library Quarterly*, vol. I (1937–8), pp. 367–90.

5 See Lawrence Stone, *The Family, Sex and Marriage in England, 1500–1800* (New York, 1977), and Lois Schwoerer, "Seventeenth-Century English Women Engraved in Stone?," *Albion*, vol. 16 (1984). Ralph Houlbroke, *The English Family, 1450–1700* (London, 1984). For family violence see HEH STT Miscellaneous legal papers, Box 2, January 1, 1626; December 31, 1625.

6 Little is known about godparenting in the period; yet both at court and in the country the role had political as well as religious importance. Godparents

promised in the christening ceremony to ensure the child's correct religious upbringing. In both Catholic and Protestant ceremonies godparents renounced the Devil, made a declaration of faith on behalf of the child and took part in its naming. On Hester Temple's list, female children had two godmothers and one godfather, males had two godfathers and one godmother. It has been suggested that puritans, especially the clergy, were hostile to the institution of godparenthood, because they felt it had no basis in scripture and that religious education should be undertaken by the parents. Yet many of the godparents chosen by Hester were among the godly; Hester herself came from a strongly Protestant family. John Bossy, "Godparenthood: The Fortunes of a Social Institution in Early Modern Christianity," in Kasper Van Greyerz (ed.), *Religion and Society in Early Modern Europe, 1500–1800* (London, 1984), pp. 194–201; "Blood and Baptism: Kinship, Community and Christianity in Western Europe from the Fourteenth to the Seventeenth Centuries" in Derek Baker (ed.), *Sanctity and Secularity: The Church and the World* (New York, 1973), pp. 129–44. Ralph Houlbroke, *The English Family, 1450–1700* (London, 1984), pp. 130–1. Patrick Collinson, *The Elizabethan Puritan Movement* (London, 1967), p. 369.

7   David Cressy, "Kinship and Kin Interaction in Early Modern England," *Past and Present*, no. 113 (1986), pp. 38–69.

8   *The Visitation of the County of Buckinghamshire, made in 1634 by John Philipot, Esquire* (London, 1909). For the Temple pedigree see pp. 115–16, 211–15. Note that p. 115 gives the wrong order of birth for Hester's first eleven children. Four more were born after she made the list: Margaret, Millecent, Thomas and Miles. Presumably the last was named after Miles Sandys. Sir Francis Goodwin, son of Sir John Goodwin, one of Temple's close friends, married the daughter of Arthur, Lord Grey and Jane Sibella Grey, the godparent of Jane Temple.

9   A. M. Johnson, "Buckinghamshire, 1640–1660," MA dissertation University of Swansea, 1963, suggests that "the members of the dominant county families married only into other families within the community and into no other" (p. 18). While there was much intermarriage as, for instance, amongst the Temples, Dentons, and Verneys, this is an overstatement.

10   Sir John Goodwin sent commendations to Temple, "to my cousin" and his mother, HEH STT 853, 849. George Stratford, sending regards to his sister and signing himself "your loving brother-in-law," wrote "I have been so bold as to use your name in some weighty affairs of mine" and called him a "dear friend in whom I repose a great trust," STT 1861 March 31, 1581; Sir Christopher Hatton, the Elizabethan courtier, wrote to Temple to ask for ten good ewes: "the helps of my good friends such as you are, may yield me necessary increase towards the provision of my poor house . . . at such price as you shalbe reasonably pleased to demand. Your love and goodwill towards me shall ever make me thankfully willing to endeavor in what service I may to requite this among many like favors," STT May 15, 1584; Arthur, Lord Grey, borrowed £100, STT 949, 1586; and on June 24, 1589 asked for longer forbearance of £100 he owed him, STT 954; Goodwin borrowed £50, STT 850, 1586; asked about cousin Susan's delivery, and asked to borrow another £100, STT 852. Thomas Onley wrote to John Temple calling him cousin and recommending his nephew; Temple responded, calling him cousin, sending a gelding as a gift and inviting them to visit next Friday. Temple had £100 ready for him and was glad to hear that his cousin was better. STT 1531, STT 1949.

11 HEH STT 1837, 1838, August 31, September 3, 1597. Extended kinship connections permeate the Temple correspondence. Temple's son-in-law was referred to as "your son Mr Denton," cf. STT 1708. Miles Sandys wrote to him about the marriage of "your sister's brother's daughter," asked for a drawing of a coat of arms and arranged with Sir Robert Dormer, Sir John Goodwin, and Temple to go to sessions together, STT 1777, September 16, 1591; Temple, in reply, noted that Lord Grey had expressed "his most inward love and good will unto you," STT 1939, September 17, 1591. Writing to someone else Sandys described Temple's children's marriages: one married the eldest son of Mr F. Sanders of the Temple, the second married Mr Risley, the third Mr Denton, STT 1778.

12 HEH STT 2332, Sir Thomas Temple to Sir Peter Temple, at Stowe, July 14, 1634, from Wolverton. Temple pointed out that the book's discussion of virtues and vices included "a view of hunting immoderately . . . one of those infirmities, to which [Longueville] . . . was subject." Temple supported Longueville, whom he described as "being of noble and ancient birth" in a Star Chamber case. HEH STT Miscellaneous Papers, Box 2 [1628]. He asked his granddaughter Anna Temple to spare a while longer the book of Revelation of St John the Apostle "which hath been once read over to me and I have read the one half thereof once again and I shall desire to read the same again as indeed our great mysteries I cannot so swiftly run over."

13 See Perez Zagorin, *Rebels and Rulers, 1500–1650* (2 vols; Cambridge, 1982); *The Court and the Country* (New York, 1970). H. G. Koenigsberger, *Estates and Revolutions* (Ithaca, 1971).

14 David Underdown, *Somerset in the Civil War and Interregnum* (Newton Abbot, 1973); John Morrill, *The Revolt of the Provinces* (London, 1976), pp. 97–111, 196–200.

15 For work on localities see Peter Clark, *English Provincial Society from the Reformation to the Revolution: Religion, Politics and Society in Kent, 1500–1640* (Hassocks, 1977); Anthony Fletcher, *A County Community in Peace and War* (London, 1975); *Reform in the Provinces, the Government of Stuart England* (New Haven, 1986); Ann Hughes, *Politics, Society and Civil War in Warwickshire, 1620–1660* (Cambridge, 1987); Clive Holmes, *Seventeenth Century Lincolnshire* (Lincoln, 1988); William Hunt, *The Puritan Moment: The Coming of the Revolution in an English County* (Cambridge, Mass., 1983). A. Hassell Smith, *County and Court: Government and Politics in Norfolk 1558–1603* (Oxford, 1974). Diarmaid MacCulloch, *Suffolk and the Tudors* (Oxford, 1986).

16 Johnson, "Buckinghamshire, 1640–1660," pp. 1–7, points out that four of these families, the Hampdens, the Verneys, the Tyrringhams and the Cheyneys, had held important positions in the county as sheriffs and members of parliament for 200 years. Other old families included the Darrells, the Bulstrodes and the Grenvilles. Seven families became prominent in the early sixteenth century: the Lees, the Dormers, who were related to a sixteenth-century sheriff of London and Lord Mayor, the Dentons, whose family had court ties to Henry VIII, the Wallers, the Piggotts, the Longuevilles and the Crokes. The Goodwins became "perhaps the most important family in the county." Ten more families came to prominence after 1550, often arriving from another county. These included the Pakingtons who bought Aylesbury Manor in 1551 and dominated the elections thereafter, the Chesters, the Andrewes, the Barringers, the Borlases, the Bowyers, Londoners and relatives of Sir William Bowyer, Teller of the Exchequer, the Clarkes, the Temples, the Fortescues, the Winwoods, the

Whitelockes, the Bennetts, the Pyes and the Drakes. Two-thirds of the leading gentry families lived in the Vale in northern Buckinghamshire.

17 HEH STT 2546 Nicholas West, Miles Sandys, John Borlase, John Croke, Griffith Hampden to my Lord of Bedford, October 1, 1584. Sources for justices of the peace in Buckinghamshire can be found in Thomas G. Barnes and A. Hassell Smith, "Justices of the Peace from 1558 to 1688," *BIHR*, vol. 32 (1959), pp. 237–9.

18 Griffith Hampden's will, PROB 11/79, 29 Harrington f. 218v; I am grateful to Conrad Russell for this reference. Miles Sandys, PROB 11/97, 65 Woodhall, ff. 199–200. Woodcocke later published a sermon dedicated to Sir Alexander Hampden, Griffith's grandson, in which he praised him for naming him to his ministry in Great Hampden where he had served three generations of his family. *A Godly and Learned Answer to a Lewd and Unlearned Pamphlet: Intituled, a Few Plaine and Forcible reasons for the Catholic Faith*. STC 25965 London, 1608.

19 Griffith Hampden received the dedication of a very interesting volume, presumably a spoof: James Glaucus, *A Knowledge for Kings, and a Warning for Subjects: Conteyning the moste Excellent and Worthy History of the Raellyans Perverted State, and Government of their Commonwealth: No Less Rare, Then Strange and Wonderfull: . . .* The dedication ended by asking God to preserve "you and yours in that course and race of true godlynes which you have begon to fulfill . . . From Colshill, in the Parish of Amersomm, the 11th day of November, By your worships to commaund William Cleaver Scholemaster." The volume, which purports to be a Latin translation from the Greek, describes "the commonwealth of the Raellyans, an unruly idolatrous people, drowned in ignorance." The Raellyans gathered together to choose a king "thinking thereby theyr governaunce, not onely to become civile: but also theyr estate better and happyer, and that theyr countrey shoulde the rather be dreaded", B2. The book continues with a debate on whether or not to choose a king.

20 In his will John Borlase left 100 angels to the Countess of Warwick, a well-known puritan patron. PROB11/81 36 Nevell, 1593. The preamble to his will does not use Calvinist language but emphasizes his religious beliefs and his wish to be buried "without pomp after the worldly fashion but in such short as shalbe seemly for a Christian." See Peck, "Goodwin v. Fortescue: The Conttext of Parliamentary Dispute," *Parliamentary History*, vol. 3 (1985), pp. 151–65. Susan Spencer Temple left silver and plate to Lord Saye and Sele, her son-in-law, who was also a well-known puritan patron, in her will in 1611, HEH, STT Personal Box 6, no. 13.

21 See Peter Allibond, trans., Jean de L'Espine, *Comfort for an Afflicted Conscience* (London, 1591), King's College, Cambridge copy, STC 15510.5 1591-C4 for this dedication.

22 HEH STT Personal Box 4, (17).

23 PRO PROB 11/82, 80 Nevell, f. 263v, October 14, 1593. Grey's will was witnessed by the Countess of Bedford and Thomas Sparke, a Calvinist minister, of whom Grey was patron. Grey's daughter Bridget was named after the wife of the second Earl of Bedford.

24 Hester Wotton was godmother to her namesake, Hester Temple, daughter of Hester and Sir Thomas, born in 1589, HEH STT Personal Box 5. Edward, Lord Wotton wrote Sir John Temple that his daughter Katherine had come, was very welcome and very fair. "For the green sickness, which indeed she seemeth to be a little entered into, I doubt not but by God his help the exercise which

she shall take with my daughter her bedfellow and companion will so rid her of it." STT 2583, March 23, 1591. Wotton paid Temple's "cousin" £100 for him; STT 2582; on February 24, 1603 Wotton wrote him from the court with a legal document, and noted he "would have willingly entertained party you wrote for had my number not been so full that I cannot without great inconveniency take any more." STT 2585.

25 PRO PROB 11/101, 32 Bolein, ff. 249v–251.

26 HEH STT 2338 October 19, 1613.

27 Clive Holmes, "The County Community in Early Stuart Historiography," *Journal of British Studies*, vol. 19 (1980), pp. 54–73.

28 Richard Cust, "News and Politics in Early Seventeenth-Century England," *Past and Present*, no. 112 (1986), pp. 60–90; F. J. Levy, "How Information Spread Among the Gentry, 1550–1640," *Journal of British Studies*, vol. 21 (1982), pp. 11–34.

29 HEH STT 1807, 1808, March 10, 21, 1581.

30 HEH STT 2383, Sir A. Throckmorton to John Temple, "Your man tells me you say the nearness of the road where I remain affordeth me rumors whereof you desire to be partaker such as they be I will not make dainty of. Credit them with your discretion." Throckmorton described the Essex revolt: "Blount should kept the uttergate, that Sir John Davies should have made good the Hall, Sir Charles Davers taken the Presence and guard chamber, Sir F. Gorges the watergate."

31 HEH STT 1323 [1616].

32 HEH STT 2581 February 1, 1599 Box 3, (9). (Nephew is crossed out, apparently Wotton had originally mistaken the nature of the family tie); STT 1444 January 9, 1599, Sir Thomas Lucy, Richard Verney, W. Combe to John Temple, Warwickshire:

> Whereas we find that the inhabitants of Brayles are not able to relieve the poor of their parish we therefore have thought good (according to the statute made for the relief of the poor) to tax, rate and assess the pastures of Burton Dassett at 13s 4d weekly to be paid to the church wardens and overseers of the said parish after the sight and receipt of these our letters. All which we thought good to signify unto you who (as we are informed) occupy two parts of them and with our very hearty commendations we leave you to the tuition of the Almighty.

33 HEH STT 942 Fulke Greville to Sir Richard Verney, February 3, 1599; Greville added the postscript that Wotton's care "is equal both for his neighbors and tenants."

34 HEH STT 2584 March 4, 1599 [1600?]. Although the letter appears dated a year later it is more likely a month.

35 Quoted in Lamar Hill, *Bench and Bureaucracy* (Stanford, 1988), p. 232. *CSPD 1625–6*, p. 132 (October 24, 1625).

36 *CSPD 1631–1633*, December 23, 1631, p. 209.

37 For a discussion of the changing character of the lord lieutenancy in the seventeenth century, see Victor Stater, "The Lord Lieutenancy in England, 1625–1688: The Crown, Nobility and Local Governance" (PhD thesis, University of Chicago, 1988).

38 J. C. Sainty, *Lieutenants of the Counties, 1585–1642*, BIHR Supp. (London, 1970).

39 HEH EL 1692, April 1, 1608.

40 J. P. Collier, *The Egerton Papers*, Camden Society, Vol. 12 (London, 1840), pp. 350–7. PROB 11/128 128 Cope, ff. 488v–491v, November 16, 1616. Dormer left

money to the poor of several towns in Buckingham and provided for the giving
of shirts and smocks on Maundy Thursday. He made no mention of the elect
in the will.

41 HEH EL 6322 Sir Thomas Tyrringham to the Earl of Bridgewater, November
    27, 1630; EL 6527, Edmund Pye to Bridgewater, October 13, 1635.
42 HEH EL 1695, EL 1694, September 16, 1616, EL 1698, February 24, 1617; STT
    Personal Box 7 (3). Stater, "The Lord Lieutenancy in England, 1625–1688," p.
    37.
43 HEH EL 1696, December 17, 1616.
44 HEH EL 6456, March 31, 1617; EL 6465 Buckingham to Egerton, May 14, 1617;
    for correspondence between Buckingham and Egerton over the earldom see
    HEH EL 6455, March 23, 1617; EL 6457, April 1, 1617; EL 6458 April 15, 1617;
    EL 6460, April 23, 1617; EL 6461 [c. 1617]; EL 6462, April 28, 1617; EL 6463,
    April 30, 1617; EL 6464; EL 6466, May 26, 1617; EL 6467; EL 6468; EL 6459,
    Egerton to Lady Compton, April 16, 1617.
45 S. R. Gardiner, *The Fortescue Papers*, Camden Society, n.s. Vol. 1 (1871), p. 209.
    Croke was also the uncle of Henry Croke, Clerk of the Pipe.
46 J. Bruce, *Letters and Papers of the Verney Family Down to the End of the
    Year 1639*, Camden Society, o.s., Vol. 56 (London, 1853), p. 106, Sir Richard
    Graham to Sir Edmund Verney, Oatlands, June 30, 1622.
47 *CSPD 1625–6*, p. 224, January 18, 1626, Sir William St. Leger to
    Buckingham.
48 *CSPD 1625–6*, pp. 106, 112.
49 HEH STT Military Box 1 (15). See Richard Cust, *The Forced Loan* (Oxford, 1987),
    pp. 97–8, 119–21, 162–4, 206n.
50 *CSPD 1631–3*, p. 418; *CSPD 1633–4*, p. 237. Stone, *The Crisis of the Aristocracy*
    (Oxford, 1965), p. 659.
51 Lipscomb, *The History and Antiquities of Buckinghamshire*, Vol. III, p. 290.
52 Anna Sophia was named after Queen Anne, James I's consort.
53 *CSPD 1628–9* p. 337, September 25, 1628; *CSPD 1629–31*, p. 322, September
    8, 1628, Sec. Conway to Council. HEH STT Personal Box 8 (8), September
    28, 1628.
54 HEH STT Military Box 1 (22), August 10, 1626. There are no letters between 1629
    and 1642. *CSPD 1631–3*, p. 184, November 18, 1631. Among the defaulters were
    John Fleetwood of Great Missenden, Edward Bulstrode of Chilton, William Pen
    of Penn, and the constables of Chalfont St. Giles.
55 STC 20347, John Prideaux, *Concio Habita Oxoniae ad Artium Baccalaureos*,
    February 22, 1626; Philip Massinger, *A New Way to Pay Old Debts* (London,
    1633), A2-2v; "Divers Italian Princes, and Lords of eminent rank in England have
    not disdain'd to receive, and read poems of the nature." Massinger pinned his
    hopes on Dormer who "have ever expressed yourself a favorer and friend to
    the muses." Gervase Markham dedicated one edition of *Markham's Masterpiece*,
    about curing diseases in horses, to Dormer.
56 William Foster, Dormer's chaplain, also dedicated to him a tract attacking as
    "magical and unlawful" weapon-salve, a nostrum claiming to heal by applying
    salve to the weapon that had caused the wound. STC 11204 William Foster, *The
    Means to Keepe Sin From Reigning in Our Mortall Body. A Sermon Preached at
    Paul's Cross May 26 1629*. STC 11203 William Foster, *Hoplocrisma-spongus: or
    a sponge to wipe away the weapon salve*.
57 HEH EL 1698 February 24, 1617; STT Personal Box 7 (6) April 9, 1618; STG
    Military Box (1), April 8, 1619; STT Military Box 1 (11), [1622]; (12), October

29, 1624; (15), 1625; the order in 1624 was Sir Thomas Temple, Sir William Clerke, Sir Francis Goodwin, Sir Thomas Tyrringham, Sir William Borlase, Sir Thomas Denton and Sir Edward Tyrrell; STT 2429, Sir Edward Tyrrell to Sir Thomas Temple, January 2, 1627.

58 BL Egerton Mss 860, Letterbook relating to the Lord Lieutenants of Kent, Buckinghamshire and Middlesex 1604–28, f. 48v. In 1625 the deputy lieutenants were listed in this order: Sir Thomas Temple, baronet, Sir Edmund Verney, Sir Francis Goodwin, Sir Thomas Tyrringham, Sir William Borlase, Sir Thomas Denton, Sir Edward Tyrrell, Sir William Clerke.

59 HEH STT Personal, Box 8 (8), September 28, 1628: Sir Thomas Temple and Sir Edward Tyrrell, knights and baronets, Sir Edmund Verney, knight Marshall to his Majesty, Sir Francis Goodwin, Sir Thomas Tyrringham, Sir Thomas Denton, Sir William Borlase the younger and Sir Francis Clark.

60 PRO LC 5/183, f. 117v. *CSPD 1625–1626*, p. 56. Peter Verney, *The Standard Bearer*, pp. 26–28, J. Bruce, *Letters and Papers of the Verney Family Down to the End of the Year 1639*, Camden Society, o.s., Vol. 56 (London, 1853); F. P. Verney, *Memoirs of the Verney Family During the Civil War* (4 vols; New York, 1892–9); Miriam Slater, *Family Life in the Seventeenth Century* (London, 1984).

61 F. P. Verney, *Memoirs of the Verney Family*, pp. 181–4.

62 See Lockyer, *Buckingham*, p. 62.

63 HMC *Downshire* Vol. III, p. 381, Abraham Williams to William Trumbull, October 14, 1612.

64 NRA 7371, Pakington Mss 211, 301.

65 HEH STT Personal, Box 6 (12); *CSPD 1625–1626*, p. 324. HEH STT 2421, July 6, 1624, STT 2422, October 17, 1625, both Sir Edward Tyrrell to Sir Peter Tyrrell; STT 2428, December 4, 1625, Sir Edward Tyrrell to Sir Thomas Temple.

66 HEH STT Personal, Box 6 (12). In his memoranda, Sir Thomas Temple noted "to pay £80 the 27th of June for the Lord Say which I owe to his Lordship for my son Lenthall." In the 1630s he was involved in a suit in Chancery with Lord Saye. In the Easter term of 1629, remembrances for Lady Hester Temple included: "to move my Lord of Northampton to be a good enemy in Bentlies cause."

67 *The Visitation of the County of Buckinghamshire* (London, 1909).

68 PRO, List and Indexes, List of Sheriffs, Bedfordshire and Buckinghamshire 1575–1640. A. M. Johnson, "Buckinghamshire, 1640–1660," p. 332: Buckinghamshire gentlemen who had incomes from their estates of £1,000 or more: Sir William Andrewes, Sir Thomas Temple's son-in-law £1,000; Sir William Bowyer, £1,000; Richard Barringer, £2,000; Sir John Borlase, £4,000; Simon Bennett, £3,000; John Clerke, £2,500; Sir Anthony Chester, £1,600; Cheyney [no first name], £2,000; Sir William Drake, £3,000; Sir Robert Dormer, £3,000; John Dormer, £2,000; Robert Dormer, Earl of Carnarvon, £7,000; Sir John Fortescue, £2,000; Sir John Hampden, £2,500; Sir Richard Ingoldsby, £1,000; Sir Edward Longueville, Sir Thomas Temple's son-in-law, £1,500; Thomas Lee, £1,800; Sir [blank] Lee, £4,000; Sir Richard Piggott, £1,500; Sir Peter Temple, £3,000; William Tyrringham, £1,300; Sir Ralph Verney, £1,400; Edmund Waller, £2,000. The list of yearly estate values is recorded in Richard Grenville's ms. notebook, Buckinghamshire Record Office.

69 See Nichols, *Progresses*, (4 vols; London, 1828), I, 165, June 1603. Sir John Fortescue's son, Francis, was made a Knight of the Bath at the coronation. The king visited Sir John Fortescue at Hendon, where he knighted Sir William Fleetwood; I, 189–92, June 27, 1603: the king and queen went to Salden

House built by Sir John Fortescue, and knighted Sir Francis Cheyney, Sir Henry Longueville, Sir Henry Drury, Sir William Borlase, Sir Thomas Denton, Sir Anthony Tyrringham, Sir John Sandys, all of Buckinghamshire. I, 193: Shortly after visiting Fortescue, King James visited Aylesbury where he and Queen Anne were entertained by Sir John Pakington. At Great Hampden, he knighted Sir Alexander Hampden and, at Great Missenden, seat of Sir William Fleetwood, he knighted among others Sir Gerrard Fleetwood, William's brother. The estate of Great Missenden had been Crown property and was confirmed by Letters Patent to Sir William Fleetwood in 1612. Fleetwood was related to Sir William Fleetwood, Surveyor-General of Prince Henry's Household. I, 428: Sir Thomas Piggott of Doddershall, Buckinghamshire, was knighted at Whitehall, April 1604; I, 454: Sir Christopher Piggott of Buckinghamshire was knighted, August 6, 1604 at Theobalds; Sir Richard Ingoldsby was knighted in April 1604 and served as sheriff the year after.

70 See Peck, "Court Patronage and Government Policy: The Jacobean Dilemma," G. Lytle and S. Orgel (eds), *Patronage in the Renaissance*, pp. 42–3.

71 G. E. C[okayne] *Complete Baronetage*, Vols. I and II.

72 Penry Williams, "Court and Polity under Elizabeth I," *Bulletin of the John Rylands University Library of Manchester*, vol. 65 (1983), pp. 259–86.

73 HMC *De Lisle*, Vol. II, pp. 133, 140. October 21, 1604, Goodwin to Sidney, reports that there was an undue grant of timber of Whaddon Chase to Joseph Mine for "his service to my Lord Treasurer that was . . . If you give way to it I shall nevertheless attain my own end which is only your Lordship's information." p. 140.

74 HMC *Salisbury* Vol. 18, p. 26, January 20, 1606, Goodwin to Salisbury.

75 *CSPD 1631–3*, p. 116. Sir Francis Goodwin to Secretary Dorchester. Because Sir John Sidley was about to purchase the manor of More, which had previously belonged to the Earl of Bedford and now to the Lord Chamberlain (Pembroke), Sir Francis asked the Secretary to report to Sir John claims which Sir Francis had as a result of his suretyship for a large debt of the late Earl and Countess of Bedford.

76 See Peck, "Goodwin v. Fortescue: The Local Context of Parliamentary Dispute," *Parliamentary History* vol. 3 (1985), pp. 151–65. For Goodwin's connections to Essex see HMC *Salisbury*, Vol. X, p. 324, Goodwin to Essex, September 24, 1600; *CSPD 1631–3*, p. 116, Goodwin to Secretary Dorchester, July 29, 1631. BL Add. Mss 11402: A letter to the bailiffs and burgesses of the town of Buckingham.

> Whereas we have understood that in that town of Buckingham there is a place of one of the burgesses of parliament void by the death of Sir Edward Tyrrell, knight, for the supply whereof there is a writ awarded to the sheriff and a warrant thereupon directed unto you for as much as we are well persuaded of the loyalty and good affection of Sir Francis Goodwin, knight, towards his Majesty and the state, as also of his sufficiency to discharge whatsoever shalbe recommended unto him for the good of that Town to which he is by habitation so near a neighbor. Although we have been informed that there hath been some mediation used for some other where there was no notice taken of his willingness to take that charge upon him yet such is our opinion and the honest respect which you do carry to those desires which should proceed from us, when they are grounded upon so just foundation as we have thought good to require you in this case so far to regard our commendation as to bestow your voices upon Sir Francis Goodwin whereby you shall not only make the election proper for your own occasions but also give us cause to think that we have interest in your goodwill whereof we shall return you our thankful acceptation.

77 BL Stowe Mss, 502, f. 50, 20 James I "Abstract of the grants of all offices and places . . . James I, Charles I, as they are recorded in the Exchequer."

78 Derek Hirst, *The Representative of the People?* (Cambridge, 1975, Mark Kishlansky, *Parliamentary Selection* (Cambridge, 1986).

79 Peck, "Goodwin v. Fortescue." For another interpretation see Kishlansky, *Parliamentary Selection*, pp. 63–5.

80 McClure (ed.), *Letters of John Chamberlain*, Vol. I, pp. 518–19.

81 Dorothy Pakington had exercised her power to return candidates in the Elizabethan period. See Kishlansky, *Parliamentary Selection*, p. 42.

82 Evangeline de Villiers, "Parliamentary Boroughs Restored by the House of Commons 1621–1641," *English Historical Review*, vol. 67 (1952), pp. 175–202. See Derek Hirst, *The Representative of the People?* on the size of the Buckinghamshire electorate.

83 de Villiers, "Parliamentary Boroughs Restored by the House of Commons, 1621–1641," p. 189. Gruenfelder suggests that Pye was a favorite client of the Duke of Buckingham and might have been his nominee. Gruenfelder, *Influence in Early Stuart Elections, 1604–1640* (Columbus, Ohio, 1981), pp. 147, 149. Hampden, who sat in the parliaments of 1621 and 1626, had close ties to Sir John Eliot and drew up considerations on Buckingham's impeachment in 1626.

84 Derek Hirst, *Representative of the People?*, p. 240 n54.

85 de Villiers, "Parliamentary Boroughs Restored by the House of Commons, 1621–1641," p. 190; Mary Frear Keeler, "The Election at Great Marlow in 1640," *Journal of Modern History*, vol. 14 (1942), pp. 433–48. Lawyers who had moved to Buckinghamshire in the seventeenth century such as Sir Edward Coke and William Hakewell found seats for the county or the newly restored boroughs in the 1620s parliaments, as did Bulstrode Whitelocke in the Short Parliament.

86 Gruenfelder, *Influence in Early Stuart Elections, 1604–1640*, pp. 230–251.

87 See Russell, *The Crisis of Parliaments*, p. 377ff.

88 Johnson, "Buckinghamshire, 1640–1660," pp. 72–3.

89 Quoted in Johnson, "Buckinghamshire, 1640–1660," p. 70.

90 ibid., p. 72. The large turnout strongly contrasted, Johnson suggests, with the refusal of the county to assemble at musters in the mid-1630s.

91 HEH STT 900: in 1608 when the Privy Council asked for a list of freeholders from the book of Subsidy for the preparation of jury panels, they complained about "sparing the principal gentlemen." HEH STT 901: A conflict over purveyance for the navy arose in 1612 and 1613. The Privy Council wrote to the justices of Buckinghamshire, that they had received their letters of 26 December last

> wherein you complain of the small rates . . . for the carriage of timber for the navy and do insist much upon the length of the way to and fro between the place where the timber lieth and the waterside which as you pretend causeth such backwardness in the county that without some further addition of allowance your endeavours will little avail as is expedient for Her Majesty's service.

The Council replied that officers of the navy had complained that 2,000 loads were to be carried by Buckinghamshire for the use of the navy,

> whereof when you were last before us you did undertake that 400 loads should be carried to the waterside the last year past, there is not yet carried above 200

loads and that the rest remaineth uncarried to the great prejudice of the service. Notwithstanding that some of the high constables have levied divers sums of money in their several divisions for the whole quantity of 400 loads. And having compounded with certain poor men for the carriage of some part of that proportion do detain the moneys from them.

The Privy Council required them to carry loads requested by the navy officers or "otherwise make your speedy repair before us."

92 HEH STT Military Box, Box 1 (19); STT 2456, January 25, 1626, Duke of Buckingham to his deputy lieutenants.
93 Bruce, *Verney Papers*, pp. 118–22. In the end Hampden paid only £10, not the £13 6s 8d that he was assessed (p. 126). In 1620 the Crown raised a free gift to support the Palatinate. Among those who subscribed was John Hampden.
94 HEH STT 2470, Privy Council to Duke of Buckingham STT 2465, December 31, 1625, enclosing STT 2470, Duke of Buckingham to deputy lieutenants of Buckinghamshire.
95 Bruce, *Verney Papers*, p. 122.
96 HEH STT 582, January 1626; STT 579, December 14, 1625; STT 580, December 20, 1625, Sir Thomas Denton to Sir Thomas Temple. At much the same time Temple was trying to have Denton and Sir Thomas Tyrringham bind to good behavior his son-in-law, Sir William Andrewes, who had been abusing his wife, Temple's daughter, STT 2342, January 11, 1626; STT 2340.
97 BL Egerton Mss 860 ff.51, 59; HEH STT 2457, August 10, 1620; STT 2469, April 12, 1622.
98 PRO SP 16/34/69, c. August 1626. Richard Cust, "Charles I, the Privy Council and the Forced Loan," *Journal of British Studies*, 24 (April 1985), p. 221, suggests that the approach the Privy Council adopted for the collection of the benevolence (free gift) was that of "holding large meetings and simply stating to the country the nature of the emergency." It was only with the Forced Loan that the Council instructed that the subsidymen were to be dealt with individually so that they would not be influenced by others. The Council's response, however, to Buckinghamshire's public meetings indicates that it did not want large meetings held even for the free gift.
99 PRO SP 16/34/70. The justices sent along a report of Goodwin's speech at Stony Stratford:

> I am commanded by these gentlemen to give you an account why you are now called together. It cannot be unknown unto you by what you have heard out of other shires, besides the directions itself that it is for a gratuity and free gift unto his Majesty which you are to understand to be for the defence of the kingdoms, and therefore for the defence of yourselves. In that subsidy men were set for, it was not intended it should go in the way and course of subsidies, but because the ablest men were always in the subsidies you were now, and wilbe sent for, as men of ability and fittest to give. To that end the gentlemen here present have likewise taken order, that the next time you shall not be troubled to come altogether to one place, but they will come hence unto you, and have prefixed Saturday the 23rd of September for Newport and Bucks which is the market days for both hundreds respectively according to precepts, which between this and that shalbe sent unto you which will fit you best, for your harvest likewise that the service was so important, that new letters were sent down unto us, and that you would seriously consider of it and give liberally for I have it took good effect in other counties.

100 *Acts of the Privy Council, 1626*, pp. 230, 241, 242.

101 See also HEH HM45148. This examination of Sir William Coryton, a Cornish gentleman, concerning his refusal to subscribe to the forced loan is not in the *CSPD* or *APC*.

102 Johnson, "Buckinghamshire, 1640–1660," p. 37.

103 PRO C. 115, M 24, no. 7758, January 15, 1627.

104 Quoted in Johnson, "Buckinghamshire, 1640–1660," p. 38. HEH STT 2343, January 3, 1627, Sir Thomas Temple to Sir Thomas Tyrringham; STT 577, Sir Thomas Denton to Sir Peter Temple, May 31, 1627, from Whitehall.

105 HEH STT Mil, Box 1, no. 4. There was a close relationship between musters and taxation. The 1522 muster roll, used not only to certify arms but also to provide a valuation of lands and goods for a forced loan in 1523, was copied in the Jacobean period probably for "a local man of prominence . . . as a reference book to wealth in Buckinghamshire," perhaps the Earl of Bedford, perhaps Francis Cheyney or William Fleetwood. A. C. Chibnall (ed.), *The Certificate of Musters for Buckinghamshire in 1552*, Buckinghamshire Record Society, vol. 17 (1973), p. 9.

106 HEH STT Mil, Box 1, nos. 12, 13, 14.

107 Johnson, "Buckinghamshire, 1640–1660," p. 38.

108 HEH STT Personal Box 8 (2), 1626. The Temple Manuscripts show a striking increase in formal Crown orders to its deputy lieutenants and justices of the peace from about 1618 on.

109 Fleetwood cast his differences with the deputy lieutenants in religious language, December 14, 1627:

> Every one that doeth evil hateth the light, neither cometh to the light, lest his deeds should be reproved. But he that doeth truth cometh to the light, that his deeds may be made manifest, that they are wrought in God. They are the words of our Saviour, gentlemen, and therefore I may make bold to build upon them, and not to shun to appear in any light whereby my actions may be discovered, I not being conscious to myself to have done ought that is evil concerning any of those points touched in your letter. In the name of God, therefore, certify what you please. All the favor I desire of you is no more but that when you certify you will vouchsafe to send me a copy of it.

Fleetwood's letter was directed to Sir Edmund Verney, Sir Francis Goodwin, Sir Thomas Tyrringham, Sir Thomas Denton and Sir Francis Clark. Goodwin sent along the letter to Verney saying, "You prophesied right of the answer, which if it be not really and by the effects replied upon, we shalbe sure that markets in the country and ordinary tables at London will ring of our letters." J. Bruce, *Letters and Papers of the Verney Family*, p. 128.

110 PRO SP 16/92/69, Sir William Fleetwood to Council from Missenden, Buckinghamshire.

111 HEH STT Parliament Box 1, no 13. The Remonstrance was prepared by parliament after King Charles's answer to the Petition of Right was found unsatisfactory in 1628. "As for the preferments which we bestow we . . . give them as rewards of desert and pains. But as the preferments . . . [are] ours so will we be judge of the desert Our self and not be taught by a remonstrance." An annotation in a contemporary hand states "This I made by the king's command who had then a purpose to publish it in print. The then Chancellor of the Exchequer Sir Richard Weston was joined with me to make the preface. But the king's mind altered not to publish it." See Maija

Jansson and William B. Bidwell (eds), *Proceedings in Parliament*, 628 (6 vols; New Haven, Conn., 1983), Vol. VI, pp. 52–6.

112 Fleetwood's will: December 8, 1630, PROB11/159, 16 St. John, f. 118.

113 Maija Jansson and William Bidwell (eds), *Proceedings in Parliament, 1625*, (New Haven, 1987), pp. 204–6, 215, 218, 226 and 226n; 297. In Buckinghamshire, Sir Thomas Temple, Sir Thomas Denton and Sir Thomas Tyrringham examined local recusants. HEH STT Religious 1625.

114 PROB11/166, 72 Seager, August 27, 1634.

115 Cliffe, *The Puritan Gentry* (London, 1984), *passim*. Cliffe includes Ingoldsby and Whitelocke among the puritan gentry in Buckinghamshire.

116 The Temples continued to have ties to the godly. Ferdinando Pulton wrote to John Temple in March 1599 desiring "that God will make you for the time present a good member of the Church militant here in earth and after this life a glorious member of the Church triumphant ... besides the particular friendship between you and me in worldly causes, and some private affairs." Because he thought him a man also of humble mind and meek spirit, he sent him pictures and engravings, specifically, the Prince of Death and a dead corpse. HEH STT Box 3. In an undated letter between 1614 and 1637 John Temple wrote to Sir Thomas Temple recommending the bearer,

> Thomas Wilroy hath bin commended unto me by a faithful minister who was chaplain in Sir Horatio Vere's house and was this last year by my Lady Dorset presented into a benefice here in Warwickshire; he hath married a brother-in-law's daughter of mine by my wife's side a very famous and worthy preacher, this bearer threatened for entertaining this preacher and being good friend ... Good brother do for him for my sake the best help you can; for not only the two preachers' sakes but for the most worthy generals whom I am most bound unto and love dearly.

Temple referred to Sir Horace and Sir Francis Vere, STT 1955.

117 Bezaleel Carter dedicated *Christ His Last Will, and John His Legacy* in 1621 to "the right worshipfull and zealous gentlewoman Mistresse Borlace of Little Merlow, and to the noble and learned Gentleman Sir William Borlace the elder, her sonne ... and to the vertuous and elect Lady, the Lady Marie Borlace, his wife." Carter claimed that when he had given the sermon he had been labelled "a man of a turbulent spirit ... let him judge that reads over this following Discourse, which I wrote out (hearing myself to bee so traduced) I will not say verbatim, for asmuch as my manner is not to write out all I speak, and when I have it perfectly by heart to repeat it *syllabice* according as I wrote it." A3–3v.

118 *CSPD 1634–5*, p. 149, July 14, 1634. Johnson, "Buckinghamshire, 1640-1660," pp. 321–2; E. R. C. Brinkworth, "The Laudian Church in Buckinghamshire," *Birmingham University Historical Journal*, vol. 5, no. 1 (1955), pp. 31–59.

119 Quoted in Johnson, "Buckinghamshire, 1640–1660," p. 44.

120 ibid. p. 45. Of Brent's orders a Buckinghamshire justice supposedly told an Arminian cleric: "I doe assure you neyther clergiemen nor laymen (if they bee gentlemen or men of any wealth) do keepe them, but laugh and jeer at them." Quoted in Fletcher, *A County Community in Peace and War: Sussex 1600–1660*, pp. 89–90.

121 *CSPD 1634–5*, p. 250. Many of the leading families, the Temples, the Fleetwoods, the Cheyneys amongst them, had high pews; see PRO SP 16/366/79.

122 Quoted in C. G. Bonsey and J. G. Jenkins (eds), *Ship Money Papers and Sir Richard Grenville's Notebook*, Buckinghamshire Record Society (1965), vol. 13, p. xiv. See Peter Lake, "The Collection of Ship Money in Cheshire during the Sixteen-thirties: A Case Study of Relations between Central and Local Government," *Northern History*, 17 (1981), pp. 44–71, who suggests that although Cheshire continued to collect almost all of its assessment up to 1639 "It may be that ship money, by placing the King's authority at the center of a claim for extra-parliamentary taxation; played a key role in forcing opposition to royal policy out of conventional, localist forms into more general, ideological modes of expression."

123 *Ship Money Papers*, p. 22.

124 ibid., p. 33.

125 ibid., p. 38.

126 Quoted in Johnson, "Buckinghamshire, 1640–1660," p. 42.

127 Nelson P. Bard, "The Ship Money Case and William Fiennes, Viscount Saye and Sele," *BIHR*, vol. 50 (1977), pp. 182–3.

128 Quoted in Johnson, "Buckinghamshire, 1640–1660," p. 51ff.

129 ibid. pp. 54–5; Mary Frear Keeler, *The Long Parliament* (Philadelphia, 1954), pp. 35–6; "The Election at Great Marlow in 1640," *Journal of Modern History*, vol. 14 (1942), pp. 433–48.

130 Johnson, "Buckinghamshire, 1640–1660," pp. 54–60; see Keeler, *The Long Parliament, passim.*

131 Johnson, "Buckinghamshire, 1640–1660," pp. 60–5.

132 ibid., pp. 77–9, 237–9. Johnson's thesis is the fullest and best discussion of Buckinghamshire politics during the Civil War.

133 HEH Stowe Mss Grenville Correspondence, STG Box 11 (14), Sir Bevil Grenville to Sir Jonathan Trelawney [1642].

> The barbarous and implacable enemy (not withstanding his Majesty's gracious proceedings with them) do continue their insolencies and rebellions in the highest degree and are united in a body of great strength, so as you must expect, if they be not prevented and mastered near their own homes they will be troublesome in ... the remotest places ere long.

134 William Seward, *Anecdotes* (London, 1796), III, pp. 287–90.

135 PRO STAC 5 G3/19, June, 39 Elizabeth. I am grateful to John Ferris and Alan Davidson for allowing me to see the History of Parliament Trust's transcript of this case.

136 Folger Shakespeare Library, T3501.5, *The Two Petitions of the Buckinghamshire Men Delivered the XI*[th] *of January, one to the Peers, the other to the House of Commons in the behalfe of Mr Hamden, Burgess for their Shire etc. They being 4000 that came on horseback to deliver them ... January 12, 1642.* (London, 1642). The five members were Hampden, John Pym, William Strode, Sir Arthur Haaselrig and Denzil Holles.

137 Quoted in Douglas J. Elliott, *Buckingham, the Loyal and Ancient BBorough* (London, 1975), pp. 110–11.

138 Joan Thirsk, *The Rural Economy of England* (London, 1984), pp. vii–ix; 101ff. Joan Thirsk has investigated an estate in northern Buckinghamshire that had belonged to the Duke of Buckingham and during the Civil War was granted to Major General Philip Skippon. Unlike the disposal of other royalist land Skippon sold 20 different parcels to 27 different buyers, most of them local yeomen and husbandmen. Buckinghamshire was an area in which complaints

about enclosure went back to the rising of 1549. Both Thomas Piggott and Arthur, Lord Grey, were accused of enclosure. The latter had written to Sir John Temple that the inhabitants of Westbury claimed common in his woods and thereby offered "hard dealing with me." He asked Temple to take the matter into his examination and ordering. Acquainting him with his grief therein, he commented, "I love not ... to trouble with the common sort," HEH STT 950, May 17, 1586. In 1607 Buckinghamshire was one of the counties involved in the Midland revolt in which one of the major issues was enclosure, indeed, Buckinghamshire had seen one of the greatest rates of enclosure in the preceding years of 1603–7. The higher percentage of acreage converted to pasture was in northern Buckinghamshire where Whaddon and Stony Stratford were located. E. F. Gay, "The Midland Revolt and the Inquisitions of Depopulation of 1607," *Transactions of the Royal Historical Society*, n.s. vol. 18 (1904), pp. 195–244.

139 Cust, "The Forced Loan," *JBS*, Vol. 24 (April 1985), pp. 208–35.

140 *CSPD 1628–1629*, p. 73, April 14, 1628.

141 Quoted in Cust, "Charles I, the Privy Council and the Forced Loan," *JBS*, vol. 24 (April 1985), p. 217, from *CSPV 1625–6*, p. 528.

142 Godfrey Davies, "The Political Career of Sir Richard Temple (1634–97) and Buckingham Politics," *Huntington Library Quarterly*, vol. 4 (1940), pp. 47–83; Mark Kishlansky, *Parliamentary Selection*, pp. 201–23.

143 National Register of Archives, Buckinghamshire Record Office, Drake Family Manuscripts.

Chapter 5:
Corruption and early modern administration: the case of the navy

1   For a discussion of the seventeenth-century navy see Michael Oppenheim, *A History of the Administration of the Royal Navy and of Merchant Shipping in Relation to the Navy, from MDIX to MDCLX* (London, 1896); A. P. McGowan, "The Royal Navy under the First Duke of Buckingham, Lord High Admiral, 1618–1628," PhD thesis, University of London, 1967; McGowan (ed.), *The Jacobean Commissions of Enquiry, 1608 and 1618* (Navy Records Society, 1971), W. G. Perrin (ed.), *The Autobiography of Phineas Pett* (Navy Records Society, 1918); Oppenheim (ed.), *The Naval Tracts of William Monson*, 5 vols (Navy Records Society, 1902–1914); D. B. Quinn and A. N. Ryan, *England's Sea Empire 1550–1642*, (London, 1983); Michael Duffy (ed.), *The Military Revolution and the State 1500–1800* (Exeter, 1980); Peck, *Northampton: Patronage and Policy at the Court of James I* (London, 1982), pp. 152–6; Michael Young, *Service and Servility* (Woodbridge, Suffolk, 1986), pp. 45–58, 73–92, 186–204; R. W. Kenny, *Elizabeth's Admiral: The Political Career of Charles Howard, Earl of Nottingham, 1536–1624* (Baltimore, 1970); Brian Quintrell, "Charles I and his Navy in the 1630s," *The Seventeenth Century*, vol. 3 (1988), pp.159–79. Andrew Thrush kindly shared his work on naval administration, to appear in his thesis "The Caroline Navy under Charles I, 1625–40." Queen Elizabeth also built three large vessels of at least 800 tons at the beginning of her reign although the Admiralty recommended only one. Glasgow, "The Maturing of Naval Administration, 1556–1564," *Mariner's Mirror*, vol. 56 (1970), p. 14. The origins of the *Prince Royal*, 1,200 tons, the first new ship of the reign and the largest built in the reign, may have lain similarly in

the royal wish for display. See Oppenheim, *A History of the Administration of the Royal Navy*, p. 203.

2 Magdalene College Cambridge, Pepys Mss 2871, p. 593, November 8, 1619. I am very grateful to the staff of the Pepys Library at Magdalene College Cambridge, for their assistance. According to John Chamberlain, the two ships were named *Buckingham's Entrance* and *Reformation*. N. E. McClure (ed.), *The Letters of John Chamberlain* (Philadelphia, 1939), Vol. 2, pp. 271–2. See Young, *Service and Servility*, p. 75. W. Salisbury, "A Draught of a Jacobean Three Decker. The *Prince Royal?*," *Mariner's Mirror*, vol. 47 (1961), pp. 170–7, suggests a draught at the National Maritime Museum provides information about Phineas Pett's innovations in naval architecture, including a much fuller body to bear the weight of armament and a third deck.

3 See BL Harleian Mss 7009; Magdalene College Cambridge, Pepys Mss 2878, pp. 380–3, pp. 446–8. "Considerations offered to the Prince concerning the building of his ship," probably by Phineas Pett who was in Prince Henry's service. C. S. Knighton, *Catalogue of the Pepys Library*, Vol. V, pt. ii (Cambridge, 1981), p. 150. Prince Henry had been a supporter of Phineas Pett since the shipwright had built him a small ship when Henry was a child. Sir Roy Strong, *Henry, Prince of Wales and England's Lost Renaissance* (London, 1986). The naval officers were frequently in communication with Prince Henry and in 1612 he issued orders to Captain Thomas Button on the better government of his ships and men "employed about the full and perfect discovery of the Northwest Passage." Library of Congress, British Manuscripts Project, Alnwick Mss 112/5.

For a different view of Prince Henry's role see C. D. Penn, *The Navy under the Early Stuarts* (London, 1920): "All the efforts of the King would have been useless and ineffectual had not the heir to the throne, by a whole-hearted and patriotic display of devotion to his country's interests, taken upon himself the task of infusing life into the dockyard administration."

4 Michael Young, *Service and Servility*, pp. 45–92; Menna Prestwich, *Cranfield* (Oxford, 1966), pp. 211–19.

5 Linda Levy Peck, *Northampton: Patronage and Policy at the Court of James I* (London, 1982), pp. 146–67. In 1608 the king visited the dockyards as a judge, to decide the merits of the shipbuilders and officeholders under attack by the commissioners. In 1618, he visited it as a proponent of reform. Oppenheim, *A History of the Administration of the Royal Navy*, p. 205; McGowan, *The Jacobean Commissions of Enquiry*, xxvi.

6 Buckingham told his client Lionel Cranfield that the king "will give all encouragement ... and sufficient testimony to the world of his good acceptance of their endeavours that are instruments in doing so good and important a service ... my respect to no man no matter how dear shall ever divert me from furthering his Majesty's service." Quoted in A. P. McGowan, "The Royal Navy under the First Duke of Buckingham, Lord High Admiral, 1618–1628," PhD thesis, University of London, 1967, p. 9.

7 Aylmer, "Bureaucracy," *The New Cambridge Modern History*, vol. 13 (1979), pp. 164–76.

8 See Michael Roberts, "The 'Military Revolution.' 1560–1660," *Essays in Swedish History* (London, 1967), pp. 195–225; Geoffrey Parker, *The Military Revolution, Military Innovation and the Rise of the West, 1500–1800* (Cambridge, 1988); John Brewer, *The Sinews of Power* (New York, 1989).

9 Geoffrey Parker, *The Military Revolution* pp. 92–6. Colin Martin and Geoffrey Parker, *The Spanish Armada* (New York, 1988); M. J. Rodriguez-Salgado (ed.),

Armada, 1588–1988 (London, 1988); Garrett Mattingly, *The Armada* (Boston, 1959).

10   Brian Quintrell, "Charles I and his Navy in the 1630s." D. B. Quinn and A. N. Ryan, *England's Sea Empire, 1550–1642*, pp. 220–1, 234. "These greater ships will carry with them more power and honour, and keep the seas with more respect and command and when there is need of small ships they may be had from the merchants." Quotation from the 1618 naval commission report, Quinn and Ryan, *England's Sea Empire, 1550–1642*, p. 222.

11   Duffy (ed.), *The Military Revolution and the State*, p. 82; Parker, *The Military Revolution*, pp. 90–1.

12   Conrad Russell, "Monarchies, Wars and Estates in England, France and Spain, c. 1580–1640," *Legislative Studies Quarterly*, vol. 7 (1982), pp. 205–20.

13   Magdalene College Cambridge, Pepys Mss 2876, p. 653, [n.d.]. Pepys's collections for his history of the royal navy are among his modern manuscripts at Magdalene College Cambridge. See C. S. Knighton, *Catalogue of the Pepys Library*, vol. V, pt. ii. As his collections demonstrate, Pepys was particularly alert to the problems of corrupt practices.

14   Brian Quintrell, "Charles I and his Navy in the 1630s," pp. 159–79.

15   Magdalene College Cambridge, Pepys Mss 1876, pp. 644–8; see BL Cotton Mss Otho E IX, "The strength and military glory of your State has been of late the Navy Royal, for preparation in thrifty order (lest the just charge which is great augmented to private ends might wear out and discontinue), providence of the wise and elder age has ordered an office consisting of five chief and many subordinate ministers." Cotton contrasted the ideal with the real: "it rests now to present to your Majesty . . ., what proportion the present state holds to this rule of laudable institution and honest service."

16   Aylmer, *The King's Servants* (London, 1961); *The State's Servants* (London, 1973); "Bureaucracy," *The New Cambridge Modern History*, vol. 13, pp. 164–76.

17   Peck, *Northampton*, pp. 155–6.

18   James Spedding (ed.), *The Letters and the Life of Francis Bacon*, vol. 6 (London, 1872), p. 341, October 9, 1618, Bacon to the Marquis of Buckingham. Bacon urged that the king "fall upon a middle proportion between that of the commissioners and that of the officers."

19   Aylmer, *The State's Servants*, pp. 139–40; Joel Hurstfield, *Freedom, Corruption and Government in Elizabethan England* (Cambridge, Mass., 1973), pp. 163–82.

20   Michael Young, *Service and Servility: The Life and Work of Sir John Coke* (Woodbridge, Suffolk, 1986), pp. 54–5.

21   Quoted in J. R. Tanner, *Two Discourses of the Navy, 1638 and 1659 by John Holland also a Discourse of the Navy 1660 by Sir Robert Slingsbie*, Navy Records Society, Vol. 7 (London, 1896), p. xxxv. Pepys's transcript of the index to Arthur Trevor's papers, Pepys Mss 2829, includes entries under fees, ill counsel, monopolies and a great many under-offices including "not consistent one with another," "sold, a crime," "several offices in one person," "officers of the king made by others a crime," The issues examined were problems throughout the sixteenth and seventeenth centuries.

22   See Oppenheim, *Administration of the Royal Navy*, p. 197.

23   McGowan (ed.), *The Jacobean Commissions of Inquiry of 1608 and 1618*, pp. 262–81. The figures have been rounded off to the nearest pound sterling.

24   McGowan, ed., *The Jacobean Commissions of Inquiry, 1608 and 1618*, pp. 273–4.

25   C. S. L. Davies, "The Administration of the Royal Navy under Henry VIII: The

origins of the Navy Board," *English Historical Review*, vol. 80 (1965), pp. 267–88.

26   Tom Glasgow Jr., "The Maturing of Naval Administration, 1556–1564," *Mariner's Mirror*, vol. 56 (1970), pp. 3–25. See Oppenheim, *Administration of the Royal Navy*, p. 112.

27   Quoted in Ronald Pollitt, "Rationality and Expedience in the Growth of Elizabethan Naval Administration," paper delivered at the Third Naval History Symposium, United States Naval Academy, Annapolis, Maryland, Fall, 1977.

28   See Ronald Pollitt, "Rationality and Expedience in the Growth of Elizabethan Naval Administration." See also the Report of the 1608 naval commission, PRO SP 14/41, f. 5, which focuses on the post Hawkins era. The papers collected by the commission include a letter from Edward Dalton to Langford referring to the officers' sharing of press money, February 17, 1595–1596. National Maritime Museum, CAD/A/13, Oversize volume, f. 53.

29   Magdalene College Cambridge, Pepys Library, 2876, pp. 559–60.

30   See John Brewer, *Sinews of Power*, p. 11.

31   See Robert W. Kenny, *Elizabeth's Admiral: The Political Career of Charles Howard, Earl of Nottingham, 1536–1624* (Baltimore, 1970); Howell A. Lloyd, "Corruption and Sir John Trevor," *Transactions of the Honourable Society of Cymmrodorion* (1974–5), pp. 77–102. Quinn and Ryan, *England's Sea Empire, 1550–1642*, pp. 216–17, suggest that the behaviour of Mansell, Trevor and Phineas Pett, the shipwright, in using the *Resistance*, fitted out at royal expense, as a merchantman for their own private profit, reflected "the survival of the medieval concept of the navy as . . . the interchangibility of the warship and the merchantman."

32   See National Maritime Museum, CAD/A/13, Northampton's comments on answers to interrogatories. Northampton's work book for the commission of 1608 was recently purchased by the National Maritime Museum. The volume is filled with depositions taken down in Northampton's own hand, his interrogatories, comments on depositions and confessions, and material in Sir Robert Cotton's hand, and, possibly, that of John Griffiths, Northampton's secretary. The volume reveals how a seventeenth-century investigative commission went about its business, including its strategy to bring pressure on officials to testify against their superiors and the specific questions to be posed to various witnesses. For a calendar of the documents in the volume see A. P. McGowan, "Further Papers from the Commission of Enquiry, 1608," *The Naval Miscellany*, vol. 5, Navy Records Society, vol. 125 (1984), pp. 1–14.

33   National Maritime Museum, CAD/A/13, ff, 145–6. Magdalene College, Cambridge, Pepys Mss 2878, provides material on the commission.

34   Tom Glasgow, Jr. "The Maturing of Naval Administration, 1556–1564," *Mariner's Mirror*, vol. 56 (January 1970), pp. 3–25.

35   Alan McGowan, "The Royal Navy under the First Duke of Buckingham, Lord High Admiral, 1618–1628," pp. 6–7.

36   Magdalene College Cambridge, Pepys Mss 2786, pp. 632ff, copied from BL Cotton Mss Otho E IX.

37   See also Magdalene College Cambridge, Pepys Mss 2875, pp. 144–5, articles touching the survey of Her Majesty's ships since 1579, which focused on diversion of stores:

> Whereas Her Majesty has also been given to understand that diverse abuses (since her coming to the throne) have been committed by the officers themselves especially in the embezzling away of both the timber provided for the building and repairing the said ships, as also in embezzling of her Majesty's provision out of Her Majesty's

storehouses, to inquire thereof where the said abuses and spoils have been so committed and to devise some such orders and rules how the said abuses may be prevented.

38 Magdalene College, Cambridge, Pepys Mss 2876, pp. 632–3. Burghley also noted recent increases in wages: "To consider how the rates of numbers of men in the Queen's ships are from the year 1585 diminished in the respect of the increase of … from 23 shillings … for wages and victuals to 28 shillings a month which is the new rate. To consider how this rate is to be observed when new ships shall be built."

39 National Maritime Museum, CAD/A/13, pp. 145–6.

40 Aylmer, *The King's Servants*, p. 166.

41 ibid., pp. 207–8.

42 McGowan, "The Royal Navy under the First Duke of Buckingham," p. 7.

43 National Maritime Museum, CAD/A/13, f. 59.

44 Peck, *Northampton*, p. 153.

45 Magdalene College, Cambridge, Pepys Mss 2876, pp. 644–8. Given his experience in the late Elizabethan navy, Sir John Coke was alert to new procedures even twenty years later. When Captain Pennington was to receive payment of £3 per diem, Coke urged that it went "beyond any former precedent and drawing with it a precedent." The Commissioners wished to divide the payment between wages at 30s a day and 30s for travelling charges giving such reasons as the danger of the time of infection. Coke pointed out that it was all one to the captain but would prevent future inconvenience, Pepys Mss 2875, p. 219. In fact it prevented a wage increase. The commissioners relied both on administrative precedent and practical knowledge. Investigating wormy timber in ships at Portsmouth in 1630, the naval officers called on a number of ancient seamen and secured the certification of 13 denying the existence of worms. Of these one was 72, 6 were in their sixties, 2 in their fifties, 2 in their forties and 2 in their thirties. Another deponent was 80 or so, p. 231.

46 McGowan, "The Royal Navy under the First Duke of Buckingham," pp. 255–6.

47 Aylmer, "Attempts at Administrative Reform," *English Historical Review*, vol. 72 (1957), pp. 239–40. A Jacobean victualling contract described its purpose as

the ease and commodity of His Majesty's subjects in excluding of purveyors in these sea-causes, as also for the well and assured provision of His Majesty's navy and for the avoiding of the uncertainty of the surcharges and losses that have grown in those services in the time of the late Queen's Majesty deceased as since His Majesty's coming.

Pepys Mss 2875, pp. 303–16; the contract drawn up in 1623 looked back to the contract drafted February 3, 1613/1614; that of 1636 looked back to that of the early 1620s. Oxford, Bodleian Library, Bankes Mss 42/17, 42/18, 64/21, 59/31, 42/52.

48 McGowan, "The Royal Navy under the First Duke of Buckingham," pp. 239–44, 246, 251–4.

49 Aylmer, *The King's Servants*, pp. 93–4.

50 Glasgow, "Maturing of Naval Administration, 1556–1564," *Mariner's Mirror*, Vol. 56 (1970), p. 10 and note 2.

51 Magdalene College, Cambridge, Pepys Mss 2871, p. 573.

52 Bodleian Library, Oxford, Bankes Mss, May 8, 1637, 63/24–26. A witness claimed to have heard that Yonge had sold four or five barrels at £4 each.

53 See Peck, *Northampton*, pp. 152–6; Kenny, *Nottingham*, pp. 295–9; Young, *Service and Servility*, pp. 15–32, 45–58. Office was treated legally as private property up until the nineteenth century which explains why even the most corrupt were allowed to sell their offices upon dismissal. See Introduction.

54 Magdalene College, Cambridge, Pepys Mss 2876, pp. 669–73, 635–8; National Maritime Museum, CAD/A/13, ff. 59, 145–6.

55 National Maritime Museum, CAD/A/13, ff. 145–6.

56 Beinecke Library, Yale University, Osborne Mss 631, Northampton's translation, "The sum of diverse directions of government which Charles V left to his son," Phillip II; BL Cotton Mss Titus B IV, f. 100v; Add. Mss 9334, f. 20.

57 Magdalene College Cambridge, Pepys Mss 2870, pp. 545–74. Collections from letterbook of Sir Henry Withrington, Knight Marshall of Berwick during Lord Hunsdon's government 1582–92, p. 551, May 18, 1590; p. 553, October 15, 1590; p. 571, November 27, 1592.

58 Magdalene College Cambridge, Pepys Mss 2878, p. 462.

59 BL Add. Mss 9334, p. 33; Cotton Mss Titus B V, f. 283.

60 National Maritime Museum, CAD/A/13, f. 112.

61 National Maritime Museum, CAD/A/13, ff. 109–11; f. 60; oversize volume, page on timber in the king's wood (no pagination).

62 Quoted in McGowan, "The Royal Navy under the First Duke of Buckingham," p. 38.

63 Magdalene College Cambridge, Pepys Mss 2878, p. 381. Kenrick Edisbury, the nail keeper, was to be made clerk of the survey and his place to be sold for what he paid for it.

64 McGowan, "The Royal Navy under the First Duke of Buckingham," pp. 27–31.

65 Magdalene College, Cambridge, Pepys Mss 2871, pp. 587–9.

66 Magdalene College, Cambridge, Pepys Mss 2876, p. 611, Nottingham to John Legatt, June 21, 1600. Writing from the court, the Lord Admiral ended the letter "your Lord and Master."

67 PRO SP 14/53/18. March 13, 1610. Salisbury had promised Sir Henry Goodere the escheat of Anthony Bennett, John King and others, but he reported that "it is bruited that this cause shall not receive an ordinary trial at Newgate but shall by special warrant be brought before my Lord Admiral." *CSPD 1603–10*, pp. 279, 416, 592, 607, 608. By 1619 King had become Postmaster of Southwark, *CSPD 1611–18*, p. 601. Nottingham instructed the Clerks of the Signet to stay the grant of the deanery of Ely to anyone since the king had long since granted it to him for Dr Clement Smith. Sir John Trevor tried to find a way around the king's *Book of Bounty* and the contractors for Crown lands. PRO SP 14/53/38, March 24, 1610; SP 14/53/26, Sir John Trevor to Edward Anthony, March 20, 1610. For Trevor's career see Howell A. Lloyd, "Corruption and Sir John Trevor," *Transactions of the Honorable Society of Cymmrodorion* (1974–5).

68 Magdalene College Cambridge, Pepys Mss 2875, pp. 260–1.

69 Magdalene College Cambridge, Pepys Mss 2871, pp. 587–9. This undated document refers to Mr Baker, who died in 1613, as deceased and occurs in the midst of other material from the 1619 commission in the Pepys Mss.

70 Magdalene College Cambridge, Pepys Mss 2871, pp. 183–202. Monson and Bingley had personal connections to Northampton.

71 McGowan, "The Royal Navy under the First Duke of Buckingham," pp. 31–8, 195. For a discussion of this problem in the late eighteenth century which links the diversion of supplies from the dockyards to wages fixed in the 1690s and price

rises after 1760, see R. J. B. Knight, "Pilfering and Theft from the Dockyards at the Time of the American War of Independence," *Mariner's Mirror*, vol. 61 (1975), pp. 215–25.

72 National Maritime Museum, CAD/A/13 f. 105ff, confession of Thomas Venables and William Ward, taken down in Northampton's own hand.

73 National Maritime Museum, CAD/A/13. ff. 145–6.

74 National Maritime Museum, CAD/A/13/ Oversize documents, Duffield's confession, marked 321. The king allowed a retinue of ten to the captain supposed to do service "as any other seafaring man." Button was also accused of protecting a pirate in exchange for two chests of sugar. Magdalene College Cambridge, Pepys Mss 2878, f. 733, Sir Robert Mansell's clerk paid wages for the *Advantage* on the testimony of the captain and purser without other warrant; although the true wages were £22 8s 2d, the clerk paid £148 3s 1d.

75 The commissioners of 1618 were eager to have the findings of the 1608 investigation. See Peck, *Northampton*, pp. 152–6.

76 McGowan, "The Royal Navy under the First Duke of Buckingham," p. 16. Young, *Servility and Service*, pp. 45–8.

77 McGowan, "The Royal Navy under the First Duke of Buckingham," p. 50 and n, points out that the *Bonaventure* had been broken up in 1611 but still charged to the king at £63 per annum; the *Advantage*, severely damaged in fire in 1613 and not repaired, was still charged to the king at £104 9s 5d per annum; the *Charles*, disposed of in Scotland in 1616, was still charged at £60 15s 10d per annum.

78 McGowan, "The Royal Navy under the First Duke of Buckingham," pp. 51–3 and 53n; some of those discharged would be found other jobs.

79 It is not surprising that Coke chose that date since it was the year when he and Fulke Greville were removed from the navy.

80 Magdalene College Cambridge, Pepys Mss 2871, p. 563. This sort of inappropriate specialization is discussed in Edmund Morgan's "The Labor Problem at Jamestown," *American Historical Review*, vol. 76 (1971), pp. 595–611. The commissioners questioned whether "Idlers must of necessity be aboard the ships as cooks, stewards, surgeons, pursers … etc. which fill up the book with names but in a fight or stress of weather are not useful." p. 564.

81 Magdalene College Cambridge, Pepys Mss 2871, pp. 568–70, 573–5.

82 McGowan, 'The Royal Navy under the First Duke of Buckingham,' pp. 50–88.

83 ibid., pp. 95–8.

84 ibid., pp. 111–21. While historians have argued that the sailors went unpaid until 1629, McGowan argues that Buckingham actually paid more than 50 per cent of it.

85 McGowan, "The Royal Navy under the First Duke of Buckingham," pp. 81–5, 265.

86 ibid., pp. 266–71, 274–5. Sir John Coke was dissatisfied, arguing that "The Commission looks too far back whereas it should look on the present state of the navy and the causes why the same is defective without laying any aspersion or imputation on the Commissioners of the Navy who are most of them persons of quality and worthy and such as have received neither reward nor thanks for their pains."

87 ibid., p. 276. The Privy Council faced the problem squarely: although the commission had been effective in peacetime, the urgent requirements of the

country at war demanded a less cumbersome administration. Michael Young, *Service and Servility*, pp. 186–92.

88 McGowan, "The Royal Navy under the First Duke of Buckingham," p. 279.

89 ibid., pp. 282–4.

90 ibid., p. 284. See BL Add. Mss 37816, ff. 35v–6, July 8, 1625. These recommendations were not accepted without exception.

91 ibid., pp. 138–9. Aylmer has suggested that the extent of Buckingham's patronage may also have been at issue: "Attempts at Administrative Reform, 1625–1640," p. 236n.

92 McGowan, "The Royal Navy under the First Duke of Buckingham," pp. 278–300. By the 1670s, despite the chronic problems of early modern bureaucracy, focus had turned to controlling those dockyard customs that cut down productivity. In 1673 the Navy Board "carried out a time and motion study for the spinning of cables and other ropeyard work." R. V. Saville (ed.), "The Management of the Royal Dockyards, 1672–1678," Navy Records Society, vol. 125 (1984), pp. 94–142.

93 National Maritime Museum, CAD/A/13, f. 51.

94 Maija Jansson and William B. Bidwell (eds), *Proceedings in Parliament, 1625* (New Haven, 1987), p. 417. Sir John Coke, the most active of the naval commissioners, replied "there is no fault in the provision, therefore desires it may be searched into and examined and his and their credits who have been employed in it to stand or fall as it should appear unto the House."

95 *Proceedings in Parliament, 1625*, pp. 392–400.

96 ibid., p. 399. Invoking precedents from the thirteenth century on, he attacked new offices with large fees, "old unprofitable offices which the King may justly take away with law, love of the people, and his own honor;" free board at court or new rates which "make the leak greater," and he called for "every officer to live on his office," to make do that is with his official fees. The Master of the ordnance was an office established in the reign of Henry VIII and was held by no one of lower status than a knight from its institution with Sir Christopher Morris. If Coke is mistaken about the "tradesmen" who held the office before 20 Henry VIII, he is correct that the nobility had taken over the office from the second year of Elizabeth's reign.

97 ibid., p. 658. Coke attacked "such men as leap from the shop to the Green Cloth; by occasion whereof he named Sir Lionel Cranfield and Sir Simon Harvey." Cranfield, the most important administrative reformer of the period, was impeached in 1624. See Prestwich, *Cranfield*. Harvey, as the monarch's chief purveyor, overcharged the counties, illegally took goods from merchants, refused to recompense county provisioners and mismanaged the royal Household. See the Grievance presented to the king by the House of Commons in 1624.

98 ibid., pp. 405, 547. In Sir John Eliot's version of the speech, Heath described himself as having "two capacities, one as a member of that House, the other as a servant to the King."

99 *Proceedings in Parliament, 1625*, pp. 402, 405–6.

100 See Quintrell, "Charles I and his Navy in the 1630s," *The Seventeenth Century*, vol. 3 (1988), pp. 159–79. Andrew Thrush's dissertation "The Navy Under Charles I, 1625–40" will illuminate further issues raised here.

101 See, for instance, Magdalene College Cambridge, Pepys Mss 2875, pp. 317–18, December, 1626. Order in Council for the former Commissioners of the Navy to survey the navy.

102 Quoted in Gordon, "The Collection of Ship Money in the Reign of Charles I," *TRHS*, 3rd ser., Vol. 4 (1910), p. 153.

103 Oxford, Bodleian, Duke Humfrey's Library, Bankes Mss transcripts, 42/17, June, 1636, 42/18, 64/21, 59/31, 42/52. The final draft of the contract is in *Foedera*, xx, 103–107. Bankes examined the proposal and noted a few changes, e.g. victuals lost due to accident, not to neglect, would not be charged to Crane. The former contract had penalized under-officers 8s a ton for cask misspent which was now raised to 12s "to be answered by stoppage of their wages." Bankes queried this item, perhaps because the witholding of seaman's wages in the 1620s had provoked riots. There was a John Crane who was a captain at Berwick in the 1590s.

104 Oppenheim, *A History of the Administration of the Royal Navy*, p. 238.

105 Sir Charles Petrie (ed.), *The Letters of King Charles I* (London, 1935), pp. 92–4. For a discussion of ship money and its collection see R. J. W. Swales, "The Ship Money Levy of 1628," *BIHR*, 50 (1977); Peter Lake, "The Collection of Ship Money in Cheshire during the Sixteen-thirties," *Northern History*, 17 (1981); M. D. Gordon, "The Collection of Ship Money in the Reign of Charles I". 3rd series, 4 *TRHS* (1910).

106 Quoted in Gordon, "The Collection of Ship Money in the Reign of Charles I," p. 145; Brian Quintrell, "Charles I and his Navy in the 1630s," *Seventeenth Century*, pp. 159–79; Derek Hirst, *Authority and Conflict, England, 1603–1658* (Cambridge, 1986). Kevin Sharpe, "The Personal Rule of Charles I," in Tomlinson (ed.), *Before the English Civil War* (London, 1983), pp. 69–70, argues that ship money specifically grew out of diplomatic negotiations with Spain. Kenyon, *The Stuart Constitution*, pp. 90–1, 98–104. *CSPD 1633–1634*, pp. 563–4, April 23, 1634, Charles expressed indignation to Archbishop Laud about the questioning of efforts to raise money to repair St Paul's "as if the work were pretended by the king to get money together, and then to turn it to other uses."

107 Magdalene College Cambridge, Pepys Mss 2877, pp. 127–36.

108 Michael Young, *Service and Servility*, pp. 210–13.

109 M. D. Gordon, "The Collection of Ship Money in the Reign of Charles I," p. 142. See Kevin Sharpe, "The Personal Rule of Charles I," p. 69.

110 Gordon, "The Collection of Ship Money in the Reign of Charles I," pp. 142–4. 'The annual average spent by the Navy Treasurer was £103,000 in 1625–30; £46,000 in 1631–1634, and £143,000, of which £91,000 came from ship money in 1635–40.'

111 The Treasurer of the Navy was asked by the Lord Treasurer to advance £16,000 because the plague was cutting down on the speed with which ship money was being collected, and "the moneys unpaid were destined for the mariners' wages." Quoted in Gordon, "he Collection of the Ship Money in Reign of Charles I," p. 144.

112 Kenyon, *The Stuart Constitution*, p. 89.

113 Quoted in Oppenheim, *The Administration of the Royal Navy*, pp. 258–9; Aylmer, *The King's Servants*, p. 78.

114 Magdalene College Cambridge, Pepys Mss 1875, pp. 346–60.

115 Pepys Mss 1875, pp. 346–60. "In former times before the reformation made by the late commissioners of the navy there were diverse prerequisites pertinent to his place which since are cut off and no benefit at all left him but his bare fee out of the Exchequer." p. 351.

116 PRO SP 16/338/86, November, 1636. The years 1636–1638 were the last period of naval reform before the Civil War. Aylmer, "Attempts at Administrative Reform,

1625–1640," pp. 237–8. The Commissioners for the Admiralty were to complete business and to call to account all Vice Admirals and others accountable for any profits, droits, or perquisites of the Admiralty accrued to His Majesty from the death of the late Duke of Buckingham to the grant of that office to the Earl of Northumberland. PRO SO 3/11, May, 1638.

117 Aylmer, "Attempts at Administrative Reform, 1625–1640," p. 237n. Aylmer asks "Had someone, perhaps Northumberland, at last begun to grasp that there were only three alternatives: legitimate perquisites, illegitimate ones, or bigger salaries from the Crown?"

118 Oppenheim, *A History of the Administration of the Royal Navy*, pp. 260–2.

119 Magdalene College Cambridge, Pepys Mss 2878, pp. 371–2, Thomas Norris to Sir Robert Cotton, February 21, 1608. Norris advised that de..iled information be sought from lower officials to use against their superiors. Sir Peter Buck should not know "he is to be deposed to anything more than to some few general interrogatories to prove the real and general corruptions of the office."

120 Magdalene College Cambridge, Pepys Mss 2878, pp. 380–3. Northampton supported those officials who aided the 1608 commission. Sir Henry Palmer, Controller of the Navy, did not have the right to name his deputy. Based on Northampton's recommendation the king allowed Palmer to name his son as his deputy.

Chapter 6:
Corruption and the economy

1 Robert Fletcher, "A Brief and True Discourse of the King's Majesty's Carttakers," National Library of Wales, Carreg-lwyd Mss 634. The following paragraphs are based on this manuscript. See also Pauline Croft, "Parliament, Purveyance and the City of London, 1589–1608," *Parliamentary History*, vol. 4 (1985), pp. 9–34.

2 Douglass C. North, "A Framework for Anlayzing the State in Economic History," *Explorations in Economic History*, vol. 16 (1979), pp. 249–59.

3 *OED*; Sir Edward Coke defined a monopoly as

> an institution or allowance by the king by his grant, commission or otherwise, to any person or persons, bodies politic or corporate of or for the sole buying, selling, making, working or using of anything whereby any person or persons, bodies politic or corporate are sought to be restrained of any freedom or liberty that they had before, or hindered in their lawful trade.

Quoted in Elizabeth Read Foster, "Procedure against Patents and Monopolies, 1621–1624," in W. A. Aiken and B. D. Henning (eds), *Conflict in Stuart England* (New York, 1960), pp. 59–85.

4 Jacob Van Klavern, "Corruption as an Historical Phenomenon", in A. Heidenheimer, M. Johnston and V. LeVine (eds), *Political Corruption*, Second edn (New Brunswick, New Jersey, 1989), pp. 73–86.

5 Rent-seeking is defined technically as "the excess value of resources above their opportunity costs given by differing sets of property rights," Robert Ekelund and Robert Tollison, *Mercantilism as a Rent-Seeking Society, Economic Regulation in Historical Perspective* (College Station, 1981). Tollison, "Rent Seeking: A Survey," *Kyklos*, Vol. 35 (1982), pp. 575–602; Jagdish N. Bhagwati and T. N.

Srinvasan, "Revenue Seeking: A Generalization of the Theory of Tariffs," *Journal of Political Economy*, vol. 88 (1980), pp. 1069–88.

6   Eleanor Searle, *Lordship and Community Battle Abbey and its Banlieu 1066–1538* (Toronto, 1974). Battle Abbey was established to honor William the Conqueror's victory at the Battle of Hastings in 1066.

7   See Maurice W. Beresford, "The Common Informer, the Penal Statutes and Economic Regulation," *Economic History Review*, 2nd ser. vol. X, No. 2 (1957), pp. 226–8.

8   Joan Thirsk, *Economic Policy and Projects: The Development of a Consumer Society in Early Modern England* (Oxford, 1978); see also W. H. Price, *The English Patents of Monopoly* (Cambridge, Mass., 1913); J. Gough, *The Rise of the Entrepreneur* (London, 1969).

9   Thirsk, *Economic Policy and Projects*. pp. 52, 58–9, 61, 75.

10 Quoted in Price, *English Patents of Monopoly* pp. 23–4.

11 ibid. p. 164. The judges noted that "it is inconvenient that the forfeitures upon penal laws or others of like nature should be granted to any before the same be received or vested in his Majesty by due and lawful proceedings."

12 Maurice W. Beresford, "The Common Informer, the Penal Statutes and Economic Regulation," *Economic History Review*, 2nd ser. Vol. X, no. 2 (1957), pp. 232–3.

13 Thirsk, *Economic Policy and Projects*, pp. 99–100.

14 See Elizabeth Read Foster, "The procedure of the House of Commons against Patents and Monopolies, 1621–1624," in Aiken and Henning (eds), *Conflict in Stuart England*, pp. 59–85.

15 *Statutes of the Realm*, vol. 4, part 2, 21 James I c. 3, pp. 1212–14. Foster, "The Procedure of the House of Commons against Patents and Monopolies, 1621–1624," pp. 59–85; Stephen D. White, *Sir Edward Coke and the "Grievances of the Commonwealth," 1621–1628* (Chapel Hill, 1979), pp. 115–35.

16 *Proceedings in Parliament, 1625* pp. 303–10.

17 Oxford, Bodleian, Bankes Mss. An extensive calendar of most of the manuscripts is available at Duke Humfreys library.

18 Oxford, Bodleian, Bankes Mss. Industrial patents requested included the ironworks in the Forest of Dean (5/50, 9/45, December 12, 1637), production of iron without charcoal (11/10, 11/9 January 24, 1636), alum mines (6/19 May 8, 1637, 65/8 August 5, 1637, 6/8 c. 1637, 7/1 August 31, 1625, 6/4–5, 13/5 no date, 12/5), the glass patent (9/43 June 26, 1635), draining of the fens (65/75), making and selling iron ordnance (66/9, 5/33), inventions for surveying and navigation (5/32 June 6, 1634), the cloth trade (5/60), new way of heating ovens with coal (11/58 June 17, 1636, 11/66 May 17, 1636), making of strong waters and vinegar (6/17), making of latin wire (9/1), the erection of snow houses and the right to sell snow and ice preserved in them (11/1 June 12, 1637), perpetual motion engines (11/7 January 4, 1636), draining water from mines (11/11 August 31, 1637), making salt from sea water (11/32 February 1637), making sword blades (11/20 November 17, 1634), boiling vessels without smoke (11/40 April 28, 1636), making cases for looking glasses (11/44 March 12, 1636), paper making (11/48/49, February 26, 1634–5. 11/50), engine for cutting timber into thin pieces (11/50 October 31, 1635), gold weights and balances (11/72 September 21, 1637), new invention of great vessels of liquor with less fuel and smoke (11/19, January 4, 1636).

19 The curing of rotten sheep (9/14), taming and breeding wild fowls (11/27 April 14, 1638), manuring and improving land (11/36 December 14, 1636), (50/36) (11/65 June 1, 1636), a new way of speedy setting of corn (111/39 January 4, 1639–40) and the planting of madder (9/15, 12/16, 1636), production of saffron (11/8 May 22, 1636).

20 Oxford, Bodleian, Bankes Mss transcript 59/14.

21 Oxford, Bodleian, Bankes Mss. The penal law and regulatory projects requested in the 1630s included the enforcement of the assize of bread on which Bankes was to certify the fitness of the request before the king declared his pleasure (59/9); the grant to the king's laundress of the register of the commission of bankrupts throughout the country with the exception of London, the licensing of stairs, ladders and trap-doors on the Thames (59/16 April 1636), the establishment of a commission to inquire into those who have "by colour of their places … greatly oppressed many subjects by suing in the king's name for debts," the establishment of an office of surveyors and receivers of the king's fines in all his courts requested by one of the king's Household officials Thomas Jermyn (59/22, April 1636), commission for defective titles (59/24), gold and silver wire (65/30 15 November, 1638 dated from "The Golden Fleece") commission for abuse of receivers (65/39 March 22 1638/9), searching and viewing of silk stockings (67/1 1638), licensing of the export of calfskins (67/4 December 3, 1635, 5/54), licensing of the import of latin wire (67/5, 50/15, 9/1), licensing of transporting of remnants of woollen cloth, old shoes, lantern horns, cuttle bone or cuttle shell (67/12 May 15, 1636), duties on tin (9/47, February 2, 1639, 5/52 late 1639, early 1640), sea coal patent (5/53) licensing to sell wines at retail (5/61), relieving alehouses of penal laws used for private profit by informers in exchange for rent (9/7 March 26, 1637) (9/8 July 31, 1635), better planting of brewhouses (6/5); licensing of wine casks (6/11 November 1637).

22 Oxford, Bodleian, Bankes Mss. New offices included offices for tarring of sugar chests (5/62), postmaster (5/63). King's Remembrancer (5/64 1640), office to register foreigners; registering and bookkeeping in all fairs and markets in return for 100 marks a year (11/21 October 2, 1634), license to print books of fees (11/51 September 13, 1635), patent for the sole putting to hire of footcloth horses in order to avoid too many coachers (11/64 February 1640), office for registrar and assistants to enter all sea contracts for ship's freights and men's wages and to arbitrate all differences concerning wages without suit or loss of time; sole trade to Barbery (11/38 March 1639); requiring merchants to land at Raphe's Quay (11/15 June 1635, 5/79), commission to look into abuses in gold and silver thread (9/22 December 1, 1635); fines levied in cases of unjust suits to go king's servant (9/27 November 19, 1638), duty on beaver hats (9/37 March 27, 1639), patentees of fines in Court of Common Pleas requesting proclamation by which abuses of informers discovered and reformed whereby king and patentees lose fines (9/35 February 23, 1637), surrender of patent to compound and grant pardons and licenses to such as had purchased land in mortmain (11/75 December 17, 1640); rent of tithes of Exmoor (11/47 June 24, 1638), the lease of oyster boats in order to bring down the cost of oysters (11/12 January 14, 1637).

23 Gerald Aylmer has noted the use of royal commissions for both purposes, and the overlapping of personnel on reform commissions and commissions which functioned as patentees. "So the same administrative instrument

served the most diverse purposes: economy and reform, or monopoly and exploitation." "Attempts at Administrative Reform, 1625–40," *English Historical Review*, p. 232.

24 Oxford, Bodleian, Bankes Mss transcript 59/21, March 14, 1639.

25 See Peter Clark, *The English Alehouse*; Menna Prestwich, *Cranfield*; S. K. Roberts, "Alehouses, Brewing and Government under the Early Stuarts," *Southern History*, Vol. II (1980), pp. 45–71.

26 Oxford, Bodleian, Bankes Mss 37/30, 37/36, 37/29, 37/28, 55/84; *Rymer's Foeodera*, vol. XX, pp. 174–7; *CSPD 1637*, pp. 564–5.

27 Maurice W. Beresford, "The Common Informer, the Penal Statutes and Economic Regulation," *Economic History Review*, 2nd ser. vol. X, no. 2 (1957), pp. 221–37; Geoffrey Elton, "Informing for Profit," *Cambridge Historical Journal*, vol. 11 (1954), 149–67. For a discussion of agents and corrupt practices see Susan Rose-Ackerman, *Corruption*, pp. 6–10.

28 Beresford, "The Common Informer, the Penal Statutes and Economic Regulation," p. 222.

29 Ibid., p. 225.

30 Joan Thirsk and J. P. Cooper, *Seventeenth Century Economic Documents* (London, 1970), pp. 237–9.

31 Margaret Gay Davies, *The Enforcement of English Apprenticeship, 1563–1642* (Cambridge, Mass., 1956), pp. 40, 57–59. Davies argues that the fines obtainable from successful prosecutions were reduced by customary allowance of mitigated forfeiture and composition. Norman Jones, *God and the Moneylenders: Usury and the Law in Elizabethan England* (Cambridge, 1989).

32 Davies, *English Apprenticeship*, p. 60.

33 ibid., pp. 64–76; see also *The Lord Coke his Speech and Charge*, (London, 1607).

34 Davies, *English Apprenticeship*, p. 74 and n.

35 Thirsk and Cooper, *Seventeenth Century Documents*, pp. 235–7.

36 Beresford, "The Common Informer, the Penal Statutes and Economic Regulation," pp. 226, 233–5.

37 See Bodleian, Bankes Mss.

38 Christopher Clay, *Economic Expansion and Social Change: England 1500–1700* (2 vols; Cambridge, 1984), Vol. II, p. 237; Beresford, "The Common Informer, the Penal Statutes and Economic Regulation," p. 237.

39 Clay, *Economic Expansion and Social Change*, Vol. I, pp. 43–4.

40 ibid., pp. 68–9, 82, 118, 121.

41 Joan Thirsk, *The Agrarian History of England, 1500–1640* (Cambridge, 1965), pp. 228–38; 39 Elizabeth I, c. 2 (1597–9).

42 *Ibid.*, p. 236–7; E. F. Gay, "The Midland Revolt and the Inquisitions of Depopulation of 1607," *Transactions of the Royal Historical Society*, vol. 18 (1904), pp. 195–244.

43 Beresford, "The Common Informer, the Penal Statutes and Economic Regulation," pp. 226–8, 238.

44 Thirsk, *The Agrarian History of England, 1500–1640*, p. 237.

45 Allegra Woodworth, "Purveyance for the Royal Hoousehold in the Reign of Queen Elizabeth," Transactions of the American Philosophical Society, n.s. vol. 35, pt. 1 (1935); A. Hassell Smith, *County and Court*, pp. 293–304, National Library of Wales, Carreg-lwyd Mss. 634.

466 See G. D. Ramsay, "The Smuggler's Trade," *TRHS* 5th ser. vol. 2 (1952), pp. 131–57; Neville Williams, *Contraband Cargoes; Seven Centuries of Smuggling*

(London, 1959); David Harris Sacks, *Trade, Society and Politics in Bristol 1500–1640*, (2 vols, New York, 1985).

47 Ramsay, "The Smuggler's Trade," p. 139. See *Letters and Papers of Henry VIII*, XVI, no. 169.

48 Ramsay, "The Smuggler's Trade," pp. 137–8.

49 Sacks, *Trade, Society and Politics*, pp. 731–4, 737.

50 Quoted in ibid., p. 727.

51 Ramsay, "The Smuggler's Trade," pp. 142–3.

52 Quoted in ibid., pp. 144–5. Sacks, *Trade, Society and Politics*, p. 728. Waiters were at times smugglers themselves.

53 Quoted in Ramsay, "The Smuggler's Trade," p. 147. Looking at the export of tin, Ramsay points out that it was notorious for smuggling. Its export in London was in the hands of the Levant merchants, but he argues that much of the tin exported was neither shipped through London nor entered in the customs records. In 1593 the Crown received only £28 in export duties from the outports.

54 ibid., pp. 145–7, 156–7; K. M. Andrews, *Trade, Plunder and Settlement* (Cambridge, 1984), pp. 15, 359.

55 See, for instance, R. Ashton, *The City and the Court* (Cambridge, 1979), pp. 20–25; HMC *Salisbury*, vol. 16, p. 319, September 28, 1604.

56 Clay, *Economic Expansion and Social Change: England 1500–1700*, vol II, p. 254.

57 ibid., pp. 64–6.

58 ibid., p. 77.

59 ibid., pp. 77–8.

60 PRO SO 3/11, February 1634; By this renewal of the patent Mansell paid the king £150 a year rent but Scotland was omitted from the patent.

61 Eleanor S. Godfrey, *The Development of English Glassmaking 1560–1640* (Chapel Hill, 1975), pp. 75–80, 255–6. There was no substantial monetary advantage to the Crown from the rents. Another example is Sir Arthur Ingram's role in the alum industry. See Anthony Upton, *Sir Arthur Ingram* (Oxford, 1961). I am grateful to my students Bernard Adams and Catherine Stafford for interesting papers on the glass and alum projects.

62 Aylmer, *The King's Servants* pp. 239–52, 332–3.

63 W. D. Rubinstein, "The End of 'Old Corruption' in Britain, 1780–1860," *Past and Present*, no. 101 (November 1983), pp. 55–6.

64 Similar transfer payments within the political elite occurred through the Court of Wards. A biological lottery determined who won and who lost through "fiscal feudalism" when the Crown determined who administered lands owned by a minor who held land by knight service. See Lawrence Stone, *Family and Fortune: Studies in Aristocratic Finance* (Oxford, 1973), Joel Hurstfield, *The Queen's Wards* (London, 1958). Similarly, the administration of the Crown lands was also subject to charges of corrupt practices and the policy of using the forest laws and Crown lands, and knighthood as a way of raising fines by composition was a form of rent-seeking by the Crown itself.

65 Samuel Huntington, *Political Order in Changing Societies* (New Haven, 1968), p. 69; See Heidenheimer (ed.), *Political Corruption* (2nd edn, New Brunswick, N. J., 1989) for a selection of articles dealing with this topic. On the problem of defining economic growth see R. M. Hartwell, "Economic Growth before the Industrial Revolution," in his *The Industrial Revolution and Economic Growth* (London, 1971), pp. 21–41.

66 James C. Scott, "Proto-Corruption in Early Stuart England," *Comparative Political Corruption* (Englewood Cliffs, N. J., 1972), pp. 37–55. Huntington, *Political Order in Changing Societies*, p. 59.

67 Nathaniel H. Leff in Heidenheimer (ed.), *Political Corruption*, pp. 389–405.

68 Robert Ashton, *The City and the Court* (Cambridge, 1979), pp. 5–42; T. K. Rabb, *Enterprise and Empire: Merchant and Gentry Investment in the Expansion of England* (Cambridge, 1967).

69 Ashton, *The City and the Court*, pp. 27, 16–28; A. P. Newton, "The Establishment of the Great Farm of the Customs," *TRHS*, 4th ser., I (1918), 119–55.

70 Ashton, *The City and the Court*, pp. 88, 98–111; Lawrence Stone, *Family and Fortune: Studies in Aristocratic Finance* (Oxford), 1973, pp. 14–15, 26–7, 58; Linda Levy Peck, *Northampton: Patronage and Policy at the Court of James I* (London, 1982), pp. 131–8. It may be, however, that the customs farmers enjoyed increased profits even if these were not passed on to the Crown or its officials.

71 Ashton, *The City and the Court*, pp. 16–17, 27–8. Menna Prestwich, *Cranfield: Politics and Profits under the Early Stuarts* (Oxford, 1966), pp. 49–157.

72 Ashton, *The City and the Court*, pp. 15–16, citing the work of R. G. Lang.

73 Astrid Friis, *Alderman Cockayne's Project and the Cloth Trade* (London, 1927); Barry Supple, *Commercial Crisis and Change in England* (Cambridge, 1959), pp. 3–51; Peck, *Northampton*, pp. 71–2, 77, 96–7. See also Thirsk, *Economic Policy and Projects*.

74 Quoted in E. Lipson, *The Economic History of England* (London, 1947), vol. III, pp. 372–3; see also Anthony Upton, *Sir Arthur Ingram* (Oxford, 1961).

75 Thirsk, *Economic Policy and Projects*; B. A. Holderness, *Pre-Industrial England: Economy and Society, 1500–1750* (London, 1976), pp. 83–116. C. Wilson and Geoffrey Parker, *An Introduction to the Sources of European Economic History, 1500–1800* (Ithaca, 1977), pp. 115–54.

76 See Joel Hurstfield, *The Queen's Wards* (London, 1958); "Church and State, 1558–1612: The Task of the Cecils", in *Freedom, Corruption and Government* (Cambridge, Mass., 1973).

77 The following discussion of Robert Cecil's finances is drawn from Stone, *Family and Fortune*, pp. 3–91. For a thoughtful analysis of the problem of analyzing corrupt practices in the early modern period see Hurstfield, "Political Corruption in Modern England: The Historian's Problem" in *Freedom, Corruption and Government*, pp. 137–62.

78 Stone, *Family and Fortune*, p. 283.

79 Jan de Vries, *The Economy of Europe in an Age of Crisis, 1600–1750* (Cambridge, 1976), pp. 198–9.

80 Stone, *Family and Fortune*, pp. 48–9, 59–61, 91, 96, 105, 106. Cecil did invest in privateering in the 1590s but that was an area of investment no longer available after peace was made with Spain in 1604. See K. R. Andrews, "Caribbean Rivalry and the Anglo-Spanish Peace of 1604," *History*, vol. 59 (Fall, 1974), pp. 1–17.

81 Roger Lockyer, *Buckingham, The Life and Career of George Villiers, First Duke of Buckingham, 1592–1628* (London, 1981), pp. 61–63, 211–13, 412–413.

82 A. P. P. Keep, "Star Chamber Proceedings against the Earl of Suffolk and Others," *English Historical Review*, vol. XIII (1898), pp. 716–29; Stone, *Family and Fortune*, pp. 268–85.

83 Keep, "Star Chamber Proceedings," *EHR*, vol. XIII (1898), p. 729.

84 Joan Thirsk (ed.), *The Agrarian History of England, 1500–1640* (Cambridge, 1967), p. 695; C. Wilson and G. Parker, *Sources of European Economic History*, p. 121.

85 Thirsk, *Agrarian History*, p. 641; Wilson and Parker, *Sources of European Economic History*, pp. 128–9.

86 Scott, "Proto-Corruption in Early Stuart England," *Comparative Corruption*, pp. 45, 47, 54.

87 National Museum of Scotland, Gordon Cumming Mss Deposit 175, Box 65, no. 276.

88 G. Batho, "Landlords in England," in Thirsk (ed.), *The Agrarian History of England, 1500–1640*, p. 289.

89 C. B. Phillips (ed.) *Lowther Family Estate Books, 1617–1675*, Surtees Society, vol. 191, p. 41.

90 Jan de Vries, *The Economy of Europe*, pp. 210–35. De Vries provides an illuminating discussion of the way in which government office and favor attracted some segments of the bourgeoisie *away* from productive investments, not only in England but in the Netherlands, France and Spain.

91 See Peck, "Corruption and Political Development in Early Modern Europe: The British Case," in A. Eisenstadt, A. Hoogenboom and H. Trefousse (eds), *Before Watergate*, pp. 35–49.

92 Robert Ekelund and Robert Tollison, *Mercntilism as a Rent-Seeking Society, Economic Regulation in Historical Perspective* (College Station, 1981).

93 Ekelund and Tollison, *Mercantilism as a Rent-Seeking Society*; Tollison, "Rent Seeking: A Survey," *Kyklos*, vol. 35 (1982), pp. 575–602; Jagdish N. Bhagwati and T. N. Srinvasan, "Revenue Seeking: A Generalization of the Theory of Tariffs," *Journal of Political Economy*, vol. 88 (1980), pp. 1069–88.

94 Pauline Croft, "Free Trade and the House of Commons, 1605–1606," *Economic History Review*, 2nd ser. vol. 28 (1975), pp. 17–27; Ashton, *The City and the Court*; Rabb, *Enterprise and Empire*.

95 Conrad Russell, *Parliaments and English Politics, 1621–1629* (Oxford, 1979).

96 Aylmer, *The King's Servants* (London, 1961); *The State's Servants* (London, 1973).

Chapter 7:
Corruption and political ideology

1 PRO SP 14/111/17, 18, November 1619.
2 See, for instance, Hurstfield, *Freedom, Corruption and Government in Elizabethan England* (Cambridge, Mass., 1973), pp. 137–62, 183–96, 294–325.
3 For a discussion of the technical meaning of scripts in linguistic theory see Victor Raskin, "On Possible Applications of Script-Based Semantics," in P. C. Bjarkman and Victor Raskin (eds), *The Real-World Linguist* (Norwood, N. J., 1986), pp. 19–45.
4 See Arnold Heidenheimer's review of John Noonan, *Bribery*, in *Corruption and Reform*, Vol. 2 (1986).

Secular social scientists interested primarily in the private regarding abuse of public offices constitute one stream. Historically oriented political theorists interested more in the maintenance and decay of models of statecraft and civic virtue constitute another. A third more intermittent stream harkens still further back to roots of contemporary ethical standards in the Old and New Testaments, and deals with problems more in terms of moral basis of individual behavior.

Heidenheimer places Noonan's book in the last category.

5   See *OED*.

6   W. J. Jones discusses the judicial aspect of English administrators in *Politics and the Bench* (London, 1971), p. 16.

7   See "The Emperor Charles V's Political Instructions to his son Philip II," translated by Henry Howard, in which sale of office is seen as preferable to impositions, B. L. Lansdowne Mss. 792.

8   *Bracton on the Laws and Customs of England* (ed.) Samuel E. Thorne (Cambridge, Mass., 1968), Vol. II., pp. 49, 59, 64.

9   Lawrence Stone, *Family and Fortune: Studies in Aristocratic Finance* (Oxford, 1973), pp. 28, 283.

10   Michael Dalton, *The Countrey Justice* (London, 1618), pp. 4–5. Citing Ecclesiastes 20 and 28, Dalton urged justices of the peace to arm themselves with "the fear of God, the love of Truth and Justice; and with the authority and knowledge of the laws and statutes of this realm". Dalton warned them that justice could be perverted in many ways. Amongst them were "favor; when they seek to please their friend, neighbor, or others" and "covetousness; when they receive or expect fee, gift or reward: for as the wiseman saith, 'Rewards and gifts do blind the eyes of the wise, and make them dumb that they cannot reprove faults'."

11   J. S. Cockburn, *A History of English Assizes, 1558–1714* (Cambridge, 1972), pp. 58–9

12   Richard Fitz-Nigel, *Dialogus de Scaccario* [Dialogue of the Exchequer], trans. and ed. Charles Johnson (London, 1950), p. 120. I am grateful to Scott Waugh for this reference.

13   Quoted in Ralph V. Turner, *The English Judiciary in the Age of Glanvill and Bracton* (Cambridge, 1985), pp. 286–7. For a discussion of the problems of gift-giving and bribery in the period of the baronial revolt see Scott L. Waugh, "Reluctant Knights and Jurors: Respite Exemptions and Public Obligations in the Reign of Henry II," *Speculum*, vol. 58 (1983), pp. 937–86.

14   Such payment might have been given previously for his services as an attorney. Robert C. Palmer, *The County Courts of Medieval England* (Princeton, 1982).

15   William Holdsworth, *A History of English Law* (Boston, 1923), Vol. II, pp. 294–99.

16   Quoted in the Introduction to Sir John Fortescue, *The Governance of England* (Oxford, 1926), p. 22.

17   Fitzherbert, *The New Boke of Justices of the Peas* (London, 1538), f. 24; Lambarde, *Archeion: or a Discourse upon the High Courts of Justice in England* (eds) C. McIlwain and P. Ward (Cambridge, 1957), pp. 106–12.

18   J. S. Cockburn, *A History of English Assizes, 1558–1714* (Cambridge, 1972), pp. 90–1, 103–7, 116–17, 222–3. Such indictments were typical of early modern government. See for example the grievances of corruption in justice in the *cahiers* of 1614 in Jeffrey Sawyer, "Judicial Corruption and Legal Reform in Early Seventeenth-Century France," *Law and History Review* (1988), vol. 6, pp. 95–117.

19   Sir Edward Coke, *The Lord Coke, his Speech and Charge. With a Discoverie of the Abuses and Corruption of Officers* (London, 1607), Bi.

20   Sir Edward Coke, *The Lord Coke, Bv. Plutarch's Miscellanies and Essays*, (ed.) W. W. Goodwin (Boston, 1889), Vol. V, pp. 116–17, tells a similar story about

Cleon. See also R. W. Dent, *John Webster's Borrowing* (Berkeley, 1960), pp. 62–3, for a parallel in Webster's *Appius and Virginia*.

21 Sir Edward Coke, *The Lord Coke*, Bv.

22 For a similar rhetoric see Thomas Scot's sermon *God and the King* (London, 1631) pp. 16–17:

> I Hope ye will as well look to the fingers of those about you. Let it not be with you, as with many great ones, who are said to allot no other wages or reward to their servants, but their avales of this nature ... but I beseech you remember that publick places, afford not means of pleasuring private friends, but follow that memorable example of Cleon, who being called to the government of the Commonwealth, assembled all his intimate friends, and disclaimed all inward amity with them. And most truly saith Tully, he deprives himself of the office of a friend, who takes upon himself the person of a judge.

J. S. Cockburn, *A History of English Assizes, 1558–1714*, pp. 49–51, 227. Cockburn suggests that this prohibition was directed at Coke himself who had "ridden the Norfolk Circuit continuously since 1606".

23 National Library of Wales, Carreg-Lwyd Mss 634, "A view of certain evils grievously complained upon which in the next parliament may be remembered and reformed."

24 Fletcher, "A view of certain evils," pp. 1–4. Fletcher described his associates:

> Thomas Knarisborough, a notable Bribing and corrupt carttaker who hath sithens put a way or sold his office ... Edward Coosyn a most sly subtle and cunning Bribing wretched fellow ... unconscionable ... hath also sold his office of groom carttaker to his man who when he was servant to Coosyn, he was not inferior to his Master for bribery and exaction.

25 On the Great Contract see A. G. R. Smith, "Crown, parliament and Finance: the Great Contract of 1610," in P. Clark, A. G. R. Smith and N. Tyacke (eds), *The English Commonwealth* (Leicester, 1979), pp. 111–27; Pauline Croft, "Parliament, Purveyance and the City of London, 1589–1608," *Parliamentary History*, vol. 4 (1985), pp. 9–34.

26 Fletcher, "A view of certain evils," pp. 6–7; Under Elizabeth, Lord North, Treasurer of the Household, named his own servants as carttakers of London although known to be abusive to the commonwealth and his own conscience. 'It is this office that troublith his ghost and his grave because the same doth trouble the whole commonwealth'.

27 Thomas Pestell, *The Churl's Sickness* (London, 1615), pp. 2–3.

28

> Is it not an high point of base foolery for a man to sit over his earthly trash, like an hen or a brood-goose; and in the meantime to neglect the inward and spiritual riches of the soul? As though a Noble man or great personage should trifle out his time in buying pins? Nay worse, plain muck (sayeth the scripture) and dung: and therefore the Apostle calls it filthy lucre.

Pestell invoked Latimer's sermon before Edward VI in which he denounced covetousness. "And therefore it so fits the time, that if with Old Latimer I should cry nothing but beware of covetousness, it would (peradventure) prove a sufficient preservative against this poison which St. Paul calls ... the root of all evil." See Noonan, *Bribery*, pp. 313–15 for Latimer's sermon, and Joel Hurstfield, "Corruption and Reform under Edward VI and Mary: The Example of Wardship," *Freedom, Corruption and Governmennt*, pp. 163–82. Pestell's sources included the Bible, Seneca, Horace and Cicero.

29 Pestell, *The Churl's Sickness*, pp. 18–21. Until the middle of the eighteenth century, Ronald Bushman argues, the focus of charges of corruption in the American colonies was not legislative manipulation or the Walpole political system but the greed of their rulers. Cotton Mather accused the governor of Connecticut of covetousness. "Sir your snare has been that thing, the hatred whereof is most expressly required of the ruler, namely Covetousness … The main channel of that Covetousness has been the reign of bribery, which you, Sir, have set up in the land, where it was hardly known till you brought it in fashion." Quoted in Richard L. Bushman, "Corruption and Power in Provincial America," in *The Development of a Revolutionary Mentality* (Washington, D.C., 1972).

30 Pestell, *The Churl's Sickness*, pp. 21–2.

31 John Squire, *A Sermon Preached at the Hartford Assizes* (London, 1618), pp. 1, 13, 14. As Squire put it, "not our friends as the Pharisees, the Athenians or the Romans would have it but every man."

32 Samuel Burton, *A Sermon Preached at the General Assizes in Warwick* (London, 1620).

33 Pemberton, *The Charge of God and the King, to Judges and Magistrates for Execution of Justice* (London. 1619).

34 ibid., pp. 25–6.

35 Anthony Cade, *A Sermon of the Nature of Conscience* … (London, 1621), pp. 1–22.

36 Robert Bolton, "Funeral notes upon my patron, Sir Augustine Nicolls," in *Mr Bolton's Last and Learned Worke of the Foure Last Things* (London, 1633), AIV–2. "What is outward preferment, to the losse, or certaine hazard of a good conscience … the name of Christian is a name both of Honour and Valour, and begets better spirits then either Romane or Grecian; let Machiavell and other Atheists say what they will." Edward Bagshawe's dedication to Francis Nicolls.

37 Bolton, "Funeral notes," pp. 154–5, 164–6; "when any good patriote which in some high place like a strong pillar opposes the corruptions and popery of the times: or any faithfull pastor … is taken away; that we take it to heart … to make our selves ready against an evill day." He was afraid, he said, that some heavy thing was in preparation because sins had grown to such a height (p. 157).

38 See J. G. A. Pocock, "Virtue and Commerce in the Eighteenth Century;" *Journal of Interdisciplinary History*, vol. 3 (1972–3), pp. 19–34. Bolton, "Funeral Notes," p. 165.

39 David Heyd, *Supererogation* (Cambridge, 1988). I am grateful to Knut Haakonson for drawing this work to my attention.

40 Robert Bolton, *Two Sermons Preached at Northampton* (London, 1635), pp. 33–4.

41 See Heyd, *Supererogation*, pp. 3, 40–9.

42 Anthony Cade, *A Sermon of the Nature of Conscience which may well be tearmed a Tragedy of Conscience in her First, Wakening, Secondly, Wrastling, Thirdly, Scourging* (London, 1621), A2v., pp. 9–10. Cade also paid homage to his superiors:

The blessings of good Princes, good Judges and Magistrates in executing good Lawes, all men may feele no man can express. Well then may I gratulate our Common wealth, that is so much blessed with wise and worthy men, such as your honours chosen out and set up by our most gratious and juditious king, to preserve our customes, and execute good laws, to the strength, growth, wealth, and happiness of our nation.' Samuel Garey, *Jenticulum Judicum: or a Breakefast for the Bench* (London, 1623) spoke also of the corruption of commonwealths; his sources included Seneca, Ovid, Socrates, Plato, Demosthenes, Aristotle, and Aquinas.

43 Samuel Ward, "Jethro's Justice of Peace" (London, 1618). "The scripture is the best man of counsell for the greatest Statesman in the world: THIS little portion thereof containing in it more then all Lipsius his Bee-hive, or Machiavels Spider-web", p. 4.

44 Ward, *Jethro's Justice of Peace*, pp. 9–12. Ward likened the sale of civil office to simony, pp. 11–12, 51.

45 ibid., p. 52.

46 ibid., pp. 37–8.

47 ibid., pp. 46–50. Of the godly magistrate he wrote: "one of these is worth a thousand of the common sort," pp. 39–40. Attacking covetousness he cited Tiberious, "Buy the truth and sell it not."

48 ibid., p. 53. Ward also attacked mercenary lawyers, extorting officers of justices "as invent pullies and winches for extraordinary fees; An Utopia I fear some will say, too good to be true, objecting to me as to Cato, that he not discerning the times hee lived in, looked for Plato's Commonwealth in the dreggs of Romulus." (p. 63).

49 ibid., pp. 53. See also Samuel Garey, *Jenticulum Judicum*, pp. 5, 14–16. Ward included in his attack not only judicial corruption but the gentry's control of elections.

> How grossely is the countrey wronged and befooled, chiefly in the choys of such, as into whose hands they put their lives and lands at Parliaments, by a kind of Conge desliers, usually sent them by some of the Gentry of the shires, perswading (if not prescribing the very cople they must chuse... This text bids you know and stand fast in your lawfull liberties of election, which that you may not abuse). (pp. 13–14).

The system of justice was like clockwork in which any part out of order would "disorder all." Writing from Prussia, Nathanial Ward added his own postscript to the sermon.

> I fear that the corruption of our times is growne so gross ... I had myself added thereto a project and persuasion for the redress of many abuses crept into offices and officers.., but fearing I have learned too much bluntnesse and plumpness of speech among the Lutherans, which is here as pirme [sic] a quallitie, as smoothness with you, as also loath to meddle out of mine orb, in my second thoughts I suppressed it. (p. 72).

50 Pierre Bourdieu, *Outline of a Theory of Practice* (Cambridge, 1977), pp. 193–7.

51 B. L. Harleian Mss 787; quoted in Nott, *The Works of Henry Howard, Earl of Surrey, and of Sir Thomas Wyatt, the Elder* (2 vols; London, 1816), vol. II, p. lxxxviii.

52 A recent discussion of such literature is in Malcom Smuts, *Court Culture and the Origins of a Royalist Tradition in Early Stuart England* (Philadelphia, 1987),

pp. 73–116; see too the discussion in Perez Zagorin, *The Court and the Country* (New York, 1970), pp. 40–73.

53 See John Salmon, "Seneca and Tacitus in Jacobean England," Peck (ed.), in *The Mental World of the Jacobean Court*, Cambridge University Press, forthcoming.

54 William Camden, *Remaines Concerning Britaine* (London, 1614), p. 198.

55 See Beatrice White, *A Cast of Ravens* (New York, 1965); A. Amos, *The Great Oyer of Poisoning* (London, 1846); Peck, *Northampton*, pp. 38–40. Northampton had died in 1614.

56 These were John Buckeridge and Thomas Bilson.

57 See Sir Walter Davenport's Commonplace book, Chester Record Office, CR/63/2/1, which contains material on the Essex divorce and Overbury murder, and scurrilous verses on Carr and Buckingham; I am grateful to Richard Cust for this reference. See also James Sanderson, "Poems on an Affair of State – The Marriage of Somerset and Lady Essex," in *RES* n.s. 17 (1966).

58 Christopher Hill, "The Norman Yoke," in *Puritanism and Revolution* (London 1958). Citation of the Norman Yoke did not signify opposition to the court. Some members of the Society of Antiquaries who were court officials viewed the Norman Conquest in a similar way.

59 Richard Niccols, *Sir Thomas Overburies Vision* (London, 1616), p. 13, STC 18524. In the margin Niccols cites "Out of a register book of the acts of the Bishop of Rochester in Stowes Survay."

60 This invocation of a heroic Essex was echoed in Thomas Scott's "Robert Earl of Essex, His Ghost" (Printed in Paradise, 1624) which attacked peace with Spain.

61 Niccols, *Sir Thomas Overburies Vision* pp. 21–2, 40–2.

62 ibid., p. 44.

63 ibid., p. 48. The poem ends with an apotheosis of king and land sounding much like John of Gaunt's speech in Shakespeare's *Richard II* even to referring to England as "an other Eden." It may be asked whether the poet meant to suggest the more unhappy conclusion of John of Gaunt's speech. "O England, O thrise happie land,/ Who of all Iles most gracefully dost stand/ Upon this earths broad face, like *Venus* spot/ Upon her Cheeke; Thou onely garden plot,/ Which as an other Eden Heav'n hath chose/ In which the tree of life and knowledge grows." At this point Niccols changes to a positive view of King James in contrast to John of Gaunt's criticism of Richard II.

"Happie in all, most happie in this thing'/ In having such a holy, happy King; /A King, whose faith in Arms of proofe doth fight/ 'Gainst that seven-headed beast, and all his might:/ A King, whose justice will at last not faile,/ To give to each his owne in equal scale:/ a King, whose love dove-like with wings of fame,/ To all the world doth happy peace proclaim' (p. 52.)

64 A3v–4. "Machiavell knowing the venome of this vice [envy], gave his sonne this last and not least instruction: that hee should not bee envious, but to doe ... such deeds that others may envy thee, for to be envied is the token of good desert, but to be envious, the signe of a foolish nature, which verefies the saying of Marcus Tullius, the Orator." (London, 1616), B3v. STC 18919.3.

65 *The Bloody Downfall*, A4v–B

66 ibid., B4–4v, C4, C2–C2v.

67 A.D. B., *The Court of ... James the First, King of Great Britain, France and Ireland: etc. With Divers Rules, Most Pure Precepts, and Selected Definitions Lively* (London, Printed by Edw. Griffin, 1619), pp. 2–3. The satirical nature of

this dedication is suggested by the later passage in which the author warns against advancing the young (p. 149).

68   A.D. B., *the Court of ... James the First*, pp. 15–20. There is a general rumor that good men are not to be found at court,

> some no doubt may say, that I doe but wash an Aethiopian-Blackmoore, in inviting and inciting Courtiers to such integritie of life ... thou shalt still be if of a right and upright courage and condition; yea, and from this fountaine, thou shalt derive all those silver streames, and comfortable currents ... Launch out into this ... turbulent Sea of the Court, and undoubtedly thou shalt vanquish and overcome the infinite swarme of ... prodigious monsters of impietie ... let not the Philosophie of effeminate and faint-hearted men distract ... hearken to God the fountaine of infallible and invincible veritie itselfe.

69   Kenneth Muir and Patricia Thompson, *The Collected Poems of Sir Thomas Wyatt* (Liverpool, 1969), p. 91.

70   A.D. B. *The Court of ... James the First* pp. 15–17, 22–3; "'tis trash, trumpery, and meere foppery for ... he which will in this sence be good and godly, must onely leave the Court, but even the whole world. For if we love and beleeve, if we will heare and beare the Truth; is it possible I pray, that any thing can be absolutely cleane and pure, in this uncleane and obscene scene of the world?" The note in the margin reads "Nothing in this life is absolutely good."

71   A.D. B., *The Court of ... James the First*, p. 25. The author urged the study of law, languages and eloquence especially histories and antiquities, citing Cicero, Plato, Salust and Polybius. "If therefore (Friendly courtier) thou wouldst not continually, shewe thyself a childe, and non-proficient, in the court of thy Prince, be not (I say) rude, but well read, and a skilfull Antiquary in Histories and Chronicles" (p. 22).

72   A.D. B. *The Court of ... James the First*, pp. 104–5. "Seeing that courtiers set councell at saile and sell their Princes secrets, it were very materiall that he would take a special care that nothing at court might be vendible, and that thereby hee open not a gap to ambition and corruption" (p. 109).

73   A.D. B., *The Court of ... James the First*, pp. 147–50,

74   PRO SP 14/71 6, 8 October, 1612, Somerset to Northampton. The favorite wrote, "I am the courtier whose hand never tooke bribes;" Cam. Univ. Lib. Mss Dd.3.63, ff. 54–6v (1613), Northampton to Somerset, "If ever I played any part artificially to give your lordship satisfaction... it is in Cranfield's matter... I told him as a true friend ... than an offer of 2,000 marks should have been made to your Lordship lately for the matter of the wines which he had valued to you at one ... I wished him to consider of how great value your favor was likely to be to him."

75   BL Cotton Mss Galba E I, f.262, October 25 1612. Sir Charles Cornwallis, as English Ambassador to Spain, took monies from the Spanish for which he was called to task by Salisbury who was himself taking a Spanish pension.

76   PRO SP 94/21 f. 200, December 16, 1615? The cipher for this letter is PRO SP 106/4, ff. 22v–23. For a discussion of the Spanish pensioners see S. R. Gardiner, *The History of England from the Accession of James I to the Outbreak of the Civil War* (London, 1883–4), vol. II, pp. 216–17; Charles Carter, "Intelligence from England, Spanish Hapsburg Policy-Making and its Informational Base, 1598–1625," PhD thesis Columbia University, 1962, pp. 172–5; Charles Carter, *The Secret Diplomacy of the Hapsburgs, 1598–1625* (New York, 1964); A. J. Loomie, *Spain and the Jacobean Catholics, 1603–12*, Catholic Record Society,

Vol. 64 (London, 1973); PRO 31, 12/35, October 17, 1614, Sarmiento to King Phillip III. Henry Lonchay and Joseph Cuvelier (eds), *Correspondance de la Cour d'Espagne sur les Affaires des Pay-Bas au XVII siecle* (6 vols; Brussels, 1923–37), Vol. 1, no. 330, p. 152.

77 PRO SP 94/20 f. 59v, September 9, 1615. For cipher see PRO SP 106/4, f. 26.

78 See Thomas Scott, *Vox Populi, Vox Coeli*; Sir Walter Scott (ed.), *A Collection of Scarce and Valuable Tracts*, Somers Tracts (13 vols; London 1809–15), Vol. 2, pp. 513–17, 584; L. B. Wright, "Propaganda against James I's Appeasement of Spain," *Huntington Library Quarterly*, vol. 6 (1942–43), p. 52.

79 Millar MacClure, *The Paul's Cross Sermons* (Toronto, 1958), pp. 141, 248, 228.

80 "Tom Tell-Troath," *Somers Tracts*, Vol. 2, p. 473.

81 For the Suffolk trial see HMC Salisbury Mss, Vol. 22, pp. 96–113; PRO SP 14/111/17, 18; *English Historical Review*, vol. 13, pp. 716–29. HMC Salisbury Mss, Vol. 22, p. 98, Sir John Finet to the Earl of Salisbury, October 27–29, 1619: "when Cortin sued for his debt of £18,000 from the King, Sir John Townsend demanded of him £3,000, and said what is it to give £3,000 to such a man as my Lord, be it but to purchase his favor."

82 HMC Salisbury Mss, Vol. 22., pp. 107–8, Finet to [Salisbury], November, 14 1619.

83 HMC Salisbury Mss, Vol. 22, p. 101. Finet to Salisbury, October 29, 1619.

84 PRO SP 14/111/17.

85 PRO SP 14/111/17. f. 33v. "Invoking the civil law they proved they might take gifts."

86 HMC Salisbury Mss, Vol. 22, p. 108; PRO SP 14/111/17, f34v.

87 PRO SP 14/111/18. "Concerning several sums of monies taken corruptly for rewards and gratuities", Suffolk admitted that his wife had received some of these but that he had repaid them. Suffolk denied private gain from His Majesty's public services "or that his wife or Sir John Bingley hath at any time by color of his office, unlawfully, corruptly ... received any sum or sums of money of any person that was to receive monies out of His Majesty's Exchequer." He denied frauds or deceits committed to the dishonor of the king or the disservice of the state.

88 HMC Salisbury Mss, pp. 106–8. The discussion of the eleven-day trial comes amidst discussion of reversions and payments to Ambassador Dudley Carleton. The Messenger of the Chamber asked for remuneration for five months' "troublesome service in suit between Crown and Earl of Suffolk."

89 HMC Salisbury Mss, Vol. 22, pp. 109–13.

90 ibid., p. 113; Bacon then placed the corrupt practices in a larger political context:

> How completely happy the king were if his treasury and state of means were settled, what honour he had obtained above any of his predecessors as to have deserved the title of Uniter of Britain and the Planter of Ireland; how glorious the church here was, like a firmament of stars; that the nobility were not now as in times past the shadowers and overawers of the King and Crown, nor oppressors of the subject; that the judges were never more learned, never more just, the justices of peace never more diligent and dutiful in their places ... nothing wants but treasure, which whosoever destroys wounds the state to death or cuts a main sinew and maims it.

He continued:

> In the country the fields grew every day more and more from deserts to gardens, the city never more populous nor flourishing, the navy never in so good way for

service, the merchant never farther more industriously trafficking, the king admired in his government at home and working great effects abroad by his reputation; the Prince a singular hope.

Both Coke and Bacon focused on the harm done to the king's finances by corrupt practices.

91 PRO SP 14/111/8: Thomas Locke to Dudley Carleton, November 6, 1619. At the same time that Locke wrote of the Suffolks' trial, Sir Thomas Edmondes described to Carleton how he had solicited "due respect ... according to the quality of your Lordship's special merit" from English merchants, "having forgotten upon the conclusion of the last Treaty with the States the extraordinary care and pains which your Lordship had formerly taken in the same business." They "really intended to give your Lordship very honorable contentment as soon as Sir Thomas Smith's indisposition will permit." Thus, while delayed in responding to Carleton because of the "great cause of the Earl of Suffolk," Edmondes solicited gratuities on behalf of Carleton. PRO SP 14/111/30, Edmondes to Carleton, November 18, 1619. Note also James I's comment to parliament in 1621 that the court had learned that "everyday was not to be a Christmas."

Chapter 8:
The language of corruption:
a discourse of political conflict

1 Wallace Notestein, Frances Helen Relf and Hartley Simpson (eds), *Commons Debates, 1621* (7 vols; New Haven, 1935), Vol. II, p. 224.

2 For a discussion of the revival of impeachment see Colin Tite, *Impeachment and Parliamentary Judicature in Early Stuart England* (London, 1974); Clayton Roberts, *The Growth of Responsible Government in Early Stuart England* (Cambridge, 1966).

3 Quoted in Conrad Russell, *Parliaments and English Politics, 1621–1629* (Oxford, 1979), p. 111.

4 T. B. Howell, *A Complete Collection of State Trials* ... (London, 1816), Vol, II, p. 1093.

5 *Commons Debates, 1621*, Vol. II, pp. 237–42.

6 Howell's *State Trials*, Vol. II, p. 1097; *Commons Debates, 1621*, Vol. II, p. 240.

After some reluctation within me, I am resolved to speak what my conscience moves me unto. I speak for the good of my country, the honor of my king, and advancement of justice. Justice is the fountain, the king the head thereof, clear as the waters of Shiloh, pure as the rivers of Damascus. But there is a derivative justice brought unto us by channels. Those are often muddy and more bitter than the waters of Marah. Such waters flow (as it should seem) abundantly in Chancery.

7 He was the recipient of many dedications including, as we have seen, those of Samuel Ward, which had focused on the problems of corruption. Howell's *State Trials*, Vol. II, pp. 1102–4. For a discussion see Joel Hurstfield, *Freedom, Corruption and Government in Elizabethan England* (Cambridge, Mass., 1973) pp. 145–7; Jonathan Marwil, *The Trials of Counsel* (Detroit, 1976). Thomas Bushell, *The First Part of Youth's Errors* (London, 1628), claimed that Bacon's

under-officers, of whom he was one, were responsible for the bribery that brought about Bacon's downfall. I am grateful to Jackson Boswell for this reference.

8   Quoted in Robert Zaller, *The Parliament of 1621* (Berkeley, Calif. 1971) p. 86.

9   George Roberts (ed.), *The Diary of Walter Yonge*, Camden Society, o.s. Vol. 41 (London, 1848), p. 37.

10   Howell, *State Trials*, Vol. II, p. 1113. Quoted in Zaller, *The Parliament of 1621*, p. 98.

11   Howell, *State Trials*, Vol. II, pp. 1146–54. Sir Henry Withrington said "the corrupt judges before and since the conquest hanged (I see by report), and I hope our causes shall have the same success." *Commons Debates, 1621*, Vol. III, pp. 54–5, April 23, 1621.

12   *Commons Debates, 1621*, Vol. III, pp. 16–17, 52.

13   ibid., Vol. II, pp. 313–14. See Tite, *Impeachment and Parliamentary Judicature in Early Stuart England*, pp. 133–5. Coke drew on historical precedents from before the Conquest and from Cicero.

14   Clayton Roberts, *The Rise of Responsible Government*, pp. 31–2.

15   *Commons Debates, 1621*, Vol III, p. 98, April 27, 1621.

16   Sir Robert Phelips said

> Although judges do not good things for reward or commendation but because they are good and just, yet they know that there is no man so void of humanity but for good done will return that honor which is due unto them foor the same. Since therefore they have been so careful for our good and liberty, let us do that may be for their honor by punishing those that have scandalized them touching the undue procuring of the fees aforesaid.

17   *Commons Debates, 1621*, Vol. II, pp. 327–8.

18   ibid., Vol. IV, p. 267. In the latter case, concealers of bribes and those who confessed were treated differently. "For if such information may not be given with impunity, there would be no discovery" of the bribery.

19   Thomas Scott, B. D., *The Projector* (London, 1623), p. 33. It is difficult to disentangle Thomas Scot of Ipswich from Thomas Scott, B. D., and others of the same name. I have followed the attributions in the revised *STC*.

20   Thomas Scot of Ipswich, *Vox Dei* (London, 1623), p. 37.

21   Robert Ruigh, *The Parliament of 1624* (Cambridge, Mass., 1971), pp. 303–44; Ruigh stresses that the lead in the Commons was taken by Sir Miles Fleetwood, an official in the Court of Wards. On Cranfield's impeachment see also Menna Prestwich, *Cranfield* (Oxford, 1966); Tite, *Impeachment and Parliamentary Judicature*; Elizabeth R. Foster, *The House of Lords, 1603–1649* (New Haven, 1983); William Cobbett, *Parliamentary History of England* (London, 1806), Vol. 1, pp. 1411–77.

22   Quoted in W. J. Jones, *Politics and the Bench* (London, 1971), p. 160. See his discussion of the relationship of judges and administrators: "Most major officials were judges, and most judges were administrators." pp. 16–17.

23   See A. R. Braunmuller, "To the Globe I Rowed," *English Literary Renaissance* (in press), Jerzy Limon, *Dangerous Matter, English Drama and Politics in 1623/1624* (Cambridge, 1986), Thomas Cogswell, "Thomas Middleton and the Court, 1624," *HLQ*, vol. 47 (1984). There is only one contemporary, John Woolley, who suggested that the Prince and Buckingham saw the play but others thought Middleton must have had powerful support.

24   Thomas Scot, *Vox Dei* (London, 1623) was originally preached at assizes March 20, 1622. HEH 69395 is the copy belonging to the Earl of Bridgewater, son

of Lord Chancellor Ellesmere. Frontispiece, pp. 58–9. Favor, like Bracton's definition of the gift, is given freely. Scot refers to favor as a blessing and identifies corruption with ambition in his address to the reader.

25   House of Lords Record Office (RO), Manuscript Journal of the House of Lords (MS L J), p.614, May 15, 1626 (Yale Center for Parliamentary History transcript [Yale transcript]), p. 734. For a discussion of the parliamentary session of 1626, see Russell, *Parliaments and English Politics, 1621–1629*, pp. 260–323; and Tite, *Impeachment and Parliamentary Judicature*, pp. 178–218. For another discussion of the 1626 debates, see Michael Young, "Buckingham, War and Parliament: Revisionism Gone too Far," *Parliamentary History*, vol. 4 (1985), pp. 45–69; Peck, " 'For a King not to be Bountiful were a Fault': Perspectives on Court Patronage in Early Stuart England," *Journal of British Studies*, vol. 25 (1986), pp. 51–8.

26   BL Harleian Mss 5007, ff. 1–3v (Yale Center for Parliamentary History microfilm). Although there was no exact precedent, Selden argued the right to proceed by "parliament law, that is either done in parliament, or allowed there for good law: and so the lords protested anciently that they would proceed neither by common law, nor by civil law." f. 5.

27   BL Harleian Mss, 5007, ff. 5–7v.

28   BL Harleian Mss, 5007, f.14.

29   Hampshire Record Office, Jervoise Mss 07, ff. 1–2. I am grateful to Conrad Russell for lending me this transcript. See BL Harl. 5007 for another version. Pym stated that "every offence presupposeth a duty." As a sworn councillor to the king, Pym argued that the duke's duty was "to preserve his Majesty's honor and service before his own pride."

30   Hampshire Record Office, Jervoise Mss 07, ff. 3–5. (BL Harl. 5007 reads "master" not "minister"). Such liberality to Buckingham, his family and associates had great cost:

> They have been a great burden to the kingdom by the gifts and pensions already received and yet stand in need of more for the future support of their dignities. . . . The commonwealth hath been bereaved of the use and employment of so much public treasure in a time of great want and greater occasion than the state had in many ages, when the expenses of the king's court can hardly be supplied, when the forts and castles are unfurnished, when the seas have been unguarded . . . to the dishonor of the nation, the damage of the subject and hazard of the whole kingdom . . . Most of the customs of Ireland, and that of poundage there, and other subsidies of that country, have been . . . proper for the defence of that kingdom; And that these come yearly through his hands.

31   Hampshire Record Office, Jervoise Mss 07, f. 8.

32   BL Harleian Mss 5007, ff. 41–3.

33   Howell, *State Trials*, Vol. II, pp. 1308–9, 1315–6. Buckingham had procured the Lord Treasurership for the Lord Mandeville for £20,000. Thus of the Lord Admiralty, the charge read,

> Whereas, by the laws and statutes of this kingdom of England, if any person whatsoever give or pay any sum of money, fee, or reward, directly or indirectly, for any office or offices, which in any wise touch or concern the administration or execution of justice . . . the same person is immediately, upon the same fee, money, or reward given or paid, to be adjudged a disabled person in the law, to . . . enjoy the said offices or offices.

And article 10 read "no Place of Judicature in the courts of justice of our sovereign lord the king, nor other like preferments given by the kings of this realm, ought to be procured by any subject whatsoever for any reward, bribe or gift."

34 Hampshire Record Office, Jervoise Mss 07, f. 3.
35 House of Lords RO, MS L J, pp. 610–12, May 15, 1626 (Yale transcript, pp. 721–8). For John Pym's speech on the eleventh and twelfth articles of impeachment that was reported in the House of Lords, see Hampshire Record Office, Jervoise Mss 07.
36 BL Harl. 5007, ff. 29–29v.
37 BL Harl. 5007, f. 30.
38 Christopher Sherland's speech, BL Harl. Mss 5007, ff. 30–1. The report of Sherland's speech is HLRO, MS L J, pp. 610–12, May 15, 1626 (Yale transcript, pp. 721–8). In the House of Lords, Sherland's points were made slightly differently: the sale of honors "soils the most beautiful flower of the crown and makes it vile and cheap in the eyes of the lookers on."
39 BL Harl. 5007, f. 31.
40 HLRO, MS L J, p. 662, June 8, 1626 (Yale transcript, pp. 949–50, 962).
41 HLRO, MS L J, p. 657, June 8, 1626 (Yale transcript, pp. 930–1). In the *Basilikon Doron* James I had explicitly advised Prince Henry against having a favorite: "Use not one in all things lest he wax proud, and be envied of his fellows," pp. 32–3.
42 Russell, *Parliaments and Politics, 1621–1629*, pp. 291, 319.
43 PRO C 115, N5, no. 8633, March 25, 1626, James Palmer to Scudamore.
44 HARO Sherfield Mss 44M/69/xxv/1. June 3, 1626. "Sherfield," *British Radicals in the Seventeenth Century*. The date is suggestive; it is during the period that the Lords heard the charges against Buckingham. I am grateful to Wilfred Prest for this reference. For other views of Sherfield see P. Slack, "Religious Protest and Urban Authority; The Case of Henry Sherfield, Iconoclast, 1633," *Studies in Church History* (1972) and F. R. Raines (ed.), *The Journal of Nicholas Assheton*, Chetham Society (1848), pp. 114–16 where Sherfield is described as "an odious hypocrite." I am grateful to Paul Hardacre for this reference. Other charges against Buckingham included exhausting and misemploying the king's revenue and giving physic to the king, suggesting that he had poisoned him. Four concerned his activities during the war with France and Spain.
45 Tite, *Impeachment and Parliamentary Judicature*, pp. 211–12.
46 Quoted in Harry F. Snapp, "The Impeachment of Roger Maynwaring," *Huntington Library Quarterly*, vol. 30 (1967), p. 219. In the proceedings against Maynwaring, Lord Saye and Sele attacked him for covetousness and flattery using the familiar language of contemporary sermons, p. 226.
47 *CJ*, I, p. 514. At the beginning of Charles's first parliament in 1625, Coke said:

> Not now to have any committee of grievances or courts of justice 1) in respect of the plague, 2ly) because this the 1st beginning of the new king's reign, wherein no grievances as yet. 3ly) Because grievances preferred last parliament to the late king, whereof no answer, which preferred too late. To petition the king now for an answer to those grievances: for though the prince gone, the king liveth, no interregnum.

48 *CJ*, I, p. 874; *Commons Debates 1628*, (6 volumes, New Haven, 1977–82), Vol. II, pp. 53, 55, 66; Vol. III, pp. 44, 54. Another version reads:

An act against giving any money for any judicial place. That the party shall forfeit 10 times the value of that he gives, and also that every party that is to be admitted shall take an oath that he gave no reward or fee. And if any judge shall receive any fee or reward for any plea pending before him, he shall forfeit 100 times as much, and be fined and ransomed, and shall be in danger of a *praemunire*, and he that gives any such fee shall forfeit 20 times as much.

The third version reads: "An act against procuring places of judicature for money, and receiving bribes; the penalty to forfeit ten times the value, then fined and imprisoned and ransomed at the King's pleasure," p. 66. Vol. III, p. 44, committed Tuesday, Court of Wards. Mr Spencer added "Though judges do not buy their places, yet they buy serjeants' places which is a step to that. I desire the committee may consider as well of the buying their places." Vol. III, p. 54. April 23, 1628.

49 *CJ*, I, p. 920. Complaints against the buying of offices in the middle of the sixteenth century had concerned the church not the state. Bills against abuses in the ecclesiastical courts continued to be brought forward in the early Jacobean period.

50 John Rushworth, *Historical Collections of Private Passages of State ... The Third Part* (London, 1692), pp. 438–51, *The Grand Remonstrance*, clause 57; Edward Reynolds, *The Shields of the Earth* (London, 1634).

51 Mary Anne Everett Green (ed.), *Diary of John Rous*, Camden Society, vol. 66, pp. 50–1, 62. Ramsey's sermon was preached, Rous thought, on the text of Isaiah 1.26, "And I will restore thy judges as at the first, and thy counsellors as at the beginning; afterward thou shalt be called the city of righteousness, the faithful city." I am grateful to Esther Cope for this reference.

See HEH EL6879, "Sermon preached at Ludlow by Mr. T. L. September 24, 1637". The author described God as the great judge and the magistrate, as his deputy, the physician of the body politic. "Justice was anciently painted blind to show that no favor be given to persons but it was not meant to blind as not to discern causes ... By him kings reign and judges rule, by him shall kings and judges be called to account and reckoning ... The robes of peace covering corruption are worse to the poor than hostile invasion." Like Thomas Scot and many other preachers he cited Cicero's injunction "he hath put off the person of a judge that puts on the person of a friend." I am grateful to Margo Todd for this reference.

52 W. L., Esquire, *The Courts of Justice Corrected and Amended* (London, 1642).

53 ibid., pp. 9–12.

The Prince of the people being the well-head of Justice is abused in his vicarie: good men sobbing for grief, and naughty packs laughing in their sleeves at it, who also do evermore requite such their misbegotten favor with this thankfulness, that their tongues do continually itch until they have blabbed abroad all the manner and means of achieving their injurious desires and corrupt conquests.

The remedy to all these evils lay in the judge himself, who may "with a lofty look take it unkindly at the hands of his better, equal or inferior friends; blaming them with the touch of his credit for their so unadvised tampering with him in matter of his judicial and sworn duty."

54 William Lamont, *Godly Rule* (London, 1969), pp. 46–7, 49, 179–80.

55 See also HEH EL 6870, Ralph Crane, "The Faultie Favorite," dedicated to the Earl of Bridgewater as a new year's gift, which the author suggested be placed in the

corner of his library "in some corner, and there under fix, in Capital Letters (Honor and Bounty)," p. 4, HEH EL 6870.

56 *DNB*; *CSPD 1628–9*, p. 483, February, 1629. He noted that "The man recommended is honest, learned and witty; one sign whereof Sir Robert Aytoun loves him. In a word he is Mr. John Echelin's brother." Carr composed a metrical version of psalms to fit music he had heard them sung to in the Low Countries.

57 Robert Bolton, *Instructions for a Right Comforting Afflicted Consciences* (London, 1631). Bolton urged Carr to "trample upon, with an holy contempt; and noble disdain, the ... pestilent sweetness of worldly pleasures and vanishing glister of all earthly glory" by embracing Jesus. A–A4v.

58 Bolton, *Instructions for a Right Comforting Afflicted Consciences*, A2, praised King James who had been a great opponent of Rome and criticized Jesuits influenced by Machiavelli.

> Without sanctification by special grace the rarest endowments degenerate: wisdom into crafts; power into private revenge. Valor into violence; prudence into plotting their own ends; courage into foolhardiness, to uphold a faction; all of them are basely and unworthily made subordinate and serviceable only to the setting forward and safeguarding their own outward felicity.

59 Quoted in David Lindley (ed.), *The Court Masque* (Manchester, 1984), p.2.

60 For a discussion of the early Stuart masque see Stephen Orgel, *The Illusion of Power* (Berkeley, 1975); Orgel, *The Jonsonian Masque* (Cambridge, Mass., 1965) and Orgel and Roy Strong (eds), *Inigo Jones* (London, 1973); David Lindley, *The Court Masque* (Manchester 1984); Leah Marcus, "Masquing Occasions and Masque Structures," *Research Opportunities in Renaissance Drama*, vol. 24 (1981), pp. 7–16; Kevin Sharpe, *Criticism and Compliment* (Cambridge, 1987) and Lindley's extensive bibliography.

61 Sharpe, *Criticism and Compliment* pp. 25–7, 214–23; Marcus, "Masquing Occasions and Masque Structures," pp. 7–16.

62 Bulstrode Whitelock, *Memorials of the English Affairs, from the beginnings of the reign of Charles the First to the happy restoration of King Charles the Second* (4 vols; Oxford, 1853 [reprint of 1732 edition]), p. 20. James Shirley, *The Triumph of Peace* in *The Dramatic Works and Poems of James Shirley, with notes by William Gifford and Alexander Dyer*, (London, 1833), Vol. VI, pp. 258 and 258n.

> the first, a Jockey with a bonnet on his head, upon the top of it a whip, he seeming much to observe and affect a bridle which he had in his hand; the second a Country fellow ... a wheel with a perpetual motion on his head ... the third, a grim Philosophical-faced fellow, in his gown ... a furnace upon his head, and in his hand a lamp; the fourth, in a case of black leather ... with glass eyes, and bellows under each arm; the fifth, a Physician, on his head a hat with a bunch of carrots, a capon perched upon his fist; the sixth, like a Seaman, a ship upon his head and holding a line and plummet in his hand. Next these, rode so many beggars in timorous looks and gestures, as pursued by two Mastives that came barking after them.

63 *The Triumph of Peace*, pp. 268–71.

64 Oxford, Bodleian, Bankes Mss; and see Chapter 6.

65 Thomas Carew, *Coelum Britanicum. A Masque at White-Hall in the Banqueting–House, on Shrove Tuesday-Night, the 18 of February, 1633* (London, 1634), in Rhodes Dunlop (ed.), *The Poems of Thomas Carew* (Oxford, 1949), pp. 151–85.

The image of the king as the embodiment of virtue was symbolized in the English coronation service when the Archbishop of Canterbury presented the new monarch with the royal scepter, "the rod of virtue." *Liber Regalis*, Roxborough Club (London, 1870).

66   Carew *Coelum Britannicum*, pp. 156, 158. Both "freeborne god" and "freeborne courtier," the latter in A.D. B., *The Court of . . . James the First* (London, 1619), are of course, puns on the freeborn Englishman. The end of the masque celebrates the love of the two monarchs:

> Those sacred seeds of Love
> Which no Power can but yours dispence,
> Since you the patterne beare from hence.
> Then from your fruitful race shall flow
> Endless Succession,
> Scepters shall bud, and Lawrels blow
> 'Bout their Immortall Throne
> Propitious Starres shall crowne each birth,
> Whilst you rule them, and they the Earth.

[lines 1128–38]

67   See for example J. P. Kenyon, *The Stuart Constitution* (2nd edn, Cambridge, 1986), p. 9; Johann Sommerville, *Politics and Ideology in England 1603–1640* (London, 1986) pp. 3–4; Mark Kishlansky, *Parliamentary Selection* (Cambridge, 1986), pp. 8, 225–7.

68   *The Speeches of the Lord Digby in the High Court of Parliament Concerning Grievances and the Triennial Parliament, The Lord Digbyes Speech the 9 of November* (London, 1641), pp. 2–3, 7–9.

69   *Articles Exhibited in Parliament Against William, Archbishop of Canterbury* (London, 1640).

70   *Depositions and articles against Thomas, Earl of Strafford, 16 February 1640–1641* (London, 1641).

71   John Pym, *The Declaration of John Pym, Esquire, upon the Whole Matter of the Charge of High Treason against Thomas Earl of Strafford*, 12 April 1641, pp. 10–11.

72   "The Accusation and Impeachment of John Lord Finch, Baron of Fordwich, Lord-Keeper of the Great-Seal of England by the House of Commons," *Harleian Miscellany*, (10 vols 1808–1813), Vol. V, pp. 566–9.

73   Martin Butler, "A Case Study in Caroline Political Theatre: Braithwaite's 'Mercurius Britannicus'," *The Historical Journal*, vol. 27 (1984), pp. 947–53. Other plays included Richard Brome, *The Antipodes* (1638) and *A Jovial Crew* (1641) and William Cavendish, *The Variety* (c. 1641).

74   Stephen F. Black, "The Courts and Judges of Westminster Hall During the Great Rebellion, 1640–1660," *The Journal of Legal History*, vol. 7 (1986), p. 24.

75   Quoted in S. R. Gardiner, *The History of England, 1603–1642* (London, 1884), Vol. IX, pp. 238–9.

76   *CJ*, Vol. II, p. 438.

77   John Rushworth, *Historical Collections*, "The Grand Remonstrance," clauses 27, 48, 106, 115–19, 140, 203, pp. 438–61.

78   Rushworth, *Historical Collections*, p. 438.

Conclusion

1 See for instance J. P. Kenyon, *The Stuart Constitution* (2nd edn, Cambridge, 1986), p. 9. But see also Johann Sommerville, *Politics and Ideology* (London, 1986), who argues that there were strikingly different views of the English monarchy in the seventeenth century.

2 For the complex meaning of early Stuart ideas of kingship see Jenny Wormald, 'James VI and I, *Basilikon Doron* and the *Trew Law of Free Monarchies*: the Scottish Context and the English Translation'; Paul Christianson, "Royal and Parliamentary Voices on the Ancient Constitution, ca. 1604–1621;" J. P. Sommerville, "James I and the Divine Right of Kings: English Politics and Continental Theory," in Linda Levy Peck (ed.), *The Mental World of the Jacobean Court* (Cambridge, forthcoming) and Peck, "Early Stuart Political Thought," in J. G. A. Pocock (ed.), *British Political Thought, 1500–1800* (forthcoming).

3 See R. W. Dent, *John Webster's Borrowing* (Berkeley, Calif., 1960), pp. 174–6.

4 See *The New Catholic Encyclopedia*, Vol. 7 (Washington, D.C., 1967), pp. 566–7.

5 Webster, Dedication, *The Dutchesse of Malfy*, lines 3–6.

6 Gerard Malynes, *The Center of the Circle of Commerce* (London, 1623), STC 17221.

7 Edward Jorden, *A Brief Discourse of a Disease Called the Suffocation of the Mother* (London, 1603), ff. 16v, 20. I am grateful to Gail Paster for this reference.

8 A contemporary described the spread of disease throughout the whole body:

> In venomous and infectious diseases ... the malignity creeping from one part to another doth alter the quality of the parts as it goeth, and at the last is communicated to the principal parts, as the head, heart, liver, lungs, etc. ... In these Fevers also many times humors are so plentifully sent up unto the braine, as by custome or long continuance they breede some proper affect there. Jorden, *A Disease Called the Suffocation of the Mother*, f. 7v.

9 L. J. Rather, "Pathology at Mid-Century," in Allen G. Debus (ed.), *Medicine in Seventeenth Century England* (London, 1974), p. 73.

10 P. R. Seddon, *Letters of John Holles, 1587–1637*, Thoroton Society (Nottingham, 1986), Vol. 3, pp. 525–9. According to Seddon's edition the speech is dated April 1615. The more likely occasion for the drafting of such a speech was the meeting of the Addled Parliament when the issue of the baronets was debated on May 23, 1614. A petition, entitled "Motives to Induce Knights, Citizens, and Burgesses of the Commons House of Parliament to Petition his Majesty for the Revoking and Abolishing of the Degree of Baronets Erected by his Highness's Letters Patent," had been submitted to parliament. It stated "Nothing is more commended than honor springing out of virtue and desert, but to purchase honor with money (as baronets have done) is a temporal simony and dishonorable to the state." Sir Edwin Sandys in his report on the petition called the baronetage "a temporal simony and mercenary order," BL Add. 48101, Maija Jansson, *Proceedings in Parliament, 1614*, pp. 321–9. Jansson's edition reads "syndory [sic]." Jansson prints the petition, pp. 328–9. The similarity between Holles's speech and the petition suggests, first, that the speech was prepared for delivery during the parliament of 1614, perhaps at the committee appointed to consider the petition to which Holles had been named. There is no evidence that Holles's

speech was ever delivered. Holles urged the king to avoid ennobling those of the poor condition of the Venetian and German nobility, "who there begg as ordinarily with their Pantalons round capps, and their Countships on their backs, as our poore heer with their brattes and patch cotes." Holles pointed out that statute provided that barons who could not provide the prescribed number of knights' fees could be degraded and there was precedent in the past of those who had voluntarily quit their baronies when they could not support them. His precedents ranged from the Romans to those "who garded the person of Harrie the 7th at Bosworth field ... faith and corage was their tutchestone which would admitt no base metall into that refined and spyrtfull fellowship."

11 Holles' language is not only harsh but occasionally oblique: shew bread translated the Hebrew for the twelve loaves placed before the Lord every Sabbath; *corona muralis* was the crown bestowed by the Romans on a soldier who first scaled a wall in battle; tapsters were keepers of taverns.

12 Quoted in J. R. Brown, *The Duchess of Malfi* (Cambridge, Mass., 1964), p. xxxix from G. C. Moore (ed.), *Gabriel Harvey's Marginalia* (Stratford on Avon, 1913), p. 142.

13 PRO SP 14/92/12, May 6, 1617.

14 N. E. McClure (ed.), *The Letters of John Chamberlain* (2 vols; Philadelphia, 1939), Vol. II, pp. 70–1.

> The greatest part of the prime Scotts are here still and make no great haste homeward, which perhaps may be for want of moyens (as they term yt) to carrie them along, and shew themselves in equipage among theyre countrifolks. Indeed for all these summes of monie that have ben borrowed, we are still in great streights, and payments are made very slowly even where there is great neede.

15 Quoted in Roger Lockyer, *Buckingham* (London, 1981), p. 38.

16 Quoted in John Kenyon, *The Stuart Constitution* (Cambridge, 1986), p. 16.

17 *The Speeches of the Lord Digby in the High Court of Parliament Concerning Grievances and the Triennial Parliament, The Lord Digbyes Speech the 9 of November* (1641), pp. 2–3.

18 HEH STT 2383, *The Speeches of the Lord Digby ... 9 of November*, pp. 7–9. "By insensible pores (as Hippocrates saith, our bodies are transpirable, and transmeable) is conveyed from one part to another: whether it be a vapor or a humor, as wee doe commonly observe in the fits of fevers, where a vapor arising from the part affected, disperseth itself through the whole body." Jorden, *A Disease Called the Suffocation of the Mother*, f. 7v.

19 Thomas P. Slaughter (ed.), *Ideology and Politics on the Eve of the Restoration: Newcastle's Advice to Charles II* (Philadelphia, 1984).

20 Slaughter (ed.), *Ideology and Politics*, pp. 52–6, 58–9.

21 ibid., pp. 47–51.

22 ibid., pp. 47–8. Newcastle recalled that neither the Earl of Pembroke nor the Earl of Arundel had achieved their desire to be named to the king's Bedchamber either by King James or King Charles.

23 Felicity Heal, "The Idea of Hospitality in Early Modern England," *Past and Present*, no. 102 (1984), pp. 66–93.

24 John Pocock, *The Machiavellian Moment* (Cambridge, 1975).

25 See Joyce Appleby's special edition of *The American Quarterly* (1986).

26 Pocock, *The Machiavellian Moment*, pp. 333–60.

27 Indeed, J. H. Hexter asked in his study of *The Machiavellian Moment*, "how the devil did republican thought, of all things, get a footing in England, of

all places, in the first place?" *On Historians* (Cambridge, Mass., 1979), p. 288.

28 Blair Worden, "Classical Republicanism and the Puritan Revolution," in Jones, Pearl and Worden (eds), *History and Imagination* (London, 1981), pp. 182–3.

29 Thomas Scot, *Vox Dei* (London, 1623), p. 42.

30 R. W. Hunt, "The Deposit of Latin Classics in the Twelfth-Century Renaissance," *Classical Influences on European Culture, A.D. 500–1500* (Cambridge, 1971), pp. 52–3. The conventionally negative view of Machiavelli in Tudor England continued in the early Stuart period with even greater attention focused on the conflict between the values of religion and Machiavelli's vision of politics. Thomas Scott, B. D., in his 1616 sermon delivered before the king deliberately eschewed Florentine political thought. "As it hath no rellish of Italian courtship or craft, so neither hath it any touch of Romish poyson: but proceeds from the simplicitie of Gods holy spirit, which teacheth a foolishnes wherewithal to overthrow the wisdom of all Machiavellists," *Christ's Politician and Solomon's Puritan*, A2v. See for example, Thomas Scot of Ipswich, *God and the King*, (London, 1631), pp. 16–17.

31 Cicero, *De Officiis*, Book III, iv, 19, vii, 32.

32 Quoted in Conrad Russell, *Parliaments and English Politics, 1621–1629*, (Oxford, 1979), p. 380n.

33 PRO SP38/18, March 23, 1639.

34 Total expenditures for the Household and other Household departments rose from £222,429 under James II, to £308,445 under William III and then receded to £259,493 under Anne, and £272,454 under George I. Within the totals the Household annual accounts themselves followed the same pattern: James II, £76,784; William III, £99,145; Anne, £89,828; George I, £87,252. But official salaries rose from £13,798 under James II to £21,469 under William III; under Anne they were £20,221 and they then rose under George I to £29,040. I am grateful to Robert Bucholz for allowing me to quote from his paper "Queen Anne and the Decline of Court Culture."

35 Quoted in G. A. Holmes and William Speck (eds), *The Divided Society* (London, 1967), p. 142; from G. Parke (ed.), *Letters and Correspondence of Henry St. John, Lord Viscount Bolingbroke* (1798), Vol. I, pp. 245–6.

36 Mark Kishlansky, *Parliamentary Selection* (Cambridge, 1986), pp. 20, 120–1.

37 G. A. Holmes, "The Attack on 'The Influence of the Crown,' 1702–1716," in his *Politics, Religion and Society in England, 1679–1742* (London, 1986), pp. 35–56.

38 See for example Clayton Roberts, *Schemes and Undertakings: A Study of English Politics in the Seventeenth Century* (Columbus, 1985).

39 See Isaac Kramnick, *Bolingbroke and his Circle, The Politics of Nostalgia in the Age of Walpole* (Cambridge, Mass., 1968).

40 Quoted in Kramnick, *Bolingbroke and his Circle*, pp. 121–4.

41 For an analysis of "Old corruption" in the eighteenth and nineteenth centuries see William Rubinstein, "The End of 'Old Corruption' in Britain, 1780–1860," *Past and Present*, 101 (1983).

42 Machiavellis, *The Prince*, Quentin Skinner and Russell Price (eds), (Cambridge, 1988).

43 *The Prince*, pp. 56 and 56n.

44 John Guy, "The Politics of Counsel," in Dale Hoak (ed.), *Tudor Political Culture*, forthcoming.

Selected Bibliography

Manuscripts

British Library

Additional Manuscripts

4107   Sir Robert Ayton to the Duke of Buckingham
5832   Schedule of grants to Duke of Buckingham and Kindred
11402 Letter to the bailiffs and burgesses of the town of Buckingham.
12497 Sir John Fortescue's means of gain, November 26, 1608.
27404 Accounts of Sir George Carew, knight, Receiver General to Queen Anne,
       September 29, 1605 to September 29, 1606.
35832 Sir Edward Conway to Henry Gibb
37816 Nicholas correspondance.
38139 Queen Anne's officers.
48101 Parliamentary papers, 1614
48150 Yelverton Mss 161, part 2 Robert Beale's formulary book for clerk of Privy
       Council.

Cotton Manuscripts

Galba E I   Sir Thomas Studder to Earl of Northampton
Otho E IX   Sixteenth and seventeenth century naval documents
Titus B V   projects
Titus B VII   French ordinance concerning petitions
Vaspasian Cx Cornwallis correspondence

Egerton Manuscripts

860   Letterbook relating to the Lord Lieutenants of Kent, Buckinghamshire and
      Middlesex 1604–1628; Sir Henry Wotton to Sir William Becher; formulary
      book.

Harleian

87   Simond D'Ewes collections
5007 John Pym's charges against the Duke of Buckingham 1626.

289

6987   King James to Lionel Cranfield
7009   Naval officers to Prince Henry

Lansdowne Manuscripts

792   "The Emperor Charles V's Political Instructions to his son Phillip II," translated by Henry Howard.

Stowe Manuscripts

502   Abstract I "Abstract of the grants of all offices and places . . . James I, Charles I, as they are recorded in the Exchequer."
57   Oath of Queen Anne's servants.
743   Lord Keeper Williams to Duke of Buckingham.

Royal Manuscripts

136   "Les nos et les gages des officiers et serviteurs domestiques de la feu Reine d'Angleterre."

Cambridge University

Dd.3.63, ff. 54–6v (1613), Northampton to Somerset.

Magdalene College Manuscripts

Pepys Mss 2425 Cecil–Parry correspondence.
Pepys Mss 2829 Transcript of Index to Trevor Papers.
Pepys Mss 2870 Letterbook of Sir Henry Withrington, Knight Marshall of Berwick, 1582–92.
Pepys Mss 2871, 2875, 2876, 2877, 2878 Collections of sixteenth and seventeenth-century navy records.

Chester Record Office

CR/63/2/1 Sir Walter Davenport's Commonplace book.

Folger Shakespeare Library

Gb10   Sir Ralph Winwood's Letterbook
Xd 428, Cavendish Talbot Mss nos 120, 127, 128, 130, 131.
Losely Mss

Hampshire Record Office

Jervoise Mss 07 Impeachment charges against the Duke of Buckingham
Sherfield Mss 44M/69/xxv/1 June 3, 1626.

Selected Bibliography

Henry E. Huntington Library

Bridgewater Manuscripts

EL Egerton, Ellesmere and Bridgewater Correspondence 1603–40.
EL 6870 "The Faultie Favorite," by Ralph Crane
EL 6879 "Sermon preached at Ludlow by Mr T. L., September 24, 1637."

Hastings Manuscripts

HM 45148 Examination of Sir William Coryton concerning refusal to subscribe to the forced loan.

Stowe Collection, Temple Manuscripts

STT Temple correspondence 1500–1653.
STT Literature
STT Military Box 1.
STT Miscellaneous legal papers, Box 2, January 1, 1625–6.
STT Miscellaneous Papers, Box 2, [1628].
STT Parliament, Box I.
STT Personal Boxes 4, 5, 6, 7, 8.

Stowe Collection, Grenville Manuscripts

STG Correspondence 1603–40.
STG Military Box.

Library of Congress

Microfilm: Alnwick Mss 112/5.

National Library of Wales

Carreg-lwyd Mss 634 Robert Fletcher's tract on purveyance.

National Maritime Museum

CAD/A/13 (2 volumes) Work book for the naval commission of 1608.

National Museum of Scotland

Gordon Cumming Mss Deposit 175, Box 65, no, 276.

National Register of Archives

NRA 7829 Buckinghamshire Record Office, Drake Family Manuscripts.
NRA 7371, Pakington Mss 211, 301.

Nottingham University Library

Newcastle Ms. NEC 15404, and NEC 15405; Yale Center for Parliamentary History microfilms.

Oxford University

Tanner Manuscripts

75 Sir Charles Cornwallis's correspondence.

Bankes Manuscripts

Petitions and grants of patents and licenses, 1630s.

Public Record Office

Chancery

C. 115, M24, nos 7750, 7758, 7759. Archbishop Laud to Sir John Scudamore.
C. 115, N5, nos 8628–69, Scudamore papers.

Exchequer

E 315/107, 138, 470 Queen Anne's accounts.
E 163/14/8 justices of the peace 1584–7.

Lord Chamberlain's Office

L. C. 5/183 Discharge from royal service of carpenter who claimed to be a stage player.

Prerogative Court of Canterbury

PROB 11 Wills
PROB 11/79, 29 Harrington, Griffith Hampden.
PROB 11/97, 65 Woodhall, Miles Sandys.
PROB 11/81 36 Nevell, John Borlase.
PROB 11/82, 80 Nevell, Arthur, Lord Grey.
PROB 11/101, 32 Bolein, Sir John Temple.
PROB 11/128 128 Cope, Sir Robert Dormer.
PROB 11/159, 16 St. John, Sir William Fleetwood.
PROB 11/166 72 Seager, Sir Francis Goodwin.

Signet Office

SO 3/5 – SO 3/11 James I–Charles I.

Star Chamber

STAC 5 Elizabeth.
STAC 8 James I.

Selected Bibliography

State Papers

14	State Papers, James I.
16	State Papers, Charles I.
31	Gondomar's Correspondence.
78	Cecil–Parry Correspondence
94	Sir John Digby's diplomatic dispatches.
106	Cipher for diplomatic dispatches.

List and Indexes

Bedfordshire and Buckinghamshire sheriffs 1575–1640,

Yale University Library

Yale Parliamentary Diaries Center

Microfilms, reproductions and transcripts.
House of Lords Record Office:
Proxies for 1626.
Manuscript Journal of the House of Lords 1626

Printed Works: Primary Sources

"The Accusation and Impeachment of John Lord Finch, Baron of Fordwich, Lord-Keeper of the Great-Seal of England by the House of Commons," *Harleian Miscellany*, (10 vols, 1808–1813), Vol. V, pp. 566–69.

The Acts of the Parliaments of Scotland (ed.) T. Thomson (Edinburgh, 1966).

Acts of the Privy Council of England, 1603–1604, 1613–1640 (46 vols; London, 1890–1964).

A Declaration of His Majesty's royal pleasure, in what sort he thinketh fit to enlarge, or reserve himself in matter of bountie (London, 1610).

Anderson, Sir Edmund, *Les Reportes du Treserudite Edmund Anderson ... Seigniour Chief Justice del Common-Bank* (London, 1664). *A Repertory of the Inrolments of the Patent Rolls of Chancery in Ireland Commencing with the Reign of King James I*, I, pt. 2.

Articles Exhibited in Parliament Against William, Archbishop of Canterbury (London, 1640).

Akrigg, G. P. V. (ed.), *Letters of King VI and James I* (Berkeley, 1984).

B, A. D., *The Court of ... James the First, With Divers Rules, Most Pure Precepts, and Selected Definitions Lively* (London, 1619).

The Bloody Downfall of Adultery, Murder, Ambition ... (London, 1615).

Bolton, Robert, *Instructions for a Right Comforting Afflicted Consciences* (London, 1631).

Bolton, Robert, "Funeral notes upon my patron, Sir Augustine Nicolls," in *Mr Bolton's Last and Learned Worke of the Foure Last Things* (London, 1633).

Bolton, Robert, *Two Sermons Preached at Northampton* (London, 1635).

Bonsey, C. G. and Jenkins, J. G. (eds), *Ship Money Papers and Sir Richard Grenville's Notebook*, Buckinghamshire Record Society, vol. 13 (1965).

293

Bracton on the Laws and Customs of England (ed.) Samuel E. Thorne (4 vols; Cambridge, Mass., 1968), Vol. II.

Brent, Nathaniel, *A Discourse Consisting of Motives for Enlargement and Freedom of Trade*, April 11, 1645.

Bruce, John (ed.), *Correspondence of King James VI of Scotland with Sir Robert Cecil and Others in England*, Camden Society, o.s. Vol. 78 (1861).

Bruce, J., *Letters and Papers of the Verney Family Down to the End of the Year 1639*, Camden Society, o.s. Vol. 56 (London, 1853).

Burton, Samuel, *A Sermon Preached at the General Assizes in Warwick* (London, 1620).

Bushell, Thomas, *The First Part of Youths Errors* (London, 1628).

Cabala, Sive Scrinia Sacra (London, 1691).

Cade, Anthony, *A Sermon of the Nature of Conscience ... preached before the right honorable Sir Henry Hobart, knight and Baronet, Lord Chief Justice of the Common Pleas and Sir Edward Bromley, knight, one of the Barons of the Exchequer, at the Assizes at Leicester, 1620, July 25* (London, 1621).

A Calendar of the Talbot Papers.

Calendar of State Papers, Domestic Series, 1547–1625 (12 vols; London, 1856–9).

Calendar of State Papers, Domestic Series, 1625–1649 (24 vols; London, 1858–97).

Calendar of the State Papers Ireland 1600–1625 (13 vols; London, 1870–1910).

Camden, William, *Remaines Concerning Britaine* (London, 1614).

Carew, Thomas, *Coelum Britanicum. A Masque at White-Hall in the Banqueting-House, on Shrove Tuesday-Night, the 18 of February, 1633* (London, 1634), in Rhodes Dunlop (ed.), *The Poems of Thomas Carew* (Oxford, 1949).

Carter, Bezaleel, *Christ His Last Will, and John His Legacy* (London, 1621).

Cawdry, Robert, *A Table Alphabeticall* (London, 1604).

Chibnall, A. C. (ed.), *The Certificate of Musters for Buckinghamshire in 1522*, Buckinghamshire Record Society, Vol. 17 (1973).

Cicero, *De Officiis.*

Cobbett, William, *Parliamentary History of England* (36 volumes; London, 1806–20), Vol. 1.

Coke, Sir Edward, *The Lord Coke, his Speech and Charge. With a Discovery of the Abuses and Corruption of Officers* (London, 1607).

Coke, Sir Edward, *The First Part of the Institutes of the Lawes of England* (London, 1628).

Coke, Sir Edward, *The Third Part of the Institutes of the Laws of England* (London, 1644).

Collier, J. P., *The Egerton Papers*, Camden Society, o.s. vol. 12 (London, 1840).

Dalton, Michael, *The Countrey Justice* (London, 1618).

Day, Angel, *The English Secretorie* (London, 1592).

Despositions and articles against Thomas, Earl of Strafford, 16 February 1640–1641 (London, 1641).

The English Reports (176 vols; London, 1900–1930).

Erasmus, Desiderius, *Apophthegmes*, trans. Nicholas Udall (London, 1542; reprint, Amsterdam, 1969).

Fitzherbert, Sir Anthony, *The New Boke of Justices of the Peas* (London, 1538).

Fitz-Nigel, Richard, *Dialogus de Scaccario*, trans. and ed. Charles Johnson (London, 1950).

Foster, Elizabeth Read (ed.), *Proceedings in Parliament, 1610* (2 vols; New Haven, 1966).

Foster, William, *The Means to Keepe Sinne From Reigning in Our Mortall Body. A Sermon Preached at Paul's Cross May 26 1629* (London, 1629).

Foster, William, *Hoplocrisma-spongus: or a sponge to wipe away the weapon salve* (London, 1631).

Gardiner, S. R., *The Fortescue Papers*, Camden Society, n.s. Vol. 1 (London, 1871).

Garey, Samuel, *Jenticulum Judicum: or a Breake-fast for the Bench, Preached in Two Sermons at Thetford, 1619* (London, 1623).

Goodman, Godfrey, *The Court of James I* (ed.) J. S. Brewer (2 vols; London, 1839).

Glaucus, James, *A Knowledge for Kings, and a Warning for Subjects: Conteyning the moste Excellent and Worthy History of the Raellyans Perverted State, and Government of Their Common Wealth ... First written in Latine, by James Glaucus a Germaine: and now translated into English by William Clever, Scholemaster* (London, 1576).

A godly and learned answer to a Lewd and unlearned Pamphlet: Intituled, A Few Plaine and Forcible reasons for the Catholic Faith (London, 1608).

Green, Mary Anne Everett (ed.), *Diary of John Rous*, Camden Society, Vol. 66 (London, 1856).

Historical Manuscripts Commission Reports:
    Fourth Report, Appendix, Denbigh, Vol. 5.
    Thirteenth Report, Appendix IV (London, 1892).
    De L'Isle and Dudley Manuscripts, Vol. II (London, 1934).
    Marquis of Downshire Manuscripts, Vol. III (London, 1938–40).
    Hastings Manuscripts Vol. II (London, 1930).
    Duke of Portland Manuscripts, Vol. IX (London, 1905).
    Marquis of Salisbury's Manuscripts (24 vols London, 1883–19).

Howell, T. B., *A Complete Collection of State Trials ...*, (21 vols; London, 1816).

Jansson, Maija (ed.), *Proceedings in Parliament, 1614 (House of Commons)*, Memoirs of the American Philosophical Society, Vol. 172 (Philadelphia, 1988).

Jansson, Maija and Bidwell, William, (eds), *Proceedings in Parliament, 1625* (New Haven, 1987).

Johnson, Robert B., Keeler, Mary Frear, Jansson, Maija, Bidwell, William B. (eds), *Commons Debates 1628* (6 vols, New Haven, 1977–82),

Journals of the House of Commons (London, 1742).

L., W., Esquire, *The Courts of Justice Corrected and Amended* (London, 1642).

Lambarde, William, *Archeion, or a Discourse upon the High Courts of Justice in England* (eds) C. McIlwain and P. Ward (Cambridge, 1957).

Larkin, James F. and Hughes, Paul L., *Stuart Royal Proclamations* (2 vols; Oxford, 1973).

Les Reports del Cases in Camera Stellata, 1593 to 1609 (London, 1894).

L'Espine, Jean de, *Comfort for an Afflicted Conscience*, trans. Peter Allibond (London, 1591). King's College Cambridge copy, STC 15510.5 1591–C4.

"Letterbook of Sir Arthur Chichester, 1612–1614", *Analecta Hibernica*, no. 8, pp. 5–177.

Legge, J. Wickham, (ed.), *The Coronation Order of King James I* (London, 1902).

Liber Regalis, Roxborough Club (London, 1870).

Lonchay, Henri and Cuvalier, Joseph (eds), *Correspondance de la Cour d'Espagne sur les Affaires des Pays-Bas au XVII siecle*, Vol. 1 (Brussels, 1923).

Loomie, A. J. (ed.) *Ceremonies of Charles I* (New York, 1987).

Massinger, Philip, *A New Way to Pay Old Debts* (London, 1633).

McClure, N. E. (ed.), *The Letters of John Chamberlain* (2 vols; Philadelphia, 1939).

McGowan, A. P. (ed.), *The Jacobean Commissions of Enquiry, 1608 and 1618*, Navy Records Society (London, 1971).

McIlwain, C. H. (ed.), *The Political Works of James I* (New York, 1965).

Machiavelli, *The Prince* (eds) Quentin Skinner and Russell Price, (Cambridge, 1988).

Malynes, Gerard, *The Center of the Circle of Commerce* (London, 1623).

Markham, Gervase, *Marlham's Maister-peece* (London, 1631).

The Mirrour of Complements (London, 1631).

Niccols, Richard, *Sir Thomas Overburies Vision* (London, 1616).

Nichols, John, *The Progresses ... of Elizabeth I* (4 vols; London, 1828).

Notestein, Wallace, Relf, Frances Helen and Simpson, Hartley (eds), *Commons Debates, 1621* (7 vols; New Haven, 1935).

Oppenheim, Michael (ed.), *The Naval Tracts of William Monson*, Navy Records Society, (5 vols, London, 1902–1914).

Osborne, Francis, *Some Traditional Memoyres on the Raigne of King James the First* (London, 1658).

Pemberton, *The Charge of God and the King, to Judges and Magistrates for Execution of Justice In a Sermon Preached at the Assizes at Hartford* (London, 1619).

Pestell, Thomas, *Morbus epidemicus, or The Churl's Sickness* (London, 1615).

Perrin, W. G. (ed.), *The Autobiography of Phineas Pett*, Navy Records Society (London, 1918).

Petrie, Sir Charles (ed.), *The Letters of King Charles I* (London, 1935), pp. 92–4.

Plowden, Edmund, *Les Commentaries on Les Reportes des Dyvers Cases* (London, 1613).

Plutarch's Miscellanies and Essays, (ed.) W. W. Goodwin (5 vols; Boston, 1889), Vol. V.

Prideaux, John, *Certaine Sermons Preached by John Prideaux* (Oxford, 1636).

Prideaux, John, *Concio Habita Oxoniae ad Artium Baccalaureos* (Oxford, 1626).

Pym, John, *The Declaration of John Pym, Esquire, upon the Whole Matter of the Charge of High Treason against Thomas Earl of Strafford, April 12, 1641* (London, 1641).

Reynolds, Edward, *The Shields of the Earth* (London, 1634).

Roper, William, *The Life of Sir Thomas More* (London, 1822).

Rushworth, John, *Historical Collections of Private Passages of State ... The Third Part* (London, 1692).

Sainty, J. C., *Lieutenants of the Counties, 1585–1642*, Bulletin of the Institute of Historical Research, special supplement no. 8 (London, 1970).

Scot, Thomas, of Ipswich, *Of God and the King, in a sermon preached at the assizes holden at Bury S. Edmunds June 13 1631* (Cambridge, 1633).

Scot, Thomas, of Ipswich, *Vox Dei ... In a Sermon preached the Twentieth of March, 1622. At the assizes holden in St. Edmunds Bury* (London, 1623).

Scott, Thomas, B. D. *Christs Politician, and Salomons Puritan, Delivered in Two Sermons Preached Before the King's Majestie*, (London, 1616).

Scott, Thomas, B. D. *The Projector* (London [i.e. Holland], 1623).

Scott, Thomas, B. D. *Robert Earle of Essex, His Ghost* (Printed in Paradise, [London], 1624).

Scott, Thomas, B. D. *Vox Coeli* (London, 1624). The revised STC attributes this to John Reynolds.

Scott, Thomas, *Vox Populi* (London, 1620).

Scott, Sir Walter (ed.), *A Collection of Scarce and Valuable Tracts* [Somers Tracts] (13 vols; London, 1809–15).

Seddon, Peter (ed.), *Letters of John Holles*, Thoroton Society Record Series (3 vols; Nottingham, 1975–86).

Seneca, *On Benefits* in *The Workes of Lucius Annaeas Seneca, both morrall and naturall*, trans. Thomas Lodge (London, 1614).

The work of L. A. Seneca concerning Benefiting. trans. A. Golding (London, 1578).

de Seyssel, Claude, *The Monarchy of France*, trans. J. H. Hexter, ed. D. R. Kelly (New Haven, Conn., 1981).

Shirley, James, *The Triumph of Peace* in *The Dramatic Works and Poems of James Shirley, with notes by William Gifford and Alexander Dyer* (London, 1833), Vol. VI.

Smith, L. P., (ed.), *The Life and Letters of Sir Henry Wotton* (2 vols; Oxford, 1907).

Spedding, James (ed.), *The Letters and the Life of Francis Bacon* (7 vols; London, 1861–1874).

The Speeches of the Lord Digby in the High Court of Parliament Concerning Grievances and the Triennial parliament, The Lord Digbyes Speech the 9 of November (London 1641).

Squire, John, *A Sermon Preached at the Hartford Assizes* (London, 1618).

Statutes of the Realm (to 1713) (11 vols; London, 1810–28).

Stoughton, John, "The Magistrates Commission," in *Choice Sermons Preached Upon Selected Occasions* (London, 1640).

Tanner, J. R., *Two Discourses of the Navy, 1638 and 1659 by John Holland also a Discourse of the Navy 1660 by Sir Robert Slingsbie*, Navy Records Society, Vol. 7 (London, 1896).

The Two Petitions of the Buckinghamshire Men January 12, 1642 (London, 1642), Folger Shakespeare Library T3501.5.

"Tom Tell-Troath," *Somers Tracts* (13 vols; London, 1809–15), Vol. 2.

"Truth Brought to Light," *Somers Tracts* (London, 1809), Vol. II

Verney, F. P., *Memoirs of the Verney Family During the Civil War* (4 vols; New York, 1892–9).

The Visitation of the County of Buckinghamshire, made in 1634 by John Philipot, Esquire (London, 1909).

Ward, Samuel, *Jethro's Justice of Peace*, (London, 1618).

Webster, John, *The Tragedy of the Duchesse of Malfy* (London, 1623).

Weldon, Anthony, *The Court and Character of King James* (London, 1650).

Whitelocke, Bulstrode, *Memorials of the English Affairs, from the beginnings of the reign of Charles the First to the happy restoration of King Charles the Second* (4 vols; Oxford, 1853 [reprint of 1732 edition]).

Wilson, Arthur, *The History of Great Britain Being the Life and Reign of King James I* (London, 1653).

Printed Works: Secondary Sources

Adams, Simon, "Faction, Clientage and Party, English Politics, 1550–1603," *History Today*, Vol. 32 (1982), pp. 33–9.

Alexander, Michael Van Cleave, *Charles I's Lord Treasurer* (Chapel Hill, 1975).

Amos, A., *The Great Oyer of Poisoning* (London, 1846).

Amussen, Susan, *An Ordered Society: Gender and Class in Early Modern England* (Oxford, 1988).

Andrews, K. R., "Caribbean Rivalry and the Anglo–Spanish Peace of 1604," *History*, Vol. 59 (Fall, 1974), pp. 1–17.

Andrews, K. R. *Trade, Plunder, and Settlement* (Cambridge, 1984).

Appleby, Joyce, "Republicanism and Ideology," in "Republicanism in the History and Historiography of the United States," special issue of *The American Quarterly*, Vol. 37 (1985), pp. 461–73.

Ashton, Robert, *The City and the Court* (Cambridge, 1979).

Aylmer, G. E. "Attempts at Administrative Reform, 1625–40," *English Historical Review*, vol. 72 (1957), pp. 229–59.

Aylmer, G. E., "Bureaucracy," *The New Cambridge Modern History*, Vol. 13 (1979), pp. 164–76.

Aylmer, G. E., *The King's Servants* (London, 1961).

Aylmer, G. E., *The State's Servants* (London, 1973).

Beresford, Maurice W., "The Common Informer, the Penal Statutes and Economic Regulation," *Economic History Review*, 2nd ser., vol. 10 (1957), pp. 221–37.

Bhagwati, Jagdish N. and Srinvasan, T. N., "Revenue Seeking: A Generalization of the Theory of Tariffs," *Journal of Political Economy*, vol. 88 (1980), pp. 1069–88.

Bagwell, Richard, *Ireland Under the Stuarts* (London, 1909).

Barcroft, John H., "Carleton and Buckingham: The Quest for Office," in Howard S. Reinmuth (ed.), *Early Stuart Studies* (Minneapolis, 1970), pp. 122–36.

Bard, Nelson P., "The Ship Money Case and William Fiennes, Viscount Saye and Sele," *Bulletin of the Institute of Historical Research*, vol. 50 (1977), pp. 177–84.

Barnes, Thomas G. and Hassell Smith, A., "Justices of the Peace from 1558 to 1688," *Bulletin of the Institute of Historical Research*, vol. 32 (1959), pp. 237–9.

Barnes, Thomas G., *List and Index to the Proceedings in Star Chamber for the Reign of James I* (3 vols; Chicago, 1975).

Barnes, Thomas G., *Somerset 1625–1640: a County's Government during the "Personal Rule"*, (Oxford, 1961).

Barroll, Leeds, "The Literary Patronage of the Court of Queen Anne," in L. L. Peck (ed.), *The Mental World of the Jacobean Court* (Cambridge, forthcoming).

Batho, G., "Landlords in England," in Joan Thirsk (ed.), *The Agrarian History of England, 1500–1640* (Cambridge, 1967), pp. 256–356.

Black, Stephen F., "The Courts and Judges of Westminster Hall During the Great Rebellion, 1640–1660," *The Journal of Legal History*, vol. 7 (1986), pp. 23–52.

Bossy, John, "Godparenthood: The Fortunes of a Social Institution in Early Modern Christianity," in Kasper Van Greyerz (ed.), *Religion and Society in Early Modern Europe, 1500–1800* (London, 1984), pp, 194–201.

Bossy, John, "Blood and Baptism: Kinship, Community and Christianity in Western Europe from the Fourteenth to the Seventeenth Centuries" in Derek Baker (ed.), *Sanctity and Secularity: The Church and the World* (New York, 1973), pp. 129–44.

Bourdieu, Pierre, *Outline of a Theory of Practice* (Cambridge, 1977).

Braddock, Robert, "The Rewards of Office Holding in Tudor England," *Journal of British Studies*, vol. 14 (1975), pp. 29–47.

Braunmuller, A. R., "The Earl of Somerset as Collector and Patron," in Peck (ed.), *The Mental World of the Jacobean Court* (Cambridge, forthcoming).

Braunmuller, A. R., "To the Globe I Rowed," *English Literary Renaissance* (forthcoming).

Brewer, John, *The Sinews of Power* (New York, 1989).

Brinkworthm, E. R. C., "The Laudian Church in Buckinghamshire," *Birmingham University Historical Journal*, vol. 5, (1955), 31–59.

Brown, J. R., *The Duchess of Malfi* (Cambridge, Mass., 1964).

Bushman, Richard L., "Corruption and Power in Provincial America," in *The Development of a Revolutionary Mentality* (Washington, D.C., 1972).

Butler, Martin, "A Case Study in Caroline Political Theatre: Braithwaite's 'Mercurius Britannicus'," *Historical Journal*, vol. 27 (1984), pp. 947–53.

Calder, Isabel MacBeath (ed.), *Letters of John Davenport, Puritan Divine* (New Haven, 1937).

Carleton, Charles, *Archbishop William Laud* (London, 1987).

Carter, Charles, *The Secret Diplomacy of the Hapsburgs, 1598–1625* (New York, 1964).

Christianson, Paul, "Royal and Parliamentary Voices on the Ancient Constitution, ca. 1604–1621," In L. L. Peck, *The Mental World of the Jacobean Court* (Cambridge, forthcoming).

Clark, Peter, *The English Alehouse: A Social History, 1200–1830* (London, 1983).

Clark, Peter, *English Provincial Society from the Reformation to the Revolution: Religion, Politics and Society in Kent, 1500–1640* (Hassocks, 1977).

Cliffe, J. T., *The Puritan Gentry* (London, 1984).

Cockburn, J. S., *A History of English Assizes 1558–1714* (Cambridge, 1972).

Cockayne, G. E. C., *Complete Baronetage*, (Exeter, 1900), vols I and II.

Cogswell, Thomas, "Thomas Middleton and the Court, 1624: A Game at Chess in Context," *Huntington Library Quarterly*, vol. 47 (1984), pp. 273–88.

Collinson, Patrick, *The Elizabethan Puritan Movement* (London, 1967).

Cooper, J. P., *Land, Men and Beliefs: Studies in Early Modern History* (eds) G. E. Aylmer and J. S. Morrill (London, 1983), pp. 17–42.

Cressy, David, "Kinship and Kin Interaction in Early Modern England," *Past and Present*, no. 113 (1986), pp. 38–69.

Croft, Pauline, "Free Trade and the House of Commons, 1605–1606," *Economic History Review*, 2nd ser. vol. 28 (1975), 17–27.

Croft, Pauline, "Parliament, Purveyance and the City of London, 1589–1608," *Parliamentary History*, vol. 4 (1985), pp. 9–34.

Cuddy, Neal, "The Revival of the Entourage: The Bedchamber of James I, 1603–1625," in David Starkey (ed.), *The English Court* (London, 1987), pp. 173–225.

Cust, Richard, "Charles I, the Privy Council and The Forced Loan," *Journal of British Studies*, vol. 24 (1985), pp. 208–35.

Cust, Richard, *The Forced Loan* (Oxford, 1987).

Cust, Richard, "News and Politics in Early Seventeenth Century England," *Past and Present*, no. 112 (1986), pp. 60–90.

Davies, C. S. L., "The Administration of the Royal Navy under Henry VIII: The Origins of the Navy Board," *English Historical Review*, vol. 80 (1965), pp. 267–88.

Davies, Godfrey, "The Political Career of Sir Richard Temple (1634–97) and Buckingham Politics," *Huntington Library Quarterly*, vol. 4 (1940), pp. 47–83.

Davies, Margaret Gay, *The Enforcement of English Apprenticeship* (Cambridge Mass., 1956).

Davis, Natalie, *The Gift in Sixteenth Century France* (University of Wisconsin Press, forthcoming).

Dent, R. W., *John Webster's Borrowing* (Berkeley, Calif., 1960).

Dickson, Donald R., *The Fountain of Living Waters* (Columbia, Mo., 1987).

Dietz, F. C., "The Receipts and Issues of the Exchequer during the Reigns of James I and Charles I," *Smith College Studies in History*, Vol. XIII, no. 4 (1928), pp. 158–71.

Donagan, Barbara, "A Courtier's Progress: Greed and Consistency in the Life of the Earl of Holland," *Historical Journal*, vol. 19 (1976), pp. 317–53.

Duffy, Michael (ed.), *The Military Revolution and the State 1500–1800* (Exeter, 1980).

Dunham, W. H., *Lord Hastings' Indentured Retainers, 1461–1483* (Hamden, Conn., 1970).

Edwards, Robert Dudley and O'Dowd, Mary, *Sources for Early Modern Irish History, 1534–1641* (Cambridge, 1985).

Eisenstadt, S. N., and Roniger, Louis, "Patron–Client Relations as a Model of Structuring Social Exchange," *Comparative Studies in Society and History*, vol. 22 (1980), pp. 42–77.

Eisenstadt, S. N. and Roniger, Louis, "The Study of Patron-Client Relations and Recent Developments in Sociological Theory," in S. N. Eisenstadt and R. Lemarchand (eds), *Political Clientalism, Patronage and Development* (London, 1981), pp. 271–329.

Ekelund, Robert and Tollison, Robert, *Mercantilism as a Rent-Seeking Society, Economic Regulation in Historical Perspective* (College Station, 1981).

Elliott, Douglas J., *Buckingham, the Loyal and Ancient Borough* (London, 1975).

Elton, Geoffrey, "Informing for Profit," *Cambridge Historical Journal*, vol. 11 (1954), 149–67.

Elton, Geoffrey, "The Points of Contact," in *Studies in Tudor and Stuart Politics and Government* (3 vols; Cambridge, 1974–83), vol. III, 3–57.

Ferris, J. P. (ed.), *The House of Commons, 1604–1629* (forthcoming).

Fletcher, Anthony, *A County Community in Peace and War: Sussex 1600–1660* (London, 1975).

Fletcher, Anthony, *Reform in the Provinces, The Government of Stuart England* (New Haven, 1986).

Fogle, French, "Such a Rural Queen: The Countess Dowager of Derby as Patron," in F. Fogle and L. Knafla (eds), *Patronage in Late Renaissance England* (Los Angeles, 1983).

Foster, Elizabeth Read, *The House of Lords, 1603–1649* (New Haven, 1983).

Foster, Elizabeth Read, "The Procedure of the House of Commons Against Patents and Monopolies, 1621–1624," in W. A. Aiken and B. D. Henning (eds), *Conflict in Stuart England* (New York, 1960), pp. 59–85.

Friis, Astrid, *Alderman Cockayne's Project and the Cloth Trade* (London, 1927).

Gardiner, Samuel Rawson, *The History of England from the Accession of James I to the Outbreak of the Civil War* (10 vols; London, 1883–4).

Gay, Edwin F., "The Rise of an English Country Family: Peter and John Temple to 1603," *Huntington Library Quarterly*, vol. I (1937–8), pp. 367–90.

Gay, Edwin F., "The Midland Revolt and the Inquisitions of Depopulation of 1607," *Transactions of the Royal Historical Society*, n.s. vol. 18 (1904), pp. 195–244.

Given-Wilson, C. J., *The Royal Household and the King's Affinity: Service, Politics and Finance in England, 1360–1413* (New Haven, 1986).

Glasgow Jr., Tom, "The Maturing of Naval Administration, 1556–1564," *Mariner's Mirror*, vol. 56 (1970), pp. 3–25.

Godfrey, Eleanor S., *The Development of English Glassmaking 1560–1640* (Chapel Hill, 1975).

Gordon, M. D. "The Collection of Ship Money in the Reign of Charles I," *Transactions of the Royal Historical Society*, 3rd ser., vol. 4 (1910), pp. 141–62.

Gough, J., *The Rise of the Entrepreneur* (London, 1969).

Gruenfelder, John K., *Influence in Early Stuart Elections, 1604–1640* (Columbus, Ohio, 1981).

Guy, John, *Tudor England* (Oxford, 1988).

Harding, Robert, "Corruption and the Moral Boundaries of Patronage in the Renaissance," in Guy Lytle and Stephen Orgel (eds), *Patronage in the Renaissance* (Princeton, 1981), pp. 47–64.

Harris, Barbara, *Edward Stafford, Third Duke of Buckingham* (Stanford, 1986).

Harris, Barbara, "Gender and Politics," *Historical Journal* (forthcoming).

Hartwell, R. M., "Economic Growth before the Industrial Revolution," in his *The Industrial Revolution and Economic Growth* (London, 1971), pp. 21–41.

Heal, Felicity, "The Idea of Hospitality in Early Modern England," *Past and Present*, no. 102 (1984), pp. 66–93.

Heidenheimer, Arnold (ed.), *Political Corruption*, (1st edn, New York, 1970; 2nd edn, New Brunswick, New Jersey, 1989).

Hexter, J. H., *On Historians* (Cambridge, Mass., 1979).

Heyd, David, *Supererogation* (Cambridge, 1988).

Hibbard, Caroline, "The Court and Household of a Queen Consort: Henrietta Maria, 1625–1642," in Ronald G. Asch and Adolph M. Birke (eds) *Princes, Patronage and the Nobility: The Court at the Beginning of the Modern Age* (Oxford University Press, forthcoming).

Hill, Christopher, "The Norman Yoke," in *Puritanism and Revolution* (London, 1958).

Hill, Lamar, *Bench and Bureaucracy* (Stanford, 1988).

Hirst, Derek, *Authority and Conflict, England, 1603–1658* (Cambridge, 1986).

Hirst, Derek, *The Representative of the People?* (Cambridge, 1975).

Holderness, B. A., *Pre-Industrial England: Economy and Society, 1500–1750* (London, 1976), 83–116.

Holdsworth, William, *A History of English Law* (13 vols, Boston, 1923–52), Vol. II.

Holmes, Clive, "The County Community in Early Stuart Historiography," *Journal of British Studies*, vol. 19 (1980), pp. 54–73.

Holmes, Clive, *Seventeenth Century Lincolnshire* (Lincoln, 1988).

Holmes, G. A., "The Attack on 'The Influence of the Crown,' 1702–1716," in his *Politics Religion and Society in England, 1679–1742* (London, 1986), pp. 35–56.

Holmes, G. A. and Speck, William (eds), *The Divided Society* (London, 1967).

Houlbroke, Ralph, *The English Family, 1450–1700* (London, 1984).

Howarth, David, *The Earl of Arundel and his Circle* (Yale, 1985).

Hughes, Ann, *Politics, Society and Civil War in Warwickshire, 1620–1660* (Cambridge, 1987).

Hunt, R. W., "The Deposit of Latin Classics in the Twelfth-Century Renaissance," *Classical Influences on European Culture, A.D. 500–1500* (Cambridge, 1971).

Hunt, William, *The Puritan Moment: The Coming of the Revolution in an English County* (Cambridge, Mass., 1983).

Huntington, Samuel P., *Political Order in Changing Societies* (New Haven, 1968).

Hurstfield, Joel, *Freedom, Corruption and Government in Elizabethan England* (Cambridge, Mass., 1973).

Hurstfield, Joel, *The Queen's Wards* (London, 1958).

Ingram, M. J., "Communities and Courts: Law and Disorder in Early Seventeenth Century Wiltshire," in J. S. Cockburn (ed.), *Crime in England, 1550–1800* (London, 1977), pp. 123–5.

James, Mervyn, *Society, Politics and Culture* (Cambridge, 1986).

Jesse, John H., *Memoirs of the Court of England* (4 vols; London, 1840).

Jones, Norman, *God and the Moneylenders: Usury and the Law in Early Modern England* (Oxford, 1989).

Jones, W. J., *Politics and the Bench* (London, 1971).

Jordan, Constance, "Woman's Rule in Sixteenth-Century British Political Thought," *Renaissance Quarterly*, vol. 40 (1987), pp. 421–51.

Jorden, Edward, *A Brief Discourse of a Disease Called the Suffocation of the Mother* (London, 1603).

Judson, Margaret, *The Crisis of the Constitution* (New York, 1964).

Keeler, Mary Frear, *The Long Parliament* (Philadelphia, 1954).

Keeler, Mary Frear, "The Election at Great Marlow in 1640," *Journal of Modern History*, vol. 14 (1942), pp. 433–48.

Keep, A. P. P., "Star Chamber Proceedings against the Earl of Suffolk and Others," *English Historical Review*, vol. XIII (1898), pp. 716–29.

Kenny, R. W., *Elizabeth's Admiral: The Political Career of Charles Howard, Earl of Nottingham, 1536–1624* (Baltimore, 1970).

Kenyon, J. P., *The Stuart Constitution* (2nd edn, Cambridge, 1986).

Kishlansky, Mark, *Parlimentary Selection* (Cambridge, 1986).

Kishlansky, Mark, "The Emergence of Adversary Politics in the Long Parliament," *Journal of Modern History*, vol. 49 (1977), pp. 617–40.

Knafla, Louis, *Law and Politics in Jacobean England* (Cambridge, 1977).

Knight, R. J. B., "Pilfering and Theft from the Dockyards at the Time of the American War of Independence," *Mariner's Mirror*, vol. 61 (1975), pp. 215–25.

Knighton, C. S., *Catalogue of the Pepys Library*, vol. V, pt. ii (Cambridge 1981).

Koenigsberger, H. G., *Estates and Revolutions* (Ithaca, 1971).

Kramnick, Isaac, *Bolingbroke and his Circle, The Politics of Nostalgia in the Age of Walpole* (Cambridge, Mass., 1968).

Lake, Peter, "The Collection of Ship Money in Cheshire during the Sixteen-thirties: A Case Study of Relations between Central and Local Government," *Northern History*, vol. 17 (1981), pp. 44–71.

Lamont, William, *Godly Rule* (London, 1969).

Laqueur, Thomas, "The Queen Caroline Affair: Politics as Art in the Reign of George IV," *Journal of Modern History*, vol. 54 (1982), pp. 417–66.

Lee, Maurice, *The Road to Revolution* (Urbana, 1985).

Leff, Nathaniel H., "Economic Development Through Bureaucratic Corruption," in Arnold Heidenheimer, Michael Johnston and Victor T. LeVine (eds), *Political Corruption*, pp. 389–405.

Levy, F. J. "How Information Spread Among the Gentry, 1550–1640," *Journal of British Studies*, vol. 21 (1982), pp. 11–34.

Lewalski, Barbara J., "Lucy, Countess of Bedford: Images of a Jacobean Courtier and Patroness," in Kevin Sharpe and Stephen Zwicker (eds.), *The Politics of Discourse* (Los Angeles, 1987).

Limon, Jerzy, *Dangerous Matter, English Drama and Politics in 1623/1624* (Cambridge, 1986).

Lindley, David (ed.), *The Court Masque* (Manchester, 1984).

Lipscomb, George, *The History and Antiquities of the County of Buckingham* (4 vols; London, 1847).

Lipson, E. *The Economic History of England* (London, 1947), vol. III.

Lloyd, Howell, A., "Corruption and Sir John Trevor," *Transactions of the Honourable Society of Cymmrodorion* (1974–5), pp. 77–102.

Lockyer, Roger, *Buckingham, The Life and Career of George Villiers, First Duke of Buckingham, 1592–1628* (London, 1981).

Loomie, A. J., "The Spanish Faction at the Court of Charles I, 1630–8," *BIHR*, vol. 49 (1986), pp. 37–49.

Loomie, A. J., *Spain and the Jacobean Catholics, 1603–12*, Catholic Record Society, Vol. 64 (London, 1973).

Lytle, Guy and Orgel, Stephen (eds), *Patronage in the Renaissance* (Princeton, 1981).

MacCaffrey, Wallace, "Place and Patronage in Elizabethan Politics," in *Elizabethan Government and Society* (eds), S. T. Bindoff, J. Hurstfield and C. H. Williams (London, 1961).

MacClure, Millar, *The Paul's Cross Sermons* (Toronto, 1958).

MacCulloch, Diarmaid, *Suffolk and the Tudors* (Oxford, 1986).

MacDougall, Elisabeth B. and Miller, Naomi *Fons Sapientiae, Garden Fountains in Illustrated Books, Sixteenth–Eighteenth Centuries* (Washington, D.C., 1977).

MacFarlane, K. B., *The Nobility of Later Medieval England* (Oxford, 1973).

MacFarlane, K. B., *England in the Fifteenth Century* (London, 1981).

McGowan, A. P., "Further Papers from the Commission of Enquiry, 1608," *The Naval Miscellany*, vol.5, Navy Records Society, Vol. 125 (1984), pp. 1–14.

Marcus, Leah, "Masquing Occasions and Masque Structures," *Research Opportunities in Renaissance Drama*, vol. 24 (1981), pp. 7–16.

Markham, C. R., *The Fighting Veres* (London, 1878).

Martin, Colin and Parker, Geoffrey, *The Spanish Armada* (New York, 1988).

Marwil, Jonathan, *The Trials of Counsel* (Detroit, 1976).

Mattingly, Garrett, *The Armada* (Boston, 1959).

Mattingly, Garrett, *Renaissance Diplomacy* (Baltimore, 1964).

Mauss, Marcel, *The Gift: Forms and Functions of Exchange in Archaic Societies*, trans. Ian Cunnisan (Glencoe, Ill., 1954).

Maxwell-Lyte, H. C., *A History of Eton College, 1440–1910* (London, 1911).

Mendelson, Sara, *The Mental World of Stuart Women* (Brighton, 1987).

Miller, Naomi, *French Renaissance Gardens* (New York, 1977).

Montrose, Louis, "Gifts and Reasons: The Contexts of Peele's *Arraynement of Paris*," *ELH*, vol. 47 (1980), pp. 433–61.

Moody, T. W., Martin, F. X. and Byrne, F. J. (eds), *A New History of Ireland*, vol. 3: *1534–1691* (Oxford, 1976).

Morgan, Edmund, "The Labor Problem at Jamestown 1607–18," *American Historical Review*, vol. 76 (1971), pp. 595–611.

Morrill, John, *The Revolt of the Provinces* (London, 1976).

Mousnier, Roland, *La Venalité des offices en France sous Henry IV et Louis XIII* (Rouen, 1945).

Mousnier, Roland, *Les Hierarches sociales de 1450 à nos jours* (Paris, 1966).

Namier, Lewis, *England in the Age of the American Revolution* (2nd edn, New York, 1961).

Naunton, Sir Robert, *Fragmenta Regalia*, edited by J. S. Cerovski (Washington, D.C., 1985).

Neale, J. E. "The Elizabethan Political Scene," in *Essays in Elizabethan History*, (London, 1958), pp. 59–84.

Nef, J. U., *Industry and Government in France and England, 1540–1640*, American Philosophical Society, vol. XV (Philadelphia, 1940).

Newton, A. P., "The Establishment of the Great Farm of the Customs," *TRHS*, 4th ser., I (1918), 119–55.

Noonan, John, *Bribery* (New York, 1984).

North, Douglass C., "A Framework for Analyzing the State in Economic History," *Explorations in Economic History*, vol. 16 (1979), pp. 249–59.

Nye, J. S. in Arnold Heidenheimer, Michael Johnson and Victor T. Le Vine (eds), *Political Corruption* (2nd edn, New Brunswick, 1989).

Oppenheim, Michael, *A History of the Administration of the Royal Navy and of Merchant Shipping in Relation to the Navy, from MDIX to MDCLX* (London, 1896).

Orgel, Stephen, *The Illusion of Power* (Berkeley, 1975).

Orgel, Stephen, *The Jonsonian Masque* (Cambridge, Mass., 1965).

Orgel, Stephen, and Strong, Roy, (eds), *Inigo Jones and the Theatre of the Stuart Court* (London, 1973), vol. I.

Palme, Per, *Triumph of Peace* (London, 1957).

Palmer, Robert C., *The County Courts of Medieval England* (Princeton, 1982).

Parker, Geoffrey, *The Military Revolution, Military Innovation and the Rise of the West, 1500–1800* (Cambridge, 1988).

Peck, Linda Levy, "Corruption and Political Development in Early Modern Europe: The British Case," in A. Eisenstadt, A. Hoogenboom and H. Trefousse (eds), *Before Watergate: Problems of Corruption in American Society* (New York, 1978), pp. 35–49.

Peck, Linda Levy, "Court Patronage and Government Policy: The Jacobean Dilemma," in G. Lytle and S. Orgel, *Patronage in the Renaissance*, (Princeton, 1981), pp. 27–46.

Peck, Linda Levy, "Early Stuart Political Thought," in J. G. A. Pocock (ed.), *British Political Thought, 1500–1800* (forthcoming).

Peck, Linda Levy, "'For a King not to be bountiful were a fault:' Perspectives on Court Patronage in Early Stuart England," *Journal of British Studies*, vol. 25 (1986), pp. 31–61.

Peck, Linda Levy, "Goodwin v. Fortescue: The Local Context of Parliamentary Dispute," *Parliamentary History* vol. 3 (1985), 151–65.

Peck, Linda Levy, *Northampton: Patronage and Policy at the Court of James I* (London, 1982).

Penn, C. D., *The Navy under the Early Stuarts* (London, 1920).

Pocock, John, *The Machiavellian Moment* (Cambridge, 1975).

Pocock, John, "Virtue and Commerce in the Eighteenth Century," Journal of Interdisciplinary History, vol. 3 (1972–3), pp. 19–34.

Prest, Wilfred, *The Rise of the Barristers* (Oxford, 1986).

Prestwich, Menna, *Cranfield: Politics and Profits under the Early Stuarts* (Oxford, 1966).

Price, W. H., *The English Patents of Monopoly* (Cambridge, Mass., 1913).

Quinn, D. B., and Ryan, A. N., *England's Sea Empire, 1550–1642* (London, 1983).

Quintrell, Brian, "Charles I and his Navy in the 1630s," *The Seventeenth Century*, vol. 3 (1988), pp. 159–79.

Rabb, T. K., *Enterprise and Empire* (Cambridge, 1967).

Ramsay, G. D., *English Overseas Trade During the Centuries of Emergence* (London, 1957).

Ramsay, G. D. "The Smuggler Trade: A Neglected Aspect of English Commercial Development," *Transactions of the Royal Historical Society*, 5th ser., vol. 2 (London, 1952), pp. 131–57.

Raskin, Victor, "On Possible Applications of Script-Based Semantics," in P. C. Bjarkman and V. Raskin, *The Real-World Linguist* (Norwood, N. J., 1986), pp. 19–45.

Rather, L. J., "Pathology at Mid-Century," in Allen G. Debus (ed.), *Medicine in*

Seventeenth Century England (London, 1974).

Rawcliffe, Carole, "The Politics of Marriage in Later Medieval England: William, Lord Botreaux, and the Hungerfords," *Huntington Library Quarterly*, vol. 51 (Summer 1988), 161–75.

Rawcliffe, Carol, *The Staffords, Earls of Stafford and Dukes of Buckingham, 1394–1521* (Cambridge, 1978).

Rianes, F. R. (ed.), *The Journal of Nicholas Asheton*, Chetham Society (1848).

Roberts, B. Dew, *Mitre & Musket, John Williams, Lord Keeper, Archbishop of York, 1582–1650* (Oxford, 1938).

Roberts, Clayton, *The Growth of Responsible Government in Early Stuart England* (Cambridge, 1966).

Roberts, Clayton, *Schemes and Undertakings* (Columbus, 1985).

Roberts, George (ed.), *The Diary of Walter Yonge*, Camden Society, n.s. vol. 41 (London, 1848).

Roberts, Michael, "The 'Military Revolution,' 1560–1660," *Essays in Swedish History* (London, 1967), pp. 195–225.

Roberts, S. K., "Alehouse, Brewing and Government under the Early Stuarts," *Southern History*, vol. II (1980), pp. 45–71.

Rodriguez-Salgado, J. (ed.), *Armada, 1588–1988* (London, 1988).

Rogers, Malcolm, *William Dobson, 1611–1646* (London, 1983).

Rose-Ackerman, Susan, *Corruption* (New York, 1978).

Ross, Charles (ed.), *Patronage, Pedigree and Power in Later Medieval England* (Totowa, N.J., 1979).

Rowney, Ian, "The Hastings Affinity in Staffordshire and the Honour of Tutbury," *BIHR*, vol. 57 (1984), pp. 35–45.

Rubinstein, W. D. "The End of 'Old Corruption' in Britain 1780–1860," *Past and Present*, vol. 101 (November 1983), pp. 55–86.

Ruigh, Robert, *The Parliament of 1624* (Cambridge, Mass., 1971).

Russell, Conrad, *The Crisis of Parliaments* (Oxford, 1971).

Russell, Conrad, "Monarchies, Wars and Estates in England, France and Spain, c. 1580–1640," *Legislative Studies Quarterley*, vol. 7 (1982), pp. 205–20.

Russell, Conrad, *Parliaments and English Politics, 1621–1629* (Oxford 1979).

Sacks, David Harris, *Trade, Society and Politics in Bristol, 1500–1640* (2 vols, New York, 1985).

Salisbury, W., "A Draught of a Jacobean Three Decker. The *Prince Royal?*" *Mariner's Mirror*, vol. 47 (1961), pp. 170–7.

Saller, R. P., *Personal Patronage under the Early Empire* (Cambridge, 1981).

Salmon, John "Stoicism and Roman Example: Seneca and Tacitus in Jacobean England," *Journal of the History of Ideas*, vol. 50 (1989), pp. 199–225.

Sanderson, James, "Poems on an Affair of State – The Marriage of Somerset and Lady Essex," *The Review of English Studies*, n.s. vol. 17 (1966), pp. 57–61.

Saville, R. V. (ed.), "The Management of the Royal Dockyards, 1672–1678," (Navy Records Society), vol. 125, (1984), pp. 94–142.

Sawyer, Jeffrey, "Judicial Corruption and Legal Reform in Early Seventeenth-Century France," *Law and History Review*, vol. 6 (1988), pp. 95–117.

Schreiber, Roy, *The First Carlisle, Sir James Hay, First Earl of Carlisle as Courtier, Diplomat and Entrepreneur, 1580–1636*, Transactions of the American Philosophical Society, vol. 74, Part 7 (1984).

Schwoerer, Lois, "Seventeenth-Century English Women Engraved in Stone?" *Albion*, vol. 16 (1984), pp. 389–403.

Schwoerer, Lois, *Lady Rachel Russell* (Baltimore, 1988).

Scott, J. C., *Comparative Political Corruption* (Englewood Cliffs, N.J., 1972).

Scott, Sir Walter, *Secret History of the Court of James the First* (2 vols; Edinburgh, 1811).

Searle, Eleanor *Lordship and Community, Battle Abbey and its Banlieu 1066–1538* (Toronto, 1974).

Seddon, Peter, "Household Reforms in the Reign of James I," *Bulletin of the Institute Historical Research*, vol. 53 (1980), pp. 44–55.

Sharpe, J. A., *Crime in Early Modern England, 1550–1750* (London, 1984).

Sharpe, Kevin, *Criticism and Compliment* (Cambridge, 1987).

Sharpe, Kevin (ed.), *Faction and Parliament* (Oxford, 1978).

Sharpe, Kevin, "Faction at the Early Stuart Court," *History Today*, vol. 33 (1983), pp. 39–46.

Sharpe, Kevin, "The Image of Virtue: The Court and Household of Charles I, 1625–1642," in David Starkey (ed.), *The English Court*, pp. 226–60.

Sharpe, Kevin, "The Personal Rule of Charles I," in Howard Tomlinson (ed.), *Before the English Civil War* (London, 1983), pp. 53–78.

Seward, William, *Anecdotes* (London, 1796), vol. III, pp. 287–90.

Skinner, Quentin, "Ambrogio Lorenzetti: The Artist as Political Philosopher," in *Proceedings of the British Academy*, vol. 72 (1986), pp. 1–56.

Slack, Paul, "Religious Protest and Urban Authority; The Case of Henry Sherfield, Iconoclast, 1633," *Studies in Church History* (1972).

Slater, Miriam, *Family Life in the Seventeenth Century* (London, 1984).

Slaughter, Thomas P. (ed.), *Ideology and Politics of the Eve of the Restoration: Newcastle's Advice to Charles II* (Philadelphia, 1984).

Smeeton, George (ed.), *Historical and Biographical Tracts* (2 vols; Westminster, 1820).

Smith, A. G. R., *Servant of the Cecils: The Life of Michael Hickes, 1543–1612* (London, 1977).

Smith, A. G. R., "Crown, Parliament and Finance: the Great Contract of 1610," in P. Clark, A. G. R. Smith and N. Tyacke (eds), *The English Commonwealth* (Leicester, 1979), pp. 111–27.

Smith, A. Hassell, *County and Court: Government and Politics in Norfolk 1558–1603* (Oxford, 1974).

Smuts, Malcolm, *Court Culture and the Origins of a Royalist Tradition in Early Stuart England* (Philadelphia, 1987).

Smuts, Malcolm, "Cultural Diversity and Cultural Change in the Court of James I," in L. L. Peck (ed.), *The Mental World of the Jacobean Court* (Cambridge University Press, forthcoming).

Smuts, Malcolm, "The Puritan Followers of Henrietta Maria," *English Historical Review*, vol. 93 (1978), pp. 26–45.

Snapp, Harry F., "The Impeachment of Roger Maynwaring," *Huntington Library Quarterly*, vol. 30 (1967).

Sommerville, Johann, "James I and the Divine Right of Kings: English Politics and Continental Theory," in L. L. Peck (ed.), *The Mental World of the Jacobean Court* (Cambridge, forthcoming).

Sommerville, Johann, *Politics and Ideology in England, 1603–1640* (London, 1986).

Starkey, David (ed.), *The English Court* (London, 1987).

Skarkey, David, "From Feud to Faction: English Politics Circa 1450–1550," *History Today*, vol. 32 (1982), pp. 16–21.

Stone, Lawrence, *The Crisis of the Aristocracy* (Oxford, 1965).

Stone, Lawrence, *Family and Fortune: Studies in Aristocratic Finance in the Sixteenth and Seventeen Centuries* (Oxford, 1973).

Stone, Lawrence, *The Family, Sex and Marriage in England, 1500–1800* (New York, 1977).

Stone, Lawrence, "Terrible Times," *The New Republic*, May 5, 1982, pp. 32–4.

Stoye, J. W., *English Travellers Abroad, 1604–1667* (London, 1952).

Swales, R. J. W., "The Ship Money Levy of 1628," *Bulletin of the Institute of Historical Research*, vol. 50 (1977), pp. 164–76.

Swart, K. W., *The Sale of Offices in the Seventeenth Century* (The Hague, 1949).

Strong, Roy, *Art and Power* (Berkeley, Calif., 1984).

Strong, Roy, *Brittania Triumphans, Inigo Jones, Rubens and Whitehall Palace* (London, 1980).

Strong, Roy, *Henry, Prince of Wales, and England's Lost Renaissance* (New York, 1986).

Supple, Barry, *Commercial Crisis and Change in England* (Cambridge, 1959).

Thirsk, Joan (ed.) *The Agrarian History of England, 1500–1640* (Cambridge, 1967).

Thirsk, Joan, *Economic Policy and Projects: The Development of a Consumer Society in Early Modern England* (Oxford, 1978).

Thirsk, Joan, *The Rural Economy of England* (London, 1984).

Thirsk, Joan, and Cooper J. P., *Seventeenth Century Economic Documents* (London, 1970).

Thomas, David. "Financial and Administrative Developments," in Howard Tomlinson, (ed.), *Before The English Civil War* (London, 1983), pp. 103–22.

Thomson, Alexander, "John Holles," *Journal of Modern History*, vol. 8 (1936), pp. 145–72.

Tilson, Robert O., "Emergence of Black-Market: Administration, Development and Corruption in the New States" in *Bureaucratic Corruption in Sub-Saharan Africa* (ed.), M. U. Ekpo (Washington, D.C., 1979).

Tite, Colin, *Impeachment and Parliamentary Judicature in Early Stuart England* (London, 1974).

Tollison, Robert, "Rent Seeking: A Survey," *Kyklos*, vol. 35 (1982), pp. 575–602.

Turner, Ralph V., *The English Judiciary in the Age of Glanvill and Bracton* (Cambridge, 1985).

Underdown, David, *Somerset in the Civil War and Interregnum* (Newton Abbot, 1973).

Upton, Anthony, *Sir Arthur Ingram* (Oxford, 1961).

Van Klavern, Jacob, "Corruption as an Historical Phenomenon," in A. Heidenheimer, M. Johnston and V. LeVine (eds), *Political Corruption*, (2nd edn, New Brunswick, New Jersey, 1989). pp. 73–86.

Verney, Peter, *The Standard Bearer* (London, 1963).

Villiers, Evangeline de, "Parliamentary Boroughs Restored by the House of Commons 1621–1641," *English Historical Review*, vol. 67 (1952), pp. 175–202.

de Vries, Jan, *The Economy of Europe in an Age of Crisis, 1600–1750*, (Cambridge, 1976).

Wallace, John, "Timon of Athens and the Three Graces: Shakespeare's Senecan Study," *Modern Philology*, vol. 83 (1986), pp. 349–63.

Waugh, Scott L., "Reluctant Knights and Jurors: Respite Exemptions and Public Obligations in the Reign of Henry II," *Speculum*, vol. 58 (1983), pp. 937–86.

Whigham, Frank, *Ambition and Privilege, The Social Tropes of Elizabethan Courtesy Theory* (Berkeley, 1984).

White, Beatrice, *A Cast of Ravens* (New York, 1965).

White, Stephen D., *Sir Edward Coke and the "Grievances of the Commonwealth," 1621–1628* (Chapel Hill, 1979).

Williams, Neville, *Contraband Cargoes: Seven Centuries of Smuggling* (London, 1959).

Williams, Neville, *Thomas Howard ... Fourth Duke of Norfolk* (New York, 1964).

Williams, Penry, *The Tudor Regime* (Oxford, 1979).

Williams, Penry, "Court and Polity Under Elizabeth I," *Bulletin of the John Rylands University Library of Manchester*, vol. 65 (1983), pp. 259–86.

Willson, D. H., *King James VI and I* (London, 1956).

Wilson, C. and Parker, Geoffrey, *An Introduction to the Sources of European Economic History, 1500–1800* (Ithaca, 1977), pp. 115–154.

Woodworth, Allegra, "Purveyance for the Royal Household in the Reign of Queen Elizabeth," *Transactions of the American Philosophical Society*, n.s. vol. 35, pt. 1 (1945).

Worden, Blair, "Classical Republicanism and the Puritan Revolution," in H. Lloyd Jones, V. Pearl and B. Worden (eds), *History and Imagination: Essays in Honour of H. R. Trevor-Roper* (London, 1981), pp. 182–200.

Wormald, Jenny, "James VI and I, *Basilikon Doron* and the *Trew Law of Free Monarchies*: The Scottish Context and the English Translation," in L. L. Peck (ed.), *The Mental World of the Jacobean Court* (Cambridge, forthcoming).

Wormald, Jenny, "James VI and I: Two Kings or One?' *History*, vol. 68 (1983), pp. 187–209.

Wright, L. B. "Propaganda against James I's 'Appeasement' of Spain," *Huntington Library Quarterly*, vol. 6 (1942–43), pp. 149–72.

Wrightson, Keith, *English Society, 1580–1680* (London, 1982).

Youings, Joyce, *Sixteenth Century England* (London, 1984).

Young, Michael, "Buckingham, War and Parliament: Revisionism Gone too Far," *Parliamentary History*, vol. 4 (1985), pp. 45–69.

Young, Michael, *Service and Servility: The Life and Work of Sir John Coke* (Woodbridge, Suffolk, 1986).

Zagorin, Perez, *The Court and the Country* (New York, 1970).

Zagorin, Perez, *Rebels and Rulers, 1500–1650* (2 vols: Cambridge, 1982).

Zaller, Robert, *The Parliament of 1621*, (Berkeley, Calif., 1971).

Unpublished theses and papers

Bucholz, Robert, "Queen Anne and the Decline of Court Culture," paper presented to Huntington Library seminar on British History, May 17 1986.

Carter, Charles, "Intelligence from England, Spanish Hapsburg Policy-Making and its Informational Base, 1598–1625," PhD thesis, Columbia University, 1962.

Hibbard, Caroline, "Aristocratic Women at Court," paper delivered at the Berkshire conference, June, 1987.

Johnson, A. M., "Buckinghamshire, 1640–1660," MA dissertation, University of Swansea, 1963.

McGowan, A. P., "The Royal Navy under the First Duke of Buckingham, Lord High Admiral, 1618–1628," PhD thesis, University of London, 1967.

Peck, Linda Levy, "Benefits, Brokers and Beneficiaries: Reading Buckingham's Patronage," paper delivered at Reading University Conference on Patronage, Politics and Literature, July, 1989.

Pollitt, Ronald, "Rationality and Expedience in the Growth of Elizabethan Naval Administration," paper delivered at the Third Naval History Symposium, United States Naval Academy, Annapolis, Maryland, Fall, 1977.

Shepherd, Robert P., "Royal Favorites in the Political Discourse of Tudor and Stuart England," PhD thesis, Claremont, 1985.

Starkey, David, "The King's Privy Chamber, 1485–1547," PhD thesis, University of Cambridge, 1973.

Stater, Victor, "The Lord Lieutenancy in England, 1625–1688: The Crown, Nobility and Local Governance," PhD thesis, University of Chicago, 1988.

Tighe, William, "The Gentlemen Pensioners in Elizabethan Politics and Government," PhD thesis, University of Cambridge, 1983.

Index

See conclusion for these eg 213-215
+ just before for military role in creaty
problems leading to CW